PLATO: SYMPOSIUM

für Heather

Advisory Editor: M.M. Willcock

PLATO

SYMPOSIUM

Edited with an introduction, translation and commentary by

C.J. Rowe

ARIS & PHILLIPS LTD – WARMINSTER – ENGLAND

British Library Cataloguing-in-Publication Data
A catalogue record of this book is available from the British Library

ISBNS
0 85668 614 X   cloth
0 85668 615 8   limp

Printed and published in England by Aris & Phillips Ltd, Teddington House, Warminster, Wiltshire BA12 8PQ

Contents

Preface

The *Symposium* is probably one of the widest read, and most admired, of all Plato's works, and countless essays and books have been written about it. Despite that, the modern reader will find relatively little to help him or her understand the dialogue as a whole, and readers without a good grasp of Greek are especially poorly served (as they are for much of ancient Greek literature). My own main emphasis, in accordance with the aims of the Aris & Phillips series, is on explicating Plato in a way that will also make him more accessible to those with little or no Greek. Those who wish to grapple more immediately with the intricacies of Plato's Greek in any case already have Sir Kenneth Dover to help them through, and the existence of his edition has made it possible for me mostly to dispense with detailed linguistic comment, leaving the translation – itself frequently influenced by Dover's insights, and sometimes even borrowing his rendering of individual phrases and words – to indicate my detailed construal of the text .

Apart from the relative spareness of its treatment of the finer points of Greek, the chief feature of the commentary is its preoccupation with attempting to understand the *argument* which informs the dialogue and its various parts. I have been concerned always to ask why any of the characters says what he says, or does what he does, in terms of the overall design of the *Symposium*. It is, above all, a careful work of art. We should never be misled by its apparent realism into assuming that things in it happen, as they might in real life, by accident, happy or otherwise (which is not of course to assert that that everything in it is there by intention). There no doubt was an actual symposium at Agathon's after his first victory as a tragic poet, and perhaps the guests there were actually the ones who are present in Plato's version. In Plato's version, however, they say and do what he makes them say or do – or if not, what they say and do always seems to fit together remarkably well. (Some of the things *Socrates* is 'reported' as saying in fact could not have been said by him, if our historical evidence is to be relied on.) Maybe real life might for once have imitated the unity of a literary work. But since we cannot establish that it did, and the chances are that it did not, we may as well get on, as I have done, and treat the *Symposium* as a literary construct, which borrows historical figures and a broadly historical context for its own purposes (cf. Wallace Stegner's epigraph to his *Angle of Repose*, 1971).

My starting-point, as always, has been the need to explain Plato to myself. I have begun, not from the vast secondary literature (of which a reasonable selection is given in the bibliography), but from what was intended to be a fresh confrontation with the text itself. The result is a reading which will in some major respects be at least a partly unfamiliar one, although in others it will inevitably overlap to some degree with the readings of others. I have tried to indicate those places where I have consciously borrowed from other scholars; but in general I have not specified points of disagreement, preferring to argue for positive conclusions whose usefulness is meant to be measured by the strength of the arguments for them.

Over three years of gestation, I have been helped considerably by a series of seminars, first at the University of Macerata, and then at the Universities of Wisconsin-Madison, Edinburgh and London, at which I was allowed to present a gradually evolving set of five lectures on the *Symposium* and profit from detailed discussion with suitably sceptical audiences (the lectures in their original form, with a sample of the discussion that took place in Macerata, are be published separately – in Italian – by Academia Verlag, Sankt Augustin). I also presented a fairly developed version of the same material to a mixed graduate and undergraduate class in Durham. It has been a salutary process. Those who have helped me with their comments are too numerous to list, but among them are Maurizio Migliori, Anthony Price, M.M.McCabe, David Levene, and above all Terry Penner, whose influence on the present volume is out of all proportion to the single acknowledgement to him that it contains. Our continuing philosophical conversations, on and around Socrates and Plato, have taught me what living dialogue can be, and have given a new sense of purpose, even of exhilaration, to the present exploration of a written one.

Finally, I should like to thank Aris & Phillips, and especially Adrian Phillips, for their commitment to a project which has missed its deadlines with predictable regularity; the University of Durham, for the grant of a term's research leave; the Hellenic Center in Washington, D.C., for generous hospitality as well as use of its fine resources at a crucial moment in the preparation of the volume; and Heather Rowe and Malcolm Willcock, for help with proof-reading, and with last-minute tidying of the translation.

Durham, August 1998

Introduction

1.1. Much of the information that might be expected in an introduction will, in this volume, be found embedded in the commentary, and may be discovered through the medium of the index at the end. This approach reflects a particular view (which I attempt to justify below) of what a Platonic dialogue is: a fiction controlled by its author, in which the various elements tend to be shaped to fit their context. So for example I think it unhelpful to begin by giving a separate sketch of the characters in the *Symposium*, which might imply that the work was in some strong sense historical, and designed to reflect what those characters were in real life. Rather, I think, the characters interest Plato just to the extent that they serve his purposes in writing: he *uses* them, no doubt leaving them recognizable as who they are, but building in just so much of them as suits him, and suppressing or inventing the rest.

1.2. The point applies with special force in the case of Socrates. By the end of the *Symposium*, we have an extraordinarily vivid portrait of an individual called 'Socrates'; and no doubt the real Socrates *was* an extraordinary figure, with many of the aspects the dialogue attributes to him. At the same time, since Plato is clearly using 'Socrates' for a purpose (broadly, as I shall suggest, to advance the claims of philosophy), there is no compulsion on us to believe that it is intended as a faithful historical portrait. Indeed, if what is 'reported' about the party is fictional, we are already at least to some extent committed to the opposite view (we may also, and particularly, wonder about what Plato puts into Socrates' mouth, and the extent to which this can be regarded as properly 'Socratic': see below). Of course, the *Symposium* might still reflect Plato's genuine view of the man, and there might well have been – at least in his view – just that harmony between the man and his work (philosophy) that the dialogue suggests. However other writers, notably Xenophon, paint rather different, though overlapping, pictures of Socrates, which cannot easily be written off as mere failures of perception. Moreover, Plato's own portrayal of him is far from constant, even if it contains many recurrent features.

1.3. Under these circumstances, it seems unwise to insist on the historicity of the Socrates of the *Symposium*, except in broad terms, and sensible to treat him as at least in part an idealized figure. In this context, it is worth bearing in mind that the largest part of the direct description of Socrates is in the form of a deliberate eulogy (by Alcibiades), which is likely to fall under the general description that the Socrates of the dialogue at one point gives of the genre as the other characters have understood it: as a matter of collecting together all the most splendid things one can think of saying of something, and applying them to the subject in hand whether they really belong to it or not. Admittedly, Alcibiades includes some *criticism* of Socrates, but that criticism itself will count as praise from Socrates' own perspective. If no corrections of the eulogy are made, that is perhaps partly just because what Plato wants to emerge is a paradigm for purposes of emulation; whether or not it is accurate, from this point of view, hardly matters – and if it is not, it is after all one person's view (Alcibiades').

1.4. My intention, then, is to review particular aspects of the dialogue – its characters, its action, and its argument – in the commentary, in the immediate contexts in which they surface; and this has the advantage that they can be discussed on the basis of a larger quantity of relevant information, most of which will come from those contexts. There are however some (other) general points which may properly be introduced before the main business of tackling the detail of the text begins. This Introduction will also sketch the main lines of the reading of the *Symposium* that will emerge, piecemeal, in the commentary.

1.5. It will be useful to begin with the briefest possible outline of the structure of the whole dialogue:

A. 'Frame' conversation. We find Apollodorus being questioned by some friends of his, somewhere very close to the end of fourth century in Athens, about a famous party that took place at Agathon's house about a dozen years before, at which there was an extended exchange of talk between Socrates and others. Lots of people have heard about it, but Apollodorus has a well-authenticated account that he got from a first-hand witness, Aristodemus. Since he likes nothing better than talking about philosophy, he is happy to oblige his friends with a full report, which occupies the whole of the rest of the dialogue.

B. Aristodemus started (Apollodorus says) with a description of how he and Socrates arrived at the party. Already there, with a few unnamed others, are Phaedrus, Pausanias, Eryximachus, Aristophanes, and Agathon (of course). A proposal that they should spend the time after dinner talking, rather than doing the usual drinking, is accepted: the subject will be *erôs*[1], or more specifically, Eros, the god Love, and each is to take his turn in giving an encomium of him.

C-G. Phaedrus gives the first speech, which is followed by speeches from Pausanias, Eryximachus, Aristophanes, and Agathon.

H. Socrates then consents to give his account of *erôs*, which he prefaces with a characteristic question-and-answer session with Agathon, at the end of which the latter admits his ignorance of what he was talking about.

I. Now Socrates drops Agathon, and continues by introducing the figure of Diotima, a wise woman with mysterious powers: she now takes over the role of questioner, while Socrates plays the role of Agathon (in conversations with Diotima, he says, he maintained just the kinds of things that Agathon did, and she treated him in precisely the way he has just treated Agathon). After a certain point the questioning gives way to virtual monologue from 'Diotima'.

J. After Socrates has finished, Alcibiades arrives, drunk and belligerent, and the original party itself begins serious drinking; but the talking also continues, with Alcibiades giving a eulogy of Socrates instead of Love.

K. There would have been further eulogies, and especially (it seems) one of Agathon by Socrates, but more drunken revellers come in, and the party gradually breaks up in disorder – except that Socrates is still talking away, with only Agathon and Alcibiades (just) awake to listen and answer his questions. When they too fall asleep, at around dawn, Socrates leaves to spend the day in his usual fashion.

2.1. The Platonic dialogues are tantalising documents, which come without even implicit instructions about how they are to be read. Each dialogue appears to be designed as a separate and self-contained entity: occasionally there are references back, or forwards, to other dialogues, in the guise of other conversations, but normally we are left to make our own connections, without knowing whether, or quite how, to make them. The *Symposium* is a case of the latter kind. We break in on a conversation, between Apollodorus and his friends, when it has already begun without us. In a sense we too are dispensable, since Apollodorus already has an audience. We *eavesdrop* on a report he has put together, based on Aristodemus' first-hand evidence, of what was said at Agathon's party. So no sign of the author, either, though Apollodorus refers to a Glaucon who is probably Plato's brother – and, strikingly, Glaucon seems to be the one who knows *least* about the party, of all the people involved in the complex business of the transmission of Aristodemus' original report.

2.2. While Plato frequently authenticates his fictions, providing them with more or less elaborate dramatic contexts, and making his characters cite their sources for ideas that *he* gives them, there is perhaps no other dialogue in which the process of authentication is carried to quite such lengths as in the *Symposium*. Yet in the very process, he allows the fictionality of the authentication to show through: whatever we may make of the badly informed Glaucon, the very attempt to create the illusion of an actual conversation, in progress as we begin to read, is itself transparent.

2.3. What, then, are we to make of an implied claim that 'what follows is the truth' which is at the same time transparently false? Apart from the point that all fictional authors, from Homer's Odysseus to modern novelists, tend to operate in the same way (see Feeney 1993)[2], it is possible to see this way of proceeding as peculiarly appropriate to an author who both wants to bring certain ideas to our attention, and at the same time typically suggests – through his characters – that all philosophical arguments and conclusions are in principle open to scrutiny. Socrates' claim to know nothing, which figures prominently in the *Symposium* itself (and is what partly accounts for the introduction of Diotima, who can advance ideas with apparent authority), is transformed in Plato into a conception of philosophy as a matter of *searching* for a truth which, perhaps, can never be grasped in its entirety, even if we may sometimes approximate to parts of it. With this conception, maybe like the original Socrates, he combines a set of convictions about what the truth might in general be like, if only we could grasp it, and about how such a grasp would improve our lives; and this combination results in a passionate commitment to philosophy, understood as *philo-sophia*, literally 'love of wisdom', which is to be expressed in a continuous process of rational inquiry.

2.4. Whatever else we may find in the *Symposium*, this understanding of the nature and importance of philosophy is central. It is initially placed centre-stage by the 'frame' conversation (see §1.5.A above); then, after it has been temporarily displaced by other, rival conceptions of the nature of intellectual excellence, in the shape of the first five contributions on the nature of *erôs*, it is reasserted in Socrates' contribution, then more indirectly by Alcibiades' speech, and finally by the closing scene. The *Symposium* as a whole is (no doubt among other things) an extended protreptic – an invitation to philosophy, on the Socratic model. As such, it reflects the central features of that model: that is, (a) advocacy of certain ideas, at least in an outline form, and (b) a clear sense of the provisionality of those ideas. The dialogue form, insofar as it creates the illusion of an actual conversation, is clearly in principle well-adapted to exhibiting just these features. After all, while a conversation may make progress, there is always likely to be something of the occasional about it (it takes place at a particular time, between particular individuals, addressing particular questions, perhaps for particular reasons ...). But this already begins to give room, too, for just that play between the ideas of the authentic and the fictional in which the opening of the *Symposium* so signally indulges.

2.5. The point sits well with one particular feature of the opening. Apollodorus specifically claims that he checked some of the details of Aristodemus' account with Socrates, who verified them. Now among those details we might expect to be the high points of the 'teaching' of 'Diotima'; and yet our evidence from other sources, especially Aristotle, suggests that those high points go beyond anything that the historical Socrates is likely to have dreamed of. In particular, 'Diotima' – who is herself, apparently, a fiction of Socrates' – has taught him a thing or two about what we traditionally refer to as 'the theory of forms', a set of metaphysical ideas which, in the kind of shape they are presented to us in the *Symposium*, belonged to Plato rather than to the real Socrates. (Broadly, Aristotle tells us that Socrates was interested in defining things, but did not treat the things he was trying to define – especially the virtues – as independent entities in their own right: what Plato calls *eidê* or *ideai*, 'forms': see §§3.6-7 below.)

2.6. So either Aristotle was mistaken, or Plato is indirectly claiming something that is historically false – or, alternatively, he is not making a *historical* claim at all. He is not saying 'Socrates said just this', when he did not; at most, he is claiming, through Apollodorus, that Socrates would not have demurred from what he is supposed to have believed on the authority of 'Diotima'. Or – what I think amounts to the same thing, insofar as 'Socrates' stands for the ideal philosopher – the claim is that the ideas in question are to be taken seriously, look philosophically defensible; and insofar as they are at bottom ideas that also appear in other dialogues, not just here in the *Symposium*, it would hardly be surprising if Plato wanted to express a degree of commitment to them (Socrates will declare himself 'convinced' of what Diotima told him). It is in *this*, fairly refined, sense, that Apollodorus is allowed to 'authenticate' Diotima's account of *erôs*. What he is claiming is literally false, or a fiction (on two levels), but in a way it is also true; and Plato too is telling the truth in a way, not lying.

3.1. Plato's symposium is an unusual one, not least because of the lack of drinking (the Greek word itself means *drinking*-party). The *Symposium* is therefore not necessarily a good source for the social historian. Nevertheless it is built around, and plays off, the context and arrangements of a typical symposium. The institution of the drinking-party was evidently central to Athenian civic, political and social life. Symposia might be public (as part of civic and/or ritual processes), or private. If they were private, they would provide a means of cementing individual and group relationships between men, whether personal, political, or of any other sort; though they would presumably have been restricted to the aristocratic and/or monied, in view of the large expenditure involved. No doubt they also provided a means of social initiation and integration for younger males. However we should not underestimate the importance of the symposium as a source of entertainment, based on drinking, talking, singing – and sex, both as a subject for talking and singing and in the form of actual sexual activity. There was a long tradition of sympotic poetry, much of which centred on erotic, and especially homoerotic, themes (sometimes addressed by an 'I' to a 'boy', with apparently pedagogic as well as erotic import: which on any occasion might have been uppermost is anybody's guess). It is this aspect of the symposium, above all, that is appropriated by Plato's version of a 'drinking-party', with its sequence of speeches on *erôs*.

3.2. It is often said that the *Symposium* is a dialogue about 'love'. However it is important to recognize from the beginning that even if the Greek word *erôs* can, in the right context, be translated as 'love',[3] its core meaning in the *Symposium* is inseparable from *sexual desire*, in a way that the meaning of our 'love' is not (except, perhaps, in the case of the love felt by the 'lover'). The standard case of *erôs*, from which most of the speakers begin, is the *erôs* felt by an older, male, lover for a younger, also male, beloved, and at least includes the desire for sexual gratification – on the part of the lover – as a central component.

3.3. Such essentially asymmetric relationships, in which the benefit to the younger partner would no doubt have varied in proportion to the quality of the older, were evidently a regular feature of Athenian society. However it would be a mistake to conclude that adult male Athenians were generally more interested, sexually, in boys than in women. Male homosexual activity was a more openly recognized feature of Athenian life than it is in most modern societies, reflecting, among other things, the fact that access to free women was relatively restricted, while access to male company, of all ages – e.g. in the gymnasia – was considerably less so (see especially Dover 1978); but 'this was basically a heterosexual society' (Parsons

1997:6, referring to Davidson 1997). We should not, in short, suppose that the ambience of the *Symposium* is representative of that of ancient Athenian society in general, even if it may – up to a point – evoke the ambience of a real symposium. It may well be that this institution itself, excluding as it did all women except professional musicians and prostitutes or *hetairai*, provided a natural environment for the privileging of sex, and affairs, between men and 'boys' (usually in late adolescence), over heterosexual sex.

3.4. Nor should we suppose that the general devaluation in the *Symposium* of heterosexual in favour of homosexual *erôs* must reflect Plato's own sexual proclivities, not least because we have no useful independent evidence as to what these might have been. If that devaluation is not fully explained by the male-orientated context of the drinking-party (as it is surely not), it is probably more fruitful to look for the remaining part of the explanation in the use that Plato wishes to make of the parallel, and the difference, between the idealized picture of the lover as *educating* his beloved, in return for sex, and the relationship between the experienced philosopher and his younger partner or partners, in which – on the Platonic model – intellectual advance is the only object of exchange. It may be useful here to remember that it is Plato, in the *Republic*, who first raises the possibility of female philosophers – and also that Diotima is a woman: if Socrates usually talks with men, that is again at least partly because women are less available.

3.5. This 'philosophical lover', who is perpetually on the look-out for beautiful young men with whom to talk, rather than to engage physically, figures prominently in the *Symposium*: he is Socrates, who lives out, so far as he can, the 'lessons' of Diotima. (Similarly, but without Diotima, in e.g. the *Lysis* and the *Phaedrus*, two other dialogues whose subject and arguments overlap with those of the *Symposium*.) The connection between Socrates, *erôs*, and philosophy is not Plato's invention. It already appears in the fragments of the dialogues of another follower of Socrates, Aeschines (see Kahn 1994), and may indeed be drawn from life, i.e. from the real Socrates. However that may be, it is pivotal to Plato's own purposes in the *Symposium* itself, insofar as he wishes to portray a revolutionary sort of 'erotic' relationship, one in which passion is directed towards talk, dialogue, and its objects, rather than sex. To such a relationship, the natural counterpoint is the sexual (but educative) one between older and younger male which all the speakers – except Aristophanes – take as their starting-point. That Plato should have made them do so is, as I have suggested, realistic enough; but the desire for realism is not his only motive. Whether or not, in another context, he seriously envisages the possibility of fruitfully philosophical, asexual relationships with women, in the *Symposium* he chooses to concentrate on that model of a relationship which stands immediately closest to what he, or his Socrates, conceives of as the ideal and indispensable kind, based on philosophical dialogue.

3.6. Such dialogue, as described in the *Symposium*,[4] will lead to an understanding of sexual *erôs* as an expression of the universal human desire for the good. Plato's (Socrates') point is often supposed to be that our erotic impulses are to be transformed, in a kind of Freudian sublimation, into a desire for something else. Rather, as I shall argue in the commentary, the point is that they themselves represent a misdirection of our desires. Philosophical reflection, in the company of others, will show us that what we really desire is not some beautiful individual, but 'procreation in the beautiful', where what is 'procreated' is 'true virtue' (what is truly good for us), against the background of an understanding of true beauty, of what beauty truly is: the (Platonic) 'form' of beauty itself.

3.7. The *Symposium* does not provide us with lavish detail about the kind of thing this is: we are not told much more than that there is such an entity ('beauty itself'), that it exists independently of particular beautiful things, which somehow 'share in' it, and that it can be grasped by rational means. The form of beauty, we gather from elsewhere, is one of a large collection of such entities, together constituting the objects of philosophical understanding. The *Symposium*, however (with an economy that is not untypical of Plato), concentrates its attention on beauty, because it is beautiful things (people) that are the objects of ordinary *erôs*, and the substitution for these of other objects of desire – or of one, the good – depends on our achieving a clearer understanding of what beauty is. In other dialogues, especially the *Republic*, there is a 'form' of the good, the highest of all, a grasp of which is essential to our achievement of our own good. Here in the erotic context of the *Symposium*, Plato has Socrates (and Diotima) talk simply, and more concretely, about our desire for the good, i.e. for what will constitute the best life for us, and about the new insight into that good which will derive from a proper insight into beauty – i.e. as residing elsewhere than in beautiful individuals. That is the main lesson that Socrates suggests he learned from Diotima, and in a way it makes the lack of information about her (Plato's) metaphysical assumptions unimportant (maybe our desires really *are* misdirected, and philosophical reflection will enable us to do better).

3.8. Socrates' account of *erôs* is frequently read as excluding attachments to individuals. In fact, it rather presupposes them, in the shape of that dialogue with like-minded others which he sees as an essential condition of philosophical progress. What is more, his notion of the good for the individual, at its highest, seems to be generous enough to include caring for others, at least insofar as it includes contributing to their intellectual improvement (this point too will be argued in detail in the commentary). What he urges, put simply, is that all the effort the ordinary lover puts into achieving his ends would be better spent in a different pursuit. Ordinary lovers go to extraordinary lengths to get what they want; the philosophical 'lover' – the kind of lover we should all be, and that Socrates himself is – sets his sights more fruitfully elsewhere. Whether there are any more general messages here about personal relationships is, I think doubtful. But once again, the *Symposium* is not about 'love', or if it is, it is about highly specific aspects of it.

4.1. The *Symposium* no doubt does give us a reasonably accurate picture of the basic arrangements of a typical (if, in this case, perhaps a particularly lavish) symposium: maybe from seven to eleven couches, each capable of holding two reclining symposiasts; dinner first, drinking later; and so on. So too with the entertainment after dinner.

> 'All of [the] forms [this might take], the singing in turn, praising, propounding and answering riddles, the new turn on the known song, are designed to keep the discourse collective, while at the same time highlighting each person's contribution. The participants must constantly respond to each other, but the full ... forms (riddle and answer, song and cap, variant heard against the known song) require the work of more than one contributor. One could say that ideally the whole symposium should create one intertextual web' (Stehle 1997:222).

This 'intertextuality', and responsiveness, is a special feature of the series of six speeches that ends with Socrates' contribution (the 'web' here in fact includes even the seventh speech, Alcibiades', despite the fact that he has not heard any of the others: here is one more difference between a literary and a real symposium). Not only does each successive speaker 'cap' the one before; they also repeatedly refer to each other, usually to take the opportunity to score points – so that the 'responsiveness' shades into competitiveness, although the tone remains light and witty almost throughout. Even Socrates' piece combines the serious with the playful, ribbing as well as correcting the others. The whole, indeed, comes as close to a comedy as anything Plato might have written, though it is a comedy which – unlike Aristophanes' own piece – overlies something more profound.

4.2. The 'capping' aspect of the first six speeches means that they already, in a sense, represent a single whole, culminating first in the speech by Agathon, the host and victorious tragedian, and then in Socrates' contribution. (They are all, of course, in any case on the same theme: see further §4.6 below.) But we should be wary of supposing that there is, or is meant to be, any sense of a gradually developing picture of *erôs* (or of *Erôs*, the god), with each speaker fitting new and better pieces to the jigsaw. Socrates, after all, prefaces his account with a general criticism of the others, and proceeds immediately to reduce Agathon's speech – which everyone else thought brilliant – to rubble. It is in any case hard to construct any joint account that might emerge from the sequence from Phaedrus to Agathon. All five are essentially individual contributions, with each attempting to go one better than the one before in an apparently haphazard way, and each proclaiming its originality; nor, in my view, is any significant point made by any of them still surviving, in the form in which it was put, by the time Socrates has finished.

4.3. If this is so, it poses in a stark form one of the standard questions about the *Symposium*: just what is the function of the first five speeches? On the face of it, there would be little point in Plato's filling a fair proportion of the whole dialogue with a set of elaborate and carefully worked disquisitions merely in order to have Socrates reject them. Nor, surely, are they ways just of portraying particular individuals, since Plato could scarcely have expected his original hearers or readers to be interested in some of them, even if they had heard of them at all. A better solution is to see the first five speakers as each representing a *type* as well as an individual: so Phaedrus is perhaps the amateur rhetorician; Pausanias the real lover (Agathon's, still, despite the fact that Agathon is now long past 'boyhood'); Eryximachus the theorizing physician; Aristophanes the comic poet; and Agathon the tragic poet. This seems to me a more satisfactory solution, but there will still be the question: why just *these* types?

4.4. It will be easiest to begin with the two poets. The way Socrates handles them is, I believe, generally consistent with the handling of poets as a class elsewhere in the dialogues: that is, as incompetent rivals to the philosopher in the education of the young, and because incompetent, also dangerous (see especially Janaway 1995). Most obviously, he spends a considerable time in demolishing Agathon, even if the demolition has some positive results; and his Diotima brushes aside Aristophanes' prize conceit[5] at a crucial point in her own account. His conversation with the pair at the end, when everyone else is either gone or asleep (something which itself underlines the poets' importance in the dialogue), also apparently consists in his 'forcing' them to agree to a thesis which is highly uncomplimentary to their poetic skills. His general verdict on Agathon's speech is that he is all style – however attractive and 'Gorgianic'[6] – and no substance. At the same time, he builds his own account on and around the ruins of Agathon's speech, saving some of its parts while transforming them into a structure that is essentially new (something he can easily do, when he pretends to borrow Agathon's whole persona: see §1.5 above). The treatment of Aristophanes, by contrast, may appear relatively gentle; but I think this is an illusion. His speech has enjoyed a fair reputation among recent commentators, not just for its inventiveness, but for more serious reasons: here, it is said, is the best or even only decent description of interpersonal love in the dialogue. I shall argue, however, that this is a misreading, and that the speech is actually meant as (and/or actually is) an imaginative but otherwise useless aetiology of *sexual intercourse* – useless, that is, except for Plato's purposes, in that it unwittingly demonstrates the unsatisfactory nature of sex as a goal. Thus Plato simultaneously criticizes both poets – both have their ignorance, and their pretensions, specifically and painfully exposed[7] – and uses them to his own ends, in the course of producing what is itself a combination of the tragic (the serious) and the comic (the playful).

4.5. One of the most striking things about Eryximachus' speech is that although he begins by saying that he will privilege his own branch of expertise (medicine), he actually spends more time on the subject of *music*. He proposes a grand theory of *erôs* as operating on a cosmic and universal scale, but gives as his most extended example the way it operates in the musical sphere. Towards the end, he caps Pausanias' introduction of two Aphrodites, Heavenly and Common, and their attendant Loves, by substituting two Loves who belong to two different Muses: Heavenly (Ourania), and Polymnia, associated with a Love that is vulgar, and needs to be 'applied with caution'. The explanation of this, I suggest, is that he is, as it were, looking at the two people who will speak after him – first Aristophanes, then Agathon. Agathon, as the tragic poet, might be expected to be associated with the Heavenly Muse; the vulgar Muse, and her Love, though Eryximachus avoids saying so (and Aristophanes goes on to try to resist the implication), must surely belong to the comic poet, Aristophanes. In this way Plato is able to mount an indirect preemptive attack on Aristophanes which forms a counterpart to Socrates' direct critique of Agathon, with Diotima's rejection of Aristophanes' main conclusion thrown in for good measure. Once again, Plato is *using* a character as part of his larger design. Eryximachus' high-faluting theory of cosmic Love itself in part prepares for Socrates' rather different broadening of the notion of *erôs*, though it is also a cameo of a particular type of 'scientific' theory.

4.6. If Eryximachus is a critic of vulgar excess, that does not prevent him from signing up to the general theme that is implicit in the decision to praise Eros, namely that *erôs* is a good thing, that lovers ought to pursue their object, and that their beloveds ought to give in to their advances. Pausanias gives the most explicit version of this theme, with the proviso that lover and beloved must both be of the right sort, and behave with the right motives (so serving the Heavenly rather than the Common Eros). It is he who most directly provides what I have called the counterpoint to Socrates', and Diotima's, vision of *erôs*, describing ordinary, common-or-garden, *erôs* at its best, i.e. as properly educative as well as sexual. Pausanias is a particularly apt choice for *this* role, insofar as no one could accuse him of aiming only for sexual gratification. We are given to understand that he is not interested in women (so constituting an exception to the rule illustrated by the others, of a kind of bisexuality), and if sex were all that he were after, there would be plenty more obvious recipients of his affections than the thirty-year-old Agathon (see §4.3 above). So when he praises the lifelong lover, he is not only praising himself (in a suitably witty way), but building an ideal of 'correct' loving which Socrates will attempt to supplant with his own.

4.7. Pausanias speech corrects Phaedrus', thus in a way itself raising the subject to a higher level. Phaedrus simply praised *erôs* in general, without explicitly distinguishing its good and less good forms, and simply assuming that it will lead to good results (especially in inspiring courageous actions). His contribution is probably the slightest of them all. It is designed to start things off, in a suitably low-key mode; but it also serves as a particularly clear illustration of the feature which Socrates will complain of in all the first five speakers (their lack of concern with what is true about their subject: see §1.2 above). Phaedrus – like Agathon, but in a different, and less showy, way – gives us a typically *rhetorical* display, in which cleverness takes priority over truth.

5. The dramatic date of the main conversation of the *Symposium* is precisely fixed: 416 B.C., not long before the disastrous Athenian expedition to Sicily, in

which Alcibiades played a leading part. But the form in which the dialogue is written – that is, in the form of a report of Aristodemus' account of that conversation – keeps us for the most part in the time of the 'frame' conversation, when the expedition is over, and Athens has suffered her final defeat in the long-running wars with Sparta. This arrangement, together with the presence of Alcibiades, may well have been meant to invite the audience of the dialogue to reflect on its contents in the light of those shattering events that took place between the two conversations: perhaps especially, to reflect on what might have been, had Alcibiades and the others listened properly to Socrates and his call to philosophy. The date of the composition of the *Symposium* itself is usually placed – on the basis of some alleged anachronisms[8] -- in the second half of the 380s; stylometric and other considerations link it with the 'middle' period of Plato's writing, along with e.g. the *Phaedo*, the *Republic* and the *Phaedrus*, in which 'forms' (see §§2.5, 3.6, 3.7 above) figure conspicuously. But given the self-contained nature of the *Symposium* (§2.1), its dating is by and large of secondary importance. The most interesting question in this area is perhaps the date of the *Symposium* relative to that of the *Lysis* and the *Phaedrus*, given the way its subject-matter overlaps with theirs: my own view, for what it is worth, is that the *Phaedrus* probably postdated the *Symposium*,[9] and that the *Lysis* is, or turned out to be, in part a sketch for it.

6. The history of the reception of the *Symposium* would occupy a book in itself. Such a book would include reference, among others, to the Stoics, Plotinus, Origen, Augustine, the Italian Renaissance, Erasmus and Muriel Spark. Such a book, however, would be chiefly about the uses to which Plato's ideas, or parts of them, have been put,[10] rather than about the *Symposium* itself; and this subject is beyond the scope of the present volume.

7. The text printed is a modified version of Burnet's, in the series of Oxford Classical texts; where I diverge significantly from Burnet (i.e. other than in matters of punctuation), his choice of reading is indicated in the minimal critical apparatus appended to the text. The sigla used in the apparatus are as follows: 'm', indicating the reading of all the main mediaeval manuscripts; 'n', indicating a reading of one or more of these; 't', indicating a reading found in ancient citations of the *Symposium*; 'p', indicating readings found in papyrus material, which represents our oldest but not necessarily most reliable evidence for the text; 'e', indicating a reading preferred or proposed by at least one editor but lacking manuscript support; and 'O', indicating Burnet's choices.

1   The general policy in this volume is to cite all Greek in transliterated form, except when commenting on specifically linguistic points. The primary aim of this policy is to give a clear indication of those (very limited) elements – those involving untransliterated Greek – which are unlikely to be of interest to the reader without Greek.

2   See Select Bibliography.

3   'Love' will in fact be the standard translation in this volume, but only for want of a better alternative.

4   But only fitfully illustrated by it (especially in Socrates' interrogation of Agathon): Socratic dialogue is essentially dialogue *between individuals*, rather than with a group. When Socrates addresses all the symposiasts together, he is behaving out of character – but then, as the *Symposium* implies, the drinking-party is not part of his natural environment.

5   Or at any rate treats it as seriously incomplete: 205d-e.

6   Socrates says that Agathon's speech reminds him of Gorgias, perhaps the best-known rhetorician of the fifth century.

7   Aristophanes more indirectly, but no less painfully (if only he were able to see it).

8   See under 'date of composition' in index.

9   See especially Rowe 1986.

10   It is the early Stoics, perhaps, who come closest to reproducing the idea of *erôs* sponsored by the Socrates of the *Symposium*: see Schofield 1991. On Plotinus, see Osborne 1994, and on Plotinus and Origen, see Rist 1964.

PLATO

SYMPOSIUM
(ΣΥΜΠΟΣΙΟΝ)

ΣΥΜΠΟΣΙΟΝ

ΑΠ. δοκῶ μοι περὶ ὧν πυνθάνεσθε οὐκ ἀμελέτητος εἶναι. καὶ   172
γὰρ ἐτύγχανον πρώην εἰς ἄστυ οἴκοθεν ἀνιὼν Φαληρόθεν· τῶν
οὖν γνωρίμων τις ὄπισθεν κατιδών με πόρρωθεν ἐκάλεσε, καὶ
παίζων ἅμα τῇ κλήσει, 'ὦ Φαληρεύς,' ἔφη, 'οὗτος
Ἀπολλόδωρος, οὐ περιμενεῖς;' κἀγὼ ἐπιστὰς περιέμεινα. καὶ   5
ὅς, 'Ἀπολλόδωρε,' ἔφη, 'καὶ μὴν καὶ ἔναγχός σε ἐζήτουν
βουλόμενος διαπυθέσθαι τὴν Ἀγάθωνος συνουσίαν καὶ   b
Σωκράτους καὶ Ἀλκιβιάδου καὶ τῶν ἄλλων τῶν τότε ἐν τῷ
συνδείπνῳ παραγενομένων, περὶ τῶν ἐρωτικῶν λόγων τίνες
ἦσαν· ἄλλος γάρ τίς μοι διηγεῖτο ἀκηκοὼς Φοίνικος τοῦ   5
Φιλίππου, ἔφη δὲ καὶ σὲ εἰδέναι. ἀλλὰ γὰρ οὐδὲν εἶχε σαφὲς
λέγειν. σὺ οὖν μοι διήγησαι· δικαιότατος γὰρ εἶ τοὺς τοῦ
ἑταίρου λόγους ἀπαγγέλλειν. πρότερον δέ μοι', ἦ δ' ὅς,
'εἰπέ, σὺ αὐτὸς παρεγένου τῇ συνουσίᾳ ταύτῃ ἢ οὔ;' κἀγὼ
εἶπον ὅτι 'παντάπασιν ἔοικέ σοι οὐδὲν διηγεῖσθαι σαφὲς ὁ   c
διηγούμενος, εἰ νεωστὶ ἡγῇ τὴν συνουσίαν γεγονέναι ταύτην
ἣν ἐρωτᾷς, ὥστε καὶ ἐμὲ παραγενέσθαι.' 'ἐγώ γε δή,' ἔφη.
'πόθεν, ἦν δ' ἐγώ, ὦ Γλαύκων; οὐκ οἶσθ' ὅτι πολλῶν ἐτῶν
Ἀγάθων ἐνθάδε οὐκ ἐπιδεδήμηκεν, ἀφ' οὗ δ' ἐγὼ Σωκράτει   5
συνδιατρίβω καὶ ἐπιμελὲς πεποίημαι ἑκάστης ἡμέρας εἰδέναι
ὅτι ἂν λέγῃ ἢ πράττῃ, οὐδέπω τρία ἔτη ἐστίν; πρὸ τοῦ δὲ
περιτρέχων ὅπῃ τύχοιμι καὶ οἰόμενός τι ποιεῖν ἀθλιώτερος ἦ   173
ὁτουοῦν, οὐχ ἧττον ἢ σὺ νυνί, οἰόμενος δεῖν πάντα μᾶλλον
πράττειν ἢ φιλοσοφεῖν.' καὶ ὅς, 'μὴ σκῶπτ',' ἔφη, 'ἀλλ'
εἰπέ μοι πότε ἐγένετο ἡ συνουσία αὕτη.' κἀγὼ εἶπον ὅτι
'παίδων ὄντων ἡμῶν ἔτι, ὅτε τῇ πρώτῃ τραγῳδίᾳ ἐνίκησεν   5
Ἀγάθων, τῇ ὑστεραίᾳ ἢ ᾗ τὰ ἐπινίκια ἔθυεν αὐτός τε καὶ οἱ
χορευταί.' 'πάνυ', ἔφη, 'ἄρα πάλαι, ὡς ἔοικεν. ἀλλὰ τίς σοι
διηγεῖτο; ἢ αὐτὸς Σωκράτης;' 'οὐ μὰ τὸν Δία,' ἦν δ' ἐγώ,   b
'ἀλλ' ὅσπερ Φοίνικι. Ἀριστόδημος ἦν τις, Κυδαθηναιεύς,
σμικρός, ἀνυπόδητος ἀεί· παρεγεγόνει δ' ἐν τῇ συνουσίᾳ,
Σωκράτους ἐραστὴς ὢν ἐν τοῖς μάλιστα τῶν τότε, ὡς ἐμοὶ
δοκεῖ. οὐ μέντοι ἀλλὰ καὶ Σωκράτη γε ἔνια ἤδη ἀνηρόμην ὧν   5
ἐκείνου ἤκουσα, καί μοι ὡμολόγει καθάπερ ἐκεῖνος διηγεῖτο.'

172a5 [Ἀπολλόδωρος] e ǀ περιμενεις n: περιμένεις n, O ǀ b3 συνδειπνεῖν n ǀ
173a6 ἦ ᾗ n: ἡ (sic) n: ἦ e

SYMPOSIUM

172 *Apollodorus*: I believe I'm not unrehearsed in relation to what you people are asking about. Just the other day I was going up to town from home, in Phalerum, and someone I know caught sight of me from some way behind, and called out jokingly: 'Hey, you – the man from Phalerum! I mean you, [a5] Apollodorus! Wait there!' And I stopped and waited. He said, 'It was only recently I was looking for you, [b1] because I wanted to find out all about the time when Agathon and Socrates and Alcibiades got together, and the others who were there at the dinner-party – I wanted to ask you what they said about love. Someone else, who'd heard about it from Phoenix the son of [b5] Philippus, did tell me, and said at the time that you knew about it too. But the truth is that he hadn't anything clear to say on the subject. So you tell me; it's most appropriate that you should report what your friend said. But first', he said, 'tell me: were you at this gathering yourself or not?' To which [c1] I replied 'It seems the person who was telling you got absolutely nothing clear at all, if you think this gathering you're asking about happened recently, so that *I* could be there.' 'I did think that', he said. 'How so, Glaucon?' I asked. 'Don't you know that Agathon has not [c5] lived here in Athens for many years, and that it's not yet three years that I've been spending time with Socrates, and have made it my business each day to know everything he is saying and doing? Before that **173** I simply rushed around this way and that, thinking I was achieving something; in fact, I was a more miserable figure than anyone you might care to mention – just like you now: I thought anything was a greater priority than doing philosophy.' 'Don't joke at me,' he said; 'just tell me when this gathering took place.' And I said [a5] 'It was when you and I were still children, when Agathon won the prize with his first tragedy, on the day after he and the members of his chorus had their sacrificial feast for his victory.' 'So apparently it really was a long time ago,' he said. 'But who [b1] told you about it? Or was it Socrates himself?' 'For heaven's sake, no!' I replied. 'It was the same person who told Phoenix. There was a man called Aristodemus, from Cydathenaeum, small, always barefoot; he had been at the gathering – he was a lover of Socrates, I think as much as anyone among those who were around [b5] at that time. However I did also later ask Socrates himself, too, about some of the things I heard from Aristodemus, and he agreed with Aristodemus' account.' 'Then why not tell

'τί οὖν,' ἔφη, 'οὐ διηγήσω μοι; πάντως δὲ ἡ ὁδὸς ἡ εἰς ἄστυ ἐπιτηδεία πορευομένοις καὶ λέγειν καὶ ἀκούειν.'

οὕτω δὴ ἰόντες ἅμα τοὺς λόγους περὶ αὐτῶν ἐποιούμεθα, ὥστε, ὅπερ ἀρχόμενος εἶπον, οὐκ ἀμελετήτως ἔχω. εἰ οὖν δεῖ c καὶ ὑμῖν διηγήσασθαι, ταῦτα χρὴ ποιεῖν. καὶ γὰρ ἔγωγε καὶ ἄλλως, ὅταν μέν τινας περὶ φιλοσοφίας λόγους ἢ αὐτὸς ποιῶμαι ἢ ἄλλων ἀκούω, χωρὶς τοῦ οἴεσθαι ὠφελεῖσθαι ὑπερφυῶς ὡς χαίρω· ὅταν δὲ ἄλλους τινάς, ἄλλως τε καὶ 5 τοὺς ὑμετέρους τοὺς τῶν πλουσίων καὶ χρηματιστικῶν, αὐτός τε ἄχθομαι ὑμᾶς τε τοὺς ἑταίρους ἐλεῶ, ὅτι οἴεσθε τὶ ποιεῖν οὐδὲν ποιοῦντες. καὶ ἴσως αὖ ὑμεῖς ἐμὲ ἡγεῖσθε κακοδαίμονα d εἶναι, καὶ οἴομαι ὑμᾶς ἀληθῆ οἴεσθαι· ἐγὼ μέντοι ὑμᾶς οὐκ οἴομαι ἀλλ' εὖ οἶδα.

ΕΤ. ἀεὶ ὅμοιος εἶ, ὦ Ἀπολλόδωρε· ἀεὶ γὰρ σαυτόν τε κακηγορεῖς καὶ τοὺς ἄλλους, καὶ δοκεῖς μοι ἀτεχνῶς πάντας 5 ἀθλίους ἡγεῖσθαι πλὴν Σωκράτους, ἀπὸ σαυτοῦ ἀρξάμενος. καὶ ὁπόθεν ποτὲ ταύτην τὴν ἐπωνυμίαν ἔλαβες τὸ μαλακὸς καλεῖσθαι, οὐκ οἶδα ἔγωγε· ἐν μὲν γὰρ τοῖς λόγοις ἀεὶ τοιοῦτος εἶ, σαυτῷ τε καὶ τοῖς ἄλλοις ἀγριαίνεις πλὴν Σωκράτους. 10

ΑΠ. ὦ φίλτατε, καὶ δῆλόν γε δὴ ὅτι οὕτω διανοούμενος καὶ e περὶ ἐμαυτοῦ καὶ περὶ ὑμῶν μαίνομαι καὶ παραπαίω;

ΕΤ. οὐκ ἄξιον περὶ τούτων, Ἀπολλόδωρε, νῦν ἐρίζειν· ἀλλ' ὅπερ ἐδεόμεθά σου, μὴ ἄλλως ποιήσῃς, ἀλλὰ διήγησαι τίνες ἦσαν οἱ λόγοι. 5

ΑΠ. ἦσαν τοίνυν ἐκεῖνοι τοιοίδε τινές – μᾶλλον δ' ἐξ ἀρχῆς ὑμῖν ὡς ἐκεῖνος διηγεῖτο καὶ ἐγὼ πειράσομαι διηγήσασθαι. **174**

ἔφη γάρ οἱ Σωκράτη ἐντυχεῖν λελουμένον τε καὶ τὰς βλαύτας ὑποδεδεμένον, ἃ ἐκεῖνος ὀλιγάκις ἐποίει· καὶ ἐρέσθαι αὐτὸν ὅποι ἴοι οὕτω καλὸς γεγενημένος.

καὶ τὸν εἰπεῖν ὅτι 'ἐπὶ δεῖπνον εἰς Ἀγάθωνος. χθὲς γὰρ 5 αὐτὸν διέφυγον τοῖς ἐπινικίοις, φοβηθεὶς τὸν ὄχλον· ὡμολόγησα δ' εἰς τήμερον παρέσεσθαι. ταῦτα δὴ ἐκαλλωπισάμην, ἵνα καλὸς παρὰ καλὸν ἴω. ἀλλὰ σύ,' ἦ δ' ὅς, 'πῶς ἔχεις πρὸς τὸ ἐθέλειν ἂν ἰέναι ἄκλητος ἐπὶ δεῖπνον;' b

'κἀγώ', ἔφη, 'εἶπον ὅτι "οὕτως ὅπως ἂν σὺ κελεύῃς".'

'ἕπου τοίνυν,' ἔφη, 'ἵνα καὶ τὴν παροιμίαν διαφθείρωμεν

d 7 μανικὸς n, O | **b 1** ἂν ἰέναι e: ἀνιέναι m

me?' he said. 'The road into town is just right for talking and listening, as we go.'

So we went on together as he proposed and had our talk about the subject, [c1] with the result that – as I said at the beginning – I'm not unrehearsed. So if I'm to tell you people too, well then, that's what I must do. In fact, quite apart from thinking I benefit from it, I myself get an amazing amount of pleasure anyway from any talking I do, or hear others doing, [c5] about philosophy; other sorts of talking, especially your rich businessmen's talk, bores me, and I pity you who are my friends because you think you're achieving something [d1] when you're achieving nothing. Maybe you in your turn suppose *I'm* in a wretched state, and I think what you think is true; however I don't just think you are, I *know* you are.

Apollodorus' Friend: You're always the same, Apollodorus; you're always insulting [d5] yourself and everyone else. You seem to me to suppose that simply everyone is in a miserable state apart from Socrates, starting with yourself. Where on earth you got that nickname of yours, 'Softy', I've personally no idea; when you talk you're always as you are now, savaging yourself and everybody else except [d10] Socrates.

[e1] *Apollodorus*: So, my dear friend, it's obvious, is it? This attitude of mine towards myself and you people means that I'm mad, off my head?

Friend: It's not worth quarrelling about these things now, Apollodorus. What about doing just what I was asking you to do, and telling us [e5] what they said?

Apollodorus: Well, it was something like this. Or rather – I'll try **174** and tell it to you from the beginning in the way Aristodemus told it to me.

What he said was that Socrates happened to meet him bathed and wearing his fine sandals, both things he rarely did; and Aristodemus asked him where he was going, to have made himself so beautiful?

[a5] Socrates said 'To dinner at Agathon's. Yesterday I avoided him, at the victory party, because I was afraid of the crowds; but I agreed that I would be there today. So I've beautified myself like this, so that my beauty matches his when I get there. But wait a minute,' he said; [b1] 'how do *you* feel about – maybe – being willing to go to the dinner, without an invitation?'

'And I said,' Aristodemus said, '"Whatever you say".'

'Well then,' said Socrates, 'follow me, and we'll make a mess of the

μεταβαλόντες, ὡς ἄρα καὶ ἀγαθῶν "ἐπὶ δαῖτας ἴασιν
αὐτόματοι ἀγαθοί". Ὅμηρος μὲν γὰρ κινδυνεύει οὐ μόνον 5
διαφθεῖραι ἀλλὰ καὶ ὑβρίσαι εἰς ταύτην τὴν παροιμίαν·
ποιήσας γὰρ τὸν Ἀγαμέμνονα διαφερόντως ἀγαθὸν ἄνδρα τὰ c
πολεμικά, τὸν δὲ Μενέλεων "μαλθακὸν αἰχμητήν", θυσίαν
ποιουμένου καὶ ἑστιῶντος τοῦ Ἀγαμέμνονος ἄκλητον ἐποίησεν
ἐλθόντα τὸν Μενέλεων ἐπὶ τὴν θοίνην, χείρω ὄντα ἐπὶ τὴν
τοῦ ἀμείνονος.' 5

ταῦτ' ἀκούσας εἰπεῖν ἔφη 'ἴσως μέντοι κινδυνεύσω καὶ
ἐγὼ οὐχ ὡς σὺ λέγεις, ὦ Σώκρατες, ἀλλὰ καθ' Ὅμηρον
φαῦλος ὢν ἐπὶ σοφοῦ ἀνδρὸς ἰέναι θοίνην ἄκλητος. ὅρα οὖν
ἄγων με τί ἀπολογήσῃ, ὡς ἐγὼ μὲν οὐχ ὁμολογήσω ἄκλητος d
ἥκειν, ἀλλ' ὑπὸ σοῦ κεκλημένος.'
'"σύν τε δύ'"', ἔφη, '"ἐρχομένω πρὸ ὁδοῦ" βουλευσόμεθα
ὅτι ἐροῦμεν. ἀλλ' ἴωμεν.'

τοιαῦτ' ἄττα σφᾶς ἔφη διαλεχθέντας ἰέναι. τὸν οὖν 5
Σωκράτη ἑαυτῷ πως προσέχοντα τὸν νοῦν κατὰ τὴν ὁδὸν
πορεύεσθαι ὑπολειπόμενον, καὶ περιμένοντος οὗ κελεύειν
προιέναι εἰς τὸ πρόσθεν. ἐπειδὴ δὲ γενέσθαι ἐπὶ τῇ οἰκίᾳ τῇ
Ἀγάθωνος, ἀνεῳγμένην καταλαμβάνειν τὴν θύραν, καί τι ἔφη e
αὐτόθι γελοῖον παθεῖν. οἷ μὲν γὰρ εὐθὺς παῖδά τινα τῶν
ἔνδοθεν ἀπαντήσαντα ἄγειν οὗ κατέκειντο οἱ ἄλλοι, καὶ
καταλαμβάνειν ἤδη μέλλοντας δειπνεῖν· εὐθὺς δ' οὖν ὡς ἰδεῖν
τὸν Ἀγάθωνα, 'ὦ', φάναι, 'Ἀριστόδημε, εἰς καλὸν ἥκεις 5
ὅπως συνδειπνήσῃς· εἰ δ' ἄλλου τινὸς ἕνεκα ἦλθες, εἰς αὖθις
ἀναβαλοῦ, ὡς καὶ χθὲς ζητῶν σε ἵνα καλέσαιμι, οὐχ οἷός τ' ἦ
ἰδεῖν. ἀλλὰ Σωκράτη ἡμῖν πῶς οὐκ ἄγεις;'

'καὶ ἐγώ', ἔφη, 'μεταστρεφόμενος οὐδαμοῦ ὁρῶ Σωκράτη
ἑπόμενον· εἶπον οὖν ὅτι καὶ αὐτὸς μετὰ Σωκράτους ἥκοιμι, 10
κληθεὶς ὑπ' ἐκείνου δεῦρ' ἐπὶ δεῖπνον.'

'καλῶς γ'', ἔφη, 'ποιῶν σύ· ἀλλὰ ποῦ ἐστιν οὗτος;'

'ὄπισθεν ἐμοῦ ἄρτι εἰσῄει· ἀλλὰ θαυμάζω καὶ αὐτὸς ποῦ 175
ἂν εἴη.'

'οὐ σκέψῃ,' ἔφη, 'παῖ,' φάναι τὸν Ἀγάθωνα, 'καὶ
εἰσάξεις Σωκράτη; σὺ δ',' ἦ δ' ὅς, 'Ἀριστόδημε, παρ'
Ἐρυξίμαχον κατακλίνου.' 5

---

b 4 Ἀγάθων' e. O | c 8 ὅρα e: ἄρα n: ἄρα n | d 3 πρὸ ὁ τοῦ e (cf. Homer,
Iliad 10.224) | e 2-3 τινα τῶν ἔνδοθεν t: τινα ἔνδοθεν m

proverb by changing it: now it'll turn out to be good men's feasts, too, that "good men [b5] go to of their own accord" That's one better than Homer: it looks as if he didn't just make a mess of this proverb, but did criminal damage to it: [c1] after making Agamemnon an exceptionally good man when it comes to warfare, and Menelaus a "soft spearfighter", when Agamemnon is sacrificing and laying on a feast Homer had Menelaus come uninvited to the banquet, an inferior to his [c5] superior's.'

When he heard this, Aristodemus said, he said 'I fear, Socrates, that I too shall fail to match up to your description, and that as in Homer's case I shall be a person of no consequence going uninvited to the feast of a man of accomplishment. So see [d1] what defence you will give for bringing me, because *I* shan't admit that I came uninvited – I shall say it was you who invited me.'

Socrates said '"As we two go together further along the way" we'll work out what we'll say. Come on, let's go.'

[d5] It was with this sort of conversation that Aristodemus said they started on the way. Well, Socrates walked along the road wrapped up somehow in his own thoughts, and got left behind, and when Aristodemus waited for him, Socrates told him to go on ahead. When he arrived at Agathon's [e1] house, he found the door already opened, and, he said, there he found himself in an amusing situation. One of the slaves inside immediately met him and took him to where the others were reclining, and he found them on the point of starting dinner; but anyway, as soon as Agathon [e5] saw him, he said, 'Aristodemus! You've come just at the right moment to dine with us; if you've come for any other reason, put it off until another occasion, because just yesterday I was looking for you in order to give you your invitation, but didn't get a glimpse of you. But what about Socrates? Why aren't you bringing him for us?'

'At this point', Aristodemus said, 'I turned round and couldn't see Socrates anywhere [e10] behind me; so I said it was actually *I* who was coming with Socrates, because he invited me to come here to dinner.'

'You were quite right to come', said Agathon; 'but where is the man?'

175 'He was behind me coming into the house just now; I'm puzzled myself to know where he can be.'

'Have a look for Socrates, slave,' said Agathon, 'and bring him in. And you,' he said, 'Aristodemus, recline [a5] beside Eryximachus.'

καὶ ἓ μὲν ἔφη ἀπονίζειν τὸν παῖδα ἵνα κατακέοιτο· ἄλλον (175)
δέ τινα τῶν παίδων ἥκειν ἀγγέλλοντα ὅτι 'Σωκράτης οὗτος
ἀναχωρήσας ἐν τῷ τῶν γειτόνων προθύρῳ ἕστηκεν, κἀμοῦ
καλοῦντος οὐκ ἐθέλει εἰσιέναι.'
'ἄτοπόν γ'', ἔφη, 'λέγεις· οὔκουν καλεῖς αὐτὸν καὶ μὴ 10
ἀφήσεις;'
καὶ ὃς ἔφη εἰπεῖν 'μηδαμῶς, ἀλλ' ἐᾶτε αὐτόν. ἔθος γάρ τι b
τοῦτ' ἔχει· ἐνίοτε ἀποστὰς ὅποι ἂν τύχῃ ἕστηκεν. ἥξει δ'
αὐτίκα, ὡς ἐγὼ οἶμαι. μὴ οὖν κινεῖτε, ἀλλ' ἐᾶτε.'
'ἀλλ' οὕτω χρὴ ποιεῖν, εἰ σοὶ δοκεῖ,' ἔφη φάναι τὸν
Ἀγάθωνα. 'ἀλλ' ἡμᾶς, ὦ παῖδες, τοὺς ἄλλους ἑστιᾶτε. 5
πάντως παρατίθετε ὅτι ἂν βούλησθε, ἐπειδάν τις ὑμῖν μὴ
ἐφεστήκῃ, ὃ ἐγὼ οὐδεπώποτε ἐποίησα· νῦν οὖν, νομίζοντες
καὶ ἐμὲ ὑφ' ὑμῶν κεκλῆσθαι ἐπὶ δεῖπνον καὶ τούσδε τοὺς c
ἄλλους, θεραπεύετε, ἵν' ὑμᾶς ἐπαινῶμεν.'
μετὰ ταῦτα ἔφη σφᾶς μὲν δειπνεῖν, τὸν δὲ Σωκράτη οὐκ
εἰσιέναι. τὸν οὖν Ἀγάθωνα πολλάκις κελεύειν μεταπέμψασθαι
τὸν Σωκράτη, ἓ δὲ οὐκ ἐᾶν. ἥκειν οὖν αὐτὸν οὐ πολὺν χρόνον 5
ὡς εἰώθει διατρίψαντα, ἀλλὰ μάλιστα σφᾶς μεσοῦν
δειπνοῦντας. τὸν οὖν Ἀγάθωνα (τυγχάνειν γὰρ ἔσχατον
κατακείμενον μόνον) 'δεῦρ',' ἔφη φάναι, 'Σώκρατες, παρ' ἐμὲ
κατάκεισο, ἵνα καὶ τοῦ σοφοῦ ἁπτόμενός σου ἀπολαύσω, ὅ σοι d
προσέστη ἐν τοῖς προθύροις. δῆλον γὰρ ὅτι ηὗρες αὐτὸ καὶ
ἔχεις· οὐ γὰρ ἂν προαπέστης.'
καὶ τὸν Σωκράτη καθίζεσθαι καὶ εἰπεῖν ὅτι 'εὖ ἂν ἔχοι,'
φάναι, 'ὦ Ἀγάθων, εἰ τοιοῦτον εἴη ἡ σοφία ὥστ' ἐκ τοῦ 5
πληρεστέρου εἰς τὸ κενώτερον ῥεῖν ἡμῶν, ἐὰν ἁπτώμεθα
ἀλλήλων, ὥσπερ τὸ ἐν ταῖς κύλιξιν ὕδωρ τὸ διὰ τοῦ ἐρίου
ῥέον ἐκ τῆς πληρεστέρας εἰς τὴν κενωτέραν. εἰ γὰρ οὕτως
ἔχει καὶ ἡ σοφία, πολλοῦ τιμῶμαι τὴν παρὰ σοὶ κατάκλισιν· e
οἶμαι γάρ με παρὰ σοῦ πολλῆς καὶ καλῆς σοφίας
πληρωθήσεσθαι. ἡ μὲν γὰρ ἐμὴ φαύλη τις ἂν εἴη, ἢ καὶ
ἀμφισβητήσιμος ὥσπερ ὄναρ οὖσα, ἡ δὲ σὴ λαμπρά τε καὶ
πολλὴν ἐπίδοσιν ἔχουσα, ἥ γε παρὰ σοῦ νέου ὄντος οὕτω 5
σφόδρα ἐξέλαμψεν καὶ ἐκφανὴς ἐγένετο πρῴην ἐν μάρτυσι
τῶν Ἑλλήνων πλέον ἢ τρισμυρίοις.'

d 6 τὸν e

He said the slave then washed him, so that he could take his place on the couch; and another of the slaves came and reported 'That Socrates has retreated into the neighbours' porch and is standing there, and though I call him he won't come in.'

[a10] 'That's a pretty strange thing you're saying', said Agathon; 'just call him, and don't let him stay there.'

[b1] Aristodemus said he intervened: 'You mustn't do that! Leave him there. This is one of his ways; sometimes he just goes off, it doesn't matter where, and stands there. He'll come presently, that's my guess. So don't disturb him. Leave him there.'

'That's what we must do, if you say so', Aristodemus said was Agathon's [b5] reply. 'You slaves, entertain the rest of us. In any case you always serve up whatever you feel like, whenever someone isn't supervising you – and supervising you is something I've never done to this day; so now imagine [c1] that I'm someone you've invited to dinner, along with the others, and see to our needs so we can applaud you.'

After that, Aristodemus said they had their dinner, and Socrates still didn't come in. The result was that Agathon kept trying to give the order 'send for [c5] Socrates!', but Aristodemus stopped him. Well, not long afterwards he arrived, having spent the time in his usual way; but by then they were pretty well in the middle of dinner. At that point, according to Aristodemus, Agathon (who as it happened was in last position on a couch by himself) said 'Come here, Socrates, and recline [d1] beside me, so that I can also have the benefit of contact with that bit of wisdom of yours, the bit that came to you in the porch. It's clear that you found what you were looking for, and have it in your possession; you wouldn't have come away before you had.'

Socrates sat himself down and said 'It would be a good thing, [d5] Agathon, if wisdom were the kind of thing that flowed from what is fuller into what is emptier in our case, if only we touch each other, like the water in cups which flows from the fuller into the emptier through the thread of wool. If wisdom [e1] too is like that, then I put a high value on reclining beside you, because then I think it's I who'll be filled from your side with quantities of beautiful wisdom. Mine, I guess, will be an inferior sort of wisdom, or even a debatable one, existing as if in a dream; whereas yours is brilliant and [e5] promises much for the future, to judge from the brightness with which it shone out from you – and you still a young man -- the other day, when it was displayed in full view with more than thirty thousand Greeks as witnesses.'

22

'ὑβριστὴς εἶ,' ἔφη,' ὦ Σώκρατες,' ὁ Ἀγάθων. 'καὶ ταῦτα
μὲν καὶ ὀλίγον ὕστερον διαδικασόμεθα ἐγώ τε καὶ σὺ περὶ
τῆς σοφίας, δικαστῇ χρώμενοι τῷ Διονύσῳ· νῦν δὲ πρὸς τὸ   10
δεῖπνον πρῶτα τρέπου.'

μετὰ ταῦτα, ἔφη, κατακλινέντος τοῦ Σωκράτους καὶ   **176**
δειπνήσαντος καὶ τῶν ἄλλων, σπονδάς τε σφᾶς ποιήσασθαι,
καὶ ᾄσαντας τὸν θεὸν καὶ τἆλλα τὰ νομιζόμενα, τρέπεσθαι
πρὸς τὸν πότον· τὸν οὖν Παυσανίαν ἔφη λόγου τοιούτου τινὸς
κατάρχειν. 'εἶεν, ἄνδρες,' φάναι, 'τίνα τρόπον ῥᾷστα   5
πιόμεθα; ἐγὼ μὲν οὖν λέγω ὑμῖν ὅτι τῷ ὄντι πάνυ χαλεπῶς
ἔχω ὑπὸ τοῦ χθὲς πότου καὶ δέομαι ἀναψυχῆς τινος, οἶμαι δὲ
καὶ ὑμῶν τοὺς πολλούς· παρῆστε γὰρ χθές. σκοπεῖσθε οὖν   b
τίνι τρόπῳ ἂν ὡς ῥᾷστα πίνοιμεν.'

τὸν οὖν Ἀριστοφάνη εἰπεῖν, 'τοῦτο μέντοι εὖ λέγεις, ὦ
Παυσανία, τὸ παντὶ τρόπῳ παρασκευάσασθαι ῥᾳστώνην τινὰ
τῆς πόσεως· καὶ γὰρ αὐτός εἰμι τῶν χθὲς βεβαπτισμένων.'   5

ἀκούσαντα οὖν αὐτῶν ἔφη Ἐρυξίμαχον τὸν Ἀκουμενοῦ 'ἦ
καλῶς', φάναι, 'λέγετε. καὶ ἔτι ἑνὸς δέομαι ὑμῶν ἀκοῦσαι·
πῶς ἔχει πρὸς τὸ ἐρρῶσθαι πίνειν Ἀγάθων;'

'οὐδαμῶς,' φάναι· 'οὐδ᾽ αὐτὸς ἔρρωμαι.'

'ἕρμαιον ἂν εἴη ἡμῖν,' ἦ δ᾽ ὅς, 'ὡς ἔοικεν, ἐμοί τε καὶ   c
Ἀριστοδήμῳ καὶ Φαίδρῳ καὶ τοῖσδε, εἰ ὑμεῖς οἱ δυνατώτατοι
πίνειν νῦν ἀπειρήκατε· ἡμεῖς μὲν γὰρ ἀεὶ ἀδύνατοι. Σωκράτη
δ᾽ ἐξαιρῶ λόγου· ἱκανὸς γὰρ καὶ ἀμφότερα, ὥστ᾽ ἐξαρκέσει
αὐτῷ ὁπότερ᾽ ἂν ποιῶμεν. ἐπειδὴ οὖν μοι δοκεῖ οὐδεὶς τῶν   5
παρόντων προθύμως ἔχειν πρὸς τὸ πολὺν πίνειν οἶνον, ἴσως
ἂν ἐγὼ περὶ τοῦ μεθύσκεσθαι οἷόν ἐστι τἀληθῆ λέγων ἧττον
ἂν εἴην ἀηδής. ἐμοὶ γὰρ δὴ τοῦτό γε οἶμαι κατάδηλον   d
γεγονέναι ἐκ τῆς ἰατρικῆς, ὅτι χαλεπὸν τοῖς ἀνθρώποις ἡ
μέθη ἐστίν· καὶ οὔτε αὐτὸς ἑκὼν εἶναι πόρρω ἐθελήσαιμι ἂν
πιεῖν οὔτε ἄλλῳ συμβουλεύσαιμι, ἄλλως τε καὶ κραιπαλῶντα
ἔτι ἐκ τῆς προτεραίας.'   5

'ἀλλὰ μήν', ἔφη φάναι ὑπολαβόντα Φαῖδρον τὸν
Μυρρινούσιον, 'ἔγωγέ σοι εἴωθα πείθεσθαι ἄλλως τε καὶ ἅττ᾽
ἂν περὶ ἰατρικῆς λέγῃς· νῦν δ᾽, ἂν εὖ βουλεύωνται, καὶ οἱ

b 8 πίνειν, Ἀγάθων\<ος\> e, O | d 8 βουλεύωνται e: βούλωνται m

'You're a downright criminal, Socrates,' said Agathon. 'On this, we'll take our rival claims to wisdom to court a bit [e10] later on, with Dionysus as judge; as for now, turn your attention to your dinner before anything else.'

176 After that, Aristodemus said, when Socrates had reclined, and he and all the rest had had dinner, they poured libations and, after a song to the god and the other usual things, turned towards drinking. Then, he said, Pausanias began an exchange [a5] of the following sort. 'Well then, gentlemen!' he said. 'What will be the easiest way for us to do our drinking? Well, I'll tell you that yesterday's drinking has really left me in a pretty bad state, and I need time to recover; I imagine [b1] most of you too feel the same, because you were there yesterday. So see how you think we can make our drinking as easy on ourselves as we can.'

Aristophanes then said 'You're absolutely right about that, Pausanias; going a bit easy on the drinking [b5] is what we need, however we can arrange it. I say that because I was myself one of those who got thoroughly soaked yesterday.'

When Eryximachus, son of Acumenus, heard this from the two of them – so Aristodemus said – he said 'I quite agree with you. And there's one more of you I want to hear from: how is Agathon? Is he feeling strong enough to drink?'

'Certainly not,' said Agathon; 'I haven't the strength either.'

[c1] 'It looks as if it will be a godsend', said Eryximachus, 'for us – for me, and Aristodemus, and Phaedrus, and these people here – if you, the best drinkers among us, have given up at this point; we're never up to it. I exclude Socrates; actually he can manage either way, so it will be fine [c5] with him whether we drink or not. In which case, since it seems to me that no one here is feeling enthusiastic about drinking large quantities of wine, perhaps I won't be so unpopular if I tell you the truth about the sort of thing [d1] drunkenness is. What I believe I have discovered from my own practice as a doctor is that being drunk is a bad thing for people generally; and I wouldn't either want to drink a lot myself, if I had the choice, or advise anyone else to do so, especially if they're still suffering from a hangover [d5] from the day before.'

Aristodemus said that Phaedrus of Myrrhinus intervened: 'Very well. It's always my rule to listen to you, especially whatever you say about doctoring; and in this case, if they think it properly through, the rest will listen

24

λοιποί.' ταῦτα δὴ ἀκούσαντας συγχωρεῖν πάντας μὴ διὰ e
μέθης ποιήσασθαι τὴν ἐν τῷ παρόντι συνουσίαν, ἀλλ' οὕτω
πίνοντας πρὸς ἡδονήν.

'ἐπειδὴ τοίνυν', φάναι τὸν Ἐρυξίμαχον, 'τοῦτο μὲν
δέδοκται, πίνειν ὅσον ἂν ἕκαστος βούληται, ἐπάναγκες δὲ 5
μηδὲν εἶναι, τὸ μετὰ τοῦτο εἰσηγοῦμαι τὴν μὲν ἄρτι
εἰσελθοῦσαν αὐλητρίδα χαίρειν ἐᾶν, αὐλοῦσαν ἑαυτῇ ἢ ἂν
βούληται ταῖς γυναιξὶ ταῖς ἔνδον, ἡμᾶς δὲ διὰ λόγων
ἀλλήλοις συνεῖναι τὸ τήμερον· καὶ δι' οἵων λόγων, εἰ
βούλεσθε, ἐθέλω ὑμῖν εἰσηγήσασθαι.'   10

   φάναι δὴ πάντας καὶ βούλεσθαι καὶ κελεύειν αὐτὸν 177
εἰσηγεῖσθαι. εἰπεῖν οὖν τὸν Ἐρυξίμαχον ὅτι 'ἡ μέν μοι ἀρχὴ
τοῦ λόγου ἐστὶ κατὰ τὴν Εὐριπίδου Μελανίππην· "οὐ γὰρ
ἐμὸς ὁ μῦθος", ἀλλὰ Φαίδρου τοῦδε, ὃν μέλλω λέγειν.
Φαῖδρος γὰρ ἑκάστοτε πρός με ἀγανακτῶν λέγει "οὐ δεινόν," 5
φησίν, "ὦ Ἐρυξίμαχε, ἄλλοις μέν τισι θεῶν ὕμνους καὶ
παίωνας εἶναι ὑπὸ τῶν ποιητῶν πεποιημένους, τῷ δὲ Ἔρωτι,
τηλικούτῳ ὄντι καὶ τοσούτῳ θεῷ, μηδὲ ἕνα πώποτε τοσούτων b
γεγονότων ποιητῶν πεποιηκέναι μηδὲν ἐγκώμιον; εἰ δὲ βούλει
αὖ σκέψασθαι τοὺς χρηστοὺς σοφιστάς, Ἡρακλέους μὲν καὶ
ἄλλων ἐπαίνους καταλογάδην συγγράφειν, ὥσπερ ὁ βέλτιστος
Πρόδικος – καὶ τοῦτο μὲν ἧττον καὶ θαυμαστόν, ἀλλ' ἔγωγε 5
ἤδη τινὶ ἐνέτυχον βιβλίῳ ἀνδρὸς σοφοῦ, ἐν ᾧ ἐνῆσαν ἅλες
ἔπαινον θαυμάσιον ἔχοντες πρὸς ὠφελίαν, καὶ ἄλλα τοιαῦτα
συχνὰ ἴδοις ἂν ἐγκεκωμιασμένα· τὸ οὖν τοιούτων μὲν πέρι c
πολλὴν σπουδὴν ποιήσασθαι, Ἔρωτα δὲ μηδένα πω ἀνθρώπων
τετολμηκέναι εἰς ταυτηνὶ τὴν ἡμέραν ἀξίως ὑμνῆσαι – ἀλλ'
οὕτως ἠμέληται τοσοῦτος θεός." ταῦτα δή μοι δοκεῖ εὖ
λέγειν Φαῖδρος. ἐγὼ οὖν ἐπιθυμῶ ἅμα μὲν τούτῳ ἔρανον 5
εἰσενεγκεῖν καὶ χαρίσασθαι, ἅμα δ' ἐν τῷ παρόντι πρέπον
μοι δοκεῖ εἶναι ἡμῖν τοῖς παροῦσι κοσμῆσαι τὸν θεόν. εἰ οὖν
συνδοκεῖ καὶ ὑμῖν, γένοιτ' ἂν ἡμῖν ἐν λόγοις ἱκανὴ διατριβή· d
δοκεῖ γάρ μοι χρῆναι ἕκαστον ἡμῶν λόγον εἰπεῖν ἔπαινον
Ἔρωτος ἐπὶ δεξιὰ ὡς ἂν δύνηται κάλλιστον, ἄρχειν δὲ
Φαῖδρον πρῶτον, ἐπειδὴ καὶ πρῶτος κατάκειται καί ἐστιν
ἅμα πατὴρ τοῦ λόγου.'   5

d 3 κάλλιστα n

[e1] too.' When they heard this everyone agreed not to carry on the party as it was at present by getting drunk, but to drink simply for the enjoyment of it.

'Well then,' said Eryximachus, 'now that this is [e5] the decision, that we're to drink as much as each of us happens to want, with no compulsion on anyone, I propose that what we should do next is to let the *aulos*-girl who came in just now go off and play her instrument to herself, or, if she likes, to the women in their quarters, and that for today we should entertain each other with talk; and if you want me to, I'm willing to [e10] propose the sort of talk it should be.'

177 Everyone said that they not only wanted him to make his proposal, but they were ordering him to make it. So Eryximachus did. He said 'I'll begin along the lines of Euripides' Melanippe: what I'm going to put to you – "the tale is not mine", but belongs to Phaedrus here. [a5] Phaedrus is always complaining to me, whenever the occasion arises: "Isn't it a terrible thing, Eryximachus,' he says, 'that while some of the gods have had hymns and paeans composed specially for them by the poets, not a single one of all [b1] the many poets there have been has ever yet composed an encomium to Love, despite his venerable age and greatness? Or again, if you like, consider the case of the sophists, I mean the respectable ones. Isn't it terrible that they write prose panegyrics of Heracles and others, as the excellent [b5] Prodicus did – in fact, that isn't so amazing, but I have actually come across a book by a clever man in which salt was the subject of amazing praise for its usefulness, and you'll see many [c1] other things of that sort given encomia: to think that people attend earnestly to things like that, when no single person has yet, to this very day, undertaken to hymn Love as he deserves! But that's a measure of the neglect there has been of so great a god." Phaedrus seems to me [c5] to be quite right about this. So I'm anxious not only to make a contribution to his cause, and do a favour for him; I also think it appropriate on the present occasion for us who are present to do honour to the god. So if [d1] you too agree with my idea, there would be enough to occupy us in discussion: what I think is that each of us, beginning from the left, should give a speech – the most beautiful he can manage – in praise of Love, and that Phaedrus should start off, in first place, since he's both reclining in first position, and is also [d5] the person who conceived the whole subject.'

'οὐδείς σοι, ὦ Ἐρυξίμαχε,' φάναι τὸν Σωκράτη, 'ἐναντία
ψηφιεῖται. οὔτε γὰρ ἄν που ἐγὼ ἀποφήσαιμι, ὃς οὐδέν φημι
ἄλλο ἐπίστασθαι ἢ τὰ ἐρωτικά, οὔτε που Ἀγάθων καὶ e
Παυσανίας, οὐδὲ μὴν Ἀριστοφάνης, ᾧ περὶ Διόνυσον καὶ
Ἀφροδίτην πᾶσα ἡ διατριβή, οὐδὲ ἄλλος οὐδεὶς τουτωνὶ ὧν
ἐγὼ ὁρῶ. καίτοι οὐκ ἐξ ἴσου γίγνεται ἡμῖν τοῖς ὑστάτοις
κατακειμένοις· ἀλλ' ἐὰν οἱ πρόσθεν ἱκανῶς καὶ καλῶς 5
εἴπωσιν, ἐξαρκέσει ἡμῖν. ἀλλὰ τύχῃ ἀγαθῇ καταρχέτω
Φαῖδρος καὶ ἐγκωμιαζέτω τὸν Ἔρωτα.'
   ταῦτα δὴ καὶ οἱ ἄλλοι πάντες ἄρα συνέφασάν τε καὶ
ἐκέλευον ἅπερ ὁ Σωκράτης. πάντων μὲν οὖν ἃ ἕκαστος εἶπεν, 178
οὔτε πάνυ ὁ Ἀριστόδημος ἐμέμνητο οὔτ' αὖ ἐγὼ ἃ ἐκεῖνος
ἔλεγε πάντα· ἃ δὲ μάλιστα καὶ ὧν ἔδοξέ μοι ἀξιο-
μνημόνευτον, τούτων ὑμῖν ἐρῶ ἑκάστου τὸν λόγον.
   πρῶτον μὲν γάρ, ὥσπερ λέγω, ἔφη Φαῖδρον ἀρξάμενον 5
ἐνθένδε ποθὲν λέγειν, ὅτι μέγας θεὸς εἴη ὁ Ἔρως καὶ
θαυμαστὸς ἐν ἀνθρώποις τε καὶ θεοῖς, πολλαχῇ μὲν καὶ ἄλλη,
οὐχ ἥκιστα δὲ κατὰ τὴν γένεσιν. 'τὸ γὰρ ἐν τοῖς b
πρεσβύτατον εἶναι τὸν θεὸν τίμιον,' ᾖ δ' ὅς, 'τεκμήριον δὲ
τούτου· γονῆς γὰρ Ἔρωτος οὔτ' εἰσὶν οὔτε λέγονται ὑπ'
οὐδενὸς οὔτε ἰδιώτου οὔτε ποιητοῦ, ἀλλ' Ἡσίοδος πρῶτον μὲν
Χάος φησὶ γενέσθαι· 5
                    αὐτὰρ ἔπειτα
    Γαῖ' εὐρύστερνος, πάντων ἕδος ἀσφαλὲς αἰεί,
    ἠδ' Ἔρος.
Ἡσιόδῳ δὲ καὶ Ἀκουσίλεως σύμφησιν μετὰ τὸ Χάος δύο
τούτω γενέσθαι, Γῆν τε καὶ Ἔρωτα. Παρμενίδης δὲ τὴν 10
γένεσιν λέγει·
    πρώτιστον μὲν Ἔρωτα θεῶν μητίσατο πάντων.
οὕτω πολλαχόθεν ὁμολογεῖται ὁ Ἔρως ἐν τοῖς πρεσβύτατος c
εἶναι. πρεσβύτατος δὲ ὢν μεγίστων ἀγαθῶν ἡμῖν αἴτιός
ἐστιν. οὐ γὰρ ἔγωγ' ἔχω εἰπεῖν ὅτι μεῖζόν ἐστιν ἀγαθὸν
εὐθὺς νέῳ ὄντι ἢ ἐραστὴς χρηστὸς καὶ ἐραστῇ παιδικά. ὃ
γὰρ χρὴ ἀνθρώποις ἡγεῖσθαι παντὸς τοῦ βίου τοῖς μέλλουσι 5
καλῶς βιώσεσθαι, τοῦτο οὔτε συγγένεια οἵα τε ἐμποιεῖν οὕτω

---

a 3-4 ἀξιομνημόνευτον εἶναι n | **b 9** Ἡ. δὲ καὶ Ἀ. σύμφησιν e: φησὶ m,
with Ἡ. δὲ καὶ Ἀ. ὁμολογεῖ after quotation in b 12 (Ἡ. δὲ καὶ Ἀ. σύμφησιν t)

'No one will vote against you, Eryximachus,' Aristodemus reported Socrates as saying. 'It's not likely that either I would say no, seeing that I claim not [e1] to know about anything *except* things erotic, or, I imagine, that Agathon and Pausanias would; nor indeed Aristophanes, since his whole business is with Dionysus and Aphrodite – nor again any of the people I see here. It isn't fair on those of us on the last [e5] couches, but it'll be enough for us if those before us give an adequate speech, or indeed a good one. Let Phaedrus begin with his encomium to Love, and good luck be with him!'

So that was what everyone else agreed to, too, and they all **178** echoed Socrates' instruction to Phaedrus to start. Aristodemus, I have to say, didn't remember everything each person said, nor in my turn do I remember everything he told me; but what he remembered best, and the people who seemed to me to say something worth remembering – I'll tell you the speech each of these gave.

[a5] First then, as I say, according to Aristodemus, Phaedrus spoke, starting from this sort of point – that Love is a great god, and an object of wonder among gods as well as men in many ways, [b1] and not least in respect of his origins. 'The god is honoured', he said, 'for being among the oldest, and evidence for this is that Love neither has any parents, nor is he said by anyone, whether layman or poet, to have them. Hesiod says that first [b5] to come into being was Chaos; "and then broad-bosomed Earth, a seat for all, safe for ever, and Love". Acusilaus too says the same as Hesiod, that these two, Earth [b10] and Love, came into being after Chaos. Parmenides says of the origin of Love "First was devised Love, of all gods". [c1] Thus it is agreed on many sides that Love was among the oldest. And being very old, he is cause of very great goods for us human beings. I cannot myself say what greater good there is for someone, from boyhood onwards, than a lover of a respectable sort, and for a lover, a beloved of the same sort. What [c5] it is that should guide human beings who mean to live well, in their whole lives: this, nothing – not kinship, or public honours, or wealth, [d1] or

καλῶς οὔτε τιμαὶ οὔτε πλοῦτος οὔτ' ἄλλο οὐδὲν ὡς ἔρως. d
λέγω δὲ δὴ τί τοῦτο; τὴν ἐπὶ μὲν τοῖς αἰσχροῖς αἰσχύνην,
ἐπὶ δὲ τοῖς καλοῖς φιλοτιμίαν· οὐ γάρ ἐστιν ἄνευ τούτων
οὔτε πόλιν οὔτε ἰδιώτην μεγάλα καὶ καλὰ ἔργα ἐξεργάζεσθαι.
φημὶ τοίνυν ἐγὼ ἄνδρα ὅστις ἐρᾷ, εἴ τι αἰσχρὸν ποιῶν 5
κατάδηλος γίγνοιτο ἢ πάσχων ὑπό του δι' ἀνανδρίαν μὴ
ἀμυνόμενος, οὔτ' ἂν ὑπὸ πατρὸς ὀφθέντα οὕτως ἀλγῆσαι οὔτε
ὑπὸ ἑταίρων οὔτε ὑπ' ἄλλου οὐδενὸς ὡς ὑπὸ παιδικῶν. ταὐτὸν e
δὲ τοῦτο καὶ τὸν ἐρώμενον ὁρῶμεν, ὅτι διαφερόντως τοὺς
ἐραστὰς αἰσχύνεται, ὅταν ὀφθῇ ἐν αἰσχρῷ τινι ὤν. εἰ οὖν
μηχανή τις γένοιτο ὥστε πόλιν γενέσθαι ἢ στρατόπεδον
ἐραστῶν τε καὶ παιδικῶν, οὐκ ἔστιν ὅπως ἂν ἄμεινον 5
οἰκήσειαν τὴν ἑαυτῶν ἢ ἀπεχόμενοι πάντων τῶν αἰσχρῶν καὶ
φιλοτιμούμενοι πρὸς ἀλλήλους, καὶ μαχόμενοί γ' ἂν μετ' 179
ἀλλήλων οἱ τοιοῦτοι νικῷεν ἂν ὀλίγοι ὄντες ὡς ἔπος εἰπεῖν
πάντας ἀνθρώπους. ἐρῶν γὰρ ἀνὴρ ὑπὸ παιδικῶν ὀφθῆναι ἢ
λιπὼν τάξιν ἢ ὅπλα ἀποβαλὼν ἧττον ἂν δήπου δέξαιτο ἢ ὑπὸ
πάντων τῶν ἄλλων, καὶ πρὸ τούτου τεθνάναι ἂν πολλάκις 5
ἕλοιτο. καὶ μὴν ἐγκαταλιπεῖν γε τὰ παιδικὰ ἢ μὴ βοηθῆσαι
κινδυνεύοντι – οὐδεὶς οὕτω κακὸς ὅντινα οὐκ ἂν αὐτὸς ὁ
Ἔρως ἔνθεον ποιήσειε πρὸς ἀρετήν, ὥστε ὅμοιον εἶναι τῷ
ἀρίστῳ φύσει· καὶ ἀτεχνῶς, ὃ ἔφη Ὅμηρος, "μένος b
ἐμπνεῦσαι" ἐνίοις τῶν ἡρώων τὸν θεόν, τοῦτο ὁ Ἔρως τοῖς
ἐρῶσι παρέχει γιγνόμενον παρ' αὑτοῦ.

'καὶ μὴν ὑπεραποθνῄσκειν γε μόνοι ἐθέλουσιν οἱ ἐρῶντες,
οὐ μόνον ὅτι ἄνδρες, ἀλλὰ καὶ αἱ γυναῖκες. τούτου δὲ καὶ ἡ 5
Πελίου θυγάτηρ Ἄλκηστις ἱκανὴν μαρτυρίαν παρέχεται ὑπὲρ
τοῦδε τοῦ λόγου εἰς τοὺς Ἕλληνας, ἐθελήσασα μόνη ὑπὲρ τοῦ
αὑτῆς ἀνδρὸς ἀποθανεῖν, ὄντων αὐτῷ πατρός τε καὶ μητρός,
οὓς ἐκείνη τοσοῦτον ὑπερεβάλετο τῇ φιλίᾳ διὰ τὸν ἔρωτα, c
ὥστε ἀποδεῖξαι αὐτοὺς ἀλλοτρίους ὄντας τῷ ὑεῖ καὶ ὀνόματι
μόνον προσήκοντας, καὶ τοῦτ' ἐργασαμένη τὸ ἔργον οὕτω
καλὸν ἔδοξεν ἐργάσασθαι οὐ μόνον ἀνθρώποις ἀλλὰ καὶ θεοῖς,
ὥστε πολλῶν πολλὰ καὶ καλὰ ἐργασαμένων εὐαριθμήτοις δή 5
τισιν ἔδοσαν τοῦτο γέρας οἱ θεοί, ἐξ Ἅιδου ἀνεῖναι πάλιν
τὴν ψυχήν, ἀλλὰ τὴν ἐκείνης ἀνεῖσαν ἀγασθέντες τῷ ἔργῳ·

e 6 [ἢ] e | b 5 οὐ μόνον ὅτι ἄνδρες n: οὐ μόνον ἄνδρες n |
c 6 ἀνιέναι e

anything else – is capable of implanting so well as love can. What is it that I refer to? The feeling of shame at shameful things, and love of honour in the case of fine ones; without these it is impossible for either a city or an individual to enact great and fine actions. [d5] I declare, then, that if a man who is in love were to be detected doing something shameful, or having something shameful done to him and failing to defend himself through a lack of manliness, he would not feel so much pain if he were seen by a father, or [e1] by friends, or by anyone else, as he would if seen by a beloved. And in the same way we observe that a beloved has a particular sense of shame towards a lover, when he is seen in some shameful situation. So if in some way it could be brought about that there was a city, or an army, [e5] of lovers and their beloveds, there is nothing that would enable them to govern their country better than their abstention from all shameful things and 179 their rivalry with each other in pursuit of honour; and if they actually fought alongside each other, such men – even a few of them – would overcome practically all human opponents. A man in love would surely find it less acceptable to be seen either breaking ranks or throwing his arms away by a beloved than by [a5] anyone else, and rather than have that happen he would choose to die many times over. Moreover, as for abandoning his beloved, or not going to his aid when he was in danger – no one is so cowardly that Love himself would not give him a courage that was inspired, to make him resemble the man who [b1] possesses supreme courage by nature; it's exactly as Homer puts it when he has the god "breathing might" into some of the heroes – this is what Love himself causes to happen to those in love.

'Moreover, when it comes to dying for others, only those who are in love are willing to do it, [b5] women too, not just men. Of that Alcestis, daughter of Pelias, supplies all of us Greeks with evidence enough, to support what I say, since she alone willingly undertook to die for her husband – when he had a father and a mother, [c1] whom she so exceeded in affection, because of her love, as to prove them alien to their son and related to him only in name, and by doing the deed she appeared not only to men but to gods to have done something so fine [c5] that although many have done many fine things, and the gods have given only a small number among them the privilege of having their souls sent back up from Hades, they sent hers up out

οὕτω καὶ θεοὶ τὴν περὶ τὸν ἔρωτα σπουδήν τε καὶ ἀρετὴν d
μάλιστα τιμῶσιν. Ὀρφέα δὲ τὸν Οἰάγρου ἀτελῆ ἀπέπεμψαν ἐξ
Ἅιδου, φάσμα δείξαντες τῆς γυναικὸς ἐφ' ἣν ἧκεν, αὐτὴν δὲ
οὐ δόντες, ὅτι μαλθακίζεσθαι ἐδόκει, ἅτε ὢν κιθαρῳδός, καὶ
οὐ τολμᾶν ἕνεκα τοῦ ἔρωτος ἀποθνῄσκειν ὥσπερ Ἄλκηστις, 5
ἀλλὰ διαμηχανᾶσθαι ζῶν εἰσιέναι εἰς Ἅιδου. τοιγάρτοι διὰ
ταῦτα δίκην αὐτῷ ἐπέθεσαν, καὶ ἐποίησαν τὸν θάνατον αὐτοῦ
ὑπὸ γυναικῶν γενέσθαι, οὐχ ὥσπερ Ἀχιλλέα τὸν τῆς Θέτιδος e
ὑὸν ἐτίμησαν καὶ εἰς μακάρων νήσους ἀπέπεμψαν, ὅτι
πεπυσμένος παρὰ τῆς μητρὸς ὡς ἀποθανοῖτο ἀποκτείνας
Ἕκτορα, μὴ ποιήσας δὲ τοῦτο οἴκαδε ἐλθὼν γηραιὸς
τελευτήσοι, ἐτόλμησεν ἑλέσθαι βοηθήσας τῷ ἐραστῇ Πατρόκλῳ 5
καὶ τιμωρήσας οὐ μόνον ὑπεραποθανεῖν ἀλλὰ καὶ ἐπαποθανεῖν 180
τετελευτηκότι· ὅθεν δὴ καὶ ὑπεραγασθέντες οἱ θεοὶ
διαφερόντως αὐτὸν ἐτίμησαν, ὅτι τὸν ἐραστὴν οὕτω περὶ
πολλοῦ ἐποιεῖτο. Αἰσχύλος δὲ φλυαρεῖ φάσκων Ἀχιλλέα
Πατρόκλου ἐρᾶν, ὃς ἦν καλλίων οὐ μόνον Πατρόκλου ἀλλ' ἄρα 5
καὶ τῶν ἡρώων ἁπάντων, καὶ ἔτι ἀγένειος, ἔπειτα νεώτερος
πολύ, ὥς φησιν Ὅμηρος. ἀλλὰ γὰρ τῷ ὄντι μάλιστα μὲν
ταύτην τὴν ἀρετὴν οἱ θεοὶ τιμῶσιν τὴν περὶ τὸν ἔρωτα, b
μᾶλλον μέντοι θαυμάζουσιν καὶ ἄγανται καὶ εὖ ποιοῦσιν, ὅταν
ὁ ἐρώμενος τὸν ἐραστὴν ἀγαπᾷ, ἢ ὅταν ὁ ἐραστὴς τὰ
παιδικά. θειότερον γὰρ ἐραστὴς παιδικῶν· ἔνθεος γάρ ἐστι.
διὰ ταῦτα καὶ τὸν Ἀχιλλέα τῆς Ἀλκήστιδος μᾶλλον 5
ἐτίμησαν, εἰς μακάρων νήσους ἀποπέμψαντες.
    'οὕτω δὴ ἔγωγέ φημι Ἔρωτα θεῶν καὶ πρεσβύτατον καὶ
τιμιώτατον καὶ κυριώτατον εἶναι εἰς ἀρετῆς καὶ εὐδαιμονίας
κτῆσιν ἀνθρώποις καὶ ζῶσι καὶ τελευτήσασιν.'
    Φαῖδρον μὲν τοιοῦτόν τινα λόγον ἔφη εἰπεῖν, μετὰ δὲ c
Φαῖδρον ἄλλους τινὰς εἶναι ὧν οὐ πάνυ διεμνημόνευε· οὓς
παρεὶς τὸν Παυσανίου λόγον διηγεῖτο. εἰπεῖν δ' αὐτὸν ὅτι
'οὐ καλῶς μοι δοκεῖ, ὦ Φαῖδρε, προβεβλῆσθαι ἡμῖν ὁ λόγος,
τὸ ἁπλῶς οὕτως παρηγγέλθαι ἐγκωμιάζειν Ἔρωτα. εἰ μὲν γὰρ 5
εἷς ἦν ὁ Ἔρως, καλῶς ἂν εἶχε, νῦν δὲ οὐ γάρ ἐστιν εἷς· μὴ
ὄντος δὲ ἑνὸς ὀρθότερόν ἐστι πρότερον προρρηθῆναι ὁποῖον
δεῖ ἐπαινεῖν. ἐγὼ οὖν πειράσομαι τοῦτο ἐπανορθώσασθαι, d
πρῶτον μὲν Ἔρωτα φράσαι ὃν δεῖ ἐπαινεῖν, ἔπειτα ἐπαινέσαι

a 5 ἀλλ' ἄρα n: ἀλλὰ n: ἀλλ' ἄμα O

of admiration for her deed; [d1] thus gods too honour especially the zeal and courage that relates to love. But Orpheus, son of Oeagrus, they sent away empty-handed from Hades, showing him a phantom of the wife for whom he had come, but not giving him the woman herself, because he seemed to them to be behaving with the usual softness of a cithara-player, and [d5] not to be brave enough to die for the sake of his love, as Alcestis did, contriving instead to enter Hades while alive. And so for this reason they punished him, and brought it about that he died [e1] at the hands of women, not treating him as they did Achilles, son of Thetis, whom they honoured and sent to the isles of the blest, because when he learned from his mother that he would die if he killed Hector, but that if he did not do that he would go home and end his life [e5] in old age, he dared to choose to go to his lover Patroclus' aid **180** and avenge him, and so not merely to die for him but to add his own death to his; and so it was that out of superlative admiration for him they honoured him more than anyone, because he set such great store by his lover. Aeschylus is talking nonsense when he claims that Achilles [a5] was in love with Patroclus, because his beauty exceeded not only Patroclus' but in fact that of all the heroes, and he was still beardless, and also much younger, as Homer says. In any case it is really true that the gods [b1] honour this courage, the kind that relates to love, most, yet they reserve more wonder and admiration, and greater benefits, for when the person who is loved shows passionate feeling for his lover, than when the lover shows it for his beloved. For a lover is something more divine than a beloved; after all, he is possessed by a god. [b5] That is why it was Achilles they honoured more, rather than Alcestis, and sent him to the isles of the blest.

'So it is that I declare Love oldest of gods, and most honoured, and with most power when it comes to the acquisition of virtue and happiness by human beings, both in life and after they have ended it.'

[c1] Phaedrus gave a speech something like this, Aristodemus said, and after Phaedrus there were some others which he was not quite able to remember; leaving these aside, he recounted Pausanias' speech. He said Pausanias said this: 'Phaedrus, our subject seems to me not to have been put forward in the right way – [c1] I mean in that we have been instructed, as we have, simply to give an encomium to Love. If Love were such that there were just one of him, that would be in order; but in fact there isn't just one of him; and if there isn't, it is more correct to preface what one says by first saying what sort of Love [d1] one should praise. So I shall try to put this right: I shall try first to indicate the Love one should praise, and then to praise him in

ἀξίως τοῦ θεοῦ. πάντες γὰρ ἴσμεν ὅτι οὐκ ἔστιν ἄνευ
Ἔρωτος Ἀφροδίτη. μιᾶς μὲν οὖν οὔσης εἷς ἂν ἦν Ἔρως· ἐπεὶ
δὲ δὴ δύο ἐστόν, δύο ἀνάγκη καὶ Ἔρωτε εἶναι. πῶς δ' οὐ δύο 5
τὼ θεά; ἡ μέν γέ που πρεσβυτέρα καὶ ἀμήτωρ Οὐρανοῦ
θυγάτηρ, ἣν δὴ καὶ Οὐρανίαν ἐπονομάζομεν· ἡ δὲ νεωτέρα
Διὸς καὶ Διώνης, ἣν δὴ Πάνδημον καλοῦμεν. ἀναγκαῖον δὴ καὶ e
Ἔρωτα τὸν μὲν τῇ ἑτέρᾳ συνεργὸν Πάνδημον ὀρθῶς
καλεῖσθαι, τὸν δὲ Οὐράνιον. ἐπαινεῖν μὲν οὖν δεῖ πάντας
θεούς, ἃ δ' οὖν ἑκάτερος εἴληχε πειρατέον εἰπεῖν. πᾶσα γὰρ
πρᾶξις ὧδ' ἔχει· αὐτὴ ἐφ' ἑαυτῆς πραττομένη οὔτε καλὴ οὔτε 181
αἰσχρά. οἷον ὃ νῦν ἡμεῖς ποιοῦμεν, ἢ πίνειν ἢ ᾄδειν ἢ
διαλέγεσθαι, οὐκ ἔστι τούτων αὐτὸ καλὸν οὐδέν, ἀλλ' ἐν τῇ
πράξει, ὡς ἂν πραχθῇ, τοιοῦτον ἀπέβη· καλῶς μὲν γὰρ
πραττόμενον καὶ ὀρθῶς καλὸν γίγνεται, μὴ ὀρθῶς δὲ αἰσχρόν. 5
οὕτω δὴ καὶ τὸ ἐρᾶν καὶ ὁ Ἔρως οὐ πᾶς ἐστι καλὸς οὐδὲ
ἄξιος ἐγκωμιάζεσθαι, ἀλλὰ ὁ καλῶς προτρέπων ἐρᾶν.

ὁ μὲν οὖν τῆς Πανδήμου Ἀφροδίτης ὡς ἀληθῶς πάνδημός
ἐστι καὶ ἐξεργάζεται ὅτι ἂν τύχῃ· καὶ οὗτός ἐστιν ὃν οἱ b
φαῦλοι τῶν ἀνθρώπων ἐρῶσιν. ἐρῶσι δὲ οἱ τοιοῦτοι πρῶτον
μὲν οὐχ ἧττον γυναικῶν ἢ παίδων, ἔπειτα ὧν καὶ ἐρῶσι τῶν
σωμάτων μᾶλλον ἢ τῶν ψυχῶν, ἔπειτα ὡς ἂν δύνωνται
ἀνοητοτάτων, πρὸς τὸ διαπράξασθαι μόνον βλέποντες, 5
ἀμελοῦντες δὲ τοῦ καλῶς ἢ μή· ὅθεν δὴ συμβαίνει αὐτοῖς ὅτι
ἂν τύχωσι τοῦτο πράττειν, ὁμοίως μὲν ἀγαθόν, ὁμοίως δὲ
τοὐναντίον. ἔστι γὰρ καὶ ἀπὸ τῆς θεοῦ νεωτέρας τε οὔσης c
πολὺ ἢ τῆς ἑτέρας, καὶ μετεχούσης ἐν τῇ γενέσει καὶ θήλεος
καὶ ἄρρενος. ὁ δὲ τῆς Οὐρανίας πρῶτον μὲν οὐ μετεχούσης
θήλεος ἀλλ' ἄρρενος μόνον, καὶ ἔστιν οὗτος ὁ τῶν παίδων
ἔρως· ἔπειτα πρεσβυτέρας, ὕβρεως ἀμοίρου· ὅθεν δὴ ἐπὶ τὸ 5
ἄρρεν τρέπονται οἱ ἐκ τούτου τοῦ Ἔρωτος ἔπιπνοι, τὸ φύσει
ἐρρωμενέστερον καὶ νοῦν μᾶλλον ἔχον ἀγαπῶντες. καί τις ἂν
γνοίη καὶ ἐν αὐτῇ τῇ παιδεραστίᾳ τοὺς εἰλικρινῶς ὑπὸ
τούτου τοῦ ἔρωτος ὡρμημένους· οὐ γὰρ ἐρῶσι παίδων, ἀλλ' d
ἐπειδὰν ἤδη ἄρχωνται νοῦν ἴσχειν, τοῦτο δὲ πλησιάζει τῷ
γενειάσκειν. παρεσκευασμένοι γὰρ οἶμαί εἰσιν οἱ ἐντεῦθεν

c 4-5 [καὶ . . . ἔρως] e

a way worthy of the god. Well, we all know that there is no Aphrodite without Love. So if there were one of her there would be one Love; [d5] but since there are in fact two, so necessarily there are two Loves too. How could we suppose that the goddesses are not two? One, I imagine, is older, motherless daughter of Heaven, the one to whom we in fact give the name Heavenly; the other, [e1] younger one is daughter of Zeus and Dione, the one we call Common. Necessarily, then, the Love who works with the second Aphrodite will himself correctly be called Common, and the other one Heavenly. Now one should praise all gods, but for now what matters is to try to say what domain falls to the lot of each Love. **181** Every action is like this: when done, in and by itself it is neither fine nor shameful. So for example with what we are doing now: whether we drink, or sing, or talk to each other, none of these things is in itself fine, but rather the manner in which it is done is what determines how it turns out, in the doing of it; if it is done [a5] in a fine way, and correctly, it becomes fine, and if incorrectly, shameful. This is how it is with loving and with Love: not all of Love is fine, or a worthy object of encomium – only the Love who impels us to love in a fine way.

'Now the Love who belongs to Common Aphrodite is truly common, [b1] and carries through with anything that happens to come his way; and this is the love that inferior people experience. In the first place people like this love women no less than boys; secondly, they love those they are in love with for their bodies rather than their souls; and thirdly, they fall in love with people who are the least [b5] intelligent possible: they have their eye simply on achieving what they want, not caring whether the way in which they get it is fine or not, and it is from this that it comes about that they do whatever comes their way – whether good, or the [c1] opposite, it's all the same to them. This is because their Love in fact comes from the goddess who not only is much younger than the other, but by reason of her birth shares in both the female and the male. The Love who belongs to Heavenly Aphrodite, by contrast, in the first place belongs to a goddess who does not share in the female but only in the male, and this love is accordingly the [c5] love of boys; secondly he belongs to one who is older, with no portion of lawlessness, and it is for this reason that those whose inspiration comes from this Love turn their attention to the male, feeling the attraction of what is by nature stronger and has a greater degree of intelligence. In fact one can recognize, among boy-lovers themselves, those who genuinely [d1] get their impulse from this love: they do not love boys, so much as those who are already beginning to be intelligent, and this occurs around the time when

34

ἀρχόμενοι ἐρᾶν ὡς τὸν βίον ἅπαντα συνεσόμενοι καὶ κοινῇ
συμβιωσόμενοι, ἀλλ' οὐκ ἐξαπατήσαντες, ἐν ἀφροσύνῃ 5
λαβόντες ὡς νέον, καταγελάσαντες οἰχήσεσθαι ἐπ' ἄλλον
ἀποτρέχοντες. χρῆν δὲ καὶ νόμον εἶναι μὴ ἐρᾶν παίδων, ἵνα
μὴ εἰς ἄδηλον πολλὴ σπουδὴ ἀνηλίσκετο· τὸ γὰρ τῶν παίδων e
τέλος ἄδηλον οἷ τελευτᾷ κακίας καὶ ἀρετῆς ψυχῆς τε πέρι
καὶ σώματος. οἱ μὲν οὖν ἀγαθοὶ τὸν νόμον τοῦτον αὐτοὶ
αὑτοῖς ἑκόντες τίθενται, χρῆν δὲ καὶ τούτους τοὺς πανδήμους
ἐραστὰς προσαναγκάζειν τὸ τοιοῦτον, ὥσπερ καὶ τῶν 5
ἐλευθέρων γυναικῶν προσαναγκάζομεν αὐτοὺς καθ' ὅσον 182
δυνάμεθα μὴ ἐρᾶν. οὗτοι γάρ εἰσιν οἱ καὶ τὸ ὄνειδος
πεποιηκότες, ὥστε τινὰς τολμᾶν λέγειν ὡς αἰσχρὸν
χαρίζεσθαι ἐρασταῖς· λέγουσι δὲ εἰς τούτους ἀποβλέποντες,
ὁρῶντες αὐτῶν τὴν ἀκαιρίαν καὶ ἀδικίαν, ἐπεὶ οὐ δήπου 5
κοσμίως γε καὶ νομίμως ὁτιοῦν πρᾶγμα πραττόμενον ψόγον
ἂν δικαίως φέροι.

'καὶ δὴ καὶ ὁ περὶ τὸν ἔρωτα νόμος ἐν μὲν ταῖς ἄλλαις
πόλεσι νοῆσαι ῥᾴδιος, ἁπλῶς γὰρ ὥρισται· ὁ δ' ἐνθάδε καὶ ἐν
Λακεδαίμονι ποικίλος. ἐν Ἤλιδι μὲν γὰρ καὶ ἐν Βοιωτοῖς, καὶ b
οὗ μὴ σοφοὶ λέγειν, ἁπλῶς νενομοθέτηται καλὸν τὸ
χαρίζεσθαι ἐρασταῖς, καὶ οὐκ ἄν τις εἴποι οὔτε νέος οὔτε
παλαιὸς ὡς αἰσχρόν, ἵνα οἶμαι μὴ πράγματ' ἔχωσιν λόγῳ
πειρώμενοι πείθειν τοὺς νέους, ἅτε ἀδύνατοι λέγειν· τῆς δὲ 5
Ἰωνίας καὶ ἄλλοθι πολλαχοῦ αἰσχρὸν νενόμισται, ὅσοι ὑπὸ
βαρβάροις οἰκοῦσιν. τοῖς γὰρ βαρβάροις διὰ τὰς τυραννίδας
αἰσχρὸν τοῦτό γε, καὶ ἥ γε φιλοσοφία καὶ ἡ φιλογυμναστία·
οὐ γὰρ οἶμαι συμφέρει τοῖς ἄρχουσι φρονήματα μεγάλα c
ἐγγίγνεσθαι τῶν ἀρχομένων, οὐδὲ φιλίας ἰσχυρὰς καὶ
κοινωνίας, ὃ δὴ μάλιστα φιλεῖ τά τε ἄλλα πάντα καὶ ὁ ἔρως
ἐμποιεῖν. ἔργῳ δὲ τοῦτο ἔμαθον καὶ οἱ ἐνθάδε τύραννοι· ὁ
γὰρ Ἀριστογείτονος ἔρως καὶ ἡ Ἁρμοδίου φιλία βέβαιος 5
γενομένη κατέλυσεν αὐτῶν τὴν ἀρχήν. οὕτως οὗ μὲν αἰσχρὸν
ἐτέθη χαρίζεσθαι ἐρασταῖς, κακίᾳ τῶν θεμένων κεῖται, τῶν
μὲν ἀρχόντων πλεονεξίᾳ, τῶν δὲ ἀρχομένων ἀνανδρίᾳ· οὗ δὲ d
καλὸν ἁπλῶς ἐνομίσθη, διὰ τὴν τῶν θεμένων τῆς ψυχῆς

---

a 6 ὁτιοῦν πρᾶγμα πραττόμεν n: ὁτιοῦν πραττόμενον n | **a 9-b 1** [καὶ ἐν
Λακεδαίμονι] e: ὁ δ' ἐνθάδε ποικίλος. ἐν Ἤλιδι μὲν γὰρ καὶ ἐν Λακεδαίμονι καὶ ... e

their beard starts growing. I think those who begin to love them from this age are ready to be with them for their whole lives, and to live a shared [d5] life in their company; not to deceive them, having taken them when they had the foolishness of the young, abandoning them with a contemptuous laugh and running off to someone else. There ought actually to be a law against loving boys, to [e1] prevent a great deal of effort being spent on something whose outcome is unpredictable: one cannot predict where boys will end up on the scale of badness and goodness, whether in relation to their souls or to their bodies. Of course good men voluntarily lay down this law for themselves; but the same sort of thing ought also [e5] to be imposed on those vulgar lovers too, just as **182** we impose a rule on them, so far as we can, not to love free women. These are the people who have brought about the reproach which causes some people to go so far as to say that it is shameful to grant favours to lovers; it is these people they are referring to when they say this, [a5] observing their inopportuneness and their injustice – because it would surely not be just for something which is done in an orderly and lawful fashion to be the object of censure.

'I next turn to the way things are laid down in relation to love: in other cities it is easy to grasp, because it has been defined in simple terms; here, and in [b1] Sparta, it is complex. In Elis and among the Boeotians, and where people are not expert at speaking, the rule is simply that it is a fine thing to grant favours to lovers, and no one, whether young or old, would say that it is shameful, I imagine so that they can spare themselves the trouble of trying [b5] to persuade the young by speaking to them, because they are incapable of speaking; whereas in Ionia, and in many places elsewhere, it is laid down as shameful, that is, where people live under the rule of non-Greeks. It is because of their tyrannies that non-Greeks make it shameful – along with love of intellectual and physical excellence; [c1] I don't think it is convenient for those in power that there should be big ideas about if these belong to their subjects, or for that matter strong friendships and partnerships, and that is just what all the other things, but especially love, most tend to bring about in us. The tyrants here in Athens themselves learned this from experience, because [c5] it was Aristogeiton's love for Harmodius, and Harmodius' affection for him, when both became firm and constant, that brought their regime to an end. Thus where it has been laid down as shameful to grant favours to lovers, the rule is there because of the failings of those who laid it down: the [d1] greed of those in power, and lack of manliness on the part of their subjects; and where the rule is simply that it is a fine thing, it is because

36

ἀργίαν. ἐνθάδε δὲ πολὺ τούτων κάλλιον νενομοθέτηται, καὶ
ὅπερ εἶπον, οὐ ῥᾴδιον κατανοῆσαι. ἐνθυμηθέντι γὰρ ὅτι
λέγεται κάλλιον τὸ φανερῶς ἐρᾶν τοῦ λάθρᾳ, καὶ μάλιστα τῶν 5
γενναιοτάτων καὶ ἀρίστων, κἂν αἰσχίους ἄλλων ὦσι, καὶ ὅτι
αὖ ἡ παρακέλευσις τῷ ἐρῶντι παρὰ πάντων θαυμαστή, οὐχ ὥς
τι αἰσχρὸν ποιοῦντι, καὶ ἑλόντι τε καλὸν δοκεῖ εἶναι καὶ μὴ e
ἑλόντι αἰσχρόν, καὶ πρὸς τὸ ἐπιχειρεῖν ἑλεῖν ἐξουσίαν ὁ
νόμος δέδωκε τῷ ἐραστῇ θαυμαστὰ ἔργα ἐργαζομένῳ
ἐπαινεῖσθαι, ἃ εἴ τις τολμῴη ποιεῖν ἄλλ' ὁτιοῦν διώκων καὶ
βουλόμενος διαπράξασθαι πλὴν τοῦτο, [φιλοσοφίας] τὰ μέγιστα 183
καρποῖτ' ἂν ὀνείδη – εἰ γὰρ ἢ χρήματα βουλόμενος παρά του
λαβεῖν ἢ ἀρχὴν ἄρξαι ἤ τινα ἄλλην δύναμιν ἐθέλοι ποιεῖν
οἷάπερ οἱ ἐρασταὶ πρὸς τὰ παιδικά, ἱκετείας τε καὶ
ἀντιβολήσεις ἐν ταῖς δεήσεσιν ποιούμενοι, καὶ ὅρκους 5
ὀμνύντες, καὶ κοιμήσεις ἐπὶ θύραις, καὶ ἐθέλοντες δουλείας
δουλεύειν οἵας οὐδ' ἂν δοῦλος οὐδείς, ἐμποδίζοιτο ἂν μὴ
πράττειν οὕτω τὴν πρᾶξιν καὶ ὑπὸ φίλων καὶ ὑπὸ ἐχθρῶν, τῶν b
μὲν ὀνειδιζόντων κολακείας καὶ ἀνελευθερίας, τῶν δὲ
νουθετούντων καὶ αἰσχυνομένων ὑπὲρ αὐτοῦ. τῷ δ' ἐρῶντι
πάντα ταῦτα ποιοῦντι χάρις ἔπεστι, καὶ δέδοται ὑπὸ τοῦ
νόμου ἄνευ ὀνείδους πράττειν, ὡς πάγκαλόν τι πρᾶγμα 5
διαπραττομένου. ὃ δὲ δεινότατον, ὥς γε λέγουσιν οἱ πολλοί,
ὅτι καὶ ὀμνύντι μόνῳ συγγνώμη παρὰ θεῶν ἐκβάντι τῶν
ὅρκων· ἀφροδίσιον γὰρ ὅρκον οὔ φασιν εἶναι. οὕτω καὶ οἱ θεοὶ
καὶ οἱ ἄνθρωποι πᾶσαν ἐξουσίαν πεποιήκασι τῷ ἐρῶντι, ὡς ὁ c
νόμος φησὶν ὁ ἐνθάδε. ταύτῃ μὲν οὖν οἰηθείη ἄν τις
πάγκαλον νομίζεσθαι ἐν τῇδε τῇ πόλει καὶ τὸ ἐρᾶν καὶ τὸ
φίλους γίγνεσθαι τοῖς ἐρασταῖς. ἐπειδὰν δὲ παιδαγωγοὺς
ἐπιστήσαντες οἱ πατέρες τοῖς ἐρωμένοις μὴ ἐῶσι διαλέγεσθαι 5
τοῖς ἐρασταῖς, καὶ τῷ παιδαγωγῷ ταῦτα προστεταγμένα ᾖ,
ἡλικιῶται δὲ καὶ ἑταῖροι ὀνειδίζωσιν ἐάν τι ὁρῶσιν τοιοῦτον
γιγνόμενον, καὶ τοὺς ὀνειδίζοντας αὖ οἱ πρεσβύτεροι μὴ d
διακωλύωσι μηδὲ λοιδορῶσιν ὡς οὐκ ὀρθῶς λέγοντας, εἰς δὲ
ταῦτά τις αὖ βλέψας ἡγήσαιτ' ἂν πάλιν αἴσχιστον τὸ
τοιοῦτον ἐνθάδε νομίζεσθαι. τὸ δὲ οἶμαι ὧδ' ἔχει· οὐχ ἁπλοῦν
ἐστιν, ὅπερ ἐξ ἀρχῆς ἐλέχθη οὔτε καλὸν εἶναι αὐτὸ καθ' αὑτὸ 5
οὔτε αἰσχρόν, ἀλλὰ καλῶς μὲν πραττόμενον καλόν, αἰσχρῶς δὲ

a 1 [φιλοσοφίας] e | b 3 αὑτοῦ e: αὐτῶν m | c 7 ἑταῖροι e: ἕτεροι m

of the mental laziness of those who laid it down. Here in Athens the rules have been arranged in a much better way; as I said, they are also not easy to grasp. If you consider that [d5] it is said to be finer to be in love openly than in secret, and most of all with the noblest and best individuals, even if they are not as beautiful as others, and again, that the encouragement that comes to the person in love from everyone is amazing (not what one would expect [e1] for someone who was doing something shameful), and people treat it as a fine thing for him if he catches his prey and shameful if he does not, and to help him try to do the catching, our customary rules give the lover licence to do, and be praised for doing, extraordinary things for which, if anyone dared to do them in pursuing and in order to **183** achieve anything else apart from this, he would earn the greatest reproaches -- for if, out of a wish to get money from someone, or access to political office, or some other kind of power, he were willing to do the sorts of things lovers do in relation to their beloveds, making his requests [a5] by supplication and entreaty, swearing oaths, sleeping in doorways, willing to submit himself to forms of slavery that no slave, even, would submit to, he would find both friends and [b1] enemies standing in the way of his acting like this, the one group reproaching him for obsequiousness and behaviour unbecoming a free man, the other remonstrating with him and being ashamed on his behalf. Yet when the lover does all these things, people even find it charming, and the rules [b5] allow him to do them with no reproach, the view being that he is trying to do something utterly fine. What is strangest, though here I only report what most people say, is that when he swears an oath, too, he alone receives divine forgiveness if he departs from the terms of his oath, because, they say, an oath prompted by Aphrodite is no oath. Thus both gods [c1] and men have allowed every licence to the man in love, according to what the rules here in Athens say. Now all this might make one think that both being in love and giving affection to lovers is regarded in this city as utterly fine. But when fathers [c5] set slave-attendants over sons who are the objects of love and forbid them to converse with their lovers, with instructions to the attendant to that effect, and the boys' contemporaries and friends call them names if they see anything of that sort [d1] going on, and in turn older people don't try to stop the name-callers, and don't tell them off for getting things wrong – anyone who judged by all *this* would rather form the opposite view, and suppose that behaviour of that sort is thought in Athens to be particularly shameful. But I think the truth of it is this. It is not [d5] a simple matter: as I said at the beginning, in and by itself it is neither fine nor shameful, but it is,

αἰσχρόν. αἰσχρῶς μὲν οὖν ἐστι πονηρῷ τε καὶ πονηρῶς χαρίζεσθαι, καλῶς δὲ χρηστῷ τε καὶ καλῶς. πονηρὸς δ' ἐστὶν ἐκεῖνος ὁ ἐραστὴς ὁ πάνδημος, ὁ τοῦ σώματος μᾶλλον ἢ τῆς e ψυχῆς ἐρῶν· καὶ γὰρ οὐδὲ μόνιμός ἐστιν, ἅτε οὐδὲ μονίμου ἐρῶν πράγματος. ἅμα γὰρ τῷ τοῦ σώματος ἄνθει λήγοντι, οὗπερ ἤρα, "οἴχεται ἀποπτάμενος", πολλοὺς λόγους καὶ ὑποσχέσεις καταισχύνας· ὁ δὲ τοῦ ἤθους χρηστοῦ ὄντος 5 ἐραστὴς διὰ βίου μένει, ἅτε μονίμῳ συντακείς. τούτους δὴ βούλεται ὁ ἡμέτερος νόμος εὖ καὶ καλῶς βασανίζειν, καὶ τοῖς 184 μὲν χαρίσασθαι, τοὺς δὲ διαφεύγειν. διὰ ταῦτα οὖν τοῖς μὲν διώκειν παρακελεύεται, τοῖς δὲ φεύγειν, ἀγωνοθετῶν καὶ βασανίζων ποτέρων ποτέ ἐστιν ὁ ἐρῶν καὶ ποτέρων ὁ ἐρώμενος. οὕτω δὴ ὑπὸ ταύτης τῆς αἰτίας πρῶτον μὲν τὸ 5 ἁλίσκεσθαι ταχὺ αἰσχρὸν νενόμισται, ἵνα χρόνος ἐγγένηται, ὃς δὴ δοκεῖ τὰ πολλὰ καλῶς βασανίζειν, ἔπειτα τὸ ὑπὸ χρημάτων καὶ ὑπὸ πολιτικῶν δυνάμεων ἁλῶναι αἰσχρόν, ἐάν b τε κακῶς πάσχων πτήξῃ καὶ μὴ καρτερήσῃ, ἄν τ' εὐεργετούμενος εἰς χρήματα ἢ εἰς διαπράξεις πολιτικὰς μὴ καταφρονήσῃ· οὐδὲν γὰρ δοκεῖ τούτων οὔτε βέβαιον οὔτε μόνιμον εἶναι, χωρὶς τοῦ μηδὲ πεφυκέναι ἀπ' αὐτῶν γενναίαν 5 φιλίαν. μία δὴ λείπεται τῷ ἡμετέρῳ νόμῳ ὁδός, εἰ μέλλει καλῶς χαριεῖσθαι ἐραστῇ παιδικά. ἔστι γὰρ ἡμῖν νόμος, ὥσπερ ἐπὶ τοῖς ἐρασταῖς ἦν δουλεύειν ἐθέλοντα ἡντινοῦν δουλείαν παιδικοῖς μὴ κολακείαν εἶναι μηδὲ ἐπονείδιστον, c οὕτω δὴ καὶ ἄλλη μία μόνη δουλεία ἑκούσιος λείπεται οὐκ ἐπονείδιστος· αὕτη δ' ἐστὶν ἡ περὶ τὴν ἀρετήν. νενόμισται γὰρ δὴ ἡμῖν, ἐάν τις ἐθέλῃ τινὰ θεραπεύειν ἡγούμενος δι' ἐκεῖνον ἀμείνων ἔσεσθαι ἢ κατὰ σοφίαν τινὰ ἢ κατὰ ἄλλο 5 ὁτιοῦν μέρος ἀρετῆς, αὕτη αὖ ἡ ἐθελοδουλεία οὐκ αἰσχρὰ εἶναι οὐδὲ κολακεία. δεῖ δὴ τὼ νόμω τούτω συμβαλεῖν εἰς ταὐτόν, τόν τε περὶ τὴν παιδεραστίαν καὶ τὸν περὶ τὴν d φιλοσοφίαν τε καὶ τὴν ἄλλην ἀρετήν, εἰ μέλλει συμβῆναι καλὸν γενέσθαι τὸ ἐραστῇ παιδικὰ χαρίσασθαι. ὅταν γὰρ εἰς τὸ αὐτὸ ἔλθωσιν ἐραστής τε καὶ παιδικά, νόμον ἔχων ἑκάτερος, ὁ μὲν χαρισαμένοις παιδικοῖς ὑπηρετῶν ὁτιοῦν 5

d 8 καλὸν δὲ   n | b 7 [ἔστι γὰρ ἡμῖν νόμος] e (with ὥσπερ or ὡς <γὰρ> in b 8) | b 8 ὅσπερ n

rather, fine if it is done in a fine way, and shameful if done in a shameful way. Doing it shamefully consists in granting favours to a disreputable person and in a disreputable way, while doing it finely consists in granting favours to a person of the right sort and in a fine way. A disreputable lover [e1] is that vulgar one, the one who is in love with the body more than with the soul; for he is not a lasting lover either, insofar as he loves something that itself does not last. As the bloom of the body, which is what he loved, fades, he "takes to his wings and is gone", with many things said and [e5] promised and none of them honoured; whereas the lover of the character which is of the right sort lasts through life, insofar as he is fused together with something lasting. It is these **184** two sorts of lovers that our rules mean to test with due care, and their upshot is: grant favours to one sort, but get away from the other. This is the reason, then, that they encourage lovers to pursue their quarry while also encouraging the quarry to run away, setting up a kind of competition or test to see to which of the two possible sorts the lover belongs to, and to which the [a5] one who is loved belongs. So this explains why, firstly, it is regarded as shameful to be quickly caught – in order that time may intervene, because time seems to be a good test of most things; and secondly why it is regarded [b1] as shameful to be caught by money or political influence, whether one is ill-treated, and gives in without resistance, or whether one is treated kindly, with offers of money or of achieving something in the city, and fails to reject them contemptuously; for none of these things seems either reliable or [b5] lasting, quite apart from the fact that a noble affection cannot possibly arise from such sources. If a beloved is to grant favours to a lover in a fine way, just one route is left by our rules. Our rule is: just as we said, in the case of lovers, that submitting oneself voluntarily to slavery [c1] of any sort whatever to one's beloved was not obsequiousness, and was above reproach, so there is also just one other kind of slavery left which is above reproach; and this is slavery that relates to excellence. For it is our considered view that if someone wishes to be of service to someone because he thinks that through [c5] him he will be a better person, as measured by some kind of wisdom, or by any other part of excellence whatever, *this* kind of voluntary slavery is not shameful, nor is it obsequiousness. These two rules – the one about [d1] the loving of boys, and the one about the pursuit of wisdom, and about the other parts of excellence – need to be combined into one, if the beloved's granting of favours to the lover is to turn out a fine thing. For when lover and beloved come together, each with his own [d5] rule, the one holding that in doing any service whatever for a beloved who has granted him favours, he would be justified in so doing, the

δικαίως ἂν ὑπηρετεῖν, ὁ δὲ τῷ ποιοῦντι αὐτὸν σοφόν τε καὶ
ἀγαθὸν δικαίως αὖ ὁτιοῦν ἂν ὑπουργῶν, καὶ ὁ μὲν δυνάμενος
εἰς φρόνησιν καὶ τὴν ἄλλην ἀρετὴν συμβάλλεσθαι, ὁ δὲ   e
δεόμενος εἰς παίδευσιν καὶ τὴν ἄλλην σοφίαν κτᾶσθαι, τότε
δὴ τούτων συνιόντων εἰς ταὐτὸν τῶν νόμων μοναχοῦ ἐνταῦθα
συμπίπτει τὸ καλὸν εἶναι παιδικὰ ἐραστῇ χαρίσασθαι, ἄλλοθι
δὲ οὐδαμοῦ. ἐπὶ τούτῳ καὶ ἐξαπατηθῆναι οὐδὲν αἰσχρόν· ἐπὶ   5
δὲ τοῖς ἄλλοις πᾶσι καὶ ἐξαπατωμένῳ αἰσχύνην φέρει καὶ μή.
εἰ γάρ τις ἐραστῇ ὡς πλουσίῳ πλούτου ἕνεκα χαρισάμενος   185
ἐξαπατηθείη καὶ μὴ λάβοι χρήματα, ἀναφανέντος τοῦ ἐραστοῦ
πένητος, οὐδὲν ἧττον αἰσχρόν· δοκεῖ γὰρ ὁ τοιοῦτος τό γε
αὑτοῦ ἐπιδεῖξαι, ὅτι ἕνεκα χρημάτων ὁτιοῦν ἂν ὁτῳοῦν
ὑπηρετοῖ, τοῦτο δὲ οὐ καλόν. κατὰ τὸν αὐτὸν δὴ λόγον κἂν εἴ   5
τις ὡς ἀγαθῷ χαρισάμενος καὶ αὐτὸς ὡς ἀμείνων ἐσόμενος
διὰ τὴν φιλίαν ἐραστοῦ ἐξαπατηθείη, ἀναφανέντος ἐκείνου
κακοῦ καὶ οὐ κεκτημένου ἀρετήν, ὅμως καλὴ ἡ ἀπάτη· δοκεῖ   b
γὰρ αὖ καὶ οὗτος τὸ καθ' αὑτὸν δεδηλωκέναι, ὅτι ἀρετῆς γ'
ἕνεκα καὶ τοῦ βελτίων γενέσθαι πᾶν ἂν παντὶ προθυμηθείη,
τοῦτο δὲ αὖ πάντων κάλλιστον· οὕτω πᾶν πάντως γε καλὸν
ἀρετῆς γ' ἕνεκα χαρίζεσθαι. οὗτός ἐστιν ὁ τῆς οὐρανίας θεοῦ   5
ἔρως καὶ οὐράνιος καὶ πολλοῦ ἄξιος καὶ πόλει καὶ ἰδιώταις,
πολλὴν ἐπιμέλειαν ἀναγκάζων ποιεῖσθαι πρὸς ἀρετὴν τόν τε
ἐρῶντα αὐτὸν αὑτοῦ καὶ τὸν ἐρώμενον· οἱ δ' ἕτεροι πάντες   c
τῆς ἑτέρας, τῆς πανδήμου. ταῦτά σοι,' ἔφη, 'ὡς ἐκ τοῦ
παραχρῆμα, ὦ Φαῖδρε, περὶ Ἔρωτος συμβάλλομαι.'

Παυσανίου δὲ παυσαμένου (διδάσκουσι γάρ με ἴσα λέγειν
οὑτωσὶ οἱ σοφοί) ἔφη ὁ Ἀριστόδημος δεῖν μὲν Ἀριστοφάνη   5
λέγειν, τυχεῖν δὲ αὐτῷ τινα ἢ ὑπὸ πλησμονῆς ἢ ὑπό τινος
ἄλλου λύγγα ἐπιπεπτωκυῖαν καὶ οὐχ οἷόν τε εἶναι λέγειν, ἀλλ'
εἰπεῖν αὐτόν (ἐν τῇ κάτω γὰρ αὐτοῦ τὸν ἰατρὸν Ἐρυξίμαχον
κατακεῖσθαι) 'ὦ Ἐρυξίμαχε, δίκαιος εἶ ἢ παῦσαί με τῆς   d
λυγγὸς ἢ λέγειν ὑπὲρ ἐμοῦ, ἕως ἂν ἐγὼ παύσωμαι.' καὶ τὸν
Ἐρυξίμαχον εἰπεῖν 'ἀλλὰ ποιήσω ἀμφότερα ταῦτα· ἐγὼ μὲν
γὰρ ἐρῶ ἐν τῷ σῷ μέρει, σὺ δ' ἐπειδὰν παύσῃ, ἐν τῷ ἐμῷ.
   5

---

d 7 ὑπουργεῖν n: ὑπουργῶν ὑπουργεῖν e, O ǀ e 2 [εἰς] e ǀ b 4-5 πᾶν
πάντως t: πάντως m ǀ d 1 τῶν ἰατρῶν n

other that in rendering any service whatever to the person who is making him wise and good, he would be justified in that, the one capable [e1] of contributing to understanding and the rest of excellence, the other wanting to acquire them for his general education and the rest of wisdom, then it is, when these rules come together, and here alone, that it comes about that it is fine for a beloved to grant favours to a lover, and under [e5] no other circumstances. In this case even being deceived is nothing to be ashamed about; in all other cases, it brings shame on someone whether he is deceived or not. **185** If someone granted favours to a lover on the basis that he was wealthy, and for the sake of his wealth, and then found himself deceived and not getting any money, because his lover was revealed to be poor, it would be just as shameful, for it seems that someone like that has revealed his own character: that he would do any service whatever for anyone whatever for the sake of [a5] money, and that is not a fine thing. By the same reasoning, then, even if someone granted favours to someone on the basis that he was a good man, and with the expectation of being a better person himself through a lover's affection, and were to be deceived, because the other person was [b1] revealed to be worthless and not in possession of excellence, nevertheless his being deceived like this is fine, for this person too, in his turn, seems to have shown what his own attitude is, that if it is for the sake of excellence, and of becoming a better person, he would be eager to do anything for anybody, and *that* is the finest thing of all; so that all [b5] granting of favours, under all circumstances, is a fine thing, if only it is for the sake of excellence. This is the love that belongs to the heavenly goddess, heavenly itself, and of great value to both city and individuals, compelling as it does the lover to take great [c1] care of himself with respect to excellence, and the loved one too; all the other loves belong to the other goddess, the common one. This, Phaedrus,' he said, 'is the best I can manage just on the spot for my contribution to you on the subject of Love.'

[c5] When Pausanias came to a pause (the experts teach me to balance things like this), Aristodemus said it was Aristophanes' turn to speak, but he happened to be having a fit of the hiccups, brought on either by overeating, or by some other cause, and wasn't able to make a speech; instead [d1] he said (the doctor Eryximachus was reclining on the couch next down from him) 'Eryximachus, it's your business either to put a stop to my hiccups or to speak for me, until I stop it myself.' To which Eryximachus said 'I'll do both: I'll [d5] speak in your place, and when you stop, you speak in mine. While

42

ἐν ᾧ δ' ἂν ἐγὼ λέγω, ἐὰν μέν σοι ἐθέλῃ ἀπνευστὶ ἔχοντι
πολὺν χρόνον παύεσθαι ἡ λύγξ· εἰ δὲ μή, ὕδατι
ἀνακογχυλίασον. εἰ δ' ἄρα πάνυ ἰσχυρά ἐστιν, ἀναλαβών τι e
τοιοῦτον οἵῳ κινήσαις ἂν τὴν ῥῖνα, πτάρε· καὶ τοῦτο ποιήσῃς
ἅπαξ ἢ δίς, καὶ εἰ πάνυ ἰσχυρά ἐστι, παύσεται.' 'οὐκ ἂν
φθάνοις λέγων,' φάναι τὸν Ἀριστοφάνη· 'ἐγὼ δὲ ταῦτα
ποιήσω.'   5

εἰπεῖν δὴ τὸν Ἐρυξίμαχον, 'δοκεῖ τοίνυν μοι ἀναγκαῖον
εἶναι, ἐπειδὴ Παυσανίας ὁρμήσας ἐπὶ τὸν λόγον καλῶς οὐχ 186
ἱκανῶς ἀπετέλεσε, δεῖν ἐμὲ πειρᾶσθαι τέλος ἐπιθεῖναι τῷ
λόγῳ. τὸ μὲν γὰρ διπλοῦν εἶναι τὸν Ἔρωτα δοκεῖ μοι καλῶς
διελέσθαι· ὅτι δὲ οὐ μόνον ἐστὶν ἐπὶ ταῖς ψυχαῖς τῶν
ἀνθρώπων πρὸς τοὺς καλοὺς ἀλλὰ καὶ πρὸς ἄλλα πολλὰ καὶ ἐν 5
τοῖς ἄλλοις, τοῖς τε σώμασι τῶν πάντων ζῴων καὶ τοῖς ἐν
τῇ γῇ φυομένοις καὶ ὡς ἔπος εἰπεῖν ἐν πᾶσι τοῖς οὖσι,
καθεωρακέναι μοι δοκῶ ἐκ τῆς ἰατρικῆς, τῆς ἡμετέρας
τέχνης, ὡς μέγας καὶ θαυμαστὸς καὶ ἐπὶ πᾶν ὁ θεὸς τείνει b
καὶ κατ' ἀνθρώπινα καὶ κατὰ θεῖα πράγματα. ἄρξομαι δὲ ἀπὸ
τῆς ἰατρικῆς λέγων, ἵνα καὶ πρεσβεύωμεν τὴν τέχνην. ἡ γὰρ
φύσις τῶν σωμάτων τὸν διπλοῦν Ἔρωτα τοῦτον ἔχει· τὸ γὰρ
ὑγιὲς τοῦ σώματος καὶ τὸ νοσοῦν ὁμολογουμένως ἕτερόν τε 5
καὶ ἀνόμοιόν ἐστι, τὸ δὲ ἀνόμοιον ἀνομοίων ἐπιθυμεῖ καὶ ἐρᾷ.
ἄλλος μὲν οὖν ὁ ἐπὶ τῷ ὑγιεινῷ ἔρως, ἄλλος δὲ ὁ ἐπὶ τῷ
νοσώδει. ἔστιν δή, ὥσπερ ἄρτι Παυσανίας ἔλεγεν τοῖς μὲν
ἀγαθοῖς καλὸν χαρίζεσθαι τῶν ἀνθρώπων, τοῖς δ' ἀκολάστοις c
αἰσχρόν, οὕτω καὶ ἐν αὐτοῖς τοῖς σώμασιν τοῖς μὲν ἀγαθοῖς
ἑκάστου τοῦ σώματος καὶ ὑγιεινοῖς καλὸν χαρίζεσθαι καὶ δεῖ,
καὶ τοῦτό ἐστιν ᾧ ὄνομα τὸ ἰατρικόν, τοῖς δὲ κακοῖς καὶ
νοσώδεσιν αἰσχρόν τε καὶ δεῖ ἀχαριστεῖν, εἰ μέλλει τις 5
τεχνικὸς εἶναι. ἔστι γὰρ ἰατρική, ὡς ἐν κεφαλαίῳ εἰπεῖν,
ἐπιστήμη τῶν τοῦ σώματος ἐρωτικῶν πρὸς πλησμονὴν καὶ
κένωσιν, καὶ ὁ διαγιγνώσκων ἐν τούτοις τὸν καλόν τε καὶ
αἰσχρὸν ἔρωτα, οὗτός ἐστιν ὁ ἰατρικώτατος· καὶ ὁ d
μεταβάλλειν ποιῶν, ὥστε ἀντὶ τοῦ ἑτέρου ἔρωτος τὸν ἕτερον
κτᾶσθαι, καὶ οἷς μὴ ἔνεστιν ἔρως, δεῖ δ' ἐγγενέσθαι,

b 5 ὁμολογοῦμεν ὡς   t, n

I'm speaking, your hiccups may stop if you hold your breath for a long time; if not, gargle [e1] with water. But if after all they turn out to be really severe, get hold of something to tickle your nose with, and sneeze; and if you do this once or twice, even if they are really severe, they'll stop.' 'Start speaking at once,' said Aristophanes; 'and I'll do [e5] as you say.'

So then Eryximachus spoke. 'Well, since Pausanias started well on his theme, but **186** failed to finish it off satisfactorily, it seems to me that my task must be to try to round off what he said. To say that Love is double, as he did, seems to me a good distinction to make. But Love is there not only in the case of human [a5] souls in relation to beautiful individuals, but also in relation to many other things and in other things – the bodies of all animals, things that grow in the earth, and practically everything that exists: this is what I think I have observed from my own expert knowledge [b1] as a doctor, as I contemplate how great and wonderful the god is, and how his influence extends to everything, both on the level of human affairs and on that of the divine. It is from medicine that I shall begin, in order that we may also give a special place to that branch of knowledge. The nature of bodies is such as to have this double Love in them: what is [b5] healthy and what is diseased in a body are by common consent different and unlike, but what is unlike desires and loves unlike things. Thus the love that exists in the case of the healthy is of one sort, and the love that exists in the case of the diseased is of another. And so just as Pausanias was saying just now that it was a fine thing [c1] to grant favours to those people who are good, and shameful to gratify those who are immoral, so too in the case of bodies themselves it is a fine thing, and imperative, to favour the good and healthy things in each body, and this is what the name "medical expertise" belongs to, whereas it is not only shameful to [c5] favour the bad and diseased things but imperative to disfavour them, if one is to be a true expert. Medical expertise, to sum it up, is knowledge of the erotic affairs of the body in relation to filling up and emptying, and the person with the best claim to possessing medical knowledge is the one who distinguishes [d1] the fine and the shameful love in these; while the one who brings about changes, so that the one kind of love is acquired instead of the other, and who knows how to produce love

44

ἐπιστάμενος ἐμποιῆσαι καὶ ἐνόντα ἐξελεῖν, ἀγαθὸς ἂν εἴη
δημιουργός. δεῖ γὰρ δὴ τὰ ἔχθιστα ὄντα ἐν τῷ σώματι φίλα 5
οἷόν τ᾽ εἶναι ποιεῖν καὶ ἐρᾶν ἀλλήλων. ἔστι δὲ ἔχθιστα τὰ
ἐναντιώτατα, ψυχρὸν θερμῷ, πικρὸν γλυκεῖ, ξηρὸν ὑγρῷ, πάντα
τὰ τοιαῦτα· τούτοις ἐπιστηθεὶς ἔρωτα ἐμποιῆσαι καὶ ὁμόνοιαν e
ὁ ἡμέτερος πρόγονος Ἀσκληπιός, ὥς φασιν οἵδε οἱ ποιηταὶ
καὶ ἐγὼ πείθομαι, συνέστησεν τὴν ἡμετέραν τέχνην. ἥ τε οὖν
ἰατρική, ὥσπερ λέγω, πᾶσα διὰ τοῦ θεοῦ τούτου κυβερνᾶται,
ὡσαύτως δὲ καὶ γυμναστικὴ καὶ γεωργία· μουσικὴ δὲ καὶ 187
παντὶ κατάδηλος τῷ καὶ σμικρὸν προσέχοντι τὸν νοῦν ὅτι
κατὰ ταὐτὰ ἔχει τούτοις, ὥσπερ ἴσως καὶ Ἡράκλειτος
βούλεται λέγειν, ἐπεὶ τοῖς γε ῥήμασιν οὐ καλῶς λέγει. τὸ ἓν
γάρ φησι "διαφερόμενον αὐτὸ αὑτῷ συμφέρεσθαι ὥσπερ 5
ἁρμονίαν τόξου τε καὶ λύρας". ἔστι δὲ πολλὴ ἀλογία
ἁρμονίαν φάναι διαφέρεσθαι ἢ ἐκ διαφερομένων ἔτι εἶναι·
ἀλλὰ ἴσως τόδε ἐβούλετο λέγειν, ὅτι ἐκ διαφερομένων
πρότερον τοῦ ὀξέος καὶ βαρέος, ἔπειτα ὕστερον b
ὁμολογησάντων γέγονεν ὑπὸ τῆς μουσικῆς τέχνης. οὐ γὰρ
δήπου ἐκ διαφερομένων γε ἔτι τοῦ ὀξέος καὶ βαρέος ἁρμονία
ἂν εἴη· ἡ γὰρ ἁρμονία συμφωνία ἐστίν, συμφωνία δὲ ὁμολογία
τις, ὁμολογίαν δὲ ἐκ διαφερομένων, ἕως ἂν διαφέρωνται, 5
ἀδύνατον εἶναι· διαφερόμενον δὲ αὖ καὶ μὴ ὁμολογοῦν
ἀδύνατον ἁρμόσαι· ὥσπερ γε καὶ ὁ ῥυθμὸς ἐκ τοῦ ταχέος καὶ
βραδέος, ἐκ διενηνεγμένων πρότερον, ὕστερον δὲ ὁμολογ- c
ησάντων γέγονε. τὴν δὲ ὁμολογίαν πᾶσι τούτοις, ὥσπερ ἐκεῖ
ἡ ἰατρική, ἐνταῦθα ἡ μουσικὴ ἐντίθησιν, ἔρωτα καὶ ὁμόνοιαν
ἀλλήλων ἐμποιήσασα· καί ἐστιν αὖ μουσικὴ περὶ ἁρμονίαν καὶ
ῥυθμὸν ἐρωτικῶν ἐπιστήμη. καὶ ἐν μέν γε αὐτῇ τῇ συστάσει 5
ἁρμονίας τε καὶ ῥυθμοῦ οὐδὲν χαλεπὸν τὰ ἐρωτικὰ
διαγιγνώσκειν, οὐδὲ ὁ διπλοῦς ἔρως ἐνταῦθά πω ἔστιν· ἀλλ᾽
ἐπειδὰν δέῃ πρὸς τοὺς ἀνθρώπους καταχρῆσθαι ῥυθμῷ τε καὶ d
ἁρμονίᾳ ἢ ποιοῦντα, ὃ δὴ μελοποιίαν καλοῦσιν, ἢ χρώμενον
ὀρθῶς τοῖς πεποιημένοις μέλεσί τε καὶ μέτροις, ὃ δὴ παιδεία
ἐκλήθη, ἐνταῦθα δὴ καὶ χαλεπὸν καὶ ἀγαθοῦ δημιουργοῦ δεῖ.

c 4 ἀλλήλοις   n | c 7 πω   e: πῶς   m | d 3 μέτροις n: ῥυθμοῖς n

in those in whom it does not exist, but should, and remove it when it is present, will be a good [d5] practitioner. For what is needed is the ability to make the things in the body that are most hostile to each other into friends, and make them love one another. The things that are most hostile to each other are those that are most opposed, cold to hot, bitter to sweet, dry to wet, everything [e1] like that; it was because he knew how to impart love and unanimity to these that our ancestor Asclepius – as these poets here tell us, and I believe them – founded our branch of expert knowledge. Thus both the whole of medicine, as I say, is governed through the agency of this god, **187** and in the same way also gymnastic training and agriculture; and it is clear to anyone who pays even small attention to the matter that music is in the same position as the things I've been talking about, as perhaps Heraclitus means to say, though so far as his actual wording goes he doesn't say it very well. He says [a5] that the one "being at variance with itself is in agreement, like a harmony of bow or lyre". But it is quite illogical to say that a harmony is at variance, or composed out of things that are still at variance. Perhaps what he meant to say was that it has come to be from [b1] the high and the low, which were previously at variance, but which then later struck an agreement under the agency of musical expertise. For surely if the high and low were still at variance, a harmony would not come from them: harmony is concord, and concord is a kind of [b5] agreement, and it is impossible for agreement to come from things at variance with each other, for so long as they are at variance with each other, and impossible in turn to harmonize what is at variance and not in agreement; just as rhythm, too, comes about from the [c1] quick and the slow, from things which had been at variance previously, but which later struck an agreement. What establishes the agreement among all these things, like medicine in its sphere, is music, by implanting in them love and unanimity with each other; and music is, in its turn, knowledge of love-matters [c5] in relation to harmony and rhythm. There is no difficulty in distinguishing what belongs to love in the structure itself of harmony and rhythm, nor is the double love yet present here; but [d1] when one needs to deploy rhythm and harmony in relation to human beings, whether one is composing, which they call musical composition, or making correct use of melodies and measures once composed, which is called education, here there really is something which is difficult, and which calls for a good practitioner.

46

πάλιν γὰρ ἥκει ὁ αὐτὸς λόγος, ὅτι τοῖς μὲν κοσμίοις τῶν 5
ἀνθρώπων, καὶ ὡς ἂν κοσμιώτεροι γίγνοιντο οἱ μήπω ὄντες,
δεῖ χαρίζεσθαι καὶ φυλάττειν τὸν τούτων ἔρωτα, καὶ οὗτός
ἐστιν ὁ καλός, ὁ οὐράνιος, ὁ τῆς Οὐρανίας μούσης Ἔρως· ὁ
δὲ Πολυμνίας, ὁ πάνδημος, ὃν δεῖ εὐλαβούμενον προσφέρειν e
οἷς ἂν προσφέρῃ, ὅπως ἂν τὴν μὲν ἡδονὴν αὐτοῦ καρπώσηται,
ἀκολασίαν δὲ μηδεμίαν ἐμποιήσῃ, ὥσπερ ἐν τῇ ἡμετέρᾳ τέχνῃ
μέγα ἔργον ταῖς περὶ τὴν ὀψοποιικὴν τέχνην ἐπιθυμίαις
καλῶς χρῆσθαι, ὥστ' ἄνευ νόσου τὴν ἡδονὴν καρπώσασθαι. καὶ 5
ἐν μουσικῇ δὴ καὶ ἐν ἰατρικῇ καὶ ἐν τοῖς ἄλλοις πᾶσι καὶ
τοῖς ἀνθρωπείοις καὶ τοῖς θείοις, καθ' ὅσον παρείκει,
φυλακτέον ἑκάτερον τὸν Ἔρωτα· ἔνεστον γάρ. ἐπεὶ καὶ ἡ τῶν 188
ὡρῶν τοῦ ἐνιαυτοῦ σύστασις μεστή ἐστιν ἀμφοτέρων τούτων,
καὶ ἐπειδὰν μὲν πρὸς ἄλληλα τοῦ κοσμίου τύχῃ ἔρωτος ἃ
νυνδὴ ἐγὼ ἔλεγον, τά τε θερμὰ καὶ τὰ ψυχρὰ καὶ ξηρὰ καὶ
ὑγρά, καὶ ἁρμονίαν καὶ κρᾶσιν λάβῃ σώφρονα, ἥκει φέροντα 5
εὐετηρίαν τε καὶ ὑγίειαν ἀνθρώποις καὶ τοῖς ἄλλοις ζῴοις τε
καὶ φυτοῖς, καὶ οὐδὲν ἠδίκησεν· ὅταν δὲ ὁ μετὰ τῆς ὕβρεως
Ἔρως ἐγκρατέστερος περὶ τὰς τοῦ ἐνιαυτοῦ ὥρας γένηται,
διέφθειρέν τε πολλὰ καὶ ἠδίκησεν. οἵ τε γὰρ λοιμοὶ φιλοῦσι b
γίγνεσθαι ἐκ τῶν τοιούτων καὶ ἄλλα ἀνόμοια πολλὰ νοσήματα
καὶ τοῖς θηρίοις καὶ τοῖς φυτοῖς· καὶ γὰρ πάχναι καὶ
χάλαζαι καὶ ἐρυσῖβαι ἐκ πλεονεξίας καὶ ἀκοσμίας περὶ ἄλληλα
τῶν τοιούτων γίγνεται ἐρωτικῶν, ὧν ἐπιστήμη περὶ ἄστρων τε 5
φορὰς καὶ ἐνιαυτῶν ὥρας ἀστρονομία καλεῖται. ἔτι τοίνυν καὶ
αἱ θυσίαι πᾶσαι καὶ οἷς μαντικὴ ἐπιστατεῖ – ταῦτα δ' ἐστὶν
ἡ περὶ θεούς τε καὶ ἀνθρώπους πρὸς ἀλλήλους κοινωνία – οὐ c
περὶ ἄλλο τί ἐστιν ἢ περὶ Ἔρωτος φυλακήν τε καὶ ἴασιν.
πᾶσα γὰρ ἀσέβεια φιλεῖ γίγνεσθαι ἐὰν μή τις τῷ κοσμίῳ
Ἔρωτι χαρίζηται μηδὲ τιμᾷ τε αὐτὸν καὶ πρεσβεύῃ ἐν παντὶ
ἔργῳ, ἀλλὰ τὸν ἕτερον, καὶ περὶ γονέας καὶ ζῶντας 5
καὶ τετελευτηκότας καὶ περὶ θεούς· ἃ δὴ προστέτακται τῇ
μαντικῇ ἐπισκοπεῖν τοὺς ἐρῶντας καὶ ἰατρεύειν, καί ἐστιν αὖ
ἡ μαντικὴ φιλίας θεῶν καὶ ἀνθρώπων δημιουργὸς τῷ d
ἐπίστασθαι τὰ κατὰ ἀνθρώπους ἐρωτικά, ὅσα τείνει πρὸς

b 5 γίγνονται e ǀ c 7 ἐρῶντας t,n: ἔρωτας n (Ἔρωτας e)

[d5] The same theme as before comes back again: that it is those people who are orderly that one must gratify, and in such a way that those who are not yet orderly might become more so, and it is these people's love that should be cherished, and this is the beautiful Love, the heavenly one, the one who belongs to the Heavenly Muse; the [e1] other one, the common one, belongs to Polymnia, and he must be applied with caution to those to whom one applies him, in order that the pleasure he brings may be enjoyed, but that he may implant no tendency to immorality, just as in the sphere of my own expertise it is a considerable task to deal properly with desires relating to the expertise [e5] of the cook, so that the pleasure may be enjoyed without ill effects. In music, then, in medicine, and in everything else, whether human or divine, one must watch out, as far as circumstances **188** permit, for each of the two kinds of Love, for both are there. Consider the constitution of the seasons of the year – it is full of both these Loves: when the things I was talking of just now, things like the hot, the cold, the dry and [a5] the wet, achieve orderliness in relation to each other, and find a controlled harmony and mixture, they come bringing well-being and health to human beings and to other living things, whether animals or plants, and do them no wrong; but when the lawless sort of Love comes more into power in relation to the seasons of the year, [b1] he does much damage and wrong. Plagues tend to arise from such things, and many other diseases of different kinds, affecting both animals and plants, for frost, hail and blight arise from excess and disorder of [b5] such things in relation to each other – erotic things; knowledge of these, relating to movements of the heavenly bodies and seasons of the year, is called astronomy. Then again, all sacrifices, and the things that are the province of the expert seer [c1] (those that have to do with the mutual relationship of gods and men), are concerned with nothing other than cherishing or curing Love. For all impiety tends to arise when one does not gratify the orderly Love, or honour him and give him pride of place [c5] in everything one does, but the other one, in relation both to parents, living or dead, and to gods; it is for just these things that the seer is enjoined to examine those who are in love and to cure them, and the seer's [d1] expertise, in its turn, is a craftsman of friendship between gods and men because of its knowledge of matters of human love, that is, those that aim at right and piety.

θέμιν καὶ εὐσέβειαν.

'οὕτω πολλὴν καὶ μεγάλην, μᾶλλον δὲ πᾶσαν δύναμιν ἔχει συλλήβδην μὲν ὁ πᾶς Ἔρως, ὁ δὲ περὶ τἀγαθὰ μετὰ 5 σωφροσύνης καὶ δικαιοσύνης ἀποτελούμενος καὶ παρ' ἡμῖν καὶ παρὰ θεοῖς, οὗτος τὴν μεγίστην δύναμιν ἔχει καὶ πᾶσαν ἡμῖν εὐδαιμονίαν παρασκευάζει, καὶ ἀλλήλοις δυναμένους ὁμιλεῖν καὶ φίλους εἶναι καὶ τοῖς κρείττοσιν ἡμῶν θεοῖς. ἴσως μὲν e οὖν καὶ ἐγὼ τὸν Ἔρωτα ἐπαινῶν πολλὰ παραλείπω, οὐ μέντοι ἑκών γε. ἀλλ' εἴ τι ἐξέλιπον, σὸν ἔργον, ὦ Ἀριστόφανες, ἀναπληρῶσαι· ἢ εἴ πως ἄλλως ἐν νῷ ἔχεις ἐγκωμιάζειν τὸν θεόν, ἐγκωμίαζε, ἐπειδὴ καὶ τῆς λυγγὸς πέπαυσαι.' 5

ἐκδεξάμενον οὖν ἔφη εἰπεῖν τὸν Ἀριστοφάνη ὅτι 'καὶ μάλ' 189 ἐπαύσατο, οὐ μέντοι πρίν γε τὸν πταρμὸν προσενεχθῆναι αὐτῇ, ὥστε με θαυμάζειν εἰ τὸ κόσμιον τοῦ σώματος ἐπιθυμεῖ τοιούτων ψόφων καὶ γαργαλισμῶν, οἷον καὶ ὁ πταρμός ἐστιν· πάνυ γὰρ εὐθὺς ἐπαύσατο, ἐπειδὴ αὐτῷ τὸν πταρμὸν 5 προσήνεγκα.'

καὶ τὸν Ἐρυξίμαχον, 'ὦγαθέ,' φάναι, 'Ἀριστόφανες, ὅρα τί ποιεῖς. γελωτοποιεῖς μέλλων λέγειν, καὶ φύλακά με τοῦ λόγου ἀναγκάζεις γίγνεσθαι τοῦ σεαυτοῦ, ἐάν τι γελοῖον b εἴπῃς, ἐξόν σοι ἐν εἰρήνῃ λέγειν.'

καὶ τὸν Ἀριστοφάνη γελάσαντα εἰπεῖν 'εὖ λέγεις, ὦ Ἐρυξίμαχε, καί μοι ἔστω ἄρρητα τὰ εἰρημένα. ἀλλὰ μή με φύλαττε, ὡς ἐγὼ φοβοῦμαι περὶ τῶν μελλόντων ῥηθήσεσθαι, οὔ 5 τι μὴ γελοῖα εἴπω — τοῦτο μὲν γὰρ ἂν κέρδος εἴη καὶ τῆς ἡμετέρας μούσης ἐπιχώριον – ἀλλὰ μὴ καταγέλαστα.'

'βαλών γε,' φάναι, 'ὦ Ἀριστόφανες, οἴει ἐκφεύξεσθαι· ἀλλὰ πρόσεχε τὸν νοῦν καὶ οὕτως λέγε ὡς δώσων λόγον. ἴσως c μέντοι, ἂν δόξῃ μοι, ἀφήσω σε.'

'καὶ μήν, ὦ Ἐρυξίμαχε,' εἰπεῖν τὸν Ἀριστοφάνη, 'ἄλλη γέ πῃ ἐν νῷ ἔχω λέγειν ἢ ᾗ σύ τε καὶ Παυσανίας εἰπέτην. ἐμοὶ γὰρ δοκοῦσιν ἄνθρωποι παντάπασι τὴν τοῦ Ἔρωτος 5 δύναμιν οὐκ ᾐσθῆσθαι, ἐπεὶ αἰσθανόμενοί γε μέγιστ' ἂν αὐτοῦ ἱερὰ κατασκευάσαι καὶ βωμούς, καὶ θυσίας ἂν ποιεῖν

d 3 εὐσέβειαν t: ἀσέβειαν m

'So much and so great is the power Love has; or rather Love taken together [d5] as a whole has all power, but it is the one who is realised with moderation and justice in relation to those things that are good, both among us and among the gods, who has the greatest power, providing us with all happiness, enabling us to associate and be [e1] friends both with each other and with the gods, who are stronger than us. Well, perhaps I too have left out many things in my praise of Love, but that was certainly not my intention. If I have left anything out, it's up to you, Aristophanes, to fill in the gaps; or if you mean to give the god a different sort of [e5] encomium, then go ahead, since your hiccups have stopped.'

189 Aristodemus said that Aristophanes took his cue, and said 'They certainly have stopped, though not until I applied the sneezing remedy, which leaves me amazed that the orderly element of the body desires the sort of noise and tickling that sneezing really is; [a5] for they stopped at exactly the moment I applied the sneezing.'

'Aristophanes, my good man,' said Eryximachus, 'just look at what you're doing. You're about to speak, and you're playing the buffoon; you're making me [b1] watch out for your own speech, in case *you* say something funny, when you could speak in peace.'

Aristophanes said with a laugh 'You're right, Eryximachus; please treat what I said as unsaid. Don't keep [b5] watch on me, because my own fear about what I'm about to say is not that I shall say things that are funny – that, after all, would be an advantage, and in the province of my Muse – but rather that I shall say things that people will laugh out of court.'

'You loosed off at me,' said Eryximachus, 'and you think you'll get away with it. [c1] Well, be careful, and remember as you're speaking that you're going to be called to account. On the other hand, perhaps I'll let you off, if that's what I decide.'

'Well now, Eryximachus', Aristophanes said: 'indeed I do mean to give a different kind of speech from the ones you and Pausanias have given. [c5] It seems to me that people have completely failed to recognize the power of Love, since if they were to recognize it, I think they would construct temples and altars to him on the largest scale, and make the largest sacrifices to him,

μεγίστας, οὐχ ὥσπερ νῦν τούτων οὐδὲν γίγνεται περὶ αὐτόν,
δέον πάντων μάλιστα γίγνεσθαι. ἔστι γὰρ θεῶν
φιλανθρωπότατος, ἐπίκουρός τε ὢν τῶν ἀνθρώπων καὶ ἰατρὸς d
τούτων ὧν ἰαθέντων μεγίστη εὐδαιμονία ἂν τῷ ἀνθρωπείῳ
γένει εἴη. ἐγὼ οὖν πειράσομαι ὑμῖν εἰσηγήσασθαι τὴν δύναμιν
αὐτοῦ, ὑμεῖς δὲ τῶν ἄλλων διδάσκαλοι ἔσεσθε. δεῖ δὲ πρῶτον
ὑμᾶς μαθεῖν τὴν ἀνθρωπίνην φύσιν καὶ τὰ παθήματα αὐτῆς· ἡ 5
γὰρ πάλαι ἡμῶν φύσις οὐχ αὐτὴ ἦν ἥπερ νῦν, ἀλλ' ἀλλοία.
πρῶτον μὲν γὰρ τρία ἦν τὰ γένη τὰ τῶν ἀνθρώπων, οὐχ
ὥσπερ νῦν δύο, ἄρρεν καὶ θῆλυ, ἀλλὰ καὶ τρίτον προσῆν e
κοινὸν ὂν ἀμφοτέρων τούτων, οὗ νῦν ὄνομα λοιπόν, αὐτὸ δὲ
ἠφάνισται· ἀνδρόγυνον γὰρ ἓν τότε μὲν ἦν καὶ εἶδος καὶ
ὄνομα ἐξ ἀμφοτέρων κοινὸν τοῦ τε ἄρρενος καὶ θήλεος, νῦν
δὲ οὐκ ἔστιν ἀλλ' ἢ ἐν ὀνείδει ὄνομα κείμενον. ἔπειτα ὅλον 5
ἦν ἑκάστου τοῦ ἀνθρώπου τὸ εἶδος στρογγύλον, νῶτον καὶ
πλευρὰς κύκλῳ ἔχον, χεῖρας δὲ τέτταρας εἶχε, καὶ σκέλη τὰ
ἴσα ταῖς χερσίν, καὶ πρόσωπα δύ' ἐπ' αὐχένι κυκλοτερεῖ,
ὅμοια πάντῃ· κεφαλὴν δ' ἐπ' ἀμφοτέροις τοῖς προσώποις 190
ἐναντίοις κειμένοις μίαν, καὶ ὦτα τέτταρα, καὶ αἰδοῖα δύο,
καὶ τἆλλα πάντα ὡς ἀπὸ τούτων ἄν τις εἰκάσειεν. ἐπορεύετο
δὲ καὶ ὀρθὸν ὥσπερ νῦν, ὁποτέρωσε βουληθείη, καὶ ὁπότε ταχὺ
ὁρμήσειεν θεῖν, ὥσπερ οἱ κυβιστῶντες καὶ εἰς ὀρθὸν τὰ σκέλη 5
περιφερόμενοι κυβιστῶσι κύκλῳ, ὀκτὼ τότε οὖσι τοῖς μέλεσιν
ἀπερειδόμενοι ταχὺ ἐφέροντο κύκλῳ. ἦν δὲ διὰ ταῦτα τρία τὰ
γένη καὶ τοιαῦτα, ὅτι τὸ μὲν ἄρρεν ἦν τοῦ ἡλίου τὴν ἀρχὴν b
ἔκγονον, τὸ δὲ θῆλυ τῆς γῆς, τὸ δὲ ἀμφοτέρων μετέχον τῆς
σελήνης, ὅτι καὶ ἡ σελήνη ἀμφοτέρων μετέχει· περιφερῆ δὲ
δὴ ἦν καὶ αὐτὰ καὶ ἡ πορεία αὐτῶν διὰ τὸ τοῖς γονεῦσιν
ὅμοια εἶναι. ἦν οὖν τὴν ἰσχὺν δεινὰ καὶ τὴν ῥώμην, καὶ τὰ 5
φρονήματα μεγάλα εἶχον, ἐπεχείρησαν δὲ τοῖς θεοῖς, καὶ ὃ
λέγει Ὅμηρος περὶ Ἐφιάλτου τε καὶ Ὤτου, περὶ ἐκείνων
λέγεται, τὸ εἰς τὸν οὐρανὸν ἀνάβασιν ἐπιχειρεῖν ποιεῖν, ὡς
ἐπιθησομένων τοῖς θεοῖς. ὁ οὖν Ζεὺς καὶ οἱ ἄλλοι θεοὶ c
ἐβουλεύοντο ὅτι χρὴ αὐτοὺς ποιῆσαι, καὶ ἠπόρουν· οὔτε

d 6 αὕτη   n | e 3 ἀνδρόγυνον γὰρ τότε   t, n

whereas, as things are now, none of these things happens in respect to him, though they ought more than anything to happen. For he is most [d1] philanthropic of gods, helper of humankind and doctor of those ills the cure of which would bring happiness to the human race on the largest scale. So I shall try to explain his power to you, and you will teach other people. First, [d5] you need to learn about the nature of human beings and what has happened to it; for our nature as it was, once upon a time, was not the same as it is now, but of a different kind. In the first place, human beings were divided into three kinds, [e1] not two as they are now, male and female – in addition to these there was also a third in which both of these had a share, one whose name now survives although the kind itself has vanished from sight; for at that time one of the kinds was androgynous, in form as well as in name shared in by both the male and the female, whereas [e5] now it does not exist except as a term of reproach. The next point is that the shape of each human being was entirely round, with back and sides making a circle, and it had four arms, an equal number of legs, and two completely similar faces on a **190** circular neck; a single head for both faces, which looked out in opposite directions; four ears; two sets of genitals; and everything else arranged as one might guess from what I have said. It moved both in an upright position, as we do now, in whichever of the two directions it wished, and also, when [a5] it launched itself into a quick run, just as tumblers bring their legs round into the upright position and tumble in a circle – well, they used the eight legs they then had to push off with, moving in quick circles. The reason why they were [b1] divided into three kinds, and kinds like this, is that the male was in the beginning born from the sun, the female from the earth, and what shared in both male and female from the moon, because the moon too shares in both; the circularity of both themselves and their movement was because of their [b5] resemblance to their parents. Well, they were terrifying in their strength and power, and their ambitions were on a large scale; they actually made an attempt on the gods, and what Homer says about Ephialtes and Otus is said about them, I mean about how they attempted to make an ascent to [c1] heaven, in order to attack the gods. So Zeus and the other gods deliberated about what they should do to them, and

γὰρ ὅπως ἀποκτείναιεν εἶχον καὶ ὥσπερ τοὺς γίγαντας
κεραυνώσαντες τὸ γένος ἀφανίσαιεν (αἱ τιμαὶ γὰρ αὐτοῖς καὶ
ἱερὰ τὰ παρὰ τῶν ἀνθρώπων ἠφανίζετο), οὔτε ὅπως ἐῷεν 5
ἀσελγαίνειν. μόγις δὴ ὁ Ζεὺς ἐννοήσας λέγει ὅτι "δοκῶ μοι",
ἔφη, "ἔχειν μηχανήν, ὡς ἂν εἶέν τε ἄνθρωποι καὶ παύσαιντο
τῆς ἀκολασίας ἀσθενέστεροι γενόμενοι. νῦν μὲν γὰρ αὐτούς", d
ἔφη, "διατεμῶ δίχα ἕκαστον, καὶ ἅμα μὲν ἀσθενέστεροι
ἔσονται, ἅμα δὲ χρησιμώτεροι ἡμῖν διὰ τὸ πλείους τὸν
ἀριθμὸν γεγονέναι· καὶ βαδιοῦνται ὀρθοὶ ἐπὶ δυοῖν σκελοῖν.
ἐὰν δ' ἔτι δοκῶσιν ἀσελγαίνειν καὶ μὴ 'θέλωσιν ἡσυχίαν 5
ἄγειν, πάλιν αὖ", ἔφη, "τεμῶ δίχα, ὥστ' ἐφ' ἑνὸς
πορεύσονται σκέλους ἀσκωλιάζοντες." ταῦτα εἰπὼν ἔτεμνε
τοὺς ἀνθρώπους δίχα, ὥσπερ οἱ τὰ ὄα τέμνοντες καὶ
μέλλοντες ταριχεύειν, ἢ ὥσπερ οἱ τὰ ᾠὰ ταῖς θριξίν· ὅντινα e
δὲ τέμοι, τὸν Ἀπόλλω ἐκέλευεν τό τε πρόσωπον μεταστρέφειν
καὶ τὸ τοῦ αὐχένος ἥμισυ πρὸς τὴν τομήν, ἵνα θεώμενος τὴν
αὑτοῦ τμῆσιν κοσμιώτερος εἴη ὁ ἄνθρωπος, καὶ τἆλλα ἰᾶσθαι
ἐκέλευεν. ὁ δὲ τό τε πρόσωπον μετέστρεφε, καὶ συνέλκων 5
πανταχόθεν τὸ δέρμα ἐπὶ τὴν γαστέρα νῦν καλουμένην, ὥσπερ
τὰ σύσπαστα βαλλάντια, ἓν στόμα ποιῶν ἀπέδει κατὰ μέσην
τὴν γαστέρα, ὃ δὴ τὸν ὀμφαλὸν καλοῦσι. καὶ τὰς μὲν ἄλλας
ῥυτίδας τὰς πολλὰς ἐξελέαινε καὶ τὰ στήθη διήρθρου, ἔχων τι 191
τοιοῦτον ὄργανον οἷον οἱ σκυτοτόμοι περὶ τὸν καλάποδα
λεαίνοντες τὰς τῶν σκυτῶν ῥυτίδας· ὀλίγας δὲ κατέλιπε, τὰς
περὶ αὐτὴν τὴν γαστέρα καὶ τὸν ὀμφαλόν, μνημεῖον εἶναι τοῦ
παλαιοῦ πάθους. ἐπειδὴ οὖν ἡ φύσις δίχα ἐτμήθη, ποθοῦν 5
ἕκαστον τὸ ἥμισυ τὸ αὑτοῦ συνῄει, καὶ περιβάλλοντες τὰς
χεῖρας καὶ συμπλεκόμενοι ἀλλήλοις, ἐπιθυμοῦντες συμφῦναι,
ἀπέθνῃσκον ὑπὸ λιμοῦ καὶ τῆς ἄλλης ἀργίας διὰ τὸ μηδὲν b
ἐθέλειν χωρὶς ἀλλήλων ποιεῖν. καὶ ὁπότε τι ἀποθάνοι τῶν
ἡμίσεων, τὸ δὲ λειφθείη, τὸ λειφθὲν ἄλλο ἐζήτει καὶ
συνεπλέκετο, εἴτε γυναικὸς τῆς ὅλης ἐντύχοι ἡμίσει, ὃ δὴ
νῦν γυναῖκα καλοῦμεν, εἴτε ἀνδρός· καὶ οὕτως ἀπώλλυντο. 5
ἐλεήσας δὲ ὁ Ζεὺς ἄλλην μηχανὴν πορίζεται, καὶ μετατίθησιν
αὐτῶν τὰ αἰδοῖα εἰς τὸ πρόσθεν· τέως γὰρ καὶ ταῦτα ἐκτὸς

d 8 ὄα   e (t): ᾠὰ   or   ᾠὰ   t, m | **e 1** [ἢ . . . θριξίν] e

were at a loss about it, because it was not open to them either to kill them, wiping out their kind with thunderbolts as they had the giants (since the honours and sacrifices [c5] they received from human beings would be wiped out with them), or to leave them to continue behaving outrageously. After thinking long and hard, Zeus said "I think I have a plan which would both allow human beings to exist and [d1] make them weaker, so that they would have to give up their immoral behaviour. For the present," he said, "I shall divide each one of them into two, the result of which will be that they will both be weaker than they are, and be more useful to us, because there will be more of them; and they'll move upright on [d5] two legs. But if I think they are still behaving outrageously, and if they are not prepared to keep their peace, then", he said, "I shall cut them into two all over again, so that they'll move around by hopping on one leg." With these words he set about cutting human beings into two, like people who cut up sorb-apples before they [e1] preserve them, or like people cutting eggs with hairs; as he cut each one, he told Apollo to twist the face and the half-neck round towards the cut, so that the spectacle of his own cutting would make the human more orderly, and as for the rest, he told [e5] Apollo to heal everything up. Apollo twisted the faces round, and drawing the skin from all sides over what is now called the belly, like a purse with a draw-string, he left a single opening which he tied off in the middle of the belly, which is what they call the navel. He smoothed out **191** the many other wrinkles, shaping the chest with the sort of tool that shoemakers use when they smooth out the wrinkles on the leather over the last; but he left a few wrinkles, the ones on the belly itself around the navel, to be a memorial of that [a5] ancient suffering. So, because their natural form had been cut in two, each half longed for what belonged to it and tried to engage with it; throwing their arms around each other and locking themselves together, because of their desire to grow back together, [b1] they died from not eating or indeed doing anything else, because they refused to do anything apart from each other. Whenever, too, any of the halves died, leaving the other half behind, the half that was left looked for another half and locked itself together with that, whether it was a whole woman's half it encountered, what [b5] we now call a woman, or a whole man's; and thus they perished. Out of pity for them Zeus came up with another plan, moving their genitals round to the front; for up till then they had these too on what

54

εἶχον, καὶ ἐγέννων καὶ ἔτικτον οὐκ εἰς ἀλλήλους ἀλλ' εἰς c
γῆν, ὥσπερ οἱ τέττιγες. μετέθηκέ τε οὖν οὕτω αὐτῶν εἰς τὸ
πρόσθεν καὶ διὰ τούτων τὴν γένεσιν ἐν ἀλλήλοις ἐποίησεν,
διὰ τοῦ ἄρρενος ἐν τῷ θήλει, τῶνδε ἕνεκα, ἵνα ἐν τῇ
συμπλοκῇ ἅμα μὲν εἰ ἀνὴρ γυναικὶ ἐντύχοι, γεννῷεν καὶ 5
γίγνοιτο τὸ γένος, ἅμα δ' εἰ καὶ ἄρρην ἄρρενι, πλησμονὴ
γοῦν γίγνοιτο τῆς συνουσίας καὶ διαπαύοιντο καὶ ἐπὶ τὰ
ἔργα τρέποιντο καὶ τοῦ ἄλλου βίου ἐπιμελοῖντο. ἔστι δὴ οὖν
ἐκ τόσου ὁ ἔρως ἔμφυτος ἀλλήλων τοῖς ἀνθρώποις καὶ τῆς d
ἀρχαίας φύσεως συναγωγεὺς καὶ ἐπιχειρῶν ποιῆσαι ἓν ἐκ
δυοῖν καὶ ἰάσασθαι τὴν φύσιν τὴν ἀνθρωπίνην. ἕκαστος οὖν
ἡμῶν ἐστιν ἀνθρώπου σύμβολον, ἅτε τετμημένος ὥσπερ αἱ
ψῆτται, ἐξ ἑνὸς δύο· ζητεῖ δὴ ἀεὶ τὸ αὑτοῦ ἕκαστος 5
σύμβολον. ὅσοι μὲν οὖν τῶν ἀνδρῶν τοῦ κοινοῦ τμῆμά εἰσιν,
ὃ δὴ τότε ἀνδρόγυνον ἐκαλεῖτο, φιλογύναικές τέ εἰσι καὶ οἱ
πολλοὶ τῶν μοιχῶν ἐκ τούτου τοῦ γένους γεγόνασιν, καὶ ὅσαι e
αὖ γυναῖκες φίλανδροί τε καὶ μοιχεύτριαι ἐκ τούτου τοῦ
γένους γίγνονται. ὅσαι δὲ τῶν γυναικῶν γυναικὸς τμῆμά
εἰσιν, οὐ πάνυ αὗται τοῖς ἀνδράσι τὸν νοῦν προσέχουσιν,
ἀλλὰ μᾶλλον πρὸς τὰς γυναῖκας τετραμμέναι εἰσί, καὶ αἱ 5
ἑταιρίστριαι ἐκ τούτου τοῦ γένους γίγνονται. ὅσοι δὲ
ἄρρενος τμῆμά εἰσι, τὰ ἄρρενα διώκουσι, καὶ τέως μὲν ἂν
παῖδες ὦσιν, ἅτε τεμάχια ὄντα τοῦ ἄρρενος, φιλοῦσι τοὺς
ἄνδρας καὶ χαίρουσι συγκατακείμενοι καὶ συμπεπλεγμένοι 192
τοῖς ἀνδράσι, καί εἰσιν οὗτοι βέλτιστοι τῶν παίδων καὶ
μειρακίων, ἅτε ἀνδρειότατοι ὄντες φύσει. φασὶ δὲ δή τινες
αὐτοὺς ἀναισχύντους εἶναι, ψευδόμενοι· οὐ γὰρ ὑπ'
ἀναισχυντίας τοῦτο δρῶσιν ἀλλ' ὑπὸ θάρρους καὶ ἀνδρείας 5
καὶ ἀρρενωπίας, τὸ ὅμοιον αὐτοῖς ἀσπαζόμενοι. μέγα δὲ
τεκμήριον· καὶ γὰρ τελεωθέντες μόνοι ἀποβαίνουσιν εἰς τὰ
πολιτικὰ ἄνδρες οἱ τοιοῦτοι. ἐπειδὰν δὲ ἀνδρωθῶσι,
παιδεραστοῦσι καὶ πρὸς γάμους καὶ παιδοποιίας οὐ b
προσέχουσι τὸν νοῦν φύσει, ἀλλ' ὑπὸ τοῦ νόμου
ἀναγκάζονται· ἀλλ' ἐξαρκεῖ αὐτοῖς μετ' ἀλλήλων καταζῆν
ἀγάμοις. πάντως μὲν οὖν ὁ τοιοῦτος παιδεραστής τε καὶ
φιλεραστὴς γίγνεται, ἀεὶ τὸ συγγενὲς ἀσπαζόμενος. ὅταν 5
μὲν οὖν καὶ αὐτῷ ἐκείνῳ ἐντύχῃ τῷ αὑτοῦ ἡμίσει καὶ ὁ

e 2-3 [ἐκ ... γίγνονται] e | b 4 μὲν οὖν m: μέντοι e

was originally their [c1] outside, and they did their begetting and child-bearing not in each other but in the ground, like cicadas. So as I say he moved their genitals to the front, and brought in reproduction through these in each other, in the female through the agency of the male, with the intention that when they [c5] locked together, if a man encountered a woman, they would breed and the race be reproduced, while at the same time even if male encountered male, there would at least be satisfaction from their intercourse, and they would pause from their search, turning to their work and taking care of the other aspects of their lives. So it is [d1] from this far back that love of one another has been inborn in human beings, a restorer of our original nature, trying to make one from two and cure human nature. Thus each of us is a tally of a human being, insofar as he has been sliced like a [d5] flatfish, making him two out of one; the quest, then, always, for each of us is for our own matching tally. Those men who are cut from the combined kind, what at that time was called "androgynous", are attracted to women, and [e1] most adulterers have their origin in this kind, and in turn those women who are attracted to men, and adulteresses, come about from this kind. Those women, on the other hand, who are cut from the whole woman do not pay very much attention to men, [e5] but are inclined more towards women, and *hetairistriai* come about from this kind. Those men who are cut from the male kind pursue male halves, and so long as they are boys, because they are slices of the male, they show affection **192** for men and enjoy lying locked in embrace with men; and these are the best of our boys and of our youth, insofar as they are most manly by nature. It is a lie to say, as some people say, that they are shameless; what makes [a5] them do this is not shamelessness but boldness, manliness, and masculinity, because they are embracing what is like them. And there's good evidence for this: such people are the only ones who as adults turn out to be real men in the political sphere. When they reach manhood, [b1] they become lovers of boys, and as for things like marriage and having children, they pay attention to them not by nature, but because they are compelled by the rules of custom; it's enough for them to live with each other without getting married. So there are no two ways about it: such a person becomes a lover of boys [b5] and someone who shows affection to lovers, because he is always embracing what is akin to him. Now whenever the lover of boys, or anyone else, encounters that very

παιδεραστὴς καὶ ἄλλος πᾶς, τότε καὶ θαυμαστὰ ἐκπλήττονται c
φιλίᾳ τε καὶ οἰκειότητι καὶ ἔρωτι, οὐκ ἐθέλοντες ὡς ἔπος
εἰπεῖν χωρίζεσθαι ἀλλήλων οὐδὲ σμικρὸν χρόνον. καὶ οἱ
διατελοῦντες μετ' ἀλλήλων διὰ βίου οὗτοί εἰσιν, οἳ οὐδ' ἂν
ἔχοιεν εἰπεῖν ὅτι βούλονται σφίσι παρ' ἀλλήλων γίγνεσθαι. 5
οὐδενὶ γὰρ ἂν δόξειεν τοῦτ' εἶναι ἡ τῶν ἀφροδισίων συνουσία,
ὡς ἄρα τούτου ἕνεκα ἕτερος ἑτέρῳ χαίρει συνὼν οὕτως ἐπὶ
μεγάλης σπουδῆς· ἀλλ' ἄλλο τι βουλομένη ἑκατέρου ἡ ψυχὴ
δήλη ἐστί, ὃ οὐ δύναται εἰπεῖν, ἀλλὰ μαντεύεται ὃ βούλεται, d
καὶ αἰνίττεται. καὶ εἰ αὐτοῖς ἐν τῷ αὐτῷ κατακειμένοις
ἐπιστὰς ὁ Ἥφαιστος, ἔχων τὰ ὄργανα, ἔροιτο· "τί ἐσθ' ὃ
βούλεσθε, ὦ ἄνθρωποι, ὑμῖν παρ' ἀλλήλων γενέσθαι;" καὶ εἰ
ἀποροῦντας αὐτοὺς πάλιν ἔροιτο· "ἆρά γε τοῦδε ἐπιθυμεῖτε, 5
ἐν τῷ αὐτῷ γενέσθαι ὅτι μάλιστα ἀλλήλοις, ὥστε καὶ νύκτα
καὶ ἡμέραν μὴ ἀπολείπεσθαι ἀλλήλων; εἰ γὰρ τούτου
ἐπιθυμεῖτε, θέλω ὑμᾶς συντῆξαι καὶ συμφυσῆσαι εἰς τὸ αὐτό, e
ὥστε δύ' ὄντας ἕνα γεγονέναι καὶ ἕως τ' ἂν ζῆτε, ὡς ἕνα
ὄντα, κοινῇ ἀμφοτέρους ζῆν, καὶ ἐπειδὰν ἀποθάνητε, ἐκεῖ αὖ
ἐν Ἅιδου ἀντὶ δυοῖν ἕνα εἶναι κοινῇ τεθνεῶτε· ἀλλ' ὁρᾶτε εἰ
τούτου ἐρᾶτε καὶ ἐξαρκεῖ ὑμῖν ἂν τούτου τύχητε." ταῦτ' 5
ἀκούσας ἴσμεν ὅτι οὐδ' ἂν εἷς ἐξαρνηθείη οὐδ' ἄλλο τι ἂν
φανείη βουλόμενος, ἀλλ' ἀτεχνῶς οἴοιτ' ἂν ἀκηκοέναι τοῦτο ὃ
πάλαι ἄρα ἐπεθύμει, συνελθὼν καὶ συντακεὶς τῷ ἐρωμένῳ ἐκ
δυοῖν εἷς γενέσθαι. τοῦτο γάρ ἐστι τὸ αἴτιον, ὅτι ἡ ἀρχαία
φύσις ἡμῶν ἦν αὕτη καὶ ἦμεν ὅλοι· τοῦ ὅλου οὖν τῇ ἐπιθυμίᾳ 10
καὶ διώξει ἔρως ὄνομα. καὶ πρὸ τοῦ, ὥσπερ λέγω, ἓν ἦμεν, **193**
νυνὶ δὲ διὰ τὴν ἀδικίαν διῳκίσθημεν ὑπὸ τοῦ θεοῦ, καθάπερ
Ἀρκάδες ὑπὸ Λακεδαιμονίων· φόβος οὖν ἔστιν, ἐὰν μὴ
κόσμιοι ὦμεν πρὸς τοὺς θεούς, ὅπως μὴ καὶ αὖθις
διασχισθησόμεθα, καὶ περίιμεν ἔχοντες ὥσπερ οἱ ἐν ταῖς 5
στήλαις καταγραφὴν ἐκτετυπωμένοι, διαπεπρισμένοι κατὰ τὰς
ῥῖνας, γεγονότες ὥσπερ λίσπαι. ἀλλὰ τούτων ἕνεκα πάντ'
ἄνδρα χρὴ ἅπαντα παρακελεύεσθαι εὐσεβεῖν περὶ θεούς, ἵνα b
τὰ μὲν ἐκφύγωμεν, τῶν δὲ τύχωμεν, ὡς ὁ Ἔρως ἡμῖν ἡγεμὼν
καὶ στρατηγός. ᾧ μηδεὶς ἐναντία πραττέτω – πράττει δ'

c 6 οὐδενὶ t: οὐδέν m | e 1 ἐθέλω n

[c1] half which belongs to him, at that point the pair are overpowered in a quite amazing way by feelings of affection and belonging and love, and they practically refuse to be separated from each other, even for a short time. And in fact these people are the ones who stay with each other throughout life, though they wouldn't [c5] even be able to say what they want for themselves from one another. For no one would suppose this to be sexual intercourse – that it is for the sake of *this* that each of the two shows such great eagerness to take pleasure in the other; it is something else that the soul of each manifestly [d1] wants, which it cannot express, but dimly grasps what it wants, and talks of it as if in riddles. And if Hephaestus were to stand over them as they lie there together, with his tools in his hands, and were to ask them "What is it, humans, that you want for yourselves from one another?" Suppose that [d5] they had no answer to give, and he put another question to them: "Is this what you desire – to be together with each other to the greatest degree possible, so as not to be separated from each other by night or [e1] by day? If this is what you desire, I am willing to fuse and melt you together, so that from being two you become one, and you both share a life in common, as a single individual, so long as you live, and in Hades too you are one instead of two, having shared a common death. See if [e5] this is what you're in love with, and if it's enough for you if you achieve this goal." We know that there is not a single person who on hearing this would persist in denying it, or would be found wanting anything else; he would simply think that he had heard what it was after all that he desired all that time, to come together and be fused with the one he loves and so from two become one. The cause is as I have said, that this was [e10] our original nature, and that we were wholes; and so the name "love" belongs **193** to the desire and pursuit of the whole. Before this, as I say, we were one, and because of our crime we were forced to live apart, as the Arcadians were by the Spartans; so there is a fear that, if we fail to behave in an orderly way towards the gods, we shall be split [a5] in half once again, and go around like the figures worked in relief on gravestones, sawn in half down our noses, becoming like dice-tallies. This is why everyone [b1] must urge pious behaviour in relation to the gods in everything, in order that we may escape the one fate, and achieve the other, as Love guides and commands us. Let no one act contrary to him – and he

ἐναντία ὅστις θεοῖς ἀπεχθάνεται· φίλοι γὰρ γενόμενοι καὶ
διαλλαγέντες τῷ θεῷ ἐξευρήσομέν τε καὶ ἐντευξόμεθα τοῖς 5
παιδικοῖς τοῖς ἡμετέροις αὐτῶν, ὃ τῶν νῦν ὀλίγοι ποιοῦσι.
καὶ μή μοι ὑπολάβῃ Ἐρυξίμαχος, κωμῳδῶν τὸν λόγον, ὡς
Παυσανίαν καὶ Ἀγάθωνα λέγω· ἴσως μὲν γὰρ καὶ οὗτοι
τούτων τυγχάνουσιν ὄντες καὶ εἰσιν ἀμφότεροι τὴν φύσιν c
ἄρρενες, λέγω δὲ οὖν ἔγωγε καθ' ἁπάντων καὶ ἀνδρῶν καὶ
γυναικῶν, ὅτι οὕτως ἂν ἡμῶν τὸ γένος εὔδαιμον γένοιτο, εἰ
ἐκτελέσαιμεν τὸν ἔρωτα καὶ τῶν παιδικῶν τῶν αὑτοῦ ἕκαστος
τύχοι εἰς τὴν ἀρχαίαν ἀπελθὼν φύσιν. εἰ δὲ τοῦτο ἄριστον, 5
ἀναγκαῖον καὶ τῶν νῦν παρόντων τὸ τούτου ἐγγυτάτω ἄριστον
εἶναι· τοῦτο δ' ἐστὶ παιδικῶν τυχεῖν κατὰ νοῦν αὑτῷ
πεφυκότων· οὗ δὴ τὸν αἴτιον θεὸν ὑμνοῦντες δικαίως ἂν d
ὑμνοῖμεν Ἔρωτα, ὃς ἔν τε τῷ παρόντι ἡμᾶς πλεῖστα ὀνίνησιν
εἰς τὸ οἰκεῖον ἄγων, καὶ εἰς τὸ ἔπειτα ἐλπίδας μεγίστας
παρέχεται, ἡμῶν παρεχομένων πρὸς θεοὺς εὐσέβειαν,
καταστήσας ἡμᾶς εἰς τὴν ἀρχαίαν φύσιν καὶ ἰασάμενος 5
μακαρίους καὶ εὐδαίμονας ποιῆσαι.

'οὗτος,' ἔφη, 'ὦ Ἐρυξίμαχε, ὁ ἐμὸς λόγος ἐστὶ περὶ
Ἔρωτος, ἀλλοῖος ἢ ὁ σός. ὥσπερ οὖν ἐδεήθην σου, μὴ
κωμῳδήσῃς αὐτόν, ἵνα καὶ τῶν λοιπῶν ἀκούσωμεν τί ἕκαστος e
ἐρεῖ, μᾶλλον δὲ τί ἑκάτερος· Ἀγάθων γὰρ καὶ Σωκράτης
λοιποί.'

'ἀλλὰ πείσομαί σοι,' ἔφη φάναι τὸν Ἐρυξίμαχον· 'καὶ
γάρ μοι ὁ λόγος ἡδέως ἐρρήθη. καὶ εἰ μὴ συνῄδη Σωκράτει 5
τε καὶ Ἀγάθωνι δεινοῖς οὖσι περὶ τὰ ἐρωτικά, πάνυ ἂν
ἐφοβούμην μὴ ἀπορήσωσι λόγων διὰ τὸ πολλὰ καὶ παντοδαπὰ
εἰρῆσθαι· νῦν δὲ ὅμως θαρρῶ.'

τὸν οὖν Σωκράτη εἰπεῖν 'καλῶς γὰρ αὐτὸς ἠγώνισαι, ὦ **194**
Ἐρυξίμαχε· εἰ δὲ γένοιο οὗ νῦν ἐγώ εἰμι, μᾶλλον δὲ ἴσως οὗ
ἔσομαι ἐπειδὰν καὶ Ἀγάθων εἴπῃ εὖ, καὶ μάλ' ἂν φοβοῖο καὶ
ἐν παντὶ εἴης ὥσπερ ἐγὼ νῦν.'

'φαρμάττειν βούλει με, ὦ Σώκρατες,' εἰπεῖν τὸν Ἀγάθωνα, 5
'ἵνα θορυβηθῶ διὰ τὸ οἴεσθαι τὸ θέατρον προσδοκίαν μεγάλην
ἔχειν ὡς εὖ ἐροῦντος ἐμοῦ.'

'ἐπιλήσμων μεντἂν εἴην, ὦ Ἀγάθων,' εἰπεῖν τὸν Σωκράτη,
'εἰ ἰδὼν τὴν σὴν ἀνδρείαν καὶ μεγαλοφροσύνην ἀναβαίνοντος b
ἐπὶ τὸν ὀκρίβαντα μετὰ τῶν ὑποκριτῶν, καὶ βλέψαντος
ἐναντία τοσούτῳ θεάτρῳ, μέλλοντος ἐπιδείξεσθαι σαυτοῦ

acts contrary to gods who is hated by them; if we become friends and [b5] are reconciled with the god, we shall find and meet the beloved who belongs to ourselves, which few people nowadays do. And Eryximachus mustn't pick up on me here and turn my speech into a comedy, by saying that I'm talking about Pausanias and Agathon; maybe they themselves [c1] really do belong to this type, and are both masculine in nature, but my point in fact applies to everyone, whether men or women – that the way to happiness for the human race would be if our love were to run its full course and each of us were to find our own [c5] beloved, returning to our original nature. If this is what is best for us, necessarily what is closest to this among the things presently available to us must also be best; and this is to find a beloved with a nature [d1] congenial to oneself – and if we are to hymn the god who is responsible for that, we would justly hymn Love, who both provides us with the greatest benefits in the present by leading us to what belongs to us, and accords us the greatest hopes for the future, that if we for our part accord piety to the gods, [d5] he will establish us in our original condition and, by healing us, make us blessed and happy.

'This, Eryximachus,' Aristophanes said, 'is my speech about Love, one of a different kind from yours. Well, as I asked, don't [e1] make a comedy out of it, because we also want to hear what the people who are left will each say – or rather what each of the two of them will say: there are Agathon and Socrates left.'

'I'll do as you say,' Eryximachus said, according to Aristodemus; 'in [e5] fact, I enjoyed listening to your speech. If I didn't know that Socrates and Agathon are experts on matters to do with love, I'd be terribly afraid that they'd be at a loss for things to say, because of the many and varied things that have already been said; as it is, I'm confident about them in spite of that.'

194 Then Socrates said 'You can say that, Eryximachus, because you've already made a fine showing in the competition; but if you were in my position, or perhaps rather the one I'll be in when Agathon too gives us a good speech, you'd be terrified and as desperate as I am now.'

[a5] 'You mean to cast a spell on me, Socrates,' replied Agathon, 'so that I'll be thrown into confusion by the thought of the audience's high expectation of a good speech from me.'

'I'd be pretty forgetful, Agathon,' replied Socrates, [b1] 'if when I'd seen your courage and self-confidence as you mounted the platform with your actors and looked straight out at such a large audience -- not in the slightest

λόγους, καὶ οὐδ' ὁπωστιοῦν ἐκπλαγέντος, νῦν οἰηθείην σε
θορυβήσεσθαι ἕνεκα ἡμῶν ὀλίγων ἀνθρώπων.' 5

'τί δέ, ὦ Σώκρατες;' τὸν Ἀγάθωνα φάναι, 'οὐ δήπου με
οὕτω θεάτρου μεστὸν ἡγῇ ὥστε καὶ ἀγνοεῖν ὅτι νοῦν ἔχοντι
ὀλίγοι ἔμφρονες πολλῶν ἀφρόνων φοβερώτεροι;'

'οὐ μεντἂν καλῶς ποιοίην,' φάναι, 'ὦ Ἀγάθων, περὶ σοῦ c
τι ἐγὼ ἄγροικον δοξάζων· ἀλλ' εὖ οἶδα ὅτι εἴ τισιν ἐντύχοις
οὓς ἡγοῖο σοφούς, μᾶλλον ἂν αὐτῶν φροντίζοις ἢ τῶν πολλῶν.
ἀλλὰ μὴ οὐχ οὗτοι ἡμεῖς ὦμεν, ἡμεῖς μὲν γὰρ καὶ ἐκεῖ
παρῆμεν καὶ ἦμεν τῶν πολλῶν· εἰ δὲ ἄλλοις ἐντύχοις σοφοῖς, 5
τάχ' ἂν αἰσχύνοιο αὐτούς, εἴ τι ἴσως οἴοιο αἰσχρὸν ὂν ποιεῖν·
ἢ πῶς λέγεις;'

'ἀληθῆ λέγεις,' φάναι.

'τοὺς δὲ πολλοὺς οὐκ ἂν αἰσχύνοιο εἴ τι οἴοιο αἰσχρὸν d
ποιεῖν;'

καὶ τὸν Φαῖδρον ἔφη ὑπολαβόντα εἰπεῖν 'ὦ φίλε Ἀγάθων,
ἐὰν ἀποκρίνῃ Σωκράτει, οὐδὲν ἔτι διοίσει αὐτῷ ὁπηοῦν τῶν
ἐνθάδε ὁτιοῦν γίγνεσθαι, ἐὰν μόνον ἔχῃ ὅτῳ διαλέγηται, 5
ἄλλως τε καὶ καλῷ. ἐγὼ δὲ ἡδέως μὲν ἀκούω Σωκράτους
διαλεγομένου, ἀναγκαῖον δέ μοι ἐπιμεληθῆναι τοῦ ἐγκωμίου τῷ
Ἔρωτι καὶ ἀποδέξασθαι παρ' ἑνὸς ἑκάστου ὑμῶν τὸν λόγον·
ἀποδοὺς οὖν ἑκάτερος τῷ θεῷ οὕτως ἤδη διαλεγέσθω.'

'ἀλλὰ καλῶς λέγεις, ὦ Φαῖδρε,' φάναι τὸν Ἀγάθωνα, 'καὶ e
οὐδέν με κωλύει λέγειν· Σωκράτει γὰρ καὶ αὖθις ἔσται
πολλάκις διαλέγεσθαι.'

'ἐγὼ δὲ δὴ βούλομαι πρῶτον μὲν εἰπεῖν ὡς χρή με εἰπεῖν,
ἔπειτα εἰπεῖν. δοκοῦσι γάρ μοι πάντες οἱ πρόσθεν εἰρηκότες 5
οὐ τὸν θεὸν ἐγκωμιάζειν ἀλλὰ τοὺς ἀνθρώπους εὐδαιμονίζειν
τῶν ἀγαθῶν ὧν ὁ θεὸς αὐτοῖς αἴτιος· ὁποῖος δέ τις αὐτὸς ὢν
ταῦτα ἐδωρήσατο, οὐδεὶς εἴρηκεν. εἷς δὲ τρόπος ὀρθὸς παντὸς 195
ἐπαίνου περὶ παντός, λόγῳ διελθεῖν οἷος οἵων αἴτιος ὢν
τυγχάνει περὶ οὗ ἂν ὁ λόγος ᾖ. οὕτω δὴ τὸν Ἔρωτα καὶ
ἡμᾶς δίκαιον ἐπαινέσαι πρῶτον αὐτὸν οἷός ἐστιν, ἔπειτα τὰς
δόσεις. φημὶ οὖν ἐγὼ πάντων θεῶν εὐδαιμόνων ὄντων Ἔρωτα, 5
εἰ θέμις καὶ ἀνεμέσητον εἰπεῖν, εὐδαιμονέστατον εἶναι αὐτῶν,
κάλλιστον ὄντα καὶ ἄριστον. ἔστι δὲ κάλλιστος ὢν τοιόσδε.

a 2 οἷος οἵων e: οἷς οἵων n: οἷος ὢν n: οἷος ὢν <οἵων> e

way overcome by the prospect of displaying compositions of your own – I
now thought you'd [b5] be overcome on account of the few of us.'

Agathon said 'What's that, Socrates? You surely don't think me so full of
the theatre that I actually don't know that to an intelligent person a few
sensible people are more frightening than a lot of stupid ones?'

[c1] 'I'd certainly be behaving badly, Agathon,' he said, 'if I entertained
any boorish opinion of you; I'm perfectly well aware that if you met some
individuals you thought to be clever, you'd care more about them than you
would about ordinary people. Now maybe we're not the ones, since we were
actually there [c5] in the theatre ourselves, and were part of the mass; but if
you did encounter other people who were actually clever, I imagine you'd
feel ashamed towards them if you thought perhaps you were doing something
that was shameful? Is that right?'

'True,' he said.

[d1] 'And towards ordinary people you wouldn't feel ashamed if you
thought you were doing something shameful?'

At that point Aristodemus said Phaedrus broke in and said 'My dear
Agathon, if you answer Socrates' question, it'll no longer matter to him in the
slightest how any [d5] of the things we're doing here turn out – so long as he
has someone to converse with, especially someone beautiful. I myself enjoy
listening to Socrates conversing, but it's my business to see to our encomium
to Love and get the required speech from each one of you; so when the two
of you have paid your dues to the god, then you can have your conversation.'

[e1] 'You're quite right, Phaedrus,' said Agathon, 'and there's nothing to
stop me giving my speech; Socrates will have plenty of other opportunities
for conversation.

'What *I* mean to do is first to say how I must say my piece, [e5] then to
say it. For all those who have spoken before me seem to me not to be
eulogizing the god but congratulating humans on the goods the god is
responsible for giving them; in virtue of his having what sort of character **195**
he gave them, no one has said. There is one correct method for any praise of
any subject, namely to describe in speech what sort of character whoever is
the subject of the speech has in virtue of which he is actually responsible for
what. Thus it is right and proper for us too to praise Love himself first for
what he is, then for his [a5] gifts. Now I for my part declare that while all
gods are happy, Love – if it is permitted and will not cause divine anger to
say it – is happiest of them, being most beautiful and best. He is most
beautiful because he has the following characteristics. [b1] First, he is

62

πρῶτον μὲν νεώτατος θεῶν, ὦ Φαῖδρε. μέγα δὲ τεκμήριον τῷ b
λόγῳ αὐτὸς παρέχεται, φεύγων φυγῇ τὸ γῆρας, ταχὺ ὂν δῆλον
ὅτι· θᾶττον γοῦν τοῦ δέοντος ἡμῖν προσέρχεται. ὃ δὴ
πέφυκεν Ἔρως μισεῖν καὶ οὐδ' ἐντὸς πολλοῦ πλησιάζειν. μετὰ
δὲ νέων ἀεὶ σύνεστί τε καί ἐστιν· ὁ γὰρ παλαιὸς λόγος εὖ 5
ἔχει, ὡς ὅμοιον ὁμοίῳ ἀεὶ πελάζει. ἐγὼ δὲ Φαίδρῳ πολλὰ
ἄλλα ὁμολογῶν τοῦτο οὐχ ὁμολογῶ, ὡς Ἔρως Κρόνου καὶ
Ἰαπετοῦ ἀρχαιότερός ἐστιν, ἀλλά φημι νεώτατον αὐτὸν εἶναι c
θεῶν καὶ ἀεὶ νέον, τὰ δὲ παλαιὰ πράγματα περὶ θεούς, ἃ
Ἡσίοδος καὶ Παρμενίδης λέγουσιν, Ἀνάγκῃ καὶ οὐκ Ἔρωτι
γεγονέναι, εἰ ἐκεῖνοι ἀληθῆ ἔλεγον· οὐ γὰρ ἂν ἐκτομαὶ οὐδὲ
δεσμοὶ ἀλλήλων ἐγίγνοντο καὶ ἄλλα πολλὰ καὶ βίαια, εἰ Ἔρως 5
ἐν αὐτοῖς ἦν, ἀλλὰ φιλία καὶ εἰρήνη, ὥσπερ νῦν, ἐξ οὗ Ἔρως
τῶν θεῶν βασιλεύει. νέος μὲν οὖν ἐστι, πρὸς δὲ τῷ νέῳ
ἁπαλός· ποιητοῦ δ' ἐστιν ἐνδεὴς οἷος ἦν Ὅμηρος πρὸς τὸ d
ἐπιδεῖξαι θεοῦ ἁπαλότητα. Ὅμηρος γὰρ Ἄτην θεόν τέ φησιν
εἶναι καὶ ἁπαλήν – τοὺς γοῦν πόδας αὐτῆς ἁπαλοὺς εἶναι –
λέγων

τῆς μέν θ' ἁπαλοὶ πόδες· οὐ γὰρ ἐπ' οὔδεος 5
πίλναται, ἀλλ' ἄρα ἥ γε κατ' ἀνδρῶν κράατα βαίνει.
καλῶ οὖν δοκεῖ μοι τεκμηρίῳ τὴν ἁπαλότητα ἀποφαίνειν, ὅτι
οὐκ ἐπὶ σκληροῦ βαίνει, ἀλλ' ἐπὶ μαλθακοῦ. τῷ αὐτῷ δὴ καὶ e
ἡμεῖς χρησόμεθα τεκμηρίῳ περὶ Ἔρωτα ὅτι ἁπαλός. οὐ γὰρ
ἐπὶ γῆς βαίνει οὐδ' ἐπὶ κρανίων, ἅ ἐστιν οὐ πάνυ μαλακά,
ἀλλ' ἐν τοῖς μαλακωτάτοις τῶν ὄντων καὶ βαίνει καὶ οἰκεῖ. ἐν
γὰρ ἤθεσι καὶ ψυχαῖς θεῶν καὶ ἀνθρώπων τὴν οἴκησιν ἵδρυται, 5
καὶ οὐκ αὖ ἐξῆς ἐν πάσαις ταῖς ψυχαῖς, ἀλλ' ᾗτινι ἂν
σκληρὸν ἦθος ἐχούσῃ ἐντύχῃ, ἀπέρχεται, ᾗ δ' ἂν μαλακόν,
οἰκίζεται. ἁπτόμενον οὖν ἀεὶ καὶ ποσὶν καὶ πάντῃ ἐν
μαλακωτάτοις τῶν μαλακωτάτων, ἁπαλώτατον ἀνάγκη εἶναι.
νεώτατος μὲν δή ἐστι καὶ ἁπαλώτατος, πρὸς δὲ τούτοις 196
ὑγρὸς τὸ εἶδος. οὐ γὰρ ἂν οἷός τ' ἦν πάντῃ περιπτύσσεσθαι
οὐδὲ διὰ πάσης ψυχῆς καὶ εἰσιὼν τὸ πρῶτον λανθάνειν καὶ
ἐξιών, εἰ σκληρὸς ἦν. συμμέτρου δὲ καὶ ὑγρᾶς ἰδέας μέγα
τεκμήριον ἡ εὐσχημοσύνη, ὃ δὴ διαφερόντως ἐκ πάντων 5
ὁμολογουμένως Ἔρως ἔχει· ἀσχημοσύνῃ γὰρ καὶ Ἔρωτι πρὸς

b 5 ἐστὶ νέος e: ἔσται e | d 5 οὐδεὶ n | e 1 τῷ αὐτῷ t, n: τὸ αὐτὸ n

youngest of the gods, Phaedrus. He himself offers good evidence for what I say, flitting as he does in flight from old age, which is something quick, plainly; at any rate it comes to us more quickly than it ought. Love, then, by his nature hates old age and does not come anywhere near it. It is with [b5] the young that he always is, and he *is* young; the old saying has it right, that like always draws near to like. I agree with Phaedrus on many other things, but on this I do not agree, that Love is more [c1] ancient than Cronus and Iapetus: I declare that he is youngest of the gods, and always young, and that those old happenings that Hesiod and Parmenides report in relation to the gods, if they were actually reporting the truth, happened through Necessity and not through Love; for they would not have been castrating each [c5] other, or tying each other up and doing all sorts of other violent things, if Love had been there among them, but there would have been affection and peace, as there is now, and has been since Love has been king of the gods. So he is young, and as well as being young he is [d1] delicate; but he lacks a poet of Homer's quality when it comes to showing his delicateness as the god he is. For Homer is declaring both the divinity and the delicateness of Atê – or at least the delicateness of her feet – when he says [d5] "hers are delicate feet; for it is not over the ground / that she approaches, but she is one who walks upon the heads of men." Well, his evidence for proclaiming her delicateness seems to me excellent – that [e1] she does not walk on something hard, but on something soft. It's the same evidence I shall myself use in relation to Love's delicateness. He does not walk on the earth, or on skulls, which in fact are not so soft, but it is in the softest things there are that he walks and makes his home. [e5] For his home is set up in the characters and souls of gods and men, and then again not in every soul, one after another, but if ever a soul he encounters has a hard character, he withdraws, and if a soft one, there he finds his home. Thus, since he lays hold of the softest in what is softest in them, both with his feet and all over, he is necessarily most delicate. **196** He is youngest, then, and most delicate, and in addition he is supple in form. For he would not be able, as he is, to enfold us completely, nor to pass in through the whole soul, first, and then to pass out again without our noticing it, if he were hard. Good evidence of his well-fitting and supple [a5] form is his gracefulness, something which it is agreed on all sides that Love possesses to a superlative degree; for ungracefulness

ἀλλήλους ἀεὶ πόλεμος. χρόας δὲ κάλλος ἡ κατ' ἄνθη δίαιτα
τοῦ θεοῦ σημαίνει· ἀνανθεῖ γὰρ καὶ ἀπηνθηκότι καὶ σώματι b
καὶ ψυχῇ καὶ ἄλλῳ ὁτῳοῦν οὐκ ἐνίζει Ἔρως, οὗ δ' ἂν εὐανθής
τε καὶ εὐώδης τόπος ᾖ, ἐνταῦθα δὲ καὶ ἵζει καὶ μένει.

'περὶ μὲν οὖν κάλλους τοῦ θεοῦ καὶ ταῦτα ἱκανὰ καὶ ἔτι
πολλὰ λείπεται, περὶ δὲ ἀρετῆς Ἔρωτος μετὰ ταῦτα λεκτέον, 5
τὸ μὲν μέγιστον ὅτι Ἔρως οὔτ' ἀδικεῖ οὔτ' ἀδικεῖται οὔτε
ὑπὸ θεοῦ οὔτε θεόν, οὔτε ὑπ' ἀνθρώπου οὔτε ἄνθρωπον. οὔτε
γὰρ αὐτὸς βίᾳ πάσχει, εἴ τι πάσχει, βία γὰρ Ἔρωτος οὐχ
ἅπτεται· οὔτε ποιῶν ποιεῖ, πᾶς γὰρ ἑκὼν Ἔρωτι πᾶν c
ὑπηρετεῖ, ἃ δ' ἂν ἑκὼν ἑκόντι ὁμολογήσῃ, φασὶ "οἱ πόλεως
βασιλῆς νόμοι" δίκαια εἶναι. πρὸς δὲ τῇ δικαιοσύνῃ
σωφροσύνης πλείστης μετέχει. εἶναι γὰρ ὁμολογεῖται
σωφροσύνη τὸ κρατεῖν ἡδονῶν καὶ ἐπιθυμιῶν, Ἔρωτος δὲ 5
μηδεμίαν ἡδονὴν κρείττω εἶναι· εἰ δὲ ἥττους, κρατοῖντ' ἂν
ὑπὸ Ἔρωτος, ὁ δὲ κρατοῖ, κρατῶν δὲ ἡδονῶν καὶ ἐπιθυμιῶν ὁ
Ἔρως διαφερόντως ἂν σωφρονοῖ. καὶ μὴν εἴς γε ἀνδρείαν
Ἔρωτι "οὐδ' Ἄρης ἀνθίσταται". οὐ γὰρ ἔχει Ἔρωτα Ἄρης, d
ἀλλ' Ἔρως Ἄρη – Ἀφροδίτης, ὡς λόγος· κρείττων δὲ ὁ ἔχων
τοῦ ἐχομένου· τοῦ δ' ἀνδρειοτάτου τῶν ἄλλων κρατῶν πάντων
ἂν ἀνδρειότατος εἴη. περὶ μὲν οὖν δικαιοσύνης καὶ
σωφροσύνης καὶ ἀνδρείας τοῦ θεοῦ εἴρηται, περὶ δὲ σοφίας 5
λείπεται· ὅσον οὖν δυνατόν, πειρατέον μὴ ἐλλείπειν. καὶ
πρῶτον μέν, ἵν' αὖ καὶ ἐγὼ τὴν ἡμετέραν τέχνην τιμήσω
ὥσπερ Ἐρυξίμαχος τὴν αὑτοῦ, ποιητὴς ὁ θεὸς σοφὸς οὕτως e
ὥστε καὶ ἄλλον ποιῆσαι· πᾶς γοῦν ποιητὴς γίγνεται, "κἂν
ἄμουσος ᾖ τὸ πρίν", οὗ ἂν Ἔρως ἅψηται. ᾧ δὴ πρέπει ἡμᾶς
μαρτυρίῳ χρῆσθαι, ὅτι ποιητὴς ὁ Ἔρως ἀγαθὸς ἐν κεφαλαίῳ
πᾶσαν ποίησιν τὴν κατὰ μουσικήν· ἃ γάρ τις ἢ μὴ ἔχει ἢ μὴ 5
οἶδεν, οὔτ' ἂν ἑτέρῳ δοίη οὔτ' ἂν ἄλλον διδάξειεν. καὶ μὲν δὴ **197**
τήν γε τῶν ζῴων ποίησιν πάντων τίς ἐναντιώσεται μὴ οὐχὶ
Ἔρωτος εἶναι σοφίαν, ᾗ γίγνεταί τε καὶ φύεται πάντα τὰ
ζῷα; ἀλλὰ τὴν τῶν τεχνῶν δημιουργίαν οὐκ ἴσμεν, ὅτι οὗ μὲν
ἂν ὁ θεὸς οὗτος διδάσκαλος γένηται, ἐλλόγιμος καὶ φανὸς 5
ἀπέβη, οὗ δ' ἂν Ἔρως μὴ ἐφάψηται, σκοτεινός;
τοξικήν γε μὴν καὶ ἰατρικὴν καὶ μαντικὴν Ἀπόλλων ἀνηῦρεν

---

b 3 ἐνταῦθα δὲ   t: ἐνταῦθα   m

and Love are always at war with one another. Beauty of complexion is indicated by the fact that the god [b1] lives among flowers; for on what is without bloom, or past blooming, whether body or soul or anything else, Love does not settle, but wherever there is a place full of flowers and fragrance, there it is that Love settles and remains.

'Well, on the subject of the god's beauty this is sufficient, and still [b5] many points remain; the next subject to be talked about is Love's virtue, and most importantly the fact that Love neither wrongs nor is wronged, neither being wronged by a god nor wronging a god, neither being wronged by a man nor wronging a man. For neither does Love himself have things done to him by force, if something is done to him, since force does not touch [c1] Love; nor, if he is the agent, does he do things by force, since everyone serves Love willingly in everything, and whatever is agreed to willingly by both sides "the laws that are kings of the city" declare to be just. As well as justice, he shares most fully in moderation. For it is agreed that [c5] moderation is nothing but mastery over pleasures and desires, and that no pleasure is stronger than Love; but if they are weaker, then they will be mastered by Love, and he will master them; and if he masters pleasures and desires, Love will be superlatively moderate. What is more, in respect of courage [d1] "not even Ares stands up to" Love. For it is not Love who is possessed by Ares, but Love who possesses Ares – for Aphrodite, so they say; and the possessor is stronger than the one possessed; but if he masters the one who is most courageous of all the rest, he will be most courageous of all. We have spoken, then, about the god's [d5] justice, moderation, and courage, and it remains to speak about his wisdom; so one must try so far as possible not to fall short. First of all – to take my turn in honouring my own expertise, [e1] as Eryximachus honoured his – the god is a poet, one wise enough to make someone else a poet too; certainly everyone who is touched by Love turns into a poet, "even if he is unmusical before". We may properly use this as evidence that Love is, in short, a poet skilled [e5] in all kinds of creation in the sphere of music; for the sorts of things one either doesn't have or **197** doesn't know, one can't give another person or teach anyone else. And then again, as for that other kind of creation, of all living creatures, who will refuse to accept that it is Love's wisdom by which all living things come into being and are born? But with the craftsmanship that belongs to the various skills, do we not recognize [a5] that whoever has this god as his teacher turns out noted and conspicuous, but whoever does not feel Love's touch stays in obscurity? Archery, furthermore, medicine, and prophecy were invented

ἐπιθυμίας καὶ ἔρωτος ἡγεμονεύσαντος, ὥστε καὶ οὗτος
Ἔρωτος ἂν εἴη μαθητής, καὶ Μοῦσαι μουσικῆς, καὶ Ἥφαιστος b
χαλκείας καὶ Ἀθηνᾶ ἱστουργίας καὶ Ζεὺς "κυβερνᾶν θεῶν τε
καὶ ἀνθρώπων". ὅθεν δὴ καὶ κατεσκευάσθη τῶν θεῶν τὰ
πράγματα Ἔρωτος ἐγγενομένου, δῆλον ὅτι κάλλους - αἴσχει
γὰρ οὐκ ἔπι ἔρως - πρὸ τοῦ δέ, ὥσπερ ἐν ἀρχῇ εἶπον, πολλὰ 5
καὶ δεινὰ θεοῖς ἐγίγνετο, ὡς λέγεται, διὰ τὴν τῆς Ἀνάγκης
βασιλείαν· ἐπειδὴ δ' ὁ θεὸς οὗτος ἔφυ, ἐκ τοῦ ἐρᾶν τῶν
καλῶν πάντ' ἀγαθὰ γέγονεν καὶ θεοῖς καὶ ἀνθρώποις.   c

'οὕτως ἐμοὶ δοκεῖ, ὦ Φαῖδρε, Ἔρως πρῶτος αὐτὸς ὢν
κάλλιστος καὶ ἄριστος μετὰ τοῦτο τοῖς ἄλλοις ἄλλων
τοιούτων αἴτιος εἶναι. ἐπέρχεται δέ μοί τι καὶ ἔμμετρον
εἰπεῖν, ὅτι οὗτός ἐστιν ὁ ποιῶν   5
    εἰρήνην μὲν ἐν ἀνθρώποις, πελάγει δὲ γαλήνην
    νηνεμίαν, ἀνέμων κοίτην ὕπνον τ' ἐνὶ κήδει.
οὗτος δὲ ἡμᾶς ἀλλοτριότητος μὲν κενοῖ, οἰκειότητος δὲ d
πληροῖ, τὰς τοιάσδε συνόδους μετ' ἀλλήλων πάσας τιθεὶς
συνιέναι, ἐν ἑορταῖς, ἐν χοροῖς, ἐν θυσίαισι γιγνόμενος
ἡγεμών· πρᾳότητα μὲν πορίζων, ἀγριότητα δ' ἐξορίζων·
φιλόδωρος εὐμενείας, ἄδωρος δυσμενείας· ἵλεως ἀγανός· 5
θεατὸς σοφοῖς, ἀγαστὸς θεοῖς· ζηλωτὸς ἀμοίροις, κτητὸς
εὐμοίροις· τρυφῆς, ἁβρότητος, χλιδῆς, χαρίτων, ἱμέρου, πόθου
πατήρ· ἐπιμελὴς ἀγαθῶν, ἀμελὴς κακῶν· ἐν πόνῳ, ἐν φόβῳ, ἐν
πόθῳ, ἐν λόγῳ κυβερνήτης, ἐπιβάτης, παραστάτης τε καὶ e
σωτὴρ ἄριστος, συμπάντων τε θεῶν καὶ ἀνθρώπων κόσμος,
ἡγεμὼν κάλλιστος καὶ ἄριστος, ᾧ χρὴ ἕπεσθαι πάντα ἄνδρα
ἐφυμνοῦντα καλῶς, ᾠδῆς μετέχοντα ἣν ᾄδει θέλγων πάντων
θεῶν τε καὶ ἀνθρώπων νόημα.   5

'οὗτος', ἔφη, 'ὁ παρ' ἐμοῦ λόγος, ὦ Φαῖδρε, τῷ θεῷ
ἀνακείσθω, τὰ μὲν παιδιᾶς, τὰ δὲ σπουδῆς μετρίας, καθ' ὅσον
ἐγὼ δύναμαι, μετέχων.'

εἰπόντος δὲ τοῦ Ἀγάθωνος πάντας ἔφη ὁ Ἀριστόδημος 198
ἀναθορυβῆσαι τοὺς παρόντας, ὡς πρεπόντως τοῦ νεανίσκου
εἰρηκότος καὶ αὐτῷ καὶ τῷ θεῷ. τὸν οὖν Σωκράτη εἰπεῖν
βλέψαντα εἰς τὸν Ἐρυξίμαχον, 'ἆρά σοι δοκῶ,' φάναι, 'ὦ

---

b 5 ἔπι   e: ἔνι   n: ἔπεστιν   t, n | c 2 πρῶτος   m: πρὸ τῶν (i.e. πρῶτον) t
| d 5 ἀγανός   e: ἀγαθός   m, O: ἀγαθοῖς   t

by Apollo with desire and love as his guide, so that he too [b1] will be a pupil of Love, and so too the Muses in music, Hephaestus in metal-working, Athena in weaving, and Zeus in the "government of gods and men". So it follows that the gods' activities were actually established after the birth among them of Love, of beauty, clearly, since there is [b5] no love for ugliness, and that before that, just as I said at the beginning, many terrible things happened among the gods, or so it is said, because Necessity was queen; but when this god was born, from the love of the [c1] beautiful all good things came about for both gods and men.

'Thus it is my view, Phaedrus, that Love, being himself first most beautiful and best, is then responsible for others' possession of things of this sort. I find myself impelled to say something [c5] in verse: he is the one who creates "peace among men, on the sea calm, / without wind, bedding of winds and sleep amidst grief". [d1] He is the one who empties us of estrangement and fills us with kinship, causing us to come together in all such gatherings as ours, acting as guide in festivals, when choruses perform, at sacrifices; bringing gentleness, excluding savagery; [d5] generous with good will, miserly with ill will; gracious, kind; a spectacle for the wise, admired by the gods; coveted by those without portion of him, prized by those with a portion; father of delicacy, daintiness, luxuriance, charms, desire, longing; caring for good, uncaring of bad; in trouble, in fear, in [e1] longing, in speaking, a steersman, defender, fellow-soldier and saviour without peer, ornament at once of all gods and all men, most beautiful and best guide, whom everyone must follow, hymning him beautifully, sharing in the song he sings to charm the mind [e5] of all gods and men.

'Let this speech from me, Phaedrus,' he said, 'stand as my dedication to the god, sharing as it does partly in play, partly in a modest seriousness, to the best of my personal ability.'

198 When Agathon had spoken, Aristodemus said, everyone present burst into applause at the appropriateness of the young man's speech both to himself and to the god. Then Socrates spoke, with a look at Eryximachus: 'Do you think, son [a5] of Acumenus,' he said, 'that I was foolish to feel the

παῖ Ἀκουμενοῦ, ἀδεὲς πάλαι δέος δεδιέναι, ἀλλ' οὐ μαντικῶς 5
ἃ νυνδὴ ἔλεγον εἰπεῖν, ὅτι Ἀγάθων θαυμαστῶς ἐροῖ, ἐγὼ δ'
ἀπορήσοιμι·'

'τὸ μὲν ἕτερον', φάναι τὸν Ἐρυξίμαχον, 'μαντικῶς μοι
δοκεῖς εἰρηκέναι, ὅτι Ἀγάθων εὖ ἐρεῖ· τὸ δὲ σὲ ἀπορήσειν,
οὐκ οἶμαι.' 10

'καὶ πῶς, ὦ μακάριε,' εἰπεῖν τὸν Σωκράτη, 'οὐ μέλλω b
ἀπορεῖν καὶ ἐγὼ καὶ ἄλλος ὁστισοῦν, μέλλων λέξειν μετὰ
καλὸν οὕτω καὶ παντοδαπὸν λόγον ῥηθέντα; καὶ τὰ μὲν ἄλλα
οὐχ ὁμοίως μὲν θαυμαστά· τὸ δὲ ἐπὶ τελευτῆς τοῦ κάλλους
τῶν ὀνομάτων καὶ ῥημάτων τίς οὐκ ἂν ἐξεπλάγη ἀκούων; ἐπεὶ 5
ἔγωγε ἐνθυμούμενος ὅτι αὐτὸς οὐχ οἷός τ' ἔσομαι οὐδ' ἐγγὺς
τούτων οὐδὲν καλὸν εἰπεῖν, ὑπ' αἰσχύνης ὀλίγου ἀποδρὰς c
ᾠχόμην, εἴ πῃ εἶχον. καὶ γάρ με Γοργίου ὁ λόγος
ἀνεμίμνησκεν, ὥστε ἀτεχνῶς τὸ τοῦ Ὁμήρου ἐπεπόνθη·
ἐφοβούμην μή μοι τελευτῶν ὁ Ἀγάθων Γοργίου κεφαλὴν
δεινοῦ λέγειν ἐν τῷ λόγῳ ἐπὶ τὸν ἐμὸν λόγον πέμψας αὐτόν 5
με λίθον τῇ ἀφωνίᾳ ποιήσειεν. καὶ ἐνενόησα τότε ἄρα
καταγέλαστος ὤν, ἡνίκα ὑμῖν ὡμολόγουν ἐν τῷ μέρει μεθ'
ὑμῶν ἐγκωμιάσεσθαι τὸν Ἔρωτα καὶ ἔφην εἶναι δεινὸς τὰ d
ἐρωτικά, οὐδὲν εἰδὼς ἄρα τοῦ πράγματος, ὡς ἔδει
ἐγκωμιάζειν ὁτιοῦν. ἐγὼ μὲν γὰρ ὑπ' ἀβελτερίας ᾤμην δεῖν
τἀληθῆ λέγειν περὶ ἑκάστου τοῦ ἐγκωμιαζομένου, καὶ τοῦτο
μὲν ὑπάρχειν, ἐξ αὐτῶν δὲ τούτων τὰ κάλλιστα ἐκλεγομένους 5
ὡς εὐπρεπέστατα τιθέναι· καὶ πάνυ δὴ μέγα ἐφρόνουν ὡς εὖ
ἐρῶν, ὡς εἰδὼς τὴν ἀλήθειαν τοῦ ἐπαινεῖν ὁτιοῦν. τὸ δὲ ἄρα,
ὡς ἔοικεν, οὐ τοῦτο ἦν τὸ καλῶς ἐπαινεῖν ὁτιοῦν, ἀλλὰ τὸ ὡς e
μέγιστα ἀνατιθέναι τῷ πράγματι καὶ ὡς κάλλιστα, ἐάν τε ᾖ
οὕτως ἔχοντα ἐάν τε μή· εἰ δὲ ψευδῆ, οὐδὲν ἄρ' ἦν πρᾶγμα.
προυρρήθη γάρ, ὡς ἔοικεν, ὅπως ἕκαστος ἡμῶν τὸν Ἔρωτα
ἐγκωμιάζειν δόξει, οὐχ ὅπως ἐγκωμιάσεται. διὰ ταῦτα δὴ 5
οἶμαι πάντα λόγον κινοῦντες ἀνατίθετε τῷ Ἔρωτι, καί φατε
αὐτὸν τοιοῦτόν τε εἶναι καὶ τοσούτων αἴτιον, ὅπως ἂν 199
φαίνηται ὡς κάλλιστος καὶ ἄριστος, δῆλον ὅτι τοῖς μὴ
γιγνώσκουσιν (οὐ γὰρ δήπου τοῖς γε εἰδόσιν), καὶ καλῶς γ'
ἔχει καὶ σεμνῶς ὁ ἔπαινος. ἀλλὰ γὰρ ἐγὼ οὐκ ᾔδη ἄρα τὸν

d 7 [τοῦ ἐπαινεῖν ὁτιοῦν] e | a 3 δήπου e: ἄν που n: που n |

fear I felt before, and that I wasn't being prophetic when I said what I was saying just now – that Agathon would speak amazingly well, and leave me at a loss?'

'On the one point,' said Eryximachus, 'that Agathon would give a good speech, I think your words were prophetic; but as for the idea that you would be at a loss, [a10] I don't think so.'

[b1] 'My dear man,' said Socrates, 'just how am I not going to be at a loss, and how would anyone else not be, if he were going to speak after the delivery of so beautiful and varied a speech as that? The rest wasn't quite as amazing, but the ending – who wouldn't [b5] have been overpowered as he listened to the beauty of its terms and expressions? I was conscious, certainly, that I wouldn't be able to say anything myself [c1] that even came near to being as beautiful as that, and I felt so ashamed that I almost took off, and would have got away if there'd been any way I could. The speech, you see, reminded me of Gorgias, so that I found myself exactly in the position Homer describes: I was afraid that Agathon would finish by sending a terrifying [c5] Gorgias' head of eloquence in his speech against *my* speech, and turn me to stone, unable to utter a word. I saw then, as I hadn't before, that I was behaving ridiculously when I agreed with you all that I'd take my turn with [d1] you in offering an encomium to Love, and declared that I was an expert in things erotic, when after all I knew nothing about the matter – I mean, how one should go about composing an encomium on anything. In my stupidity I thought that what one should do when composing encomia was to say what is true about each subject, and that with this [d5] as the basis, one should pick out the most beautiful aspects just from there and arrange them in the most attractive way possible; and I had a very lofty view of my prospects of giving a good speech, because I thought I knew the true way to praise anything whatsoever. But in fact [e1] it looks as if this wasn't after all the way to praise anything whatsoever well; the thing to do is to attribute the greatest and most beautiful characteristics possible to the thing in question, whether they are true of it or not, and if they are false, well, it's of no importance. For it seems that what was proposed was that each of us should appear to be [e5] offering an encomium to Love, not that we should actually offer him one. It's for that reason, I imagine, that you rake up everything you can think of saying and attribute it to Love, declaring **199** him of such a character and responsible for so many things, so that he will appear as beautiful and good as possible – evidently, to the ignorant sort of people (not, surely, to those with knowledge); and the praise is attractive enough, even impressive. But the truth is that I just didn't know – I see it now

τρόπον τοῦ ἐπαίνου, οὐ δ᾽ εἰδὼς ὑμῖν ὡμολόγησα καὶ αὐτὸς **(199)**
ἐν τῷ μέρει ἐπαινέσεσθαι. "ἡ δὲ γλῶσσα" οὖν ὑπέσχετο, "ἡ 6
δὲ φρὴν" οὔ· χαιρέτω δή. οὐ γὰρ ἔτι ἐγκωμιάζω τοῦτον τὸν
τρόπον· οὐ γὰρ ἂν δυναίμην. οὐ μέντοι ἀλλὰ τά γε ἀληθῆ, εἰ
βούλεσθε, ἐθέλω εἰπεῖν κατ᾽ ἐμαυτόν, οὐ πρὸς τοὺς ὑμετέρους b
λόγους, ἵνα μὴ γέλωτα ὄφλω. ὅρα οὖν, ὦ Φαῖδρε, εἴ τι καὶ
τοιούτου λόγου δέῃ, περὶ Ἔρωτος τἀληθῆ λεγόμενα ἀκούειν,
ὀνόμασι δὲ καὶ θέσει ῥημάτων τοιαύτη ὁποία ἄν τις τύχῃ
ἐπελθοῦσα.' 5

τὸν οὖν Φαῖδρον ἔφη καὶ τοὺς ἄλλους κελεύειν λέγειν, ὅπη
αὐτὸς οἴοιτο δεῖν εἰπεῖν, ταύτῃ.

'ἔτι τοίνυν,' φάναι, 'ὦ Φαῖδρε, πάρες μοι Ἀγάθωνα
σμίκρ᾽ ἄττα ἐρέσθαι, ἵνα ἀνομολογησάμενος παρ᾽ αὐτοῦ οὕτως c
ἤδη λέγω.'

'ἀλλὰ παρίημι,' φάναι τὸν Φαῖδρον· ἀλλ᾽ ἐρώτα.' μετὰ
ταῦτα δὴ τὸν Σωκράτη ἔφη ἐνθένδε ποθὲν ἄρξασθαι.

'καὶ μήν, ὦ φίλε Ἀγάθων, καλῶς μοι ἔδοξας καθηγήσασθαι 5
τοῦ λόγου, λέγων ὅτι πρῶτον μὲν δέοι αὐτὸν ἐπιδεῖξαι ὁποῖός
τίς ἐστιν ὁ Ἔρως, ὕστερον δὲ τὰ ἔργα αὐτοῦ. ταύτην τὴν
ἀρχὴν πάνυ ἄγαμαι. ἴθι οὖν μοι περὶ Ἔρωτος, ἐπειδὴ καὶ
τἆλλα καλῶς καὶ μεγαλοπρεπῶς διῆλθες οἷός ἐστι, καὶ τόδε d
εἰπέ· πότερόν ἐστι τοιοῦτος οἷος εἶναί τινος ὁ Ἔρως ἔρως, ἢ
οὐδενός; ἐρωτῶ δ᾽ οὐκ εἰ μητρός τινος ἢ πατρός ἐστιν
(γελοῖον γὰρ ἂν εἴη τὸ ἐρώτημα εἰ Ἔρως ἐστὶν ἔρως μητρὸς
ἢ πατρός), ἀλλ᾽ ὥσπερ ἂν εἰ αὐτὸ τοῦτο πατέρα ἠρώτων, ἆρα 5
ὁ πατήρ ἐστι πατήρ τινος ἢ οὔ; εἶπες ἂν δήπου μοι, εἰ
ἐβούλου καλῶς ἀποκρίνασθαι, ὅτι ἐστὶν ὑέος γε ἢ θυγατρὸς ὁ
πατὴρ πατήρ· ἢ οὔ;'

'πάνυ γε,' φάναι τὸν Ἀγάθωνα.

'οὐκοῦν καὶ ἡ μήτηρ ὡσαύτως;' ὁμολογεῖσθαι καὶ τοῦτο. e

'ἔτι τοίνυν,' εἰπεῖν τὸν Σωκράτη, 'ἀπόκριναι ὀλίγῳ πλείω,
ἵνα μᾶλλον καταμάθῃς ὃ βούλομαι. εἰ γὰρ ἐροίμην, "τί δέ;
ἀδελφός, αὐτὸ τοῦθ᾽ ὅπερ ἔστιν, ἐστί τινος ἀδελφὸς ἢ οὔ;"'
φάναι εἶναι. 5

'οὐκοῦν ἀδελφοῦ ἢ ἀδελφῆς;' ὁμολογεῖν.

---

b 4 ὀνόμασι   n: ὀνομάσει   n, O | ἄν   n: δ᾽ἄν   n: δἄν (= δὴ ἄν) e, O

– the [a5] way to praise things, and it was because I didn't know that I agreed that I'd take my turn in doing it. "It was my tongue", then, that promised, "and my mind" didn't; well, let's forget it. I'm not prepared to give another encomium in that way; I wouldn't have the capacity to do it. However, if you like, I *am* willing [b1] to say what is actually true, on my own terms, and not on those of your speeches, because by your standards I'd be a laughing-stock. So, Phaedrus, see if you want this kind of speech too – whether you want to listen to the truth being told about Love, and with whatever terms and arrangement of expressions happen to [b5] occur to me.'

modesty

Aristodemus said that Phaedrus and the others told Socrates to speak in whatever way he decided for himself that it should be done.

'Well, Phaedrus,' said Socrates, 'allow me just to put [c1] a few more little questions to Agathon, and then after I've got his agreement on these I'll speak my piece.'

'You have my permission,' said Phaedrus; 'ask away.' And after that, Aristodemus said, Socrates began, something like this:

[c5] 'Well now, my dear Agathon: you seemed to me to make a good start to your speech, when you said that one should first of all display the sort of character Love himself has, and then go on to what he does. I very much admire that way of starting off. So then, on the subject of Love, since you [d1] gave a magnificently attractive description of the other sorts of characteristics he has, please tell me this too: is Love of the sort to make him love *of* something, or of nothing? My question is not whether he is of some mother or father (for it would be ridiculous to ask whether Love *is love of* mother [d5] or father); it's rather as if I were asking the same thing about a father – is a father father of someone, or isn't he? You would surely have replied, if you wanted to give the right answer, "Yes, a father is father of a son or a daughter." Wouldn't you?'

'Absolutely', said Agathon.

[e1] 'And the same with a mother?' Agathon agreed to that too.

'Well,' said Socrates, 'answer me just a few more questions, so that you get a clearer idea of what I mean. What if I asked you "And what about a brother? Just insofar as he is a brother, is he brother of someone, or not?"' [e5] He said he was.

'Of a brother or a sister?' He agreed.

'πειρῶ δή', φάναι, 'καὶ τὸν ἔρωτα εἰπεῖν. ὁ Ἔρως ἔρως
ἐστὶν οὐδενὸς ἢ τινός;'
'πάνυ μὲν οὖν ἐστιν.' **200**
'τοῦτο μὲν τοίνυν', εἰπεῖν τὸν Σωκράτη, 'φύλαξον παρὰ
σαυτῷ μεμνημένος ὅτου· τοσόνδε δὲ εἰπέ, πότερον ὁ Ἔρως
ἐκείνου οὗ ἔστιν ἔρως, ἐπιθυμεῖ αὐτοῦ ἢ οὔ;'
'πάνυ γε', φάναι. 5
'πότερον ἔχων αὐτὸ οὗ ἐπιθυμεῖ τε καὶ ἐρᾷ, εἶτα ἐπιθυμεῖ
τε καὶ ἐρᾷ, ἢ οὐκ ἔχων;'
'οὐκ ἔχων, ὡς τὸ εἰκός γε,' φάναι.
'σκόπει δή,' εἰπεῖν τὸν Σωκράτη, 'ἀντὶ τοῦ εἰκότος εἰ
ἀνάγκη οὕτως, τὸ ἐπιθυμοῦν ἐπιθυμεῖν οὗ ἐνδεές ἐστιν, ἢ μὴ 10
ἐπιθυμεῖν, ἐὰν μὴ ἐνδεὲς ᾖ; ἐμοὶ μὲν γὰρ θαυμαστῶς δοκεῖ, ὦ b
Ἀγάθων, ὡς ἀνάγκη εἶναι· σοὶ δὲ πῶς;'
'κἀμοί', φάναι, 'δοκεῖ.'
'καλῶς λέγεις. ἆρ' οὖν βούλοιτ' ἄν τις μέγας ὢν μέγας
εἶναι, ἢ ἰσχυρὸς ὢν ἰσχυρός;' 5
'ἀδύνατον ἐκ τῶν ὡμολογημένων.'
'οὐ γάρ που ἐνδεὴς ἂν εἴη τούτων ὅ γε ὤν.'
'ἀληθῆ λέγεις.'
'εἰ γὰρ καὶ ἰσχυρὸς ὢν βούλοιτο ἰσχυρὸς εἶναι,' φάναι
τὸν Σωκράτη, 'καὶ ταχὺς ὢν ταχύς, καὶ ὑγιὴς ὢν ὑγιής – 10
ἴσως γὰρ ἄν τις ταῦτα οἰηθείη καὶ πάντα τὰ τοιαῦτα τοὺς
ὄντας τε τοιούτους καὶ ἔχοντας ταῦτα τούτων ἅπερ ἔχουσι c
καὶ ἐπιθυμεῖν (ἵν' οὖν μὴ ἐξαπατηθῶμεν, τούτου ἕνεκα λέγω)·
τούτοις γάρ, ὦ Ἀγάθων, εἰ ἐννοεῖς, ἔχειν μὲν ἕκαστα τούτων
ἐν τῷ παρόντι ἀνάγκη ἃ ἔχουσιν, ἐάντε βούλωνται ἐάντε μή,
καὶ τούτου γε δήπου τίς ἂν ἐπιθυμήσειεν; ἀλλ' ὅταν τις λέγῃ 5
ὅτι "ἐγὼ ὑγιαίνων βούλομαι καὶ ὑγιαίνειν", καὶ "πλουτῶν
βούλομαι καὶ πλουτεῖν", καὶ "ἐπιθυμῶ αὐτῶν τούτων ἃ ἔχω",
εἴποιμεν ἂν αὐτῷ ὅτι "σύ, ὦ ἄνθρωπε, πλοῦτον κεκτημένος
καὶ ὑγίειαν καὶ ἰσχὺν βούλει καὶ εἰς τὸν ἔπειτα χρόνον d
ταῦτα κεκτῆσθαι, ἐπεὶ ἐν τῷ γε νῦν παρόντι, εἴτε βούλει εἴτε
μή, ἔχεις· σκόπει οὖν, ὅταν τοῦτο λέγῃς, ὅτι 'ἐπιθυμῶ τῶν
παρόντων', εἰ ἄλλο τι λέγεις ἢ τόδε, ὅτι 'βούλομαι τὰ νῦν
παρόντα καὶ εἰς τὸν ἔπειτα χρόνον παρεῖναι.'" ἄλλο τι 5
ὁμολογοῖ ἄν;' συμφάναι ἔφη τὸν Ἀγάθωνα.
εἰπεῖν δὴ τὸν Σωκράτη, 'οὐκοῦν τοῦτό γ' ἐστὶν ἐκείνου

'Then', Socrates said, 'try to say what the case is with love too. Is Love love of nothing, or of something?'

200 'Yes, he is; certainly.'

'Well then,' said Socrates, 'keep this result by you, remembering all the time *what* it is love of. Now tell me this – does Love desire that thing he is love of, or not?'

[a5] 'Absolutely,' said Agathon.

'Does he desire and love the very thing he desires and loves as a consequence of having it, or of not having it?'

'Of not having it, probably', said Agathon.

'Then see', said Socrates, 'whether instead of your "probably" [a10] it isn't necessarily like this: that what desires desires what it lacks, or, if [b1] it doesn't lack it, it doesn't desire it? To me this looks amazingly necessary, Agathon; how about you?'

'It looks so to me too', he said.

'Well said. So will anyone wish to be tall if he is [b5] tall, or strong if he is strong?'

'From what we've agreed, it'll be impossible.'

'Yes, because the person who is these things presumably can't be lacking them.'

'True.'

'For if he did wish to be strong even when he was strong,' Socrates [b10] said, 'and quick when he was quick, and healthy when he was healthy – for maybe one might think in these and all such cases that people [c1] like that, who have the qualities in question, actually do desire the very things they have (so I'm bringing it up to prevent our being misled): if you think about it, Agathon, it's necessary that they presently have every single one of the things that they have, whether they wish it or not, [c5] and surely no one could desire *that?* Whenever anyone says "I'm healthy, and what I want is to be healthy", and "I'm wealthy and what I want is to be wealthy", and "I desire just what I have", we'll say to him "Hey, you! You've got it wrong: wealth, health, [d1] strength you already possess, and what you wish for is to possess these in the future too, since so far as the present is concerned, whether you wish it or not, you have them; so, whenever you say 'I desire the things I have', see whether you mean anything other than 'I wish to have [d5] the things I have now in the future as well'." He'd surely have to go along with us?' Aristodemus said Agathon agreed.

ἐρᾶν, ὃ οὔπω ἕτοιμον αὐτῷ ἐστιν οὐδὲ ἔχει, τὸ εἰς τὸν
ἔπειτα χρόνον ταῦτα εἶναι αὐτῷ σῳζόμενα καὶ παρόντα;'   e
'πάνυ γε,' φάναι.
'καὶ οὗτος ἄρα καὶ ἄλλος πᾶς ὁ ἐπιθυμῶν τοῦ μὴ ἑτοίμου
ἐπιθυμεῖ καὶ τοῦ μὴ παρόντος, καὶ ὃ μὴ ἔχει καὶ ὃ μή ἐστιν
αὐτὸς καὶ οὗ ἐνδεής ἐστι, τοιαῦτ' ἄττα ἐστὶν ὧν ἡ ἐπιθυμία   5
τε καὶ ὁ ἔρως ἐστίν;'
'πάνυ γ',' εἰπεῖν.
'ἴθι δή,' φάναι τὸν Σωκράτη, 'ἀνομολογησώμεθα τὰ
εἰρημένα. ἄλλο τί ἐστιν ὁ Ἔρως πρῶτον μέν τινων, ἔπειτα
τούτων ὧν ἂν ἔνδεια παρῇ αὐτῷ;'   10
'ναί,' φάναι.   201
'ἐπὶ δὴ τούτοις ἀναμνήσθητι τίνων ἔφησθα ἐν τῷ λόγῳ
εἶναι τὸν Ἔρωτα· εἰ δὲ βούλει, ἐγώ σε ἀναμνήσω. οἶμαι γάρ
σε οὑτωσί πως εἰπεῖν, ὅτι τοῖς θεοῖς κατεσκευάσθη τὰ
πράγματα δι' ἔρωτα καλῶν· αἰσχρῶν γὰρ οὐκ εἴη ἔρως. οὐχ   5
οὑτωσί πως ἔλεγες;'
'εἶπον γάρ,' φάναι τὸν Ἀγάθωνα.
'καὶ ἐπιεικῶς γε λέγεις, ὦ ἑταῖρε,' φάναι τὸν Σωκράτη·
'καὶ εἰ τοῦτο οὕτως ἔχει, ἄλλο τι ὁ Ἔρως κάλλους ἂν εἴη
ἔρως, αἴσχους δὲ οὔ;' ὡμολόγει.   10
'οὐκοῦν ὡμολόγηται, οὗ ἐνδεής ἐστι καὶ μὴ ἔχει, τούτου
ἐρᾶν;'   b
'ναί,' εἰπεῖν.
'ἐνδεὴς ἄρ' ἐστὶ καὶ οὐκ ἔχει ὁ Ἔρως κάλλος.'
'ἀνάγκη,' φάναι.
'τί δέ; τὸ ἐνδεὲς κάλλους καὶ μηδαμῇ κεκτημένον κάλλος   5
ἆρα λέγεις σὺ καλὸν εἶναι;'
'οὐ δῆτα.'
'ἔτι οὖν ὁμολογεῖς Ἔρωτα καλὸν εἶναι, εἰ ταῦτα οὕτως
ἔχει;'
καὶ τὸν Ἀγάθωνα εἰπεῖν 'κινδυνεύω, ὦ Σώκρατες, οὐδὲν   10
εἰδέναι ὧν τότε εἶπον.'
'καὶ μὴν καλῶς γε εἶπας,' φάναι, 'ὦ Ἀγάθων. ἀλλὰ   c
σμικρὸν ἔτι εἰπέ· τἀγαθὰ οὐ καὶ καλὰ δοκεῖ σοι εἶναι;'
'ἔμοιγε.'

a 5 ὁ ἔρως   n | c 1 ειπας   p: εἶπες   m, O

Socrates then said 'So this is in fact a matter of his loving what is not yet available to him, and what he does not yet have: that is, the preservation [e1] and presence to him of these things in the future?'

'Absolutely', said Agathon.

'In that case both he and everyone else who desires, desires something not available and something not present to him; and what he does not have, what he himself [e5] is not, and what he is lacking – these are the sorts of things that are the objects of desire and love.'

'Absolutely', replied Agathon.

'So then', said Socrates, 'let's reckon up together what's been said. Am I right in saying that Love is firstly of certain things, and secondly [e10] of those things of which he has a lack, whatever they may be?'

201 'Yes,' said Agathon.

'Given these points, then, remember what things you said in your speech Love is of; or if you like, I'll remind you. I think you said something to the effect that the establishment of the gods' [a5] activities came about through love of beautiful things; for – you said – there is no love of ugly things. Didn't you say something like this?'

'Yes, I did,' said Agathon.

'It's a pretty reasonable thing to say,' said Socrates; 'and if that's the case, will I be right in saying that Love is of [a10] beauty, and not of ugliness?' Agathon agreed.

'Now then, we've agreed that he loves what he lacks and does not [b1] possess?'

'Yes', he said.

'In that case Love is lacking in, and does not possess, beauty.'

'Necessarily', he said.

[b5] 'Well then: do you say that what is lacking in beauty and does not possess it in any way is beautiful?'

'Certainly not.'

'Then do you still agree that Love is beautiful, if all this is so?'

[b10] And Agathon said 'It looks very much, Socrates, as if I didn't know the slightest thing about what I said then.'

[c1] 'And yet you said it so beautifully, Agathon,' said Socrates. 'But tell me one more little thing: don't you think that what is good is also beautiful?'

'I do.'

76

'εἰ ἄρα ὁ Ἔρως τῶν καλῶν ἐνδεής ἐστι, τὰ δὲ ἀγαθὰ
καλά, κἂν τῶν ἀγαθῶν ἐνδεὴς εἴη.'   5
'ἐγώ,' φάναι, 'ὦ Σώκρατες, σοὶ οὐκ ἂν δυναίμην
ἀντιλέγειν, ἀλλ' οὕτως ἐχέτω ὡς σὺ λέγεις.'
'οὐ μὲν οὖν τῇ ἀληθείᾳ,' φάναι, 'ὦ φιλούμενε Ἀγάθων,
δύνασαι ἀντιλέγειν, ἐπεὶ Σωκράτει γε οὐδὲν χαλεπόν.'
'καὶ σὲ μέν γε ἤδη ἐάσω· τὸν δὲ λόγον τὸν περὶ τοῦ   d
Ἔρωτος, ὅν ποτ' ἤκουσα γυναικὸς Μαντινικῆς Διοτίμας, ἣ
ταῦτά τε σοφὴ ἦν καὶ ἄλλα πολλά, καὶ Ἀθηναίοις ποτὲ
θυσαμένοις πρὸ τοῦ λοιμοῦ δέκα ἔτη ἀναβολὴν ἐποίησε τῆς
νόσου – ἣ δὴ καὶ ἐμὲ τὰ ἐρωτικὰ ἐδίδαξεν· ὃν οὖν ἐκείνη   5
ἔλεγε λόγον, πειράσομαι ὑμῖν διελθεῖν ἐκ τῶν ὡμολογημένων
ἐμοὶ καὶ Ἀγάθωνι, αὐτὸς ἐπ' ἐμαυτοῦ, ὅπως ἂν δύνωμαι. δεῖ
δή, ὦ Ἀγάθων, ὥσπερ σὺ διηγήσω, διελθεῖν αὐτὸν πρῶτον, τίς
ἐστιν ὁ Ἔρως καὶ ποῖός τις, ἔπειτα τὰ ἔργα αὐτοῦ. δοκεῖ   e
οὖν μοι ῥᾷστον εἶναι οὕτω διελθεῖν, ὥς ποτέ με ἡ ξένη
ἀνακρίνουσα διῄει. σχεδὸν γάρ τι καὶ ἐγὼ πρὸς αὐτὴν ἕτερα
τοιαῦτα ἔλεγον οἷάπερ νῦν πρὸς ἐμὲ Ἀγάθων, ὡς εἴη ὁ Ἔρως
μέγας θεός, εἴη δὲ τῶν καλῶν· ἤλεγχε δή με τούτοις τοῖς   5
λόγοις οἷσπερ ἐγὼ τοῦτον, ὡς οὔτε καλὸς εἴη κατὰ τὸν ἐμὸν
λόγον οὔτε ἀγαθός.
'καὶ ἐγώ, "πῶς λέγεις," ἔφην, "ὦ Διοτίμα; αἰσχρὸς ἄρα ὁ
Ἔρως ἐστὶ καὶ κακός;"
'καὶ ἥ, "οὐκ εὐφημήσεις;" ἔφη· "ἢ οἴει, ὅτι ἂν μὴ καλὸν   10
ᾖ, ἀναγκαῖον αὐτὸ εἶναι αἰσχρόν;"
'"μάλιστά γε."   202
'"ἦ καὶ ἂν μὴ σοφόν, ἀμαθές; ἢ οὐκ ᾔσθησαι ὅτι ἔστιν τι
μεταξὺ σοφίας καὶ ἀμαθίας;"
'"τί τοῦτο;"
'"τὸ ὀρθὰ δοξάζειν καὶ ἄνευ τοῦ ἔχειν λόγον δοῦναι οὐκ   5
οἶσθ' ", ἔφη, "ὅτι οὔτε ἐπίστασθαί ἐστιν (ἄλογον γὰρ πρᾶγμα
πῶς ἂν εἴη ἐπιστήμη;) οὔτε ἀμαθία (τὸ γὰρ τοῦ ὄντος
τυγχάνον πῶς ἂν εἴη ἀμαθία;); ἔστι δὲ δήπου τοιοῦτον ἡ ὀρθὴ
δόξα, μεταξὺ φρονήσεως καὶ ἀμαθίας.'
'"ἀληθῆ", ἦν δ' ἐγώ, "λέγεις."   10
'"μὴ τοίνυν ἀνάγκαζε ὃ μὴ καλόν ἐστιν αἰσχρὸν εἶναι,   b

'In that case, if Love is lacking in what is beautiful, and what is good is [c5] beautiful, he will also be lacking in what is good.'

'There's no way, Socrates,' said Agathon, 'that I can argue against *you*; let it be as you say.'

'No, it's rather the truth, beloved Agathon,' Socrates said, 'that you can't argue with, since there's nothing difficult about arguing against Socrates.

[d1] 'You I'm going to let go now; and I'm going to turn to the account of Love that I once heard from a woman of Mantinea, Diotima, who was wise both in these things and in much else, and once, before the plague, brought about a ten-year postponement of the disease for the Athenians, [d5] when they had performed the sacrifices – she's the very person who taught me too about erotics. So it's the account she gave that I'm going to try to describe to all of you, starting from what has been agreed between myself and Agathon, and doing it all myself, in whatever way I can manage it. Now one *should* do, Agathon, as you did, first describing who [e1] Love himself is and what sort of character he has, and then going on to what he does. Well, it seems to me easiest to go about describing him in the way the Mantinean visitor once went about it, by closely questioning me. I myself was saying to her other things of pretty much the very sort that Agathon was saying to me just now, that Love was [e5] a great god, and was of beautiful things; and she then set about examining me by means of the very arguments I was using with Agathon, with the outcome that Love was neither beautiful – by my own account – nor good.

'My reaction was to say "What do you mean, Diotima? Is Love then ugly and bad?"

[e10] 'She said "Take care what you say! Or do you suppose that whatever is not beautiful is necessarily ugly?"

202 '"Yes, very much so."

'"Do you also suppose that if something is not wise, it is ignorant? Don't you see that there is something between wisdom and ignorance?"

'"What is that?"

[a5] '"Don't you recognize", she said, "that having correct beliefs, even without being able to give a rational account of them, is neither a matter of knowing (since how could something irrational be knowledge?), nor of ignorance (how could something that hits on what is the case be ignorance?)? Correct belief is, I imagine, something of the sort in question, between wisdom and ignorance."

[a10] '"What you say is true," I said.

78

μηδὲ ὃ μὴ ἀγαθόν, κακόν. οὕτω δὲ καὶ τὸν Ἔρωτα ἐπειδὴ **(202)**
αὐτὸς ὁμολογεῖς μὴ εἶναι ἀγαθὸν μηδὲ καλόν, μηδέν τι
μᾶλλον οἴου δεῖν αὐτὸν αἰσχρὸν καὶ κακὸν εἶναι, ἀλλά τι
μεταξύ", ἔφη, "τούτοιν."   5
'"καὶ μήν", ἦν δ' ἐγώ, "ὁμολογεῖταί γε παρὰ πάντων
μέγας θεὸς εἶναι."
'"τῶν μὴ εἰδότων", ἔφη, "πάντων λέγεις, ἢ καὶ τῶν
εἰδότων;"
'"συμπάντων μὲν οὖν."   10
'καὶ ἣ γελάσασα "καὶ πῶς ἄν", ἔφη, "ὦ Σώκρατες,
ὁμολογοῖτο μέγας θεὸς εἶναι παρὰ τούτων, οἵ φασιν αὐτὸν   c
οὐδὲ θεὸν εἶναι;"
'"τίνες οὗτοι;" ἦν δ' ἐγώ.
'"εἷς μέν," ἔφη, "σύ, μία δ' ἐγώ."
'κἀγὼ εἶπον, "πῶς τοῦτο", ἔφην, "λέγεις;"   5
'καὶ ἥ, "ῥᾳδίως," ἔφη. "λέγε γάρ μοι, οὐ πάντας θεοὺς
φῂς εὐδαίμονας εἶναι καὶ καλούς; ἢ τολμήσαις ἄν τινα μὴ
φάναι καλόν τε καὶ εὐδαίμονα θεῶν εἶναι;"
'"μὰ Δί' οὐκ ἔγωγ'," ἔφην.
'"εὐδαίμονας δὲ δὴ λέγεις οὐ τοὺς τἀγαθὰ καὶ τὰ καλὰ   10
κεκτημένους;"
'"πάνυ γε."
'"ἀλλὰ μὴν Ἔρωτά γε ὡμολόγηκας δι' ἔνδειαν τῶν ἀγαθῶν   d
καὶ καλῶν ἐπιθυμεῖν αὐτῶν τούτων ὧν ἐνδεής ἐστιν."
'"ὡμολόγηκα γάρ."
'"πῶς ἂν οὖν θεὸς εἴη ὅ γε τῶν καλῶν καὶ ἀγαθῶν
ἄμοιρος;"   5
'"οὐδαμῶς, ὥς γ' ἔοικεν."
'"ὁρᾷς οὖν", ἔφη, "ὅτι καὶ σὺ Ἔρωτα οὐ θεὸν νομίζεις;"
'"τί οὖν ἄν", ἔφην, "εἴη ὁ Ἔρως; θνητός;"
'"ἥκιστά γε."
'"ἀλλὰ τί μήν;"   10
'"ὥσπερ τὰ πρότερα," ἔφη, "μεταξὺ θνητοῦ καὶ
ἀθανάτου."
'"τί οὖν, ὦ Διοτίμα;"
'"δαίμων μέγας, ὦ Σώκρατες· καὶ γὰρ πᾶν τὸ δαιμόνιον
μεταξύ ἐστι θεοῦ τε καὶ θνητοῦ."   e

d 4 πῶς ἄν p, t, n: πῶς δ'ἄν n

[b1] '"Then don't insist that anything not beautiful is necessarily ugly, or that anything not good is necessarily bad. So too in the case of Love, because you yourself admit him not to be good, or beautiful, don't be any more inclined for that reason to suppose that he must be ugly and bad, but rather", she said, [b5] "suppose him to be something *between* these two things."

'"And yet", I said, "he's agreed by everyone to be a great god."

'"Do you mean," she said, "by everyone who is ignorant, or by everyone knowledgeable as well?"

[b10] '"By absolutely everyone."

'With a laugh she said "And just how, Socrates, [c1] could he be agreed to be a great god by people who say that he's not a god at all?"

'"Who are these people?" I asked.

'"You're one," she said, "and I'm one too."

[c5] 'And I said "How can you say that?"

'To which she replied "Easily. Tell me: don't you assert that all gods are happy and beautiful? Or would you be so bold as to deny that any one of the gods was beautiful and happy?"

'"Zeus! I would not," I said.

[c10] '"But isn't it those individuals who possess good and beautiful things that you call happy?"

'"Yes, certainly."

[d1] '"And yet you've agreed, in Love's case, that a lack of good and beautiful things is what makes him desire the very things he lacks."

'"Yes, I have agreed to that."

'"Then how could he be a god, if he has no portion of beautiful and [d5] good things?"

'"There's no way he could be, so it seems."

'"So", she said, "do you see that you too don't recognize Love as a god?"

'"What then", I said, "will Love be? Mortal?"

'"Certainly not that."

[d10] '"Then what?"

'"It's as in the previous cases," she said; "he's in between the mortal and the immortal."

'"What then is he, Diotima?"

'"A great spirit, Socrates; for everything of the nature of spirits [e1] is between god and mortal."

80

'" τίνα", ἦν δ' ἐγώ, "δύναμιν ἔχον;"

'" ἑρμηνεῦον καὶ διαπορθμεῦον θεοῖς τὰ παρ' ἀνθρώπων καὶ
ἀνθρώποις τὰ παρὰ θεῶν, τῶν μὲν τὰς δεήσεις καὶ θυσίας,
τῶν δὲ τὰς ἐπιτάξεις τε καὶ ἀμοιβὰς τῶν θυσιῶν, ἐν μέσῳ   5
δὲ ὂν ἀμφοτέρων συμπληροῖ, ὥστε τὸ πᾶν αὐτὸ αὑτῷ
συνδεδέσθαι. διὰ τούτου καὶ ἡ μαντικὴ πᾶσα χωρεῖ καὶ ἡ τῶν
ἱερέων τέχνη τῶν τε περὶ τὰς θυσίας καὶ τελετὰς καὶ τὰς
ἐπῳδὰς καὶ τὴν μαντείαν πᾶσαν καὶ γοητείαν. θεὸς δὲ   203
ἀνθρώπῳ οὐ μείγνυται, ἀλλὰ διὰ τούτου πᾶσά ἐστιν ἡ ὁμιλία
καὶ ἡ διάλεκτος θεοῖς πρὸς ἀνθρώπους, καὶ ἐγρηγορόσι καὶ
καθεύδουσι· καὶ ὁ μὲν περὶ τὰ τοιαῦτα σοφὸς δαιμόνιος ἀνήρ·
ὁ δὲ ἄλλο τι σοφὸς ὢν ἢ περὶ τέχνας ἢ χειρουργίας τινὰς   5
βάναυσος. οὗτοι δὴ οἱ δαίμονες πολλοὶ καὶ παντοδαποί εἰσιν,
εἷς δὲ τούτων ἐστὶ καὶ ὁ Ἔρως."

'" πατρὸς δέ", ἦν δ' ἐγώ, "τίνος ἐστὶ καὶ μητρός;"

'" μακρότερον μέν", ἔφη, "διηγήσασθαι· ὅμως δέ σοι ἐρῶ.   b
ὅτε γὰρ ἐγένετο ἡ Ἀφροδίτη, ἡστιῶντο οἱ θεοὶ οἵ τε ἄλλοι
καὶ ὁ τῆς Μήτιδος ὑὸς Πόρος. ἐπειδὴ δὲ ἐδείπνησαν,
προσαιτήσουσα οἷον δὴ εὐωχίας οὔσης ἀφίκετο ἡ Πενία, καὶ
ἦν περὶ τὰς θύρας. ὁ οὖν Πόρος μεθυσθεὶς τοῦ νέκταρος   5
(οἶνος γὰρ οὔπω ἦν) εἰς τὸν τοῦ Διὸς κῆπον εἰσελθὼν
βεβαρημένος ηὗδεν. ἡ οὖν Πενία ἐπιβουλεύουσα διὰ τὴν αὑτῆς
ἀπορίαν παιδίον ποιήσασθαι ἐκ τοῦ Πόρου, κατακλίνεταί τε   c
παρ' αὐτῷ καὶ ἐκύησε τὸν Ἔρωτα. διὸ δὴ καὶ τῆς Ἀφροδίτης
ἀκόλουθος καὶ θεράπων γέγονεν ὁ Ἔρως, γεννηθεὶς ἐν τοῖς
ἐκείνης γενεθλίοις, καὶ ἅμα φύσει ἐραστὴς ὢν περὶ τὸ καλὸν
καὶ τῆς Ἀφροδίτης καλῆς οὔσης. ἅτε οὖν Πόρου καὶ Πενίας   5
ὑὸς ὢν ὁ Ἔρως ἐν τοιαύτῃ τύχῃ καθέστηκεν. πρῶτον μὲν
πένης ἀεί ἐστι, καὶ πολλοῦ δεῖ ἁπαλός τε καὶ καλός, οἷον οἱ
πολλοὶ οἴονται, ἀλλὰ σκληρὸς καὶ αὐχμηρὸς καὶ ἀνυπόδητος
καὶ ἄοικος, χαμαιπετὴς ἀεὶ ὢν καὶ ἄστρωτος, ἐπὶ θύραις καὶ   d
ἐν ὁδοῖς ὑπαίθριος κοιμώμενος, τὴν τῆς μητρὸς φύσιν ἔχων,
ἀεὶ ἐνδείᾳ σύνοικος. κατὰ δὲ αὖ τὸν πατέρα ἐπίβουλός ἐστι
τοῖς καλοῖς καὶ τοῖς ἀγαθοῖς, ἀνδρεῖος ὢν καὶ ἴτης καὶ
σύντονος, θηρευτὴς δεινός, ἀεί τινας πλέκων μηχανάς, καὶ   5

a 1 μαντείαν   m: μαγγανείαν   e: μαγείαν   e | a 8 καὶ μητρὸς τίνος ἐστίν
p. n | b 6 εξελθων   p

'"What function does it have?" I asked.

'"That of interpreting and conveying things from men to gods and from gods to men – men's petitions and sacrifices, [e5] the gods' commands and returns for sacrifices; being in the middle between both, it fills in the space between them, so that the whole is bound close together. It is through this that the whole expertise of the seer works its effects, and that of priests, and of those concerned with sacrifices, rites, spells, **203** and the whole realm of the seer and of magic. God does not mix with man; through this it is that there takes place all intercourse and conversation of gods with men, whether awake or asleep; and the person who is wise about such things is a spirit-like man, [a5] while the one who is wise in anything else, in relation to one or other sort of expertise or manual craft, is vulgar. These spirits, then, are many and of all sorts, and one of them is Love himself."

'"And who are his father and mother?" I asked.

[b1] '"It's rather a long story to tell," she said; "but I'll tell it to you all the same. When Aphrodite was born, the gods held a feast; and among them was Resource, son of Craftiness. Their dinner over, Poverty came begging, as one might expect with festivities going on, and [b5] placed herself around the doors. Well, Resource had got drunk with nectar (wine, you see, did not yet exist), and gone out into Zeus' garden; now, weighed down with drink, he was sleeping. So Poverty plotted, because of her own [c1] resourcelessness, to have a baby from Resource, and she lay down beside him and became pregnant with Love. This is why it was Aphrodite whose follower and attendant he became, because he was conceived during her birthday party, and also because he is by nature a lover in relation to what is beautiful, [c5] and Aphrodite is beautiful. Because, then, he is son of Resource and Poverty, Love's situation is like this. First, he is always poor, and far from delicate and beautiful, as most people think he is; he is hard, dirty, barefoot, [d1] homeless, always sleeping on the ground, without blankets, stretching out under the sky in doorways and by the roadside, because he has his mother's nature, always with lack as his companion. His father's side, for its part, makes him a schemer after the beautiful and good, courageous, impetuous, and [d5] intense, a clever hunter, always weaving new devices, both

φρονήσεως ἐπιθυμητὴς καὶ πόριμος, φιλοσοφῶν διὰ παντὸς
τοῦ βίου, δεινὸς γόης καὶ φαρμακεὺς καὶ σοφιστής· καὶ οὔτε
ὡς ἀθάνατος πέφυκεν οὔτε ὡς θνητός, ἀλλὰ τοτὲ μὲν τῆς   e
αὐτῆς ἡμέρας θάλλει τε καὶ ζῇ, ὅταν εὐπορήσῃ, τοτὲ δὲ
ἀποθνήσκει, πάλιν δὲ ἀναβιώσκεται διὰ τὴν τοῦ πατρὸς φύσιν,
τὸ δὲ ποριζόμενον ἀεὶ ὑπεκρεῖ, ὥστε οὔτε ἀπορεῖ Ἔρως ποτὲ
οὔτε πλουτεῖ, σοφίας τε αὖ καὶ ἀμαθίας ἐν μέσῳ ἐστίν. ἔχει 5
γὰρ ὧδε. θεῶν οὐδεὶς φιλοσοφεῖ οὐδ' ἐπιθυμεῖ σοφὸς γενέσθαι 204
(ἔστι γάρ), οὐδ' εἴ τις ἄλλος σοφός, οὐ φιλοσοφεῖ. οὐδ' αὖ οἱ
ἀμαθεῖς φιλοσοφοῦσιν οὐδ' ἐπιθυμοῦσι σοφοὶ γενέσθαι· αὐτὸ
γὰρ τοῦτό ἐστι χαλεπὸν ἀμαθία, τὸ μὴ ὄντα καλὸν κἀγαθὸν
μηδὲ φρόνιμον δοκεῖν αὑτῷ εἶναι ἱκανόν. οὔκουν ἐπιθυμεῖ ὁ 5
μὴ οἰόμενος ἐνδεὴς εἶναι οὗ ἂν μὴ οἴηται ἐπιδεῖσθαι."

'"τίνες οὖν," ἔφην ἐγώ, "ὦ Διοτίμα, οἱ φιλοσοφοῦντες, εἰ
μήτε οἱ σοφοὶ μήτε οἱ ἀμαθεῖς;"

'"δῆλον δή", ἔφη, "τοῦτό γε ἤδη καὶ παιδί, ὅτι οἱ μεταξὺ   b
τούτων ἀμφοτέρων, ὧν ἂν εἴη καὶ ὁ Ἔρως. ἔστιν γὰρ δὴ τῶν
καλλίστων ἡ σοφία, Ἔρως δ' ἐστὶν ἔρως περὶ τὸ καλόν, ὥστε
ἀναγκαῖον Ἔρωτα φιλόσοφον εἶναι, φιλόσοφον δὲ ὄντα μεταξὺ
εἶναι σοφοῦ καὶ ἀμαθοῦς. αἰτία δὲ αὐτῷ καὶ τούτων ἡ   5
γένεσις· πατρὸς μὲν γὰρ σοφοῦ ἐστι καὶ εὐπόρου, μητρὸς δὲ
οὐ σοφῆς καὶ ἀπόρου. ἡ μὲν οὖν φύσις τοῦ δαίμονος, ὦ φίλε
Σώκρατες, αὕτη· ὃν δὲ σὺ ᾠήθης Ἔρωτα εἶναι, θαυμαστὸν
οὐδὲν ἔπαθες. ᾠήθης δέ, ὡς ἐμοὶ δοκεῖ τεκμαιρομένη ἐξ ὧν c
σὺ λέγεις, τὸ ἐρώμενον Ἔρωτα εἶναι, οὐ τὸ ἐρῶν· διὰ ταῦτά
σοι οἶμαι πάγκαλος ἐφαίνετο ὁ Ἔρως. καὶ γάρ ἐστι τὸ
ἐραστὸν τὸ τῷ ὄντι καλὸν καὶ ἁβρὸν καὶ τέλεον καὶ
μακαριστόν· τὸ δέ γε ἐρῶν ἄλλην ἰδέαν τοιαύτην ἔχον, οἵαν   5
ἐγὼ διῆλθον."

'καὶ ἐγὼ εἶπον, "εἶεν δή, ὦ ξένη, καλῶς γὰρ λέγεις·
τοιοῦτος ὢν ὁ Ἔρως τίνα χρείαν ἔχει τοῖς ἀνθρώποις;"

'"τοῦτο δὴ μετὰ ταῦτ'", ἔφη, "ὦ Σώκρατες, πειράσομαί   d
σε διδάξαι. ἔστι μὲν γὰρ δὴ τοιοῦτος καὶ οὕτω γεγονὼς ὁ
Ἔρως, ἔστι δὲ τῶν καλῶν, ὡς σὺ φῄς. εἰ δέ τις ἡμᾶς ἔροιτο·
'τί τῶν καλῶν ἐστιν ὁ Ἔρως, ὦ Σώκρατές τε καὶ Διοτίμα;'

passionate for wisdom and resourceful in looking for it, philosophizing through all his life, a clever magician, sorcerer, and sophist; his nature is neither that of an immortal, [e1] nor that of a mortal, but on the same day, now he flourishes and lives, when he finds resources, and now he dies, but then comes back to life again, because of his father's nature, and what he gets for himself is always slipping away from him, so that Love is neither resourceless at any moment, [e5] nor rich, and again is in the middle between wisdom and ignorance. This is **204** how things are: no god philosophizes, or desires to become wise (for gods *are* wise); nor, if anyone else is wise, does he philosophize. Nor, on the other hand, do the ignorant philosophize or desire to become wise; it's just this that makes ignorance so damaging, that someone who isn't an admirable person, [a5] or a wise one, nevertheless seems to himself to be quite good enough. The person who doesn't think he lacks something certainly won't desire what he doesn't think he lacks."

"'Who then, Diotima," I said, "are those who philosophize, if it is neither the wise nor the ignorant?"

[b1] "'That", she said, "is by now surely clear enough even to a child: it's those who are between these two groups, and Love will be among these. Wisdom is actually one of the most beautiful things, and Love is love in relation to what is beautiful, so that Love is necessarily a philosopher, and as a philosopher, necessarily between [b5] wisdom and ignorance. What makes him like this is again his birth: he has a father who is wise and resourceful, a mother who is not wise, and resourceless. This, then, my dear Socrates, is the nature of the spirit; as for the way you thought of Love, it's not at all [c1] surprising. To judge from the things you say, you thought Love to be what is loved, not what does the loving; that, I imagine, is why Love seemed to you to be supremely beautiful. What is loveable is in fact what is really beautiful, graceful, perfect, and [c5] to be counted as blessed; whereas what does the loving is of a quite different character, of the sort I described."

'I said "Well then, dear visitor – given that you're right: if Love is like this, what use does he have for human beings?"

[d1] "'This, Socrates," she said, "is just what I shall try to teach you next. Love's character, and his birth, are as I have said; and he is of beautiful things, according to what you say. But if someone were to ask us 'Why, Socrates and Diotima, is Love of beautiful things?' – [d5] or to put it more

ὧδε δὲ σαφέστερον· ἐρᾷ ὁ ἐρῶν τῶν καλῶν· τί ἐρᾷ;"   5
'καὶ ἐγὼ εἶπον ὅτι "γενέσθαι αὐτῷ."
'"ἀλλ᾽ ἔτι ποθεῖ", ἔφη, "ἡ ἀπόκρισις ἐρώτησιν τοιάνδε· τί
ἔσται ἐκείνῳ ᾧ ἂν γένηται τὰ καλά;"
'οὐ πάνυ ἔφην ἔτι ἔχειν ἐγὼ πρὸς ταύτην τὴν ἐρώτησιν
προχείρως ἀποκρίνασθαι.   10
'"ἀλλ᾽", ἔφη, "ὥσπερ ἂν εἴ τις μεταβαλὼν ἀντὶ τοῦ καλοῦ e
τῷ ἀγαθῷ χρώμενος πυνθάνοιτο· 'φέρε, ὦ Σώκρατες, ἐρᾷ ὁ
ἐρῶν τῶν ἀγαθῶν· τί ἐρᾷ;'"
'"γενέσθαι", ἦν δ᾽ ἐγώ, "αὐτῷ."
'"καὶ τί ἔσται ἐκείνῳ ᾧ ἂν γένηται τἀγαθά;"   5
'"τοῦτ᾽ εὐπορώτερον", ἦν δ᾽ ἐγώ, "ἔχω ἀποκρίνασθαι, ὅτι
εὐδαίμων ἔσται."
'"κτήσει γάρ", ἔφη, "ἀγαθῶν οἱ εὐδαίμονες εὐδαίμονες, 205
καὶ οὐκέτι προσδεῖ ἐρέσθαι 'ἵνα τί δὲ βούλεται εὐδαίμων
εἶναι ὁ βουλόμενος;' ἀλλὰ τέλος δοκεῖ ἔχειν ἡ ἀπόκρισις."
'"ἀληθῆ λέγεις," εἶπον ἐγώ.
'"ταύτην δὴ τὴν βούλησιν καὶ τὸν ἔρωτα τοῦτον πότερα 5
κοινὸν οἴει εἶναι πάντων ἀνθρώπων, καὶ πάντας τἀγαθὰ
βούλεσθαι αὑτοῖς εἶναι ἀεί, ἢ πῶς λέγεις;"
'"οὕτως," ἦν δ᾽ ἐγώ· "κοινὸν εἶναι πάντων."
'"τί δὴ οὖν," ἔφη, "ὦ Σώκρατες, οὐ πάντας ἐρᾶν φαμεν,
εἴπερ γε πάντες τῶν αὐτῶν ἐρῶσι καὶ ἀεί, ἀλλὰ τινάς φαμεν b
ἐρᾶν, τοὺς δ᾽ οὔ;"
'"θαυμάζω", ἦν δ᾽ ἐγώ, "καὶ αὐτός."
'"ἀλλὰ μὴ θαύμαζ᾽," ἔφη· "ἀφελόντες γὰρ ἄρα τοῦ ἔρωτός
τι εἶδος ὀνομάζομεν, τὸ τοῦ ὅλου ἐπιτιθέντες ὄνομα, ἔρωτα, 5
τὰ δὲ ἄλλα ἄλλοις καταχρώμεθα ὀνόμασιν."
'"ὥσπερ τί;" ἦν δ᾽ ἐγώ.
'"ὥσπερ τόδε. οἶσθ᾽ ὅτι ποίησίς ἐστί τι πολύ· ἡ γάρ τοι
ἐκ τοῦ μὴ ὄντος εἰς τὸ ὂν ἰόντι ὁτῳοῦν αἰτία πᾶσά ἐστι
ποίησις, ὥστε καὶ αἱ ὑπὸ πάσαις ταῖς τέχναις ἐργασίαι c
ποιήσεις εἰσὶ καὶ οἱ τούτων δημιουργοὶ πάντες ποιηταί."
'"ἀληθῆ λέγεις."
'"ἀλλ᾽ ὅμως", ἦ δ᾽ ἥ, "οἶσθ᾽ ὅτι οὐ καλοῦνται ποιηταὶ
ἀλλὰ ἄλλα ἔχουσιν ὀνόματα, ἀπὸ δὲ πάσης τῆς ποιήσεως ἓν 5

a 5 ταύτην δὲ p. n | b 4 γὰρ ἄρα p. n: γὰρ n |

clearly, the person who loves, loves beautiful things: why does he love them?"

'I said "To possess them for himself."

'"But", she said, "your answer still requires a question of the following sort: what will the person who possesses beautiful things get by possessing them?"

'I said that I didn't find *this* question at all [d10] easy to answer.

[e1] '"Well," she said, "answer as if someone changed things round, and questioned you using the good instead of the beautiful: 'Come on, Socrates: the person who loves, loves good things; why does he love them?'"

'"To possess them for himself", I said.

[e5] '"And what will the person who possesses good things get by possessing them?"

'"That", I said, "I'm better placed to answer: he'll be happy."

205 '"Yes," she said, "because those who are happy are happy by virtue of possessing good things, and one no longer needs to go on to ask 'And what reason does the person who wishes to be happy have for wishing it?' Your answer seems to be complete."

'"True," I said.

[a5] '"This wish, then, this love – do you think it common to all human beings, and that everyone wishes always to possess good things, or what's your view?"

'"The same as yours," I replied; "that it's common to everyone."

'"Why is it, then, Socrates," she said. "that we don't say that everyone is in love, [b1] if in fact everyone loves the same things, and always loves them, but rather say that some people are in love, others not?"

'"I'm surprised at it myself," I replied.

'"You shouldn't be," she said. "The fact is, as we can now see, that we separate off one kind of [b5] love and apply to it the name which belongs to the whole; we call *it* 'love', and for the other kinds we use other names."

'"Is there a similar case?"   creation .

'"There's this one. You're aware that *poiêsis* includes a large range of things: after all, what causes anything whatever to pass from not being into being is all [c1] *poiêsis*, so that the productive activities that belong to all the different kinds of expertise are in fact kinds of *poiêsis*, and their practitioners are all po[i]ets."

'"True."

'"Nevertheless", she replied, "you're aware that they're not called poets, [c5] but have other names; one part has been divided off from *poiêsis* as a

μόριον ἀφορισθὲν τὸ περὶ τὴν μουσικὴν καὶ τὰ μέτρα τῷ τοῦ ὅλου ὀνόματι προσαγορεύεται. ποίησις γὰρ τοῦτο μόνον καλεῖται, καὶ οἱ ἔχοντες τοῦτο τὸ μόριον τῆς ποιήσεως ποιηταί."

'"ἀληθῆ λέγεις," ἔφην.　10

'"οὕτω τοίνυν καὶ περὶ τὸν ἔρωτα. τὸ μὲν κεφάλαιόν ἐστι d πᾶσα ἡ τῶν ἀγαθῶν ἐπιθυμία καὶ τοῦ εὐδαιμονεῖν "ὁ μέγιστος καὶ δολερὸς ἔρως" παντί· ἀλλ' οἱ μὲν ἄλλη τρεπόμενοι πολλαχῇ ἐπ' αὐτόν, ἢ κατὰ χρηματισμὸν ἢ κατὰ φιλογυμναστίαν ἢ κατὰ φιλοσοφίαν, οὔτε ἐρᾶν καλοῦνται οὔτε 5 ἐρασταί, οἱ δὲ κατὰ ἕν τι εἶδος ἰόντες τε καὶ ἐσπουδακότες τὸ τοῦ ὅλου ὄνομα ἴσχουσιν, ἔρωτά τε καὶ ἐρᾶν καὶ ἐρασταί."

'"κινδυνεύεις ἀληθῆ", ἔφην ἐγώ, "λέγειν."

'"καὶ λέγεται μέν γέ τις", ἔφη, "λόγος, ὡς οἳ ἂν τὸ ἥμισυ ἑαυτῶν ζητῶσιν, οὗτοι ἐρῶσιν· ὁ δ' ἐμὸς λόγος οὔτε 10 ἡμίσεός φησιν εἶναι τὸν ἔρωτα οὔτε ὅλου, ἐὰν μὴ τυγχάνῃ γέ e που, ὦ ἑταῖρε, ἀγαθὸν ὄν, ἐπεὶ αὐτῶν γε καὶ πόδας καὶ χεῖρας ἐθέλουσιν ἀποτέμνεσθαι οἱ ἄνθρωποι, ἐὰν αὐτοῖς δοκῇ τὰ ἑαυτῶν πονηρὰ εἶναι. οὐ γὰρ τὸ ἑαυτῶν οἶμαι ἕκαστοι ἀσπάζονται, εἰ μὴ εἴ τις τὸ μὲν ἀγαθὸν οἰκεῖον καλεῖ καὶ 5 ἑαυτοῦ, τὸ δὲ κακὸν ἀλλότριον· ὡς οὐδέν γε ἄλλο ἐστὶν οὗ ἐρῶσιν ἄνθρωποι ἢ τοῦ ἀγαθοῦ. ἢ σοὶ δοκοῦσιν;"　206

'"μὰ Δί' οὐκ ἔμοιγε," ἦν δ' ἐγώ.

'"ἆρ' οὖν," ἦ δ' ἥ, "οὕτως ἁπλοῦν ἐστι λέγειν ὅτι οἱ ἄνθρωποι τἀγαθοῦ ἐρῶσιν;"

'"ναί," ἔφην.　5

'"τί δέ; οὐ προσθετέον", ἔφη, "ὅτι καὶ εἶναι τὸ ἀγαθὸν αὑτοῖς ἐρῶσιν;"

'"προσθετέον."

'"ἆρ' οὖν", ἔφη, "καὶ οὐ μόνον εἶναι, ἀλλὰ καὶ ἀεὶ εἶναι;

'"καὶ τοῦτο προσθετέον."　10

'"ἔστιν ἄρα συλλήβδην", ἔφη, "ὁ ἔρως τοῦ τὸ ἀγαθὸν αὑτῷ εἶναι ἀεί."

'"ἀληθέστατα", ἔφην ἐγώ, "λέγεις."

d 7 ἴσχουσιν　m: εσχον　p

whole, the part concerned with music and verse, and is given the name of the whole. This alone is called *poiêsis*, and those to whom this part of *poiêsis* belongs are called poets."

[c10] "'True," I said.

[d1] "'Well, it's the same with love too. To sum up, the whole of desire for good things and for happiness is 'the supreme and treacherous love', to be found in everyone; but those who direct themselves to it in all sorts of other ways, in business, or in [d5] their love of physical exercise, or in philosophy, are neither said to be 'in love' nor to be 'lovers', while those who proceed by giving themselves to just one kind of love have the name of the whole, 'love' – and they're the ones who are 'in love', and 'lovers'.'"

"'Very likely that's true,' I said.

[d10] "'Yes," she said, "and there's a story that's told, according to which it's those [e1] who seek the other half of themselves who are in love; but my story declares that love is neither of a half nor of a whole, unless, my friend, it turns out actually to be *good*, since people are even willing to have their own feet and hands cut off, if their own state [e5] seems to them to be a bad one. For it's not, I think, what is their own that either group is embracing, except if someone calls what is good 'what belongs to' him, and **206** 'his own', and what is bad 'alien'; since there is nothing else that people are in love with except the good. Or do you think there is?"

"'Zeus! I certainly don't", I replied.

"'Is it then true to say, without qualification, that [a5] people love what is good?"

"'Yes," I said.

"'But", she said, "oughtn't we to add that what they love includes their possessing the good?"

"'We ought."

[a10] "'And then", she said. "not only possessing it, but always possessing it?"

"'We must add that too."

"'In that case," she said, "we can sum up by saying that love is of permanent possession of what is good."

"'What you say is very true," I said.

'"ὅτε δὴ τοῦτο ὁ ἔρως ἐστὶν ἀεί," ἦ δ' ἥ, "τῶν τίνα b
τρόπον διωκόντων αὐτὸ καὶ ἐν τίνι πράξει ἡ σπουδὴ καὶ ἡ
σύντασις ἔρως ἂν καλοῖτο; τί τοῦτο τυγχάνει ὂν τὸ ἔργον;
ἔχεις εἰπεῖν;"
'"οὐ μεντἂν σέ," ἔφην ἐγώ, "ὦ Διοτίμα, ἐθαύμαζον ἐπὶ 5
σοφίᾳ καὶ ἐφοίτων παρὰ σὲ αὐτὰ ταῦτα μαθησόμενος."
'"ἀλλὰ ἐγώ σοι", ἔφη, "ἐρῶ. ἔστι γὰρ τοῦτο τόκος ἐν
καλῷ καὶ κατὰ τὸ σῶμα καὶ κατὰ τὴν ψυχήν."
'"μαντείας", ἦν δ' ἐγώ, "δεῖται ὅτι ποτε λέγεις, καὶ οὐ
μανθάνω." 10
'"ἀλλ' ἐγώ", ἦ δ' ἥ, "σαφέστερον ἐρῶ. κυοῦσιν γάρ," ἔφη, c
"ὦ Σώκρατες, πάντες ἄνθρωποι καὶ κατὰ τὸ σῶμα καὶ κατὰ
τὴν ψυχήν, καὶ ἐπειδὰν ἔν τινι ἡλικίᾳ γένωνται, τίκτειν
ἐπιθυμεῖ ἡμῶν ἡ φύσις. τίκτειν δὲ ἐν μὲν αἰσχρῷ οὐ δύναται,
ἐν δὲ τῷ καλῷ. ἡ γὰρ ἀνδρὸς καὶ γυναικὸς συνουσία τόκος 5
ἐστίν. ἔστι δὲ τοῦτο θεῖον τὸ πρᾶγμα, καὶ τοῦτο ἐν θνητῷ
ὄντι τῷ ζῴῳ ἀθάνατον ἔνεστιν, ἡ κύησις καὶ ἡ γέννησις. τὰ
δὲ ἐν τῷ ἀναρμόστῳ ἀδύνατον γενέσθαι· ἀνάρμοστον δ' ἐστὶ
τὸ αἰσχρὸν παντὶ τῷ θείῳ, τὸ δὲ καλὸν ἁρμόττον. Μοῖρα οὖν d
καὶ Εἰλείθυια ἡ Καλλονή ἐστι τῇ γενέσει. διὰ ταῦτα ὅταν
μὲν καλῷ προσπελάζῃ τὸ κυοῦν, ἵλεών τε γίγνεται καὶ
εὐφραινόμενον διαχεῖται καὶ τίκτει τε καὶ γεννᾷ· ὅταν δὲ
αἰσχρῷ, σκυθρωπόν τε καὶ λυπούμενον συσπειρᾶται καὶ 5
ἀποτρέπεται καὶ ἀνείλλεται καὶ οὐ γεννᾷ, ἀλλὰ ἴσχον τὸ
κύημα χαλεπῶς φέρει. ὅθεν δὴ τῷ κυοῦντί τε καὶ ἤδη
σπαργῶντι πολλὴ ἡ πτοίησις γέγονε περὶ τὸ καλόν, διὰ τὸ e
μεγάλης ὠδῖνος ἀπολύειν τὸν ἔχοντα. ἔστιν γάρ, ὦ
Σώκρατες," ἔφη, "οὐ τοῦ καλοῦ ὁ ἔρως, ὡς σὺ οἴει."
'"ἀλλὰ τί μήν;"
'"τῆς γεννήσεως καὶ τοῦ τόκου ἐν τῷ καλῷ." 5
'"εἶεν," ἦν δ' ἐγώ.
'"πάνυ μὲν οὖν," ἔφη. "τί δὴ οὖν τῆς γεννήσεως; ὅτι
ἀειγενές ἐστι καὶ ἀθάνατον ὡς θνητῷ ἡ γέννησις· ἀθανασίας
δὲ ἀναγκαῖον ἐπιθυμεῖν μετὰ ἀγαθοῦ ἐκ τῶν ὡμολογημένων, 207

---

b 1 τούτου e | c 5-6 [ἡ γὰρ ... ἐστίν] e | d 1 θεῷ p, n | e 7 γενεσεως
p

[b1] '"Given, then, that love is always this," she replied, "how will those pursuing it do so, and through what activity, if their intense eagerness in pursuing it is to be called love? What really is this thing that it does? Can you say?"

[b5] '"If I could, Diotima," I said, I certainly wouldn't be admiring you for your wisdom, and visiting you to learn just these very things."

'"Then", she said, " I'll tell you. It's giving birth in the beautiful, in relation both to body and to soul."

'"It would take a seer," I replied, "to see what on earth you mean; I don't [b10] understand."

[c1] '"Then I'll tell you more clearly," she said. "All human beings, Socrates, are pregnant both in body and in soul, and when we come to be of the right age, we naturally desire to give birth. We cannot do it in what is ugly, [c5] but we can in what is beautiful. The intercourse of man and woman is in fact a kind of giving birth. This matter of giving birth is something divine: living creatures, despite their mortality, contain this immortal aspect, of pregnancy and procreation. It is impossible for this to be completed in what is unfitting; and what is unfitting for everything [d1] divine is what is ugly, while the beautiful is fitting. Thus beauty is both Fate and Eileithyia for coming-into-being. For these reasons, if ever what is pregnant approaches something beautiful, it becomes gracious, melts with joy, and gives birth and procreates; but when [d5] it approaches what is ugly, it contracts, frowning with pain, turns away, curls up, and fails to procreate, retaining what it has conceived, and suffering because of it. This is why what is pregnant and already [e1] full to bursting feels the great excitement it does in proximity to the beautiful, because of the fact that the beautiful person frees it from great pain. For, Socrates," she said, "love is not, as you think, of the beautiful."

'"Well, then, what is it of?"

[e5] '"Of procreation and giving birth in the beautiful."

'"All right," I replied.

'"I can assure you it is," she said. "Why, then, is it of procreation? Because procreation is something everlasting and immortal, as far as anything can be for what is mortal; and it is immortality, **207** together with

εἴπερ τοῦ ἀγαθοῦ ἑαυτῷ εἶναι ἀεὶ ἔρως ἐστίν. ἀναγκαῖον δὴ (207)
ἐκ τούτου τοῦ λόγου καὶ τῆς ἀθανασίας τὸν ἔρωτα εἶναι."

'ταῦτά τε οὖν πάντα ἐδίδασκέ με, ὁπότε περὶ τῶν ἐρωτικῶν λόγους ποιοῖτο, καί ποτε ἤρετο "τί οἴει, ὦ Σώκρατες, 5
αἴτιον εἶναι τούτου τοῦ ἔρωτος καὶ τῆς ἐπιθυμίας; ἢ οὐκ
αἰσθάνῃ ὡς δεινῶς διατίθεται πάντα τὰ θηρία ἐπειδὰν γεννᾶν
ἐπιθυμήσῃ, καὶ τὰ πεζὰ καὶ τὰ πτηνά, νοσοῦντά τε πάντα b
καὶ ἐρωτικῶς διατιθέμενα, πρῶτον μὲν περὶ τὸ συμμιγῆναι
ἀλλήλοις, ἔπειτα περὶ τὴν τροφὴν τοῦ γενομένου, καὶ ἕτοιμά
ἐστιν ὑπὲρ τούτων καὶ διαμάχεσθαι τὰ ἀσθενέστατα τοῖς
ἰσχυροτάτοις καὶ ὑπεραποθνήσκειν, καὶ αὐτὰ τῷ λιμῷ 5
παρατεινόμενα ὥστ' ἐκεῖνα ἐκτρέφειν, καὶ ἄλλο πᾶν ποιοῦντα·
τοὺς μὲν γὰρ ἀνθρώπους", ἔφη, "οἴοιτ' ἄν τις ἐκ λογισμοῦ
ταῦτα ποιεῖν· τὰ δὲ θηρία τίς αἰτία οὕτως ἐρωτικῶς
διατίθεσθαι; ἔχεις λέγειν;" c

'καὶ ἐγὼ αὖ ἔλεγον ὅτι οὐκ εἰδείην· ἢ δ' εἶπεν, "διανοῇ
οὖν δεινός ποτε γενήσεσθαι τὰ ἐρωτικά, ἐὰν ταῦτα μὴ
ἐννοῇς;"

'"ἀλλὰ διὰ ταῦτά τοι, ὦ Διοτίμα, ὅπερ νυνδὴ εἶπον, παρὰ 5
σὲ ἥκω, γνοὺς ὅτι διδασκάλων δέομαι. ἀλλά μοι λέγε καὶ
τούτων τὴν αἰτίαν καὶ τῶν ἄλλων τῶν περὶ τὰ ἐρωτικά."

'"εἰ τοίνυν", ἔφη, "πιστεύεις ἐκείνου εἶναι φύσει τὸν
ἔρωτα, οὗ πολλάκις ὡμολογήκαμεν, μὴ θαύμαζε. ἐνταῦθα γὰρ
τὸν αὐτὸν ἐκείνῳ λόγον ἡ θνητὴ φύσις ζητεῖ κατὰ τὸ d
δυνατὸν ἀεί τε εἶναι καὶ ἀθάνατος. δύναται δὲ ταύτῃ μόνον,
τῇ γενέσει, ὅτι ἀεὶ καταλείπει ἕτερον νέον ἀντὶ τοῦ παλαιοῦ,
ἐπεὶ καὶ ἐν ᾧ ἓν ἕκαστον τῶν ζῴων ζῆν καλεῖται καὶ εἶναι
τὸ αὐτό – οἷον ἐκ παιδαρίου ὁ αὐτὸς λέγεται ἕως ἂν 5
πρεσβύτης γένηται· οὗτος μέντοι οὐδέποτε τὰ αὐτὰ ἔχων ἐν
αὑτῷ ὅμως ὁ αὐτὸς καλεῖται, ἀλλὰ νέος ἀεὶ γιγνόμενος, τὰ
δὲ ἀπολλύς, καὶ κατὰ τὰς τρίχας καὶ σάρκα καὶ ὀστᾶ καὶ e
αἷμα καὶ σύμπαν τὸ σῶμα. καὶ μὴ ὅτι κατὰ τὸ σῶμα, ἀλλὰ
καὶ κατὰ τὴν ψυχὴν οἱ τρόποι, τὰ ἤθη, δόξαι, ἐπιθυμίαι,
ἡδοναί, λῦπαι, φόβοι, τούτων ἕκαστα οὐδέποτε τὰ αὐτὰ
πάρεστιν ἑκάστῳ, ἀλλὰ τὰ μὲν γίγνεται, τὰ δὲ ἀπόλλυται. 5
πολὺ δὲ τούτων ἀτοπώτερον ἔτι, ὅτι καὶ αἱ ἐπιστῆμαι μὴ ὅτι

a 2 ἀγαθοῦ p. n: τἀγαθὸν n: ἀγαθὸν e

the good, that must necessarily be desired, according to what has been agreed before – if indeed love is of permanent possession of the good. Well, from this argument it necessarily follows that love is of immortality as well."

'All these things she taught me, then, whenever she talked [a5] about matters to do with love; and on one occasion she asked me "What do you think, Socrates, is the cause of this love, and this desire? Don't you see how terribly all animals are affected whenever they feel the desire [b1] to procreate, whether they go on foot or have wings – all of them stricken with the effects of love, first for intercourse with one another, and then also for nurturing their offspring, so that the weakest are prepared to join battle with the strongest [b5] on their offspring's behalf and even die for them, torturing themselves with hunger so as to rear them, and doing everything else necessary? Human beings", she said, "one might suppose to do this as a result of reasoning it out; but what cause makes animals be so powerfully affected [c1] by love? Can you say?"

'I replied, for my part, that I didn't know; and she said "Well, do you imagine that you'll ever become an expert in erotics, if you don't think about these things?"

[c5] '"But that's the very reason, Diotima, as I said just now, that I've come to you – because I recognize that I need teachers. Tell me the cause both of this and of everything else to do with love."

'"Well then," she said, "if you are confident that what love is of, by nature, is what we have agreed many times that it is, you have no need to be surprised. The same [d1] account applies to animals as to human beings: mortal nature seeks so far as it can to exist for ever and to be immortal. And it can achieve it only in this way, through the process of coming-into-being, because it always leaves behind something else that is new in place of the old, since even during the time in which each living creature is said to be alive and to be [d5] the same individual – as for example someone is said to be the same person from when he is a child until he comes to be an old man, and yet, if he's called the same, that's despite the fact that he's never made up from the same things, but is always being renewed, and [e1] losing what he had before, whether it's hair, or flesh, or bones, or blood, in fact the whole body. And don't suppose that this is just true in the case of the body; in the case of the soul, too, its traits, habits, opinions, desires, pleasures, pains, fears – none of these things is ever [e5] the same in any individual, but some are coming into existence, others passing away. It's much stranger even than this

αἱ μὲν γίγνονται, αἱ δὲ ἀπόλλυνται ἡμῖν, καὶ οὐδέποτε οἱ 208
αὐτοί ἐσμεν οὐδὲ κατὰ τὰς ἐπιστήμας, ἀλλὰ καὶ μία ἑκάστη
τῶν ἐπιστημῶν ταὐτὸν πάσχει. ὃ γὰρ καλεῖται μελετᾶν, ὡς
ἐξιούσης ἐστὶ τῆς ἐπιστήμης· λήθη γὰρ ἐπιστήμης ἔξοδος,
μελέτη δὲ πάλιν καινὴν ἐμποιοῦσα ἀντὶ τῆς ἀπιούσης μνήμην 5
σῴζει τὴν ἐπιστήμην, ὥστε τὴν αὐτὴν δοκεῖν εἶναι. τούτῳ
γὰρ τῷ τρόπῳ πᾶν τὸ θνητὸν σῴζεται, οὐ τῷ παντάπασιν τὸ
αὐτὸ ἀεὶ εἶναι ὥσπερ τὸ θεῖον, ἀλλὰ τῷ τὸ ἀπιὸν καὶ b
παλαιούμενον ἕτερον νέον ἐγκαταλείπειν οἷον αὐτὸ ἦν. ταύτῃ
τῇ μηχανῇ, ὦ Σώκρατες," ἔφη, "θνητὸν ἀθανασίας μετέχει,
καὶ σῶμα καὶ τἆλλα πάντα· ἀθάνατον δὲ ἄλλη. μὴ οὖν
θαύμαζε εἰ τὸ αὑτοῦ ἀποβλάστημα φύσει πᾶν τιμᾷ· ἀθανασίας 5
γὰρ χάριν παντὶ αὕτη ἡ σπουδὴ καὶ ὁ ἔρως ἕπεται."

'καὶ ἐγὼ ἀκούσας τὸν λόγον ἐθαύμασά τε καὶ εἶπον
"εἶεν," ἦν δ' ἐγώ, "ὦ σοφωτάτη Διοτίμα, "ταῦτα ὡς ἀληθῶς
οὕτως ἔχει;"

'καὶ ἥ, ὥσπερ οἱ τέλεοι σοφισταί, "εὖ ἴσθι," ἔφη, "ὦ c
Σώκρατες· ἐπεί γε καὶ τῶν ἀνθρώπων εἰ ἐθέλεις εἰς τὴν
φιλοτιμίαν βλέψαι, θαυμάζοις ἂν τῆς ἀλογίας περὶ ἃ ἐγὼ
εἴρηκα, εἰ μὴ ἐννοεῖς, ἐνθυμηθεὶς ὡς δεινῶς διάκεινται ἔρωτι
τοῦ ὀνομαστοὶ γενέσθαι καὶ 'κλέος ἐς τὸν ἀεὶ χρόνον 5
ἀθάνατον καταθέσθαι', καὶ ὑπὲρ τούτου κινδύνους τε
κινδυνεύειν ἕτοιμοί εἰσι πάντας ἔτι μᾶλλον ἢ ὑπὲρ τῶν
παίδων, καὶ χρήματα ἀναλίσκειν καὶ πόνους πονεῖν d
οὑστινασοῦν καὶ ὑπεραποθνῄσκειν. ἐπεὶ οἴει σύ", ἔφη,
" Ἄλκηστιν ὑπὲρ Ἀδμήτου ἀποθανεῖν ἄν, ἢ Ἀχιλλέα Πατρόκλῳ
ἐπαποθανεῖν, ἢ προαποθανεῖν τὸν ὑμέτερον Κόδρον ὑπὲρ τῆς
βασιλείας τῶν παίδων, μὴ οἰομένους ἀθάνατον μνήμην ἀρετῆς 5
πέρι ἑαυτῶν ἔσεσθαι, ἣν νῦν ἡμεῖς ἔχομεν; πολλοῦ γε δεῖ,"
ἔφη, "ἀλλ' οἶμαι ὑπὲρ ἀρετῆς ἀθανάτου καὶ τοιαύτης δόξης
εὐκλεοῦς πάντες πάντα ποιοῦσιν, ὅσῳ ἂν ἀμείνους ὦσι, e
τοσούτῳ μᾶλλον· τοῦ γὰρ ἀθανάτου ἐρῶσιν. οἱ μὲν οὖν
ἐγκύμονες", ἔφη, "κατὰ τὰ σώματα ὄντες πρὸς τὰς γυναῖκας
μᾶλλον τρέπονται καὶ ταύτῃ ἐρωτικοί εἰσιν, διὰ παιδογονίας
ἀθανασίαν καὶ μνήμην καὶ εὐδαιμονίαν, ὡς οἴονται, αὑτοῖς εἰς 5
τὸν ἔπειτα χρόνον πάντα ποριζόμενοι· οἱ δὲ κατὰ τὴν ψυχήν

a 5 [μνήμην] e: μνήμη p | b 4 ἀδύνατον e

with the pieces of knowledge we have: not only **208** are some of them coming into existence and others passing away, so that we are never the same even in respect to the things we know, but in fact each individual piece of knowledge is subject to the same process. For what we call 'going over' things exists because knowledge goes out of us; forgetting is the departure of knowledge, [a5] and going over something creates in us again a new memory in place of the one that is leaving us, and so preserves our knowledge in such a way as to make it seem the same. In this way everything mortal is preserved, not by always being [b1] absolutely the same, as the divine is, but by virtue of the fact that what is departing and decaying with age leaves behind in us something else new, of the same sort that it was. It is by this means, Socrates," she said, "that the mortal partakes of immortality, both body and everything else; and what is immortal partakes of it in a different way. So don't [b5] be surprised that everything by nature values what springs from itself; this eagerness, this love, that attends on every creature is for the sake of immortality."

'When I heard what she said, I was indeed surprised, and I said "Well now, most wise Diotima: is what you say really true?"

[c1] 'Like an accomplished sophist, she said "You can be sure of that, Socrates; because in fact if you'll look at human beings too, and their love of honour, you'd be surprised at their irrationality in relation to what I've talked about, if you don't think about it, and reflect on how terribly they are affected by love [c5] of acquiring a name for themselves, and 'of laying up immortal glory for all time to come', and how for the sake of that they're ready to run all risks, even more than they are for their [d1] children – they'll spend money, undergo any suffering you like, die for it. Do you think", she said, "that Alcestis would have died for Admetus, that Achilles would have added his death to Patroclus', or that your Codrus would have died before his time for the sake of his [d5] children's succession to the kingship, unless they thought at the time that there would be an immortal memory of their own courage, the one we now have of them? Far from it," she said; "I imagine it's for the sake of immortal virtue and this sort of glorious [e1] reputation that everyone does everything, the more so the better people they are, because they are in love with immortality. Those, then," she said, "who are pregnant in their bodies turn their attention more towards women, and their love is directed in this way, securing [e5] immortality, a memory of themselves, and happiness, as they think, for themselves for all time to come through having

– εἰσὶ γὰρ οὖν", ἔφη, "οἳ ἐν ταῖς ψυχαῖς κυοῦσιν ἔτι μᾶλλον **209**
ἢ ἐν τοῖς σώμασιν, ἃ ψυχῇ προσήκει καὶ κυῆσαι καὶ τεκεῖν.
τί οὖν προσήκει; φρόνησίν τε καὶ τὴν ἄλλην ἀρετήν· ὧν δή
εἰσι καὶ οἱ ποιηταὶ πάντες γεννήτορες καὶ τῶν δημιουργῶν
ὅσοι λέγονται εὑρετικοὶ εἶναι. πολὺ δὲ μεγίστη", ἔφη, "καὶ 5
καλλίστη τῆς φρονήσεως ἡ περὶ τὰ τῶν πόλεών τε καὶ
οἰκήσεων διακόσμησις, ᾗ δὴ ὄνομά ἐστι σωφροσύνη τε καὶ
δικαιοσύνη. τούτων δ' αὖ ὅταν τις ἐκ νέου ἐγκύμων ᾖ τὴν b
ψυχήν, θεῖος ὤν, καὶ ἡκούσης τῆς ἡλικίας τίκτειν τε καὶ
γεννᾶν ἤδη ἐπιθυμῇ, ζητεῖ δὴ οἶμαι καὶ οὗτος περιιὼν τὸ
καλὸν ἐν ᾧ ἂν γεννήσειεν· ἐν τῷ γὰρ αἰσχρῷ οὐδέποτε
γεννήσει. τά τε οὖν σώματα τὰ καλὰ μᾶλλον ἢ τὰ αἰσχρὰ 5
ἀσπάζεται ἅτε κυῶν, καὶ ἂν ἐντύχῃ ψυχῇ καλῇ καὶ γενναίᾳ
καὶ εὐφυεῖ, πάνυ δὴ ἀσπάζεται τὸ συναμφότερον, καὶ πρὸς
τοῦτον τὸν ἄνθρωπον εὐθὺς εὐπορεῖ λόγων περὶ ἀρετῆς καὶ
περὶ οἷον χρὴ εἶναι τὸν ἄνδρα τὸν ἀγαθὸν καὶ ἃ ἐπιτηδεύειν, c
καὶ ἐπιχειρεῖ παιδεύειν. ἁπτόμενος γὰρ οἶμαι τοῦ καλοῦ καὶ
ὁμιλῶν αὐτῷ, ἃ πάλαι ἐκύει τίκτει καὶ γεννᾷ, καὶ παρὼν καὶ
ἀπὼν μεμνημένος, καὶ τὸ γεννηθὲν συνεκτρέφει κοινῇ μετ'
ἐκείνου, ὥστε πολὺ μείζω κοινωνίαν τῆς τῶν παίδων πρὸς 5
ἀλλήλους οἱ τοιοῦτοι ἴσχουσι καὶ φιλίαν βεβαιοτέραν, ἅτε
καλλιόνων καὶ ἀθανατωτέρων παίδων κεκοινωνηκότες. καὶ πᾶς
ἂν δέξαιτο ἑαυτῷ τοιούτους παῖδας μᾶλλον γεγονέναι ἢ τοὺς d
ἀνθρωπίνους, καὶ εἰς Ὅμηρον ἀποβλέψας καὶ Ἡσίοδον καὶ
τοὺς ἄλλους ποιητὰς τοὺς ἀγαθοὺς ζηλῶν, οἷα ἔκγονα ἑαυτῶν
καταλείπουσιν, ἃ ἐκείνοις ἀθάνατον κλέος καὶ μνήμην
παρέχεται αὐτὰ τοιαῦτα ὄντα· εἰ δὲ βούλει," ἔφη, "οἵους 5
Λυκοῦργος παῖδας κατελίπετο ἐν Λακεδαίμονι, σωτῆρας τῆς
Λακεδαίμονος καὶ ὡς ἔπος εἰπεῖν τῆς Ἑλλάδος. τίμιος δὲ
παρ' ὑμῖν καὶ Σόλων διὰ τὴν τῶν νόμων γέννησιν, καὶ ἄλλοι
ἄλλοθι πολλαχοῦ ἄνδρες, καὶ ἐν Ἕλλησι καὶ ἐν βαρβάροις, e
πολλὰ καὶ καλὰ ἀποφηνάμενοι ἔργα, γεννήσαντες παντοίαν
ἀρετήν· ὧν καὶ ἱερὰ πολλὰ ἤδη γέγονε διὰ τοὺς τοιούτους
παῖδας, διὰ δὲ τοὺς ἀνθρωπίνους οὐδενός πω.

---

a 3 τεκειν   p: κυεῖν   m | **a 6** τὰ   e: τὰς p,m | **a 7** διακοσμήσεις   n |
b 2 θεῖος   p, m: ἤθεος   e | **b 3** ἐπιθυμῇ   e: επιθυμη   p: ἐπιθυμεῖ   m |
c 1 [περὶ]   e | **e 2** καλὰ   m: αλλα   p

children; whereas those who are pregnant in their souls – **209** for in fact", she said, "there are those who are pregnant in their souls still more than in their bodies, with things that it is fitting for the soul to conceive and to bring to birth. What then are these things that are fitting? Wisdom and the rest of virtue; of which all the poets are, of course, procreators, along with all those [a5] craftsmen who are said to be inventive. But by far the greatest and most beautiful kind of wisdom is the setting in order of the affairs of cities and households, which is called 'moderation' and [b1] 'justice'. When someone is pregnant with these things in his soul, from youth on, by divine gift, and with the coming of the right age, desires to give birth and procreate, then I imagine he too goes round looking for the beautiful object in which he might procreate; for he will never do so in [b5] what is ugly. So he warms to beautiful bodies rather than ugly ones, because he is pregnant, and if he encounters a soul that is beautiful and noble and naturally well-endowed, his welcome for the combination – beautiful body *and* soul – is warm indeed; to this person he is immediately full of resource when it comes to things to say about virtue, [c1] what sort of thing the good man must be concerned with, and the activities such a man should involve himself in, and tries to educate him. For I imagine it's by contact with what is beautiful, and associating with it, that he brings to birth and procreates the things with which he was for so long pregnant, both when he is present with him and when he is away from him but remembering him; and he joins with the other person in nurturing what [c5] has been born, with the result that such people enjoy a much greater partnership with each other than the one people have in their children and a firmer affection between them, insofar as their sharing is in children of a more beautiful and more immortal kind. Everyone [d1] would prefer the birth to them of children of this sort to that of human children, looking with envy at Homer and Hesiod and the other good poets, and the sort of offspring they leave behind them, which provide them with immortal glory [d5] and remembrance because they are themselves immortal; and if you'd like another example," she said, "take the sort of children Lycurgus left behind for himself in Sparta, which have been saviours of Sparta and practically of Greece. Solon too, here in Athens, is honoured for having procreated your laws, and so too are other [e1] men in many other places, among both Greeks and non-Greeks, for having achieved many conspicuously beautiful things, and procreated virtue of all sorts; and in fact in many cases cults have been set up to them because of their having had children of this sort, whereas none has ever yet been set up to anyone because of their human children.

96

'"ταῦτα μὲν οὖν τὰ ἐρωτικὰ ἴσως, ὦ Σώκρατες, κἄν σὺ 5
μυηθείης· τὰ δὲ τέλεα καὶ ἐποπτικά, ὧν ἕνεκα καὶ ταῦτα 210
ἔστιν, ἐάν τις ὀρθῶς μετίῃ, οὐκ οἶδ' εἰ οἷός τ' ἂν εἴης. ἐρῶ
μὲν οὖν", ἔφη, "ἐγὼ καὶ προθυμίας οὐδὲν ἀπολείψω· πειρῶ δὲ
ἔπεσθαι, ἂν οἷός τε ᾖς. δεῖ γάρ", ἔφη, "τὸν ὀρθῶς ἰόντα ἐπὶ
τοῦτο τὸ πρᾶγμα ἄρχεσθαι μὲν νέον ὄντα ἰέναι ἐπὶ τὰ καλὰ 5
σώματα, καὶ πρῶτον μέν, ἐὰν ὀρθῶς ἡγῆται ὁ ἡγούμενος, ἑνὸς
αὐτὸν σώματος ἐρᾶν καὶ ἐνταῦθα γεννᾶν λόγους καλούς,
ἔπειτα δὲ αὐτὸν κατανοῆσαι ὅτι τὸ κάλλος τὸ ἐπὶ ὁτῳοῦν
σώματι τῷ ἐπὶ ἑτέρῳ σώματι ἀδελφόν ἐστι, καὶ εἰ δεῖ b
διώκειν τὸ ἐπ' εἴδει καλόν, πολλὴ ἄνοια μὴ οὐχ ἕν τε καὶ
ταὐτὸν ἡγεῖσθαι τὸ ἐπὶ πᾶσιν τοῖς σώμασι κάλλος· τοῦτο δ'
ἐννοήσαντα καταστῆναι πάντων τῶν καλῶν σωμάτων ἐραστήν,
ἑνὸς δὲ τὸ σφόδρα τοῦτο χαλάσαι καταφρονήσαντα καὶ 5
σμικρὸν ἡγησάμενον· μετὰ δὲ ταῦτα τὸ ἐν ταῖς ψυχαῖς
κάλλος τιμιώτερον ἡγήσασθαι τοῦ ἐν τῷ σώματι, ὥστε καὶ
ἐὰν ἐπιεικὴς ὢν τὴν ψυχήν τις κἂν σμικρὸν ἄνθος ἔχῃ, c
ἐξαρκεῖν αὐτῷ, καὶ ἐρᾶν καὶ κήδεσθαι καὶ τίκτειν λόγους
τοιούτους καὶ ζητεῖν οἵτινες ποιήσουσι βελτίους τοὺς νέους,
ἵνα ἀναγκασθῇ αὖ θεάσασθαι τὸ ἐν τοῖς ἐπιτηδεύμασι καὶ
τοῖς νόμοις καλὸν καὶ τοῦτ' ἰδεῖν ὅτι πᾶν αὐτὸ αὑτῷ 5
συγγενές ἐστιν, ἵνα τὸ περὶ τὸ σῶμα καλὸν σμικρόν τι
ἡγήσηται εἶναι· μετὰ δὲ τὰ ἐπιτηδεύματα ἐπὶ τὰς ἐπιστήμας
ἀγαγεῖν, ἵνα ἴδῃ αὖ ἐπιστημῶν κάλλος, καὶ βλέπων πρὸς πολὺ
ἤδη τὸ καλὸν μηκέτι τὸ παρ' ἑνί, ὥσπερ οἰκέτης, ἀγαπῶν d
παιδαρίου κάλλος ἢ ἀνθρώπου τινὸς ἢ ἐπιτηδεύματος ἑνός,
δουλεύων φαῦλος ᾖ καὶ σμικρολόγος, ἀλλ' ἐπὶ τὸ πολὺ
πέλαγος τετραμμένος τοῦ καλοῦ καὶ θεωρῶν, πολλοὺς καὶ
καλοὺς λόγους καὶ μεγαλοπρεπεῖς τίκτῃ καὶ διανοήματα ἐν 5
φιλοσοφίᾳ ἀφθόνῳ, ἕως ἂν ἐνταῦθα ῥωσθεὶς καὶ αὐξηθεὶς
κατίδῃ τινὰ ἐπιστήμην μίαν τοιαύτην, ἥ ἐστι καλοῦ τοιοῦδε.
πειρῶ δέ μοι", ἔφη, "τὸν νοῦν προσέχειν ὡς οἷόν τε e
μάλιστα. ὃς γὰρ ἂν μέχρι ἐνταῦθα πρὸς τὰ ἐρωτικὰ
παιδαγωγηθῇ, θεώμενος ἐφεξῆς τε καὶ ὀρθῶς τὰ καλά, πρὸς
τέλος ἤδη ἰὼν τῶν ἐρωτικῶν ἐξαίφνης κατόψεταί τι

a 3-4 πειρω δε και συ επεσθαι p | a 7 αὐτῶν n | c 3 [και ζητεῖν] e |
d 1-3 τῷ παρ' ἑνὶ [ὥσπερ ... ἑνός,] δουλεύων e

[e5] '"Into these aspects of erotics, perhaps, Socrates, you too could **210** be initiated; but as for those aspects relating to the final revelation, the ones for the sake of which I have taught you the rest, if one approaches these correctly – I don't know whether you would be capable of initiation into *them*. Well," she said, "I'll tell you this next part, and spare no effort in doing so; and you must try to follow, if you can. It's like this," she said. "The person who turns to this [a5] matter correctly must begin, when he is young, to turn to beautiful bodies, and first, if the one leading him leads him correctly, he must fall in love with a single body and there procreate beautiful words, and then realise for himself that the beauty that there is in any body [b1] whatever is the twin of that in any other, and that if one should pursue beauty of outward form, it's quite mad not to regard the beauty in all bodies as one and the same; and having realised that, he must become a lover of all beautiful bodies, [b5] and relax this passionate love for one body, despising it and considering it a slight thing. The next stage is that he must consider beauty in souls more valuable than beauty in the body, so that if [c1] someone who is decent in his soul has even a slight physical bloom, even then it's enough for him, and he loves and cares for the other person, and gives birth to the sorts of words – and seeks for them – that will make young men into better men, in order that he may be compelled in turn to contemplate beauty as it exists in kinds of activity and in [c5] laws, and to observe that all of this is mutually related, in order that he should think beauty of body a slight thing. After activities, he must lead him to the different kinds of knowledge, in order that he may next observe the beauty that belongs to kinds of knowledge, and, gazing now towards [d1] a beauty which is vast, and no longer slavishly attached to the beauty belonging to a single thing – a young boy, some individual human being, or one kind of activity – may cease to be worthless and petty, as his servitude made him, but instead, turned towards the great sea of beauty and contemplating that, may bring to birth many [d5] beautiful, even magnificent, words and thoughts in a love of wisdom that grudges nothing, until there, with his strength and stature increased, he may catch sight of a certain single kind of knowledge, which has for its object a beauty of a sort I shall describe to you. [e1] Try", she said, "to pay as much attention to me as you can. I tell you that whoever is led by his teacher thus far in relation to love matters, and contemplates the various beautiful things in order and in the correct way, will come now towards the final goal of matters of love, and will suddenly catch sight of a [e5] beauty

98

θαυμαστὸν τὴν φύσιν καλόν, τοῦτο ἐκεῖνο, ὦ Σώκρατες, οὗ δὴ 5
ἕνεκεν καὶ οἱ ἔμπροσθεν πάντες πόνοι ἦσαν, πρῶτον μὲν ἀεὶ
ὂν καὶ οὔτε γιγνόμενον οὔτε ἀπολλύμενον, οὔτε αὐξανόμενον 211
οὔτε φθίνον, ἔπειτα οὐ τῇ μὲν καλόν, τῇ δ' αἰσχρόν, οὐδὲ
τοτὲ μέν, τοτὲ δὲ οὔ, οὐδὲ πρὸς μὲν τὸ καλόν, πρὸς δὲ τὸ
αἰσχρόν, οὐδ' ἔνθα μὲν καλόν, ἔνθα δὲ αἰσχρόν, ὡς τισὶ μὲν
ὂν καλόν, τισὶ δὲ αἰσχρόν· οὐδ' αὖ φαντασθήσεται αὐτῷ τὸ 5
καλὸν οἷον πρόσωπόν τι οὐδὲ χεῖρες οὐδὲ ἄλλο οὐδὲν ὧν
σῶμα μετέχει, οὐδέ τις λόγος οὐδέ τις ἐπιστήμη, οὐδέ που
ὂν ἐν ἑτέρῳ τινί, οἷον ἐν ζῴῳ ἢ ἐν γῇ ἢ ἐν οὐρανῷ ἢ ἔν τῳ b
ἄλλῳ, ἀλλ' αὐτὸ καθ' αὑτὸ μεθ' αὑτοῦ μονοειδὲς ἀεὶ ὄν, τὰ δὲ
ἄλλα πάντα καλὰ ἐκείνου μετέχοντα τρόπον τινὰ τοιοῦτον,
οἷον γιγνομένων τε τῶν ἄλλων καὶ ἀπολλυμένων μηδὲν ἐκεῖνο
μήτε τι πλέον μήτε ἔλαττον γίγνεσθαι μηδὲ πάσχειν μηδέν. 5
ὅταν δή τις ἀπὸ τῶνδε διὰ τὸ ὀρθῶς παιδεραστεῖν ἐπανιὼν
ἐκεῖνο τὸ καλὸν ἄρχηται καθορᾶν, σχεδὸν ἄν τι ἅπτοιτο τοῦ
τέλους. τοῦτο γὰρ δή ἐστι τὸ ὀρθῶς ἐπὶ τὰ ἐρωτικὰ ἰέναι ἢ
ὑπ' ἄλλου ἄγεσθαι, ἀρχόμενον ἀπὸ τῶνδε τῶν καλῶν ἐκείνου c
ἕνεκα τοῦ καλοῦ ἀεὶ ἐπανιέναι, ὥσπερ ἐπαναβασμοῖς
χρώμενον, ἀπὸ ἑνὸς ἐπὶ δύο καὶ ἀπὸ δυοῖν ἐπὶ πάντα τὰ
καλὰ σώματα, καὶ ἀπὸ τῶν καλῶν σωμάτων ἐπὶ τὰ καλὰ
ἐπιτηδεύματα, καὶ ἀπὸ τῶν ἐπιτηδευμάτων ἐπὶ τα καλὰ 5
μαθήματα, καὶ ἀπὸ τῶν μαθημάτων ἐπ' ἐκεῖνο τὸ μάθημα
τελευτῆσαι, ὅ ἐστιν οὐκ ἄλλου ἢ αὐτοῦ ἐκείνου τοῦ καλοῦ
μάθημα, ἵνα γνῶ αὐτὸ τελευτῶν ὅ ἐστι καλόν. ἐνταῦθα τοῦ d
βίου, ὦ φίλε Σώκρατες," ἔφη ἡ Μαντινικὴ ξένη, "εἴπερ που
ἄλλοθι, βιωτὸν ἀνθρώπῳ, θεωμένῳ αὐτὸ τὸ καλόν. ὃ ἐάν ποτε
ἴδῃς, οὐ κατὰ χρυσίον τε καὶ ἐσθῆτα καὶ τοὺς καλοὺς παῖδάς
τε καὶ νεανίσκους δόξει σοι εἶναι, οὓς νῦν ὁρῶν ἐκπέπληξαι 5
καὶ ἕτοιμος εἶ καὶ σὺ καὶ ἄλλοι πολλοί, ὁρῶντες τὰ παιδικὰ
καὶ συνόντες ἀεὶ αὐτοῖς, εἴ πως οἷόν τ' ἦν, μήτ' ἐσθίειν
μήτε πίνειν, ἀλλὰ θεᾶσθαι μόνον καὶ συνεῖναι. τί δῆτα," ἔφη,
"οἰόμεθα, εἴ τῳ γένοιτο αὐτὸ τὸ καλὸν ἰδεῖν εἰλικρινές, e
καθαρόν, ἄμεικτον, ἀλλὰ μὴ ἀνάπλεων σαρκῶν τε ἀνθρωπίνων
καὶ χρωμάτων καὶ ἄλλης πολλῆς φλυαρίας θνητῆς, ἀλλ' αὐτὸ
τὸ θεῖον καλὸν δύναιτο μονοειδὲς κατιδεῖν; ἆρ' οἴει," ἔφη,

---

c 6 καὶ ... 7 τελευτῆσαι ... d 1 ἵνα γνῶ   e: καὶ ... τελευτήσῃ ... καὶ
γνῶ   p. m: ἵνα (or ἕως ἄν) ... τελευτήσῃ ... καὶ γνῶ   e

amazing in its nature – that very beauty, in fact, Socrates, that all his previous toils were for: first, a beauty that always **211** is, and neither comes into being nor perishes, neither increases nor diminishes; secondly, one that is not beautiful in this respect but ugly in that, nor beautiful at one moment but not at another, nor beautiful in relation to this but ugly in relation to that, nor beautiful here but ugly there, because some people [a5] find it beautiful while others find it ugly; nor again will beauty appear to him the sort of thing a face is, or hands, or anything else in which a body shares, or a speech, or a piece of knowledge, nor as having [b1] a location in some other thing, such as a living creature, or the earth, or the heavens, or anything else – but rather as being always itself by itself, in its own company, uniform, with all the other beautiful things sharing in it in such a way that when they come to be and perish, *it* does not in the [b5] slightest degree become either greater or less, nor is it affected in the slightest. Well, when someone moves upwards, away from these things, through the correct kind of boy-loving, and begins to catch sight of *that* beauty, he would practically have the final goal within his reach. For this is what it is to approach love matters, or be led [c1] by someone else in them, in the correct way: beginning from these beautiful things here, one must always move upwards for the sake of that beauty I speak of, using the other things as steps, from one to two and from two to all beautiful bodies, from beautiful bodies to beautiful [c5] activities, from activities to beautiful sciences, and finally from sciences to *that* science, which is science of nothing other than that beauty [d1] itself, in order that one may finally know what beauty is, itself. It is here, my dear Socrates," said the visitor from Mantinea, "if anywhere, that life is worth living for a human being, in contemplation of beauty itself. That, if ever you see it, will not seem to you to be of the same order as gold, and clothes, and [d5] the beautiful boys and young men that now drive you out of your mind when you see them, so that both you and many others are ready, so long as you can see your beloveds and be with them always (if somehow it were possible), to stop eating and drinking, and just gaze at them and be with them. What then", she said, [e1] "do we suppose it would be like if someone succeeded in seeing beauty itself, pure, clean, unmixed, and not contaminated with things like human flesh, and colour, and much other mortal nonsense, but were able

"φαῦλον βίον γίγνεσθαι ἐκεῖσε βλέποντος ἀνθρώπου καὶ ἐκεῖνο 212
ᾧ δεῖ θεωμένου καὶ συνόντος αὐτῷ; ἢ οὐκ ἐνθυμῇ", ἔφη, "ὅτι
ἐνταῦθα αὐτῷ μοναχοῦ γενήσεται, ὁρῶντι ᾧ ὁρατὸν τὸ καλόν,
τίκτειν οὐκ εἴδωλα ἀρετῆς, ἅτε οὐκ εἰδώλου ἐφαπτομένῳ, ἀλλὰ
ἀληθῆ, ἅτε τοῦ ἀληθοῦς ἐφαπτομένῳ· τεκόντι δὲ ἀρετὴν ἀληθῆ 5
καὶ θρεψαμένῳ ὑπάρχει θεοφιλεῖ γενέσθαι, καὶ εἴπερ τῳ ἄλλῳ
ἀνθρώπων ἀθανάτῳ καὶ ἐκείνῳ;"

'ταῦτα δή, ὦ Φαῖδρέ τε καὶ οἱ ἄλλοι, ἔφη μὲν Διοτίμα, b
πέπεισμαι δ' ἐγώ· πεπεισμένος δὲ πειρῶμαι καὶ τοὺς ἄλλους
πείθειν ὅτι τούτου τοῦ κτήματος τῇ ἀνθρωπείᾳ φύσει
συνεργὸν ἀμείνω Ἔρωτος οὐκ ἄν τις ῥᾳδίως λάβοι. διὸ δὴ
ἔγωγέ φημι χρῆναι πάντα ἄνδρα τὸν Ἔρωτα τιμᾶν, καὶ αὐτὸς 5
τιμῶ τὰ ἐρωτικὰ καὶ διαφερόντως ἀσκῶ, καὶ τοῖς ἄλλοις
παρακελεύομαι, καὶ νῦν τε καὶ ἀεὶ ἐγκωμιάζω τὴν δύναμιν
καὶ ἀνδρείαν τοῦ Ἔρωτος καθ' ὅσον οἷός τ' εἰμί. τοῦτον οὖν
τὸν λόγον, ὦ Φαῖδρε, εἰ μὲν βούλει, ὡς ἐγκώμιον εἰς Ἔρωτα c
νόμισον εἰρῆσθαι, εἰ δέ, ὅτι καὶ ὅπῃ χαίρεις ὀνομάζων, τοῦτο
ὀνόμαζε.'

εἰπόντος δὲ ταῦτα τοῦ Σωκράτους τοὺς μὲν ἐπαινεῖν, τὸν
δὲ Ἀριστοφάνη λέγειν τι ἐπιχειρεῖν, ὅτι ἐμνήσθη αὐτου 5
λέγων ὁ Σωκράτης περὶ τοῦ λόγου· καὶ ἐξαίφνης τὴν αὔλειον
θύραν κρουομένην πολὺν ψόφον παρασχεῖν ὡς κωμαστῶν, καὶ
αὐλητρίδος φωνὴν ἀκούειν. τὸν οὖν Ἀγάθωνα, 'παῖδες,' d
φάναι, 'οὐ σκέψεσθε; καὶ ἐὰν μέν τις τῶν ἐπιτηδείων ᾖ,
καλεῖτε· εἰ δὲ μή, λέγετε ὅτι οὐ πίνομεν ἀλλ' ἀναπαυόμεθα
ἤδη.'

καὶ οὐ πολὺ ὕστερον Ἀλκιβιάδου τὴν φωνὴν ἀκούειν ἐν τῇ 5
αὐλῇ σφόδρα μεθύοντος καὶ μέγα βοῶντος, ἐρωτῶντος ὅπου
Ἀγάθων καὶ κελεύοντος ἄγειν παρ' Ἀγάθωνα. ἄγειν οὖν
αὐτὸν παρὰ σφᾶς τήν τε αὐλητρίδα ὑπολαβοῦσαν καὶ ἄλλους
τινὰς τῶν ἀκολούθων, καὶ ἐπιστῆναι ἐπὶ τὰς θύρας
ἐστεφανωμένον αὐτὸν κιττοῦ τέ τινι στεφάνῳ δασεῖ καὶ ἴων, e
καὶ ταινίας ἔχοντα ἐπὶ τῆς κεφαλῆς πάνυ πολλάς, καὶ εἰπεῖν·
'ἄνδρες, χαίρετε· μεθύοντα ἄνδρα πάνυ σφόδρα δέξεσθε
συμπότην, ἢ ἀπίωμεν ἀναδήσαντες μόνον Ἀγάθωνα, ἐφ' ᾧπερ
ἤλθομεν; ἐγὼ γάρ τοι', φάναι, 'χθὲς μὲν οὐχ οἷός τ' 5

a 2 ᾧ δεῖ e: ᾧ δεῖ n: ᾡδὶ n: ὃ δεῖ n: δὴ e: ἀεὶ e | d 3 αλλα
παυο[p

to catch sight of the uniformity of divine beauty itself? Do you think it's **212** a worthless life," she said, "if a person turns his gaze in that direction and contemplates that beauty with the faculty he should use, and is able to be with it? Or do you not recognize", she said, "that it is under these conditions alone, as he sees beauty with what has the power to see it, that he will succeed in bringing to birth, not phantoms of virtue, because he is not grasping a phantom, [a5] but true virtue, because he is grasping the truth; and that when he has given birth to and nurtured true virtue, it belongs to him to be loved by the gods, and to him, if to any human being, to be immortal?"

[b1] 'Well, Phaedrus, and everyone else, that's what Diotima said, and I am persuaded by her; since I am persuaded, I try to persuade everyone else too that for acquiring this possession one couldn't easily get a better co-worker with human nature than Love is. That's why [b5] I declare that everyone must honour Love, and I myself honour what belongs to him and practise it more than anyone, and call on everyone else to do so, and both now and always I eulogize the power and courage of Love to the best of my ability. So, Phaedrus, [c1] if you like, consider this speech of mine to have been given as an encomium to Love; or if you prefer, whatever and in whatever way it pleases you to name it, name it like that.'

When Socrates finished, the others praised his speech (Aristodemus said), but [c5] Aristophanes was trying to say something, because Socrates while speaking had mentioned him and *his* speech. Suddenly there was a loud banging from the door to the court, from what sounded like revellers; and [d1] an *aulos*-girl's voice could be heard. So Agathon said, "Slaves, take a look. If it's someone we know, invite them in; if it isn't, say we're not drinking but actually going off to bed."

[d5] Shortly afterwards they heard the voice of Alcibiades in the court, very drunk and shouting loudly; he was asking where Agathon was, and demanding to be taken to Agathon. So he was taken in to the party by the *aulos*-girl, who was supporting him, and by some other attendants of his; he humour positioned himself by the doors, [e1] wreathed with a thick wreath of ivy and violets, and with a mass of ribbons on his head, and said 'Greetings, gentlemen; will you accept someone who's drunk, really drunk, as a drinking-companion, or are we to leave once we've just crowned Agathon, which is what [e5] we came to do? You see,' he said, 'I wasn't able to make it

ἐγενόμην ἀφικέσθαι, νῦν δὲ ἥκω ἐπὶ τῇ κεφαλῇ ἔχων τὰς
ταινίας, ἵνα ἀπὸ τῆς ἐμῆς κεφαλῆς τὴν τοῦ σοφωτάτου καὶ
καλλίστου κεφαλὴν, ἀνειπὼν οὑτωσί, ἀναδήσω. ἆρα
καταγελάσεσθέ μου ὡς μεθύοντος; ἐγὼ δέ, κἂν ὑμεῖς γελᾶτε,
ὅμως εὖ οἶδ' ὅτι ἀληθῆ λέγω. ἀλλά μοι λέγετε αὐτόθεν, ἐπὶ **213**
ῥητοῖς εἰσίω ἢ μή; συμπίεσθε ἢ οὔ;'

πάντας οὖν ἀναθορυβῆσαι καὶ κελεύειν εἰσιέναι καὶ
κατακλίνεσθαι, καὶ τὸν Ἀγάθωνα καλεῖν αὐτόν. καὶ τὸν ἰέναι
ἀγόμενον ὑπὸ τῶν ἀνθρώπων, καὶ περιαιρούμενον ἅμα τὰς 5
ταινίας, ὡς ἀναδήσοντα, ἐπίπροσθε τῶν ὀφθαλμῶν ἔχοντα οὐ
κατιδεῖν τὸν Σωκράτη, ἀλλὰ καθίζεσθαι παρὰ τὸν Ἀγάθωνα ἐν
μέσῳ Σωκράτους τε καὶ ἐκείνου· παραχωρῆσαι γὰρ τὸν b
Σωκράτη ὡς ἐκεῖνον κατιδεῖν. παρακαθεζόμενον δὲ αὐτὸν
ἀσπάζεσθαί τε τὸν Ἀγάθωνα καὶ ἀναδεῖν.

εἰπεῖν οὖν τὸν Ἀγάθωνα 'ὑπολύετε, παῖδες, Ἀλκιβιάδην,
ἵνα ἐκ τρίτων κατακέηται.' 5

'πάνυ γε,' εἰπεῖν τὸν Ἀλκιβιάδην· 'ἀλλὰ τίς ἡμῖν ὅδε
τρίτος συμπότης;' καὶ ἅμα μεταστρεφόμενον αὐτὸν ὁρᾶν τὸν
Σωκράτη, ἰδόντα δὲ ἀναπηδῆσαι καὶ εἰπεῖν 'ὦ Ἡράκλεις,
τουτὶ τί ἦν; Σωκράτης οὗτος; ἐλλοχῶν αὖ με ἐνταῦθα
κατέκεισο, ὥσπερ εἰώθεις ἐξαίφνης ἀναφαίνεσθαι ὅπου ἐγὼ c
ὤμην ἥκιστά σε ἔσεσθαι. καὶ νῦν τί ἥκεις; καὶ τί αὖ ἐνταῦθα
κατεκλίνης; ὡς οὐ παρὰ Ἀριστοφάνει οὐδὲ εἴ τις ἄλλος
γελοῖός ἐστί τε καὶ βούλεται, ἀλλὰ διεμηχανήσω ὅπως παρὰ
τῷ καλλίστῳ τῶν ἔνδον κατακείσῃ.' 5

καὶ τὸν Σωκράτη, 'Ἀγάθων,' φάναι, 'ὅρα εἴ μοι
ἐπαμυνεῖς· ὡς ἐμοὶ ὁ τούτου ἔρως τοῦ ἀνθρώπου οὐ φαῦλον
πρᾶγμα γέγονεν. ἀπ' ἐκείνου γὰρ τοῦ χρόνου, ἀφ' οὗ τούτου
ἠράσθην, οὐκέτι ἔξεστίν μοι οὔτε προσβλέψαι οὔτε d
διαλεχθῆναι καλῷ οὐδ' ἑνί, ἢ οὑτοσὶ ζηλοτυπῶν με καὶ φθονῶν
θαυμαστὰ ἐργάζεται καὶ λοιδορεῖταί τε καὶ τὼ χεῖρε μόγις
ἀπέχεται. ὅρα οὖν μή τι καὶ νῦν ἐργάσηται, ἀλλὰ διάλλαξον
ἡμᾶς, ἢ ἐὰν ἐπιχειρῇ βιάζεσθαι, ἐπάμυνε, ὡς ἐγὼ τὴν τούτου 5
μανίαν τε καὶ φιλεραστίαν πάνυ ὀρρωδῶ.'

---

yesterday, but I've come now with my head with the ribbons on it, to crown from *my* head the head of the wisest and most beautiful man – that's my proclamation. You'll laugh at me for this, will you, because I'm drunk? I tell you – even if you do laugh, **213** all the same I *know* I'm telling the truth. Tell me at once: am I to come in on agreed terms, or not? Will you drink with me or not?'

Well, everyone shouted out that he should come in and find a couch, and Agathon called out to him. Alcibiades duly went over, [a5] led by his people, and because he was simultaneously taking off the ribbons to crown Agathon, and had them in front of his eyes, he failed to catch sight of Socrates, and sat down beside Agathon, in the [b1] middle between Socrates and him; Socrates had moved over when *he* caught sight of *him*. Once sat down, he embraced Agathon and put the ribbons on him.

Agathon said 'Slaves, take off Alcibiades' sandals, [b5] so that he can make a third on the couch.'

'Absolutely,' said Alcibiades; 'but who's this third person joining in our drinking?' As he said this he turned himself round and saw Socrates; and when he saw him he leapt up and said 'Heracles! What's this we have here? Is it Socrates? You were lying there to [c1] ambush me again, showing up suddenly as you always used to, where I least expected you to be. So why is it you've come now? And another thing – why did you choose *this* couch? I see you didn't choose to be next to Aristophanes, or someone else we laugh at, and who wants to be laughed at; you contrived instead to get a [c5] place on a couch next to the most beautiful person in the house.'

Socrates said 'Agathon, you'll defend me, won't you? My love for this person has become no slight matter. From the time I fell in love with [d1] him, I've no longer been allowed either to look at or to talk to a single beautiful person, or else *he* gets jealous and resentful, and does extraordinary things, calling me names and scarcely able to stop himself from hitting me. So watch out that he doesn't do something now, and please make peace [d5] between us, or if he tries to use force, defend me, because I'm absolutely terrified of his mad attachment to being loved.'

104

'ἀλλ' οὐκ ἔστι', φάναι τὸν Ἀλκιβιάδην, 'ἐμοὶ καὶ σοὶ
διαλλαγή. ἀλλὰ τούτων μὲν εἰς αὖθίς σε τιμωρήσομαι· νῦν δέ
μοι, Ἀγάθων,' φάναι, 'μετάδος τῶν ταινιῶν, ἵνα ἀναδήσω καὶ e
τὴν τούτου ταυτηνὶ τὴν θαυμαστὴν κεφαλήν, καὶ μή μοι
μέμφηται ὅτι σὲ μὲν ἀνέδησα, αὐτὸν δὲ νικῶντα ἐν λόγοις
πάντας ἀνθρώπους, οὐ μόνον πρῴην ὥσπερ σύ, ἀλλ' ἀεί,
ἔπειτα οὐκ ἀνέδησα.' καὶ ἅμ' αὐτὸν λαβόντα τῶν ταινιῶν 5
ἀναδεῖν τὸν Σωκράτη καὶ κατακλίνεσθαι.
    ἐπειδὴ δὲ κατεκλίνη, εἰπεῖν· 'εἶεν δή, ἄνδρες· δοκεῖτε γάρ
μοι νήφειν. οὐκ ἐπιτρεπτέον οὖν ὑμῖν, ἀλλὰ ποτέον·
ὡμολόγηται γὰρ ταῦθ' ἡμῖν. ἄρχοντα οὖν αἱροῦμαι τῆς
πόσεως, ἕως ἂν ὑμεῖς ἱκανῶς πίητε, ἐμαυτόν. ἀλλὰ φερέτω, 10
Ἀγάθων, εἴ τί ἐστιν ἔκπωμα μέγα. μᾶλλον δὲ οὐδὲν δεῖ, ἀλλὰ
φέρε, παῖ,' φάναι, 'τὸν ψυκτῆρα ἐκεῖνον,' ἰδόντα αὐτὸν 214
πλέον ἢ ὀκτὼ κοτύλας χωροῦντα. τοῦτον ἐμπλησάμενον πρῶτον
μὲν αὐτὸν ἐκπιεῖν, ἔπειτα τῷ Σωκράτει κελεύειν ἐγχεῖν καὶ
ἅμα εἰπεῖν· 'πρὸς μὲν Σωκράτη, ὦ ἄνδρες, τὸ σόφισμά μοι
οὐδέν· ὁπόσον γὰρ ἂν κελεύῃ τις, τοσοῦτον ἐκπιὼν οὐδὲν 5
μᾶλλον μή ποτε μεθυσθῇ.'
    τὸν μὲν οὖν Σωκράτη ἐγχέαντος τοῦ παιδὸς πίνειν· τὸν δ'
Ἐρυξίμαχον 'πῶς οὖν, φάναι, ὦ Ἀλκιβιάδη, ποιοῦμεν; οὕτως
οὔτε τι λέγομεν ἐπὶ τῇ κύλικι οὔτε τι ᾄδομεν, ἀλλ' ἀτεχνῶς b
ὥσπερ οἱ διψῶντες πιόμεθα;'
    τὸν οὖν Ἀλκιβιάδην εἰπεῖν 'ὦ Ἐρυξίμαχε, βέλτιστε
βελτίστου πατρὸς καὶ σωφρονεστάτου, χαῖρε.
    'καὶ γὰρ σύ,' φάναι τὸν Ἐρυξίμαχον· 'ἀλλὰ τί ποιῶμεν;' 5
    'ὅτι ἂν σὺ κελεύῃς. δεῖ γάρ σοι πείθεσθαι·
    ἰητρὸς γὰρ ἀνὴρ πολλῶν ἀντάξιος ἄλλων·
ἐπίταττε οὖν ὅτι βούλει.'
    'ἄκουσον δή,' εἰπεῖν τὸν Ἐρυξίμαχον. 'ἡμῖν πρὶν σὲ
εἰσελθεῖν ἔδοξε χρῆναι ἐπὶ δεξιὰ ἕκαστον ἐν μέρει λόγον 10
περὶ Ἔρωτος εἰπεῖν ὡς δύναιτο κάλλιστον, καὶ ἐγκωμιάσαι. οἱ c
μὲν οὖν ἄλλοι πάντες ἡμεῖς εἰρήκαμεν· σὺ δ' ἐπειδὴ οὐκ
εἴρηκας καὶ ἐκπέπωκας, δίκαιος εἶ εἰπεῖν, εἰπὼν δὲ ἐπιτάξαι
Σωκράτει ὅτι ἂν βούλῃ, καὶ τοῦτον τῷ ἐπὶ δεξιὰ καὶ οὕτω
τοὺς ἄλλους.'   5

e 1 ἀναδήσω καὶ p. n: ἀναδησώμεθα n | b 1 οὔτ' ἐπᾴδομεν n

'I'm not making peace with you,' said Alcibiades. 'But for this I'll get my own back on you on another occasion. As for now – [e1] Agathon, give me back some of the ribbons, so that I can crown *this* one's head too, this amazing head, and so he won't hold it against me that I crowned you and didn't crown him, when after all he uses words to defeat everyone in the world, not just the day before yesterday, [e5] like you, but always.' As he said this, he seized some of the ribbons, crowned Socrates, and reclined on the couch.

When he was settled in his place, he said 'Well, gentlemen, what's this? You seem to me to be sober. I obviously can't leave it to you: what we must do is drink, because that's what we agreed. So as person in charge of [e10] drinking, until such time as you drink enough, I elect – myself. Agathon, let someone bring a big cup, if there is one. No, no need – **214** you, slave,' he said, 'bring that wine-cooler,' because he'd seen that it was big enough to hold eight *kotulai*. When he'd had this filled, he first drained it himself, then ordered it refilled for Socrates, saying as he did so 'With Socrates, gentlemen, my [a5] trick gets nowhere at all; however much anyone orders him to drink, he drinks it up without the slightest increase in the chance of his getting drunk.'

Well, the slave refilled the cooler and Socrates drank from it; but Eryximachus said 'So what are we doing here, Alcibiades? Are we really [b1] passing the cup round like this, without doing any talking or any singing? Are we simply going to drink like people with a thirst on them?'

At this Alcibiades said 'Eryximachus! Best of sons to the best and most sensible father – greetings to you!'

[b5] 'And to you,' said Eryximachus; 'but what are we to do?'

'Whatever you order us to do; we have to obey you, "for a medical man is worth as much as many other men together". So give us your instructions.'

'Then listen,' said Eryximachus. 'Before you came [b10] in, we decided that each of us in turn, beginning from the left, should give [c1] a speech about Love, the most beautiful he could manage, by way of an encomium to him. Well, all the rest of us have given ours; since you haven't given yours, and you've finished your drink, the right thing is for you to do it now, and when you've given it, to give any instruction to Socrates you like – and he can then do the same with the person to his right, and so on with [c5] the rest.'

'ἀλλά, ' φάναι, 'ὦ Ἐρυξίμαχε,' τὸν Ἀλκιβιάδην, 'καλῶς μὲν λέγεις, μεθύοντα δὲ ἄνδρα παρὰ νηφόντων λόγους παραβάλλειν μὴ οὐκ ἐξ ἴσου ᾖ. καὶ ἅμα, ὦ μακάριε, πείθει τί σε Σωκράτης ὧν ἄρτι εἶπεν; ἢ οἶσθα ὅτι τοὐναντίον ἐστὶ πᾶν d ἢ ὃ ἔλεγεν; οὗτος γάρ, ἐάν τινα ἐγὼ ἐπαινέσω τούτου παρόντος ἢ θεὸν ἢ ἄνθρωπον ἄλλον ἢ τοῦτον, οὐκ ἀφέξεταί μου τὼ χεῖρε.'

'οὐκ εὐφημήσεις;' φάναι τὸν Σωκράτη. 5

'μὰ τὸν Ποσειδῶ,' εἰπεῖν τὸν Ἀλκιβιάδην, 'μηδὲν λέγε πρὸς ταῦτα, ὡς ἐγὼ οὐδ' ἂν ἕνα ἄλλον ἐπαινέσαιμι σοῦ παρόντος.'

'ἀλλ' οὕτω ποίει,' φάναι τὸν Ἐρυξίμαχον, 'εἰ βούλει· Σωκράτη ἐπαίνεσον.' 10

'πῶς λέγεις;' εἰπεῖν τὸν Ἀλκιβιάδην· 'δοκεῖ χρῆναι, ὦ e Ἐρυξίμαχε; ἐπιθῶμαι τῷ ἀνδρὶ καὶ τιμωρήσωμαι ὑμῶν ἐναντίον;'

'οὗτος,' φάναι τὸν Σωκράτη, 'τί ἐν νῷ ἔχεις; ἐπὶ τὰ γελοιότερά με ἐπαινέσει; ἢ τί ποιήσεις;' 5

'τἀληθῆ ἐρῶ. ἀλλ' ὅρα εἰ παρίης.'

'ἀλλὰ μέντοι', φάναι, 'τά γε ἀληθῆ παρίημι καὶ κελεύω λέγειν.'

'οὐκ ἂν φθάνοιμι,' εἰπεῖν τὸν Ἀλκιβιάδην. 'καὶ μέντοι οὑτωσὶ ποίησον. ἐάν τι μὴ ἀληθὲς λέγω, μεταξὺ ἐπιλαβοῦ, ἂν 10 βούλῃ, καὶ εἰπὲ ὅτι τοῦτο ψεύδομαι· ἑκὼν γὰρ εἶναι οὐδὲν 215 ψεύσομαι. ἐὰν μέντοι ἀναμιμνῃσκόμενος ἄλλο ἄλλοθεν λέγω, μηδὲν θαυμάσῃς· οὐ γάρ τι ῥᾴδιον τὴν σὴν ἀτοπίαν ὧδ' ἔχοντι εὐπόρως καὶ ἐφεξῆς καταριθμῆσαι.

'Σωκράτη δ' ἐγὼ ἐπαινεῖν, ὦ ἄνδρες, οὕτως ἐπιχειρήσω, δι' 5 εἰκόνων. οὗτος μὲν οὖν ἴσως οἰήσεται ἐπὶ τὰ γελοιότερα, ἔσται δ' ἡ εἰκὼν τοῦ ἀληθοῦς ἕνεκα, οὐ τοῦ γελοίου. φημὶ γὰρ δὴ ὁμοιότατον αὐτὸν εἶναι τοῖς σιληνοῖς τούτοις τοῖς ἐν τοῖς ἑρμογλυφείοις καθημένοις, οὕστινας ἐργάζονται οἱ b δημιουργοὶ σύριγγας ἢ αὐλοὺς ἔχοντας, οἳ διχάδε διοιχθέντες φαίνονται ἔνδοθεν ἀγάλματα ἔχοντες θεῶν. καὶ φημὶ αὖ ἐοικέναι αὐτὸν τῷ σατύρῳ τῷ Μαρσύα. ὅτι μὲν οὖν τό γε εἶδος ὅμοιος εἶ τούτοις, ὦ Σώκρατες, οὐδ' αὐτὸς ἄν που 5 ἀμφισβητήσαις· ὡς δὲ καὶ τἆλλα ἔοικας, μετὰ τοῦτο ἄκουε.

e 5 ἐπαινέσει e: ἐπαινέσεις m: ἐπαινέσαι O

'That's a fine suggestion, Eryximachus,' said Alcibiades, 'but I'm afraid it isn't fair to put up a drunken man against speeches from sober ones. And anyway, my fine friend, do you believe any [d1] of what Socrates just said? Or are you aware that the truth is completely the opposite of what he was saying? He's the one that's the problem: if ever I praise anyone in his presence, whether a god or a human being, other than him, he can't stop himself from hitting me.'

[d5] 'Take care what you say!' said Socrates.

'By Poseidon,' responded Alcibiades, 'don't you even try stopping me, because there just isn't anyone else I'd praise in your presence.'

'Then do as you say,' said Eryximachus, 'if you want to; [d10] praise Socrates.'

[e1] 'What do you mean?' said Alcibiades. 'Do you really think I should, Eryximachus? I'm to lay into the man and give him his punishment in front of you all?'

'Hey!' said Socrates. 'What have you got in mind? Will you praise [e5] me to amuse everybody? Or what will you do?'

'I'll tell the truth. Do I have your permission?'

'If it's the truth,' said Socrates, 'I'll certainly let you; indeed I order it.'

'I'll start at once,' replied Alcibiades. 'But there's [e10] a rule I want you to observe: if ever I say anything that isn't true, break in on me then and there, if **215** you like, and say it's untrue, because I shan't deliberately say anything that's not true. However if as I'm speaking my memory gets jumbled up, don't be surprised; it's not at all an easy thing for someone in my condition to recount the details of your strangeness fluently and in the proper order.

[a5] 'The way I'm going to set out to praise Socrates, gentlemen, is through images. Now *he* will probably think it's meant to amuse everybody, but the purpose of the image will in fact be to tell the truth, not to be amusing. I declare that he is most like those silenuses that [b1] sit in the statuary-shops, the ones the craftsmen make, with pipes or *auloi*, and when you open them up by taking them apart, they turn out to have statues of gods inside them. I declare, too, that he's like the satyr Marsyas. Now, that you're like [b5] them in your physical appearance, not even you, Socrates, I imagine, would dispute; but what you're going to hear next is how you

ὑβριστὴς εἶ· ἢ οὔ; ἐὰν γὰρ μὴ ὁμολογῇς, μάρτυρας
παρέξομαι. ἀλλ᾽ οὐκ αὐλητής; πολύ γε θαυμασιώτερος ἐκείνου.
ὁ μέν γε δι᾽ ὀργάνων ἐκήλει τοὺς ἀνθρώπους τῇ ἀπὸ τοῦ
στόματος δυνάμει, καὶ ἔτι νυνὶ ὃς ἂν τὰ ἐκείνου αὐλῇ, ἃ γὰρ c
Ὄλυμπος ηὔλει, Μαρσύου λέγω, τούτου διδάξαντος· τὰ οὖν
ἐκείνου ἐάντε ἀγαθὸς αὐλητὴς αὐλῇ ἐάντε φαύλη αὐλητρίς,
μόνα κατέχεσθαι ποιεῖ καὶ δηλοῖ τοὺς τῶν θεῶν τε καὶ
τελετῶν δεομένους διὰ τὸ θεῖα εἶναι. σὺ δ᾽ ἐκείνου τοσοῦτον 5
μόνον διαφέρεις, ὅτι ἄνευ ὀργάνων ψιλοῖς λόγοις ταὐτὸν
τοῦτο ποιεῖς. ἡμεῖς γοῦν ὅταν μέν του ἄλλου ἀκούωμεν
λέγοντος καὶ πάνυ ἀγαθοῦ ῥήτορος ἄλλους λόγους, οὐδὲν d
μέλει ὡς ἔπος εἰπεῖν οὐδενί· ἐπειδὰν δὲ σοῦ τις ἀκούῃ ἢ τῶν
σῶν λόγων ἄλλου λέγοντος, κἂν πάνυ φαῦλος ᾖ ὁ λέγων,
ἐάντε γυνὴ ἀκούῃ ἐάντε ἀνὴρ ἐάντε μειράκιον, ἐκπεπληγμένοι
ἐσμὲν καὶ κατεχόμεθα. ἐγὼ γοῦν, ὦ ἄνδρες, εἰ μὴ ἔμελλον 5
κομιδῇ δόξειν μεθύειν, εἶπον ὀμόσας ἂν ὑμῖν οἷα δὴ πέπονθα
αὐτὸς ὑπὸ τῶν τούτου λόγων καὶ πάσχω ἔτι καὶ νυνί. ὅταν
γὰρ ἀκούω, πολύ μοι μᾶλλον ἢ τῶν κορυβαντιώντων ἥ τε
καρδία πηδᾷ καὶ δάκρυα ἐκχεῖται ὑπὸ τῶν λόγων τῶν τούτου, e
ὁρῶ δὲ καὶ ἄλλους παμπόλλους τὰ αὐτὰ πάσχοντας·
Περικλέους δὲ ἀκούων καὶ ἄλλων ἀγαθῶν ῥητόρων εὖ μὲν
ἡγούμην λέγειν, τοιοῦτον δ᾽ οὐδὲν ἔπασχον, οὐδ᾽ ἐτεθορύβητό
μου ἡ ψυχὴ οὐδ᾽ ἠγανάκτει ὡς ἀνδραποδωδῶς διακειμένου, 5
ἀλλ᾽ ὑπὸ τουτουῒ τοῦ Μαρσύου πολλάκις δὴ οὕτω διετέθην
ὥστε μοι δόξαι μὴ βιωτὸν εἶναι ἔχοντι ὡς ἔχω. καὶ ταῦτα, ὦ
Σώκρατες, οὐκ ἐρεῖς ὡς οὐκ ἀληθῆ. καὶ ἔτι γε νῦν σύνοιδ᾽ 216
ἐμαυτῷ ὅτι εἰ ἐθέλοιμι παρέχειν τὰ ὦτα, οὐκ ἂν καρτερήσαιμι
ἀλλὰ ταὐτὰ ἂν πάσχοιμι. ἀναγκάζει γάρ με ὁμολογεῖν ὅτι
πολλοῦ ἐνδεὴς ὢν αὐτὸς ἔτι ἐμαυτοῦ μὲν ἀμελῶ, τὰ δ᾽
Ἀθηναίων πράττω. βίᾳ οὖν ὥσπερ ἀπὸ τῶν Σειρήνων 5
ἐπισχόμενος τὰ ὦτα οἴχομαι φεύγων, ἵνα μὴ αὐτοῦ καθήμενος
παρὰ τούτῳ καταγηράσω. πέπονθα δὲ πρὸς τοῦτον μόνον
ἀνθρώπων, ὃ οὐκ ἄν τις οἴοιτο ἐν ἐμοὶ ἐνεῖναι, τὸ
αἰσχύνεσθαι ὁντινοῦν· ἐγὼ δὲ τοῦτον μόνον αἰσχύνομαι. b
σύνοιδα γὰρ ἐμαυτῷ ἀντιλέγειν μὲν οὐ δυναμένῳ ὡς οὐ δεῖ
ποιεῖν ἃ οὗτος κελεύει, ἐπειδὰν δὲ ἀπέλθω, ἡττημένῳ τῆς

c 2 που τοῦ   e

resemble them in everything else too. You're a downright criminal – or do you deny it? If you don't admit it, I shall offer witnesses. So you're not an *aulos*-player? You are, and a much more amazing one than Marsyas. [c1] *He* used to charm people by means of instruments, by the power that came from his mouth, as even now does anyone who plays his compositions on the *aulos* (since what Olympus used to play, I call Marsyas', because Marsyas taught Olympus); his compositions, then, whether it's a good *aulos*-player who's playing them or a sorry *aulos*-girl, [c5] are the only ones that cause the hearer to be possessed, and indicate those who stand in need of the gods and their initiation-rites – both things that they can do because they are divine. You differ from him only to this extent, that you cause the same effect without instruments, [d1] by the use of words on their own. Thus whenever we hear anyone else uttering words of a different sort, even if he's a perfectly good speaker, it's of no concern to practically anyone; but if ever anyone hears you speaking, or your words being spoken by someone else, even if the speaker is extremely poor, [d5] whether it's a woman who's listening or a grown man or a young lad, we're all overwhelmed and possessed. Certainly, gentlemen, if it weren't for the fact that I'd appear totally drunk, I'd have told you on oath the sorts of effects I myself have felt from this man's words, and still feel even now. For [e1] whenever I hear them, I'm in the same state as the Corybantes, only much worse – heart leaping, tears pouring out under the impact of this man's words; and I observe lots of other people too experiencing the same effects. When I listened to Pericles and other good speakers, I thought they were [e5] speaking well, but I felt no effect of *this* sort, nor was my soul in confusion, or angry at the thought that my condition was that of a slave. But because of *this* Marsyas, this one here, I was frequently reduced to **216** thinking that it wasn't worth my living, in the condition I'm in. You can't deny that this is true, Socrates. What's more, even now I'm conscious that if I were prepared to listen to him, I wouldn't be able to resist, and the same things would happen to me. For he forces me [a5] to admit that although there's much that I lack myself, it's myself I neglect, and do the Athenians' business. So I forcibly stop my ears and I'm off, as if I were running away from the Sirens, to prevent my sitting there and growing old beside him. He's the only person in the world [b1] towards whom I have experienced what one wouldn't suppose I had in me – feeling ashamed towards someone, no matter who; it's only towards him that I feel it. For I'm conscious that I'm not capable of arguing against doing what he tells me to

110

τιμῆς τῆς ὑπὸ τῶν πολλῶν. δραπετεύω οὖν αὐτὸν καὶ φεύγω, 5
καὶ ὅταν ἴδω, αἰσχύνομαι τὰ ὡμολογημένα. καὶ πολλάκις μὲν
ἡδέως ἂν ἴδοιμι αὐτὸν μὴ ὄντα ἐν ἀνθρώποις· εἰ δ' αὖ τοῦτο c
γένοιτο, εὖ οἶδα ὅτι πολὺ μεῖζον ἂν ἀχθοίμην, ὥστε οὐκ ἔχω
ὅτι χρήσωμαι τούτῳ τῷ ἀνθρώπῳ.

'καὶ ὑπὸ μὲν δὴ τῶν αὐλημάτων καὶ ἐγὼ καὶ ἄλλοι πολλοὶ
τοιαῦτα πεπόνθασιν ὑπὸ τοῦδε τοῦ σατύρου· ἄλλα δὲ ἐμοῦ 5
ἀκούσατε ὡς ὅμοιός τ' ἐστὶν οἷς ἐγὼ ᾔκασα αὐτὸν καὶ τὴν
δύναμιν ὡς θαυμασίαν ἔχει. εὖ γὰρ ἴστε ὅτι οὐδεὶς ὑμῶν
τοῦτον γιγνώσκει· ἀλλὰ ἐγὼ δηλώσω, ἐπείπερ ἠρξάμην. ὁρᾶτε d
γὰρ ὅτι Σωκράτης ἐρωτικῶς διάκειται τῶν καλῶν καὶ ἀεὶ περὶ
τούτους ἐστὶ καὶ ἐκπέπληκται, καὶ αὖ ἀγνοεῖ πάντα καὶ οὐδὲν
οἶδεν, ὡς τὸ σχῆμα αὐτοῦ. τοῦτο οὐ σιληνῶδες; σφόδρα γε.
τοῦτο γὰρ οὗτος ἔξωθεν περιβέβληται, ὥσπερ ὁ γεγλυμμένος 5
σιληνός· ἔνδοθεν δὲ ἀνοιχθεὶς πόσης οἴεσθε γέμει, ὦ ἄνδρες
συμπόται, σωφροσύνης; ἴστε ὅτι οὔτε εἴ τις καλός ἐστι μέλει
αὐτῷ οὐδέν, ἀλλὰ καταφρονεῖ τοσοῦτον ὅσον οὐδ' ἂν εἷς e
οἰηθείη, οὔτ' εἴ τις πλούσιος, οὔτ' εἰ ἄλλην τινὰ τιμὴν ἔχων
τῶν ὑπὸ πλήθους μακαριζομένων· ἡγεῖται δὲ πάντα ταῦτα τὰ
κτήματα οὐδενὸς ἄξια καὶ ἡμᾶς οὐδὲν εἶναι – λέγω ὑμῖν –
εἰρωνευόμενος δὲ καὶ παίζων πάντα τὸν βίον πρὸς τοὺς 5
ἀνθρώπους διατελεῖ. σπουδάσαντος δὲ αὐτοῦ καὶ ἀνοιχθέντος
οὐκ οἶδα εἴ τις ἑώρακεν τὰ ἐντὸς ἀγάλματα· ἀλλ' ἐγὼ ἤδη
ποτ' εἶδον, καί μοι ἔδοξεν οὕτω θεῖα καὶ χρυσᾶ
εἶναι καὶ πάγκαλα καὶ θαυμαστά, ὥστε ποιητέον εἶναι 217
ἔμβραχυ ὅτι κελεύοι Σωκράτης. ἡγούμενος δὲ αὐτὸν
ἐσπουδακέναι ἐπὶ τῇ ἐμῇ ὥρᾳ ἕρμαιον ἡγησάμην εἶναι καὶ
εὐτύχημα ἐμὸν θαυμαστόν, ὡς ὑπάρχον μοι χαρισαμένῳ
Σωκράτει πάντ' ἀκοῦσαι ὅσαπερ οὗτος ᾔδει· ἐφρόνουν γὰρ δὴ 5
ἐπὶ τῇ ὥρᾳ θαυμάσιον ὅσον. ταῦτα οὖν διανοηθείς, πρὸ τοῦ
οὐκ εἰωθὼς ἄνευ ἀκολούθου μόνος μετ' αὐτοῦ γίγνεσθαι, τότε
ἀποπέμπων τὸν ἀκόλουθον μόνος συνεγιγνόμην (δεῖ γὰρ πρὸς b
ὑμᾶς πάντα τἀληθῆ εἰπεῖν· ἀλλὰ προσέχετε τὸν νοῦν, καὶ εἰ
ψεύδομαι, Σώκρατες, ἐξέλεγχε)· συνεγιγνόμην γάρ, ὦ ἄνδρες,
μόνος μόνῳ, καὶ ᾤμην αὐτίκα διαλέξεσθαι αὐτόν μοι ἅπερ ἂν
ἐραστὴς παιδικοῖς ἐν ἐρημίᾳ διαλεχθείη, καὶ ἔχαιρον. τούτων 5

a 2 ἔμβραχυ e: ἐν βραχεῖ m

do, and that whenever I leave him, I'm giving in to my desire for the [b5] honour that comes from ordinary people. In any case I'm off and away from him like a runaway slave, and when I see him I'm ashamed because of what's been agreed between us. Often [c1] I'd happily see him gone from this world; but then, if that were to happen, I'm well aware that my grief would be much greater, and so I just don't know what to do with this man.

'These then are the sorts of effects that the pipings of this satyr [c5] have had both on me and on many other people; now I'm going to tell you other things that show both how he resembles the figures I compared him to, and how amazing his power is. Believe you me, not one of you [d1] knows him; now that I've started, I'll show you. You see for yourselves that Socrates is in love with beautiful young men and is always around them, and overwhelmed; and again that he's ignorant of everything and knows nothing, so far as his appearance goes. Isn't this silenus-like? It certainly [d5] is. All of this is his outside covering, like that of the sculpted silenus; but inside, when he's opened up, you just couldn't imagine how completely full he is, fellow-drinkers, of moderation. I assure you it doesn't matter to him [e1] at all if a person is beautiful, which he looks down on to a greater degree than anyone could possibly suppose, nor if he's rich, nor if he possesses anything else that gives a man honour in the eyes of ordinary people and makes them call him blessed. He thinks that all these possessions are worthless, and that we are nothing, [e5] I tell you, and spends his whole life continually pretending and playing with people. But as soon as he comes to be in earnest, and he's opened up – I don't know if any one of you has seen the statues inside, but I *did* once see them, and they appeared to me so divine, golden, **217** so outstandingly beautiful and amazing, that I had to do, in short, whatever Socrates told me to do. Thinking that he was seriously attracted by the way I looked at my age, I thought it a real piece of luck and amazingly fortunate for me, because I was in a position to hear [a5] from Socrates everything he knew if I granted him my favours; I was amazingly proud of the way I looked. With these thoughts in my mind, whereas before it wasn't my habit to be on my own with him without an attendant, I now started sending my attendant away and getting together with Socrates on my own (I've got to [b1] tell you the whole truth: pay proper attention, you people, and Socrates, *you* challenge me if I say anything that's not true); yes, I'd be with him, gentlemen, I on my own and him on his own, and I'd be contentedly thinking that he'd immediately have the conversation with me [b5] that a lover would

112

δ' οὐ μάλα ἐγίγνετο οὐδέν, ἀλλ' ὥσπερ εἰώθει διαλεχθεὶς ἄν μοι καὶ συνημερεύσας ᾤχετο ἀπιών. μετὰ ταῦτα συγγυμνάζεσθαι προυκαλούμην αὐτὸν καὶ συνεγυμναζόμην, ὥς c τι ἐνταῦθα περανῶν. συνεγυμνάζετο οὖν μοι καὶ προσεπάλαιεν πολλάκις οὐδενὸς παρόντος· καὶ τί δεῖ λέγειν; οὐδὲν γάρ μοι πλέον ἦν. ἐπειδὴ δὲ οὐδαμῆ ταύτῃ ἤνυτον, ἔδοξέ μοι ἐπιθετέον εἶναι τῷ ἀνδρὶ κατὰ τὸ καρτερὸν καὶ οὐκ ἀνετέον, 5 ἐπειδήπερ ἐνεκεχειρήκη, ἀλλὰ ἰστέον ἤδη τί ἐστι τὸ πρᾶγμα. προκαλοῦμαι δὴ αὐτὸν πρὸς τὸ συνδειπνεῖν, ἀτεχνῶς ὥσπερ ἐραστὴς παιδικοῖς ἐπιβουλεύων. καί μοι οὐδὲ τοῦτο ταχὺ d ὑπήκουσεν, ὅμως δ' οὖν χρόνῳ ἐπείσθη. ἐπειδὴ δὲ ἀφίκετο τὸ πρῶτον, δειπνήσας ἀπιέναι ἐβούλετο. καὶ τότε μὲν αἰσχυνόμενος ἀφῆκα αὐτόν· αὖθις δ' ἐπιβουλεύσας, ἐπειδὴ ἐδεδειπνήκεμεν διελεγόμην ἀεὶ πόρρω τῶν νυκτῶν, καὶ ἐπειδὴ 5 ἐβούλετο ἀπιέναι, σκηπτόμενος ὅτι ὀψὲ εἴη, προσηνάγκασα αὐτὸν μένειν. ἀνεπαύετο οὖν ἐν τῇ ἐχομένῃ ἐμοῦ κλίνῃ, ἐν ᾗπερ ἐδείπνει, καὶ οὐδεὶς ἐν τῷ οἰκήματι ἄλλος καθηῦδεν ἢ ἡμεῖς. μέχρι μὲν οὖν δὴ δεῦρο τοῦ λόγου καλῶς ἂν ἔχοι καὶ e πρὸς ὁντινοῦν λέγειν· τὸ δ' ἐντεῦθεν οὐκ ἄν μου ἠκούσατε λέγοντος, εἰ μὴ πρῶτον μέν, τὸ λεγόμενον, οἶνος ἄνευ τε παίδων καὶ μετὰ παίδων ἦν ἀληθής, ἔπειτα ἀφανίσαι Σωκράτους ἔργον ὑπερήφανον εἰς ἔπαινον ἐλθόντα ἄδικόν μοι 5 φαίνεται. ἔτι δὲ τὸ τοῦ δηχθέντος ὑπὸ τοῦ ἔχεως πάθος κἄμ' ἔχει. φασὶ γάρ πού τινα τοῦτο παθόντα οὐκ ἐθέλειν λέγειν οἷον ἦν πλὴν τοῖς δεδηγμένοις, ὡς μόνοις γνωσομένοις τε καὶ 218 συγγνωσομένοις εἰ πᾶν ἐτόλμα δρᾶν τε καὶ λέγειν ὑπὸ τῆς ὀδύνης. ἐγὼ οὖν δεδηγμένος τε ὑπὸ ἀλγεινοτέρου καὶ τὸ ἀλγεινότατον ὧν ἄν τις δηχθείη – τὴν καρδίαν γὰρ ἢ ψυχὴν ἢ ὅτι δεῖ αὐτὸ ὀνομάσαι πληγείς τε καὶ δηχθεὶς ὑπὸ τῶν ἐν 5 φιλοσοφίᾳ λόγων, οἳ ἔχονται ἐχίδνης ἀγριώτερον, νέου ψυχῆς μὴ ἀφυοῦς ὅταν λάβωνται, καὶ ποιοῦσι δρᾶν τε καὶ λέγειν ὁτιοῦν – καὶ ὁρῶν αὖ Φαίδρους, Ἀγάθωνας, Ἐρυξιμάχους, b Παυσανίας, Ἀριστοδήμους τε καὶ Ἀριστοφάνας – Σωκράτη δὲ αὐτὸν τί δεῖ λέγειν, καὶ ὅσοι ἄλλοι; πάντες γὰρ κεκοινωνήκατε τῆς φιλοσόφου μανίας τε καὶ βακχείας. διὸ πάντες ἀκούσεσθε· συγγνώσεσθε γὰρ τοῖς τε τότε πραχθεῖσι 5

d 5 ἐδεδειπνήκεμεν   e: δεδειπνήκαμεν   t: ἐδεδειπνήκει   m Ι ἀεὶ πόρρω   t: πόρρω   p.m

have with a beloved when no one was there. But I tell you *nothing* of that sort happened at all, but he would have his habitual kind of conversation with me, and after spending the day with me he'd be off. After this [c1] I used to invite him to exercise with me, and I actually did exercise with him, thinking I'd get somewhere that way. Well, he exercised with me, and wrestled with me on many occasions with no one else there – and what can I say? I was no further forward. Since I was achieving absolutely nothing by these methods, I decided [c5] I had to try a direct assault on the man, and not give up, since I'd started the whole business; I just had to know what the matter was. So I invited him to dine with me, just as if [d1] I were a lover plotting to have his way with his beloved. He wasn't quick to accept this invitation from me either, but still in the end he said he'd come. When he came the first time, he wanted to leave immediately after dinner. On that occasion, I was ashamed not to let him go; but then I laid a new plot, and on the next occasion after [d5] we'd had dinner I kept the conversation going further and further into the night, and when he wanted to go, I used the excuse that it was late, and forced him to stay. Well, he settled down on the couch next to mine, the one on which he had dinner, and no one was sleeping in the house except [e1] us. Now up to this point in my account it could all perfectly well be told to anyone; but as for the next bit, you wouldn't have heard it from me, if first of all – as the saying goes – the truth weren't in the wine, whether without slaves present or with them, and secondly it seems to me [e5] unfair when one's involved in praising Socrates to leave a proud achievement of his in obscurity. What's more, I'm feeling what people feel when they've been bitten by the snake. I think they say that someone who's had this experience won't say **218** what it was like except to others who've been bitten, because only they will understand and be forgiving if in fact the pain caused them to lose any inhibition about what they did and said. Well, as for me, bitten as I've been by something more painful, and in the most painful place one could be bitten – because it's in my heart, or my soul, [a5] or whatever one's supposed to call it, that I've been stricken and bitten by the words that philosophy brings with her, which bite into you more fiercely than a snake, whenever they fasten onto a young man's soul that isn't without natural endowment, and make you do or say [b1] anything whatever; and then, seeing the likes of Phaedrus, Agathon, Eryximachus, Pausanias, Aristodemus and Aristophanes – and of course there's Socrates himself, and the rest of you: you've all shared in the madness and Bacchic frenzy of philosophy. That's why [b5] I'm going to tell you my story, because you'll forgive both

114

καὶ τοῖς νῦν λεγομένοις. οἱ δὲ οἰκέται, καὶ εἴ τις ἄλλος
ἐστὶν βέβηλός τε καὶ ἄγροικος, πύλας πάνυ μεγάλας τοῖς
ὠσὶν ἐπίθεσθε.

'ἐπειδὴ γὰρ οὖν, ὦ ἄνδρες, ὅ τε λύχνος ἀπεσβήκει καὶ οἱ
παῖδες ἔξω ἦσαν, ἔδοξέ μοι χρῆναι μηδὲν ποικίλλειν πρὸς c
αὐτόν, ἀλλ᾽ ἐλευθέρως εἰπεῖν ἅ μοι ἐδόκει· καὶ εἶπον κινήσας
αὐτόν, " Σώκρατες, καθεύδεις;"
'" οὐ δῆτα, ἦ δ᾽ ὅς."
'" οἶσθα οὖν ἅ μοι δέδοκται;"   5
'" τί μάλιστα;" ἔφη.
'" σὺ ἐμοὶ δοκεῖς", ἦν δ᾽ ἐγώ, "ἐμοῦ ἐραστὴς ἄξιος
γεγονέναι μόνος, καί μοι φαίνῃ ὀκνεῖν μνησθῆναι πρός με.
ἐγὼ δὲ οὑτωσὶ ἔχω· πάνυ ἀνόητον ἡγοῦμαι εἶναι σοὶ μὴ οὐ
καὶ τοῦτο χαρίζεσθαι καὶ εἴ τι ἄλλο ἢ τῆς οὐσίας τῆς ἐμῆς 10
δέοιο ἢ τῶν φίλων τῶν ἐμῶν. ἐμοὶ μὲν γὰρ οὐδέν ἐστι d
πρεσβύτερον τοῦ ὡς ὅτι βέλτιστον ἐμὲ γενέσθαι, τούτου δὲ
οἶμαί μοι συλλήπτορα οὐδένα κυριώτερον εἶναι σοῦ. ἐγὼ δὴ
τοιούτῳ ἀνδρὶ πολὺ μᾶλλον ἂν μὴ χαριζόμενος αἰσχυνοίμην
τοὺς φρονίμους, ἢ χαριζόμενος τούς τε πολλοὺς καὶ 5
ἄφρονας."

'καὶ οὗτος ἀκούσας μάλα εἰρωνικῶς καὶ σφόδρα ἑαυτοῦ τε
καὶ εἰωθότως ἔλεξεν "ὦ φίλε Ἀλκιβιάδη, κινδυνεύεις τῷ ὄντι
οὐ φαῦλος εἶναι, εἴπερ ἀληθῆ τυγχάνει ὄντα ἅ λέγεις περὶ e
ἐμοῦ, καί τις ἔστ᾽ ἐν ἐμοὶ δύναμις δι᾽ ἧς ἂν σὺ γένοιο
ἀμείνων· ἀμήχανόν τοι κάλλος ὁρῴης ἂν ἐν ἐμοὶ καὶ τῆς
παρὰ σοὶ εὐμορφίας πάμπολυ διαφέρον. εἰ δὴ καθορῶν αὐτὸ
κοινώσασθαί τέ μοι ἐπιχειρεῖς καὶ ἀλλάξασθαι κάλλος ἀντὶ 5
κάλλους, οὐκ ὀλίγῳ μου πλεονεκτεῖν διανοῇ, ἀλλ᾽ ἀντὶ δόξης
ἀλήθειαν καλῶν κτᾶσθαι ἐπιχειρεῖς καὶ τῷ ὄντι 'χρύσεα 219
χαλκείων' διαμείβεσθαι νοεῖς. ἀλλ᾽, ὦ μακάριε, ἄμεινον
σκόπει, μή σε λανθάνω οὐδὲν ὤν. ἤ τοι τῆς διανοίας ὄψις
ἄρχεται ὀξὺ βλέπειν ὅταν ἡ τῶν ὀμμάτων τῆς ἀκμῆς λήγειν
†ἐπιχειρῇ· σὺ δὲ τούτων ἔτι πόρρω."   5

'κἀγὼ ἀκούσας, "τὰ μὲν παρ᾽ ἐμοῦ", ἔφην, "ταῦτά ἐστιν,
ὧν οὐδὲν ἄλλως εἴρηται ἢ ὡς διανοοῦμαι· σὺ δὲ αὐτὸς οὕτω
βουλεύου ὅτι σοί τε ἄριστον καὶ ἐμοὶ ἡγῇ."

a 4-5 λήγειν ἐπιχειρῇ m: ἐπιλείπῃ e | a 6 παρ᾽ ἐμοῦ p, n: παρ᾽ ἐμοί n |
a 8 σοι τε οτι αριστον p

what I did then and what I'm saying now. You slaves – and anyone else here who's uninitiated and a boor – fit some biggish doors to your ears.

'Well, gentlemen, it was like this: when the lamp had been put out, and the [c1] slaves were out of the room, I decided that there was no point at all in my beating about the bush with him, and that I should freely express what I was thinking; so I gave him a nudge, and said "Socrates, are you asleep?"

'"I'm certainly not," he said.

[c5] '"Well, do you know what I've decided?"

'"What exactly?" he said.

'"You seem to me", I said, "to be the only worthy lover I've had, and you give me the impression of being shy about mentioning the subject to me. My position is as follows: I consider it quite senseless not to [c10] gratify you both in this matter and in anything else that you might ask for, from my [d1] property or my friends'. For me there's nothing more important than my becoming as good a person as possible, and in this I don't think there's any more effective collaborator for me than you. I'd feel much more shame towards people of good sense if I didn't gratify [d5] such a man than I'd feel, towards the many who have no sense, for doing it."

'He listened to me, and with great pretence of seriousness, quite in his characteristic and usual fashion, he said "My dear Alcibiades, you must really [e1] be a person of no mean quality, if indeed what you say about me is actually true, and there is in me some power which could make you a better man; it'd be an irresistible beauty that you were observing in me, and one altogether superior to your own fine looks. If then because you see it [e5] you're trying to enter into partnership with me and exchange beauty for beauty, you're meaning to get the better of me in no small way; you're trying **219** to get hold of truly beautiful things in return for only apparently beautiful ones, and you have in mind a true exchange of 'gold for bronze'. But you need to take a better look, my fine friend, in case you're mistaken about me, and I'm really nothing. The sight of the mind, I assure you, first sees sharply when the sight of the eyes starts [?] to fade [a5] from its prime; and you are still far away from that."

'When I heard this, I said "On my side, things are as I've said – I've told you exactly what's in my mind; it's for you yourself, in that case, to think out what you believe is best for you and for me."

116

'"ἀλλ'", ἔφη, "τοῦτό γ' εὖ λέγεις· ἐν γὰρ τῷ ἐπιόντι χρόνῳ βουλευόμενοι πράξομεν ὃ ἂν φαίνηται νῷν περί τε b τούτων καὶ περὶ τῶν ἄλλων ἄριστον."

ἐγὼ μὲν δὴ ταῦτα ἀκούσας τε καὶ εἰπών, καὶ ἀφεὶς ὥσπερ βέλη, τετρῶσθαι αὐτὸν ᾤμην· καὶ ἀναστάς γε, οὐδ' ἐπιτρέψας τούτῳ εἰπεῖν οὐδὲν ἔτι, ἀμφιέσας τὸ ἱμάτιον τὸ 5 ἐμαυτοῦ τοῦτον (καὶ γὰρ ἦν χειμών) ὑπὸ τὸν τρίβωνα κατακλινεὶς τὸν τουτουί, περιβαλὼν τὼ χεῖρε τούτῳ τῷ δαιμονίῳ ὡς ἀληθῶς καὶ θαυμαστῷ, κατεκείμην τὴν νύκτα c ὅλην. καὶ οὐδὲ ταῦτα αὖ, ὦ Σώκρατες, ἐρεῖς ὅτι ψεύδομαι. ποιήσαντος δὲ δὴ ταῦτα ἐμοῦ οὗτος τοσοῦτον περιεγένετό τε καὶ κατεφρόνησεν καὶ κατεγέλασεν τῆς ἐμῆς ὥρας καὶ ὕβρισεν – καὶ περὶ ἐκεῖνό γε ᾤμην τὶ εἶναι, ὦ ἄνδρες 5 δικασταί· δικασταὶ γάρ ἐστε τῆς Σωκράτους ὑπερηφανίας. εὖ γὰρ ἴστε μὰ θεούς, μὰ θεάς, οὐδὲν περιττότερον καταδεδαρθηκὼς ἀνέστην μετὰ Σωκράτους, ἢ εἰ μετὰ πατρὸς d καθηῦδον ἢ ἀδελφοῦ πρεσβυτέρου.

τὸ δὴ μετὰ τοῦτο τίνα οἴεσθέ με διάνοιαν ἔχειν, ἡγούμενον μὲν ἠτιμάσθαι, ἀγάμενον δὲ τὴν τούτου φύσιν τε καὶ σωφροσύνην καὶ ἀνδρείαν, ἐντετυχηκότα ἀνθρώπῳ τοιούτῳ 5 οἵῳ ἐγὼ οὐκ ἂν ᾤμην ποτ' ἐντυχεῖν εἰς φρόνησιν καὶ εἰς καρτερίαν; ὥστε οὔθ' ὅπως οὖν ὀργιζοίμην εἶχον καὶ ἀποστερηθείην τῆς τούτου συνουσίας, οὔτε ὅπῃ προσαγαγοίμην αὐτὸν ηὐπόρουν. εὖ γὰρ ἤδη ὅτι χρήμασί γε e πολὺ μᾶλλον ἄτρωτος ἦν πανταχῇ ἢ σιδήρῳ ὁ Αἴας, ᾧ τε ᾤμην αὐτὸν μόνῳ ἁλώσεσθαι, διεπεφεύγει με. ἠπόρουν δή, καταδεδουλωμένος τε ὑπὸ τοῦ ἀνθρώπου ὡς οὐδεὶς ὑπ' οὐδενὸς ἄλλου περιῇα. ταῦτά τε γάρ μοι ἅπαντα προυγεγόνει, 5 καὶ μετὰ ταῦτα στρατεία ἡμῖν εἰς Ποτείδαιαν ἐγένετο κοινὴ καὶ συνεσιτοῦμεν ἐκεῖ. πρῶτον μὲν οὖν τοῖς πόνοις οὐ μόνον ἐμοῦ περιῆν, ἀλλὰ καὶ τῶν ἄλλων ἁπάντων· ὁπότ' ἀναγκασθεῖμεν ἀποληφθέντες που, οἷα δὴ ἐπὶ στρατείας, 220 ἀσιτεῖν, οὐδὲν ἦσαν οἱ ἄλλοι πρὸς τὸ καρτερεῖν· ἔν τ' αὖ ταῖς εὐωχίαις μόνος ἀπολαύειν οἷός τ' ἦν τά τ' ἄλλα καὶ πίνειν οὐκ ἐθέλων, ὁπότε ἀναγκασθείη, πάντας ἐκράτει, καὶ ὃ

b 4 βέλει p. n | d 7 καρτερίαν m:]κρατειαν p | a 1 ἀποληφθέντες e: ἀπολειφθέντες m

'"Now that's a good suggestion," he said; "from now [b1] on we'll think things out and do whatever appears to the two of us to be best, both in relation to the present situation and in relation to everything else."

'Well then, when I'd heard this response to what I'd said, and having as it were loosed off my arrows, I thought he'd been hit; so I got up, and not [b5] giving him the chance to say any more, I put my himation around him (it was winter), lay down under the short cloak he – this person here – had over him, threw my arms around this [c1] truly superhuman and amazing man, and lay there all night long. You won't tell me I'm saying anything untrue here either, Socrates. Well, when I'd done all that, this man so much got the better of me, looked down on me, laughed at my beauty, [c5] treated it criminally – and it was just in *that* respect that I thought I was something, gentlemen of the jury; for it's up to you to judge Socrates' arrogance. You have my word for it, by the gods, and by the goddesses too: I got up in the morning having [d1] slept with Socrates in a way not the slightest bit more out of the ordinary than if I'd been sleeping with my father or elder brother.

'What state of mind do you think I was in after that: on the one hand thinking I'd been humiliated, on the other admiring the man for his nature, [d5] his self-control and courage, because I'd come across a person with the sort of wisdom and capacity for endurance I thought I'd never encounter? The result was that I couldn't be angry – how could I? – and deprive myself of being with this man, and yet I didn't have any idea, either, [e1] how to win him over. I knew perfectly well that he was much more completely invulnerable to money than Ajax was to iron weapons, and as for the single thing I thought I'd catch him with, he'd already evaded me. So I was at a loss, and I went round in a state of enslavement to this person unlike [e5] anyone's to anyone else. For after all of these things had happened to me, we served together on the expedition to Potidaea, and shared the same mess. The first point is that he put up with the hardships involved not only better than I did but better than everyone else: whenever **220** we were forced to go without food, as often happens on campaign, because we were cut off somewhere, the rest of them were nowhere in respect of endurance; and when it was a matter of feasting he was the only one able to take proper advantage of it, and in particular, at drinking when he didn't want to, whenever he was forced to, he

118

πάντων θαυμαστότατον, Σωκράτη μεθύοντα οὐδεὶς πώποτε 5
ἑώρακεν ἀνθρώπων. τούτου μὲν οὖν μοι δοκεῖ καὶ αὐτίκα ὁ
ἔλεγχος ἔσεσθαι. πρὸς δὲ αὖ τὰς τοῦ χειμῶνος καρτερήσεις
(δεινοὶ γὰρ αὐτόθι χειμῶνες) θαυμάσια ἠργάζετο τά τε ἄλλα,
καὶ ποτε ὄντος πάγου οἵου δεινοτάτου, καὶ πάντων ἢ οὐκ b
ἐξιόντων ἔνδοθεν, ἢ εἴ τις ἐξίοι, ἠμφιεσμένων τε θαυμαστὰ
δὴ ὅσα καὶ ὑποδεδεμένων καὶ ἐνειλιγμένων τοὺς πόδας εἰς
πίλους καὶ ἀρνακίδας, οὗτος δ' ἐν τούτοις ἐξῄει ἔχων ἱμάτιον
μὲν τοιοῦτον οἷόνπερ καὶ πρότερον εἰώθει φορεῖν, ἀνυπόδητος 5
δὲ διὰ τοῦ κρυστάλλου ῥᾷον ἐπορεύετο ἢ οἱ ἄλλοι
ὑποδεδεμένοι, οἱ δὲ στρατιῶται ὑπέβλεπον αὐτὸν ὡς
καταφρονοῦντα σφῶν. καὶ ταῦτα μὲν δὴ ταῦτα· c

οἷον δ' αὖ τόδ' ἔρεξε καὶ ἔτλη καρτερὸς ἀνὴρ
ἐκεῖ ποτε ἐπὶ στρατείας, ἄξιον ἀκοῦσαι. συννοήσας γὰρ
αὐτόθι ἑωθέν τι εἱστήκει σκοπῶν, καὶ ἐπειδὴ οὐ προυχώρει
αὐτῷ, οὐκ ἀνίει ἀλλὰ εἱστήκει ζητῶν. καὶ ἤδη ἦν μεσημβρία, 5
καὶ ἄνθρωποι ᾐσθάνοντο, καὶ θαυμάζοντες ἄλλος ἄλλῳ ἔλεγεν
ὅτι Σωκράτης ἐξ ἑωθινοῦ φροντίζων τι ἕστηκε. τελευτῶντες
δέ τινες τῶν Ἰώνων, ἐπειδὴ ἑσπέρα ἦν, δειπνήσαντες (καὶ d
γὰρ θέρος τότε γ' ἦν) χαμεύνια ἐξενεγκάμενοι ἅμα μὲν ἐν τῷ
ψύχει καθηῦδον, ἅμα δ' ἐφύλαττον αὐτὸν εἰ καὶ τὴν νύκτα
ἑστήξοι. ὁ δὲ εἱστήκει μέχρι ἕως ἐγένετο καὶ ἥλιος ἀνέσχεν·
ἔπειτα ᾤχετ' ἀπιὼν προσευξάμενος τῷ ἡλίῳ. εἰ δὲ βούλεσθε 5
ἐν ταῖς μάχαις (τοῦτο γὰρ δὴ δίκαιόν γε αὐτῷ ἀποδοῦναι)·
ὅτε γὰρ ἡ μάχη ἦν ἐξ ἧς ἐμοὶ καὶ τἀριστεῖα ἔδοσαν οἱ
στρατηγοί, οὐδεὶς ἄλλος ἐμὲ ἔσωσεν ἀνθρώπων ἢ οὗτος,
τετρωμένον οὐκ ἐθέλων ἀπολιπεῖν, ἀλλὰ συνδιέσωσε καὶ τὰ e
ὅπλα καὶ αὐτὸν ἐμέ. καὶ ἐγὼ μέν, ὦ Σώκρατες, καὶ τότε
ἐκέλευον σοὶ διδόναι τἀριστεῖα τοὺς στρατηγούς, καὶ τοῦτό
γέ μοι οὔτε μέμψῃ οὔτε ἐρεῖς ὅτι ψεύδομαι· ἀλλὰ γὰρ τῶν
στρατηγῶν πρὸς τὸ ἐμὸν ἀξίωμα ἀποβλεπόντων καὶ 5
βουλομένων ἐμοὶ διδόναι τἀριστεῖα, αὐτὸς προθυμότερος
ἐγένου τῶν στρατηγῶν ἐμὲ λαβεῖν ἢ σαυτόν. ἔτι τοίνυν, ὦ
ἄνδρες, ἄξιον ἦν θεάσασθαι Σωκράτη, ὅτε ἀπὸ Δηλίου φυγῇ 221
ἀνεχώρει τὸ στρατόπεδον· ἔτυχον γὰρ παραγενόμενος ἵππον

a 5 θαυμασιωτατον p | b 1 ἢ οὐκ p, n: οὐκ n | b 4 οὗτος δ' m:
οὗτος p | d 5-6 βουλεσθε και εν p

beat everyone – and what's [a5] most amazing of all is that no person on earth has ever yet seen Socrates drunk. That, I think, will be put to the test any time now. Again, as for feats of endurance in the cold of winter (the winters there are terrible), he did amazing things, particularly [b1] on one occasion, when there was the most terrible frost, and when everyone either didn't go outside at all, or if they did, did so wearing amazing quantities of clothing, and not just with shoes on, but with their feet wrapped up in felt and fleeces – well, *he* went out among them wearing a himation [b5] of the sort he'd been used to wearing even before it was so cold, and because he was barefoot he crossed the ice more easily than the rest with things on their feet, which made the soldiers look askance at him because they thought [c1] he was looking down on them. So much for that; but "what a thing *this* was that our enduring hero dared to do", there on the campaign, is a story worth hearing. There he was at daybreak with something on his mind, standing and reflecting on it; and when he couldn't make progress [c5] with it, he didn't give up but stood there looking for a way forward. By now it was midday, and people began to notice him; amazed, they told each other that Socrates had been standing there thinking about something since dawn. Finally [d1] when evening came some of the Ionians, after they'd finished their evening meal, took palliasses outside (it was summer at the time) and slept there in the cool, at the same time looking out to see if he'd stand there all night too. And so he did – stand there, until dawn came and the sun rose; [d5] then, with a prayer to the sun, he went off. Or again, in the battles (it's only right to pay him tribute for this) – when there was the battle which resulted in the generals actually giving the prize for valour to me, it was this man, and no one else, who saved my life, [e1] because he wasn't prepared to desert me when I'd been wounded; he succeeded in getting both my weapons and armour and myself to safety. At the time, Socrates, I did in fact urge the generals to give the prize to you – here you won't either blame me, or say I'm not telling the truth; but actually, when the [e5] generals took regard of my standing in society and proposed to give me the prize, you were more eager than the generals that I should get it rather than yourself. Then again, **221** gentlemen, it was worth just seeing Socrates, when the army was withdrawing in retreat from Delium; I happened to be there as a cavalryman,

120

ἔχων, οὗτος δὲ ὅπλα. ἀνεχώρει οὖν ἐσκεδασμένων ἤδη τῶν
ἀνθρώπων οὗτός τε ἅμα καὶ Λάχης· καὶ ἐγὼ περιτυγχάνω, καὶ
ἰδὼν εὐθὺς παρακελεύομαί τε αὐτοῖν θαρρεῖν, καὶ ἔλεγον ὅτι 5
οὐκ ἀπολείψω αὐτώ. ἐνταῦθα δὴ καὶ κάλλιον ἐθεασάμην
Σωκράτη ἢ ἐν Ποτειδαίᾳ (αὐτὸς γὰρ ἧττον ἐν φόβῳ ἦ διὰ τὸ
ἐφ’ ἵππου εἶναι), πρῶτον μὲν ὅσον περιῆν Λάχητος τῷ ἔμφρων
εἶναι· ἔπειτα ἔμοιγ’ ἐδόκει, ὦ Ἀριστόφανες, τὸ σὸν δὴ τοῦτο, b
καὶ ἐκεῖ διαπορεύεσθαι ὥσπερ καὶ ἐνθάδε, "βρενθυόμενος καὶ
τὠφθαλμὼ παραβάλλων", ἠρέμα παρασκοπῶν καὶ τοὺς φιλίους
καὶ τοὺς πολεμίους, δῆλος ὢν παντὶ καὶ πάνυ πόρρωθεν ὅτι εἴ
τις ἅψεται τούτου τοῦ ἀνδρός, μάλα ἐρρωμένως ἀμυνεῖται. διὸ 5
καὶ ἀσφαλῶς ἀπῄει καὶ οὗτος καὶ ὁ ἑταῖρος· σχεδὸν γάρ τι
τῶν οὕτω διακειμένων ἐν τῷ πολέμῳ οὐδὲ ἅπτονται, ἀλλὰ
τοὺς προτροπάδην φεύγοντας διώκουσιν.   c

'πολλὰ μὲν οὖν ἄν τις καὶ ἄλλα ἔχοι Σωκράτη ἐπαινέσαι
καὶ θαυμάσια· ἀλλὰ τῶν μὲν ἄλλων ἐπιτηδευμάτων τάχ’ ἄν
τις καὶ περὶ ἄλλου τοιαῦτα εἴποι, τὸ δὲ μηδενὶ ἀνθρώπων
ὅμοιον εἶναι, μήτε τῶν παλαιῶν μήτε τῶν νῦν ὄντων, τοῦτο 5
ἄξιον παντὸς θαύματος. οἷος γὰρ Ἀχιλλεὺς ἐγένετο,
ἀπεικάσειεν ἄν τις καὶ Βρασίδαν καὶ ἄλλους, καὶ οἷος αὖ
Περικλῆς, καὶ Νέστορα καὶ Ἀντήνορα (εἰσὶ δὲ καὶ ἕτεροι), καὶ d
τοὺς ἄλλους κατὰ ταῦτ’ ἄν τις ἀπεικάζοι· οἷος δὲ οὑτοσὶ
γέγονε τὴν ἀτοπίαν ἄνθρωπος, καὶ αὐτὸς καὶ οἱ λόγοι αὐτοῦ,
οὐδ’ ἐγγὺς ἂν εὕροι τις ζητῶν, οὔτε τῶν νῦν οὔτε τῶν
παλαιῶν, εἰ μὴ ἄρα εἰ οἷς ἐγὼ λέγω ἀπεικάζοι τις αὐτόν, 5
ἀνθρώπων μὲν μηδενί, τοῖς δὲ σιληνοῖς καὶ σατύροις, αὐτὸν
καὶ τοὺς λόγους.

'καὶ γὰρ οὖν καὶ τοῦτο ἐν τοῖς πρώτοις παρέλιπον, ὅτι
καὶ οἱ λόγοι αὐτοῦ ὁμοιότατοί εἰσι τοῖς σιληνοῖς τοῖς
διοιγομένοις. εἰ γὰρ ἐθέλοι τις τῶν Σωκράτους ἀκούειν λόγων, e
φανεῖεν ἂν πάνυ γελοῖοι τὸ πρῶτον· τοιαῦτα καὶ ὀνόματα καὶ
ῥήματα ἔξωθεν περιαμπέχονται, σατύρου δή τινα ὑβριστοῦ
δοράν. ὄνους γὰρ κανθηλίους λέγει καὶ χαλκέας τινὰς καὶ
σκυτοτόμους καὶ βυρσοδέψας, καὶ ἀεὶ διὰ τῶν αὐτῶν τὰ αὐτὰ 5
φαίνεται λέγειν, ὥστε ἄπειρος καὶ ἀνόητος ἄνθρωπος πᾶς ἂν
τῶν λόγων καταγελάσειεν. διοιγομένους δὲ ἰδὼν ἄν τις καὶ 222

b 3 φίλους p | b5 αψαιτο p | b 6 οὗτος m: αυτος p | ἑταῖρος t:
ἕτερος p. m | d 5 ἄρα εἰ n: ἄρα p. n | e 1 ἐθέλει n: εθελ[p | e 3 δή
τινα e: ἄν τινα n: τινα p. n

while he was a hoplite. Well, people were already scattered, and he was withdrawing, Laches with him. I happened along, and [a5] as soon as I saw the two of them I called out to them to keep their courage up, and kept reassuring them that I wouldn't desert them. It was there that I got an even better sight of Socrates than I did at Potidaea (I was less afraid, because I was on horseback), first of how much more composed he was than [b1] Laches; but then it seemed to me, Aristophanes, to use something you wrote, that he was making his way along there just as he does here at home, "swaggering and casting his eyes this way and that", observing people on our own side and on the enemy's in the same calm way, and making it plain to anyone, even if they were some distance away, that [b5] if anyone laid a hand on *him*, they'd meet with some pretty stiff resistance. That's why he actually got away safely, along with his companion; it's a general rule in war that people don't even try to lay a hand on someone who behaves like this, but [c1] go after those who are running away as fast as their feet will carry them.

'Well, there are many other things too that one could find to say in praise of Socrates, and amazing things at that; but whereas in the case of the other aspects of his behaviour, one might perhaps also say such things about someone else, the fact that there is no human being [c5] like him, whether among past generations or among those alive now – *that's* what deserves our complete amazement. With the sort of man Achilles was, one could compare Brasidas and others, and for [d1] Pericles' sort there'd be Nestor and Antenor (and there are others as well); and one could make similar comparisons in other cases. But as for the sort of man *this* one is, so strange is he, both in himself and in the things he says, one wouldn't come even close to finding anyone like him if one looked, whether among people now or among those [d5] in the past, unless perhaps if one were to compare him to the figures I'm talking about, not to anyone human, but to silenuses and satyrs – both him and what he says.

'In fact this was something I left out at the beginning: the things he says, too, are very like the silenuses that [e1] open up. For if one were willing to listen to what Socrates says, at first it'd appear pretty amusing: such are the terms and expressions in which it is clothed, like some mischief-making satyr's skin. For he mentions pack-asses, and things like blacksmiths, for example, and [e5] cobblers and tanners, and he always appears to be saying the same things in the same ways, so that any person with no experience of him, and no intelligence, would **222** laugh at the things he says. But if one

122

ἐντὸς αὐτῶν γιγνόμενος πρῶτον μὲν νοῦν ἔχοντας ἔνδον (222)
μόνους εὑρήσει τῶν λόγων, ἔπειτα θειοτάτους καὶ πλεῖστα
ἀγάλματ᾽ ἀρετῆς ἐν αὑτοῖς ἔχοντας καὶ ἐπὶ πλεῖστον
τείνοντας, μᾶλλον δὲ ἐπὶ πᾶν ὅσον προσήκει σκοπεῖν τῷ 5
μέλλοντι καλῷ κἀγαθῷ ἔσεσθαι.
'ταῦτ᾽ ἐστίν, ὦ ἄνδρες, ἃ ἐγὼ Σωκράτη ἐπαινῶ· καὶ αὖ ἃ
μέμφομαι συμμείξας ὑμῖν εἶπον ἅ με ὕβρισεν. καὶ μέντοι οὐκ
ἐμὲ μόνον ταῦτα πεποίηκεν, ἀλλὰ καὶ Χαρμίδην τὸν b
Γλαύκωνος καὶ Εὐθύδημον τὸν Διοκλέους καὶ ἄλλους πάνυ
πολλούς, οὓς οὗτος ἐξαπατῶν ὡς ἐραστὴς παιδικὰ μᾶλλον
αὐτὸς καθίσταται ἀντ᾽ ἐραστοῦ. ἃ δὴ καὶ σοὶ λέγω, ὦ
Ἀγάθων, μὴ ἐξαπατᾶσθαι ὑπὸ τούτου, ἀλλ᾽ ἀπὸ τῶν ἡμετέρων 5
παθημάτων γνόντα εὐλαβηθῆναι, καὶ μὴ κατὰ τὴν παροιμίαν
ὥσπερ νήπιον παθόντα γνῶναι.'
εἰπόντος δὴ ταῦτα τοῦ Ἀλκιβιάδου γέλωτα γενέσθαι ἐπὶ c
τῇ παρρησίᾳ αὐτοῦ, ὅτι ἐδόκει ἔτι ἐρωτικῶς ἔχειν τοῦ
Σωκράτους. τὸν οὖν Σωκράτη, 'νήφειν μοι δοκεῖς,' φάναι, 'ὦ
Ἀλκιβιάδη. οὐ γὰρ ἄν ποτε οὕτω κομψῶς κύκλῳ
περιβαλλόμενος ἀφανίσαι ἐνεχείρεις οὗ ἕνεκα ταῦτα πάντα 5
εἴρηκας, καὶ ὡς ἐν παρέργῳ δὴ λέγων ἐπὶ τελευτῆς αὐτὸ
ἔθηκας, ὡς οὐ πάντα τούτου ἕνεκα εἰρηκώς, τοῦ ἐμὲ καὶ
Ἀγάθωνα διαβάλλειν, οἰόμενος δεῖν ἐμὲ μὲν σοῦ ἐρᾶν καὶ d
μηδενὸς ἄλλου, Ἀγάθωνα δὲ ὑπὸ σοῦ ἐρᾶσθαι καὶ μηδ᾽ ὑφ᾽
ἑνὸς ἄλλου. ἀλλ᾽ οὐκ ἔλαθες, ἀλλὰ τὸ σατυρικόν σου δρᾶμα
τοῦτο καὶ σιληνικὸν κατάδηλον ἐγένετο. ἀλλ᾽, ὦ φίλε Ἀγάθων,
μηδὲν πλέον αὐτῷ γένηται, ἀλλὰ παρασκευάζου ὅπως ἐμὲ καὶ 5
σὲ μηδεὶς διαβαλεῖ.'
τὸν οὖν Ἀγάθωνα εἰπεῖν, 'καὶ μήν, ὦ Σώκρατες, κινδυνεύεις ἀληθῆ λέγειν. τεκμαίρομαι δὲ καὶ ὡς κατεκλίνη ἐν
μέσῳ ἐμοῦ τε καὶ σοῦ, ἵνα χωρὶς ἡμᾶς διαλάβῃ. οὐδὲν οὖν e
πλέον αὐτῷ ἔσται, ἀλλ᾽ ἐγὼ παρὰ σὲ ἐλθὼν κατακλινήσομαι.'
'πάνυ γε,' φάναι τὸν Σωκράτη, 'δεῦρο ὑποκάτω ἐμοῦ
κατακλίνου.'
'ὦ Ζεῦ,' εἰπεῖν τὸν Ἀλκιβιάδην, 'οἷα αὖ πάσχω ὑπὸ τοῦ 5
ἀνθρώπου. οἴεταί μου δεῖν πανταχῇ περιεῖναι. ἀλλ᾽ εἰ μή τι
ἄλλο, ὦ θαυμάσιε, ἐν μέσῳ ἡμῶν ἔα Ἀγάθωνα κατακεῖσθαι.'
'ἀλλ᾽ ἀδύνατον,' φάναι τὸν Σωκράτη. 'σὺ μὲν γὰρ ἐμὲ

b5 ἐξαπατᾶσθε n | d6 διαβαλεῖ e: διαβαλει p: διαβάλῃ m

were to see them being opened up, and get inside them – then first of all one will find that they are the only ones, of the things one hears, that have intelligence within them; then that they are to the highest degree divine, contain within them the greatest number of statues of virtue, and have the greatest [a5] reach – or rather, that they extend to everything that it is appropriate for the man who means to be a person of quality to consider.

'This, gentlemen, is what I have to say in praise of Socrates; and I've also mixed in with it what I hold against him, the crimes he committed against me. But I should add that I'm not [b1] the only one he's done it to: there are also Charmides, son of Glaucon, Euthydemus, son of Diocles, and a great many others, whom this man deceives in the role of lover, becoming more of a beloved himself instead of a lover. So, Agathon, I warn [b5] you too not to be deceived in this way by this man, but to take care, learning from our sufferings, not – as the proverb runs – to learn like a fool, by suffering.'

[c1] When Alcibiades had said all this, there was laughter (Aristodemus said) at his frankness, because he seemed still to be affected by love for Socrates. Socrates himself said 'I think you must be sober, Alcibiades. Otherwise there's no way you'd make such a clever attempt [c5] to disguise the actual motive behind everything you've said, putting it in at the end like an aside, as if you didn't say everything for this reason, just to cause [d1] trouble between me and Agathon, supposing that it's for me to love you and no one else, and for Agathon to be loved by you and by no one else at all. But you didn't get away with it; I've seen through this satyr-play of yours, or silenus-play. My dear Agathon, [d5] don't let him get anywhere with it; make sure *no one* causes trouble between the two of us.'

Agathon replied 'Why, Socrates, I believe you're right. I notice how he lay down on the couch in the [e1] middle between me and you, in order to separate us. So he won't get anywhere; I'll come and recline beside you.'

'Absolutely,' said Socrates; 'come here and recline below me.'

[e5] 'Zeus!' said Alcibiades. 'How the man's making me suffer again! He thinks he's got to get the better of me in every way. Well, if you won't allow anything else, my wonderful friend, at least let Agathon lie between us.'

'That's impossible,' said Socrates; 'for you praised me, and I in my turn

ἐπήνεσας, δεῖ δὲ ἐμὲ αὖ τὸν ἐπὶ δεξί' ἐπαινεῖν. ἐὰν οὖν ὑπὸ
σοὶ κατακλινῇ Ἀγάθων, οὐ δήπου ἐμὲ πάλιν ἐπαινέσεται, πρὶν 10
ὑπ' ἐμοῦ μᾶλλον ἐπαινεθῆναι; ἀλλ' ἔασον, ὦ δαιμόνιε, καὶ μὴ
φθονήσῃς τῷ μειρακίῳ ὑπ' ἐμοῦ ἐπαινεθῆναι· καὶ γὰρ πάνυ 223
ἐπιθυμῶ αὐτὸν ἐγκωμιάσαι.'

'ἰοῦ ἰοῦ,' φάναι τὸν Ἀγάθωνα, ' Ἀλκιβιάδη, οὐκ ἔσθ' ὅπως
ἂν ἐνθάδε μείναιμι, ἀλλὰ παντὸς μᾶλλον μεταναστήσομαι, ἵνα
ὑπὸ Σωκράτους ἐπαινεθῶ.' 5

'ταῦτα ἐκεῖνα', φάναι τὸν Ἀλκιβιάδην, 'τὰ εἰωθότα·
Σωκράτους παρόντος τῶν καλῶν μεταλαβεῖν ἀδύνατον ἄλλῳ.
καὶ νῦν ὡς εὐπόρως καὶ πιθανὸν λόγον ηὗρεν, ὥστε παρ'
ἑαυτῷ τουτονὶ κατακεῖσθαι.'

τὸν μὲν οὖν Ἀγάθωνα ὡς κατακεισόμενον παρὰ τῷ b
Σωκράτει ἀνίστασθαι· ἐξαίφνης δὲ κωμαστὰς ἥκειν
παμπόλλους ἐπὶ τὰς θύρας, καὶ ἐπιτυχόντας ἀνεῳγμέναις
ἐξιόντος τινὸς εἰς τὸ ἀντικρὺς πορεύεσθαι παρὰ σφᾶς καὶ
κατακλίνεσθαι, καὶ θορύβου μεστὰ πάντα εἶναι, καὶ οὐκέτι ἐν 5
κόσμῳ οὐδενὶ ἀναγκάζεσθαι πίνειν πάμπολυν οἶνον. τὸν μὲν
οὖν Ἐρυξίμαχον καὶ τὸν Φαῖδρον καὶ ἄλλους τινὰς ἔφη ὁ
Ἀριστόδημος οἴχεσθαι ἀπιόντας, ἓ δὲ ὕπνον λαβεῖν, καὶ
καταδαρθεῖν πάνυ πολύ, ἅτε μακρῶν τῶν νυκτῶν οὐσῶν, c
ἐξεγρέσθαι δὲ πρὸς ἡμέραν ἤδη ἀλεκτρυόνων ᾀδόντων,
ἐξεγρόμενος δὲ ἰδεῖν τοὺς μὲν ἄλλους καθεύδοντας καὶ
οἰχομένους, Ἀγάθωνα δὲ καὶ Ἀριστοφάνη καὶ Σωκράτη ἔτι
μόνους ἐγρηγορέναι καὶ πίνειν ἐκ φιάλης μεγάλης ἐπὶ δεξιά. 5
τὸν οὖν Σωκράτη αὐτοῖς διαλέγεσθαι· καὶ τὰ μὲν ἄλλα ὁ
Ἀριστόδημος οὐκ ἔφη μεμνῆσθαι τῶν λόγων – οὔτε γὰρ ἐξ
ἀρχῆς παραγενέσθαι ὑπονυστάζειν τε – τὸ μέντοι κεφάλαιον, d
ἔφη, προσαναγκάζειν τὸν Σωκράτη ὁμολογεῖν αὐτοὺς τοῦ
αὐτοῦ ἀνδρὸς εἶναι κωμῳδίαν καὶ τραγῳδίαν ἐπίστασθαι
ποιεῖν, καὶ τὸν τέχνῃ τραγῳδοποιὸν ὄντα καὶ κωμῳδοποιὸν
εἶναι. ταῦτα δὴ ἀναγκαζομένους αὐτοὺς καὶ οὐ σφόδρα 5
ἑπομένους νυστάζειν, καὶ πρότερον μὲν καταδαρθεῖν τὸν
Ἀριστοφάνη, ἤδη δὲ ἡμέρας γιγνομένης τὸν Ἀγάθωνα. τὸν
οὖν Σωκράτη, κατακοιμίσαντ' ἐκείνους, ἀναστάντα ἀπιέναι, καὶ
<ἓ> ὥσπερ εἰώθει ἕπεσθαι, καὶ ἐλθόντα εἰς Λύκειον,
ἀπονιψάμενον, ὥσπερ ἄλλοτε τὴν ἄλλην ἡμέραν διατρίβειν, καὶ 10
οὕτω διατρίψαντα εἰς ἑσπέραν οἴκοι ἀναπαύεσθαι.

b 8 ἓ m: εαυτον p | c 4 σωκρατη και αριστοφανη p | d 4 ὄντα και n:
ὄντα p, n | d 8-9 καὶ <ἓ> e: καὶ p, m

have to praise the person on my right. So if [e10] Agathon reclines below you, won't he praise me again, instead of being praised by me, as he should be? Come on, man, let him be – don't **223** begrudge the boy his chance to be praised by me; for I'm absolutely longing to give him an encomium.'

'Hey! Amazing!' said Agathon. 'Alcibiades, there's no way I'd stay where I am. Whatever I do, I'm going to change places, so that [a5] I can be praised by Socrates.'

'It's happening again, just as it always does,' said Alcibiades; 'when Socrates is around it's impossible for anyone else to get their share of beauties. So now see how resourceful he was in finding something persuasive to say, to make this one here lie beside *him*.'

[b1] So Agathon got up to lie down beside Socrates, but suddenly a whole crowd of revellers came to the doors, and finding them open because of someone's going out they marched straight in to the company and [b5] reclined on the couches; everything was full of uproar, and with things no longer in any sort of order they were forced to drink very large quantities of wine. So, Aristodemus said, Eryximachus and Phaedrus and some others went off, but he himself dropped off to sleep, and [c1] slept for a pretty long time, since the nights were long, waking up when it was already almost daylight and cocks were crowing. When he woke up, he saw that the others either were sleeping or had gone; the only ones still awake were Agathon, Aristophanes [c5] and Socrates, drinking from a large cup from left to right. Well, Socrates was having a conversation with them; Aristodemus said he didn't remember the rest of what was said – for one thing he hadn't [d1] been there from the beginning, and for another he was nodding off – but the gist of it, he said, was that Socrates was also forcing them to agree that it belongs to the same man to know how to compose comedy and tragedy, and that the person who is an expert tragic poet is also a comic [d5] poet. Even as they were being forced to agree to this, and not following too well, they were nodding off, and first Aristophanes fell asleep, then Agathon, as day was actually breaking. So Socrates, having put them to sleep, got up and left, with himself, Aristodemus, following him as usual; when he got to the Lyceum, [d10] he had a wash, spent the rest of the day as he did any other, and then in the evening went home to rest.

Commentary

172a1 'I believe I'm not unrehearsed in relation to what you people are asking about': a friend of Apollodorus', together with some unnamed others (rich businessmen: see 173c6) have asked – as we discover (a6-b4) – for an account of what was said at Agathon's party, the 'symposium' after which the dialogue is named. Quite why they have asked for it we are not told; but see 173c6n. The reason Apollodorus now gives as to why he is 'not unrehearsed' provides a sort of (dramatic) explanation for the polished nature of his account; at the same time, we the audience are allowed to break in, as it were, in between question and answer, as if the conversation were going on without us. On the possible motives for Plato's (hereafter 'P.') devoting such attention to achieving verisimilitude (in a way which, given that we are reading a text, itself suggests that the whole is a *fiction*), see Introduction, §2. If Agathon left Athens 'many years' ago (c4-5), and he actually left in about 408 B.C. (Bury: lxvi), then since Socrates (hereafter 'S.') is also not yet dead (Apollodorus is still spending his time with him, c5-6), the conversation must be presumed to be taking place at the very end of the fifth century – not long before the year (399 B.C.) in which, as *we* know, Athens executed the great man. Those present, of course, know nothing of that, nor of the fairly drawn-out proceedings that led up to it. There is thus no sense of the foreboding felt in those Platonic works – above all the *Apology* and the *Phaedo* – set within the broad context of S.'s trial and death; nothing to disturb the generally festive atmosphere of the whole work, beyond what we may supply for ourselves. Apollodorus is in fact the man most affected by S.'s death in the *Phaedo* (117d; cf. *Symp.* 173d7-8n.); *Symp.* helps show us why he might have been so affected. Bury: xvi n.1 favours the idea that he represents P. himself; this is certainly true at least insofar as it is Apollodorus who has put together (and 'rehearsed') the account of the 'drinking-party' (*sumposion*).

a2 'Phalerum': one of the outlying demes of Athens, to which Apollodorus belonged; on the coast, away from the urban centre of Athens ('town').

a3 'someone I know': inconspicuously named in c4 as Glaucon – who surely must be identified with the Glaucon who is one of P.'s elder brothers (but see below). This brother plays an extended role in the *Republic*, and there are several apparent connections between the beginnings of the two dialogues: in the *Republic*, S. is himself coming back to town, with Glaucon son of Ariston (Ariston being P.'s father), from the coast – in fact, the main port of Peiraeus – when someone catches sight of *him*, also from a long way off, and tells *him* to wait. If such resemblances obviously could be coincidental, their sheer number seems to make it unlikely; though if there is an intertextual reference of this sort (from *Republic* to *Symp.*, if we believe the traditional dating, and the usual hypothesis that the dialogues were written in sequence), it is anyone's guess how it should be taken. The first word of the *Republic*, *katebên* ('I went down', i.e. to the Peiraeus), has seemed to some to anticipate the philosopher's descent into the cave in Book VII, and/or the descent of the soul into Hades in Book X; one might then try to make something of the contrasting 'going up' (*aniôn*) at *Symp.* 172a2 – but if there is an ascent later in *Symp.* (in Diotima's speech), there is a parallel ascent prior to the descent in *Republic* VII, and in S.'s case 'going down' to Peiraeus is actually being followed by a 'going up', back to town. – Towards the end of *Symp.*, at 222b1-2, another and more precisely described Glaucon is mentioned, the father of Charmides. If Glaucon I is Plato's brother (see Introduction, §2.1), then this Glaucon II will be his, and so also P.'s, maternal grandfather; Glaucon II's appearance then in a way both reminds us that the identification of Glaucon I must be purely speculative, and lends support to that identification.

a3-4 'called out jokingly': lit. 'called out, and joking/playing at the same time as the calling out, said'. The joke is probably in the mock-official tone of the address. (The fact that Apollodorus has been recognized from behind makes it tempting to think there might be a play on *Phalêreus* and *phalaros*, 'bald'; but (a) we don't know that Apollodorus *was* bald, (b) probably no one in Plato's immediate audience would have known either, and (c) 'you from Phalerum' would presumably most often mean just what it says, so that no bald person from Phalerum would have had any particular reason to hear it as a reference to his baldness.) It may also be worth asking if there might not also be a covert authorial reference to the title 'Symposium': could P. be indicating what is in any case true, that what will follow is no ordinary 'drinking-party'? Or might he even be announcing the comic intent of the dialogue ('the title ... was deliberately chosen to arouse comic expectations', Cotter 1973:48)? Cf. Introduction, §4.1.

b1-3 'the time when Agathon and S. and Alcibiades got together, and the others who were there at the dinner-party': the three main characters in *Symp.* are conveniently (and inconspicuously) announced; if we should expect Aristophanes to appear in the list, we should note that P. does not see fit to have Glaucon to include him, or at any rate to have Apollodorus remember Glaucon's including him. Commentators have long noticed that *within* the dialogue, the word *sumposion* does not occur; here the words are *sunousia* ('get-together', of which the symposium appears as a species at *Laws* 652a) and *sundeipnon* ('dinner-party'). Alcibiades alone, who is not at the party, and does not know what kind of party it really is, refers to it as a *sumposion*, by introducing the cognate term *sumpotês*, 'fellow-drinker': 212e4, 213b7).

b3-4 'what they said about love': or 'what the speeches about love were'; lit. 'about the *erôtikoi logoi*, what they were' (the word *logos* covers a wide range, from 'thing said', to 'talk', 'speech', then 'reason', 'argument'). Cf. 'what your friend said', *tous tou hetairou logous* in b6-7. (An) *erôtikos logos* would perhaps typically be a form of words addressed by a lover to his quarry, real or otherwise; the speech attributed to Lysias in the *Phaedrus* gives us an example of an orator's (paradoxical) handling of the theme. The symposium, as an occasion for sexual activity as well as drinking, talking, etc., would be a natural place for such *logoi*, which were no doubt closely related to the sympotic poetry exemplified by poets like Theognis. Cf. Lasserre 1944. 'Love': on the problems of translating the word *erôs* in *Symp.*, see Introduction, §3. (As suggested there, it will not be too far wrong at least to begin by identifying 'love' in the dialogue with what is felt by someone – usually an older male – who either is or wishes to be someone else's – usually a younger male's – sexual partner.)

b4-5 'Phoenix the son of Philippus': someone otherwise unknown to us, if he is real. (Phoenix, in Homer *Iliad* 9, takes part in the embassy sent to try to reconcile Achilles with Agamemnon.) Bury:xvii thinks it 'reasonable to infer that there was already in existence, when P. wrote, at least one other account of a banquet at which S., Alcibiades and Agathon figured, and that it is P.'s intention to discredit it', and goes on to hypothesize about the identity of the author (? Polycrates: cf. 177b6n.). While this is one explanation of b5-6 'he hadn't anything clear to say on the subject', it is purely conjectural, as Bury admits; but in general it is not unlikely that P. might take a side-swipe at other, less friendly, accounts of S.

b6-7 'it's most appropriate that you should report what your friend said': i.e., as it emerges, what S. said. It is worth noting once again how carefully P. maintains the impression of a real conversation: we only gradually gather information which is already known to the speakers.

c2-3 **'if you think this gathering you're asking about happened recently':** on the dramatic dating of the dinner-party, see 173a5-6n., and Introduction, §5. Even if it is a fiction (as it is) here that oral accounts of what was said at a party up to fifteen years before were still circulating, the idea is evidently not (in a fifth-century Athenian context) impossible, even if it might be surprising; but then the party *was* a memorable one.

c4 **'Glaucon':** see a3n.

c4-5 **'Agathon has not lived here in Athens for many years':** see a1n.

c5-6 **'spending time with S.':** if he has to find out what S. is saying and doing every day (c6-7), he evidently doesn't spend *all* his time with him; since being with S. seems to mean doing philosophy, evidently he does sometimes give things priority over philosophy (cf. 173a2-3). But what normal person wouldn't?

173a2-3 **'I thought anything was a greater priority than doing philosophy':** being 'miserable' *(athlios)* is apparently a consequence of not doing philosophy. Glaucon may think this a joke ('Don't joke'), but any serious follower of S.' s – as *Symp.* itself will reveal – would have to take the idea perfectly seriously; doing philosophy means looking for wisdom *(sophia)* or knowledge, without which we are bound to 'rush around this way and that', with no sense of the direction in which our good, or happiness, lies.

a5-6 **'when Agathon won the prize with his first tragedy':** according to Athenaeus (217a), the occasion referred to is Agathon's victory at the festival of the Lenaea in January 416 B.C. ('when P. was fourteen'); evidently this would have been a fairly low-key affair, involving only two tragedians competing with two plays each. However according to Sider 1980, P. systematically attempts to mislead us into thinking that the victory was actually at the much grander City Dionysia (see esp. 175e6-7n.); and unless the presentation of Agathon's triumph in the dialogue as a whole is ironic, Sider has a point.

a6 **'sacrificial feast':** a party of thanksgiving for victory, for players and friends; the sacrifice would have ensured that there was meat to eat; and those present evidently also had a lot to drink (176a-b).

b1 **'For heaven's sake':** lit. 'by Zeus'.

b2-3 **'Aristodemus, from Cydathenaeum, small, always barefoot':** that Aristodemus has to be described in such detail (Cydathenaeum is his deme) shows that at least by comparison with Agathon, S. and Alcibiades he was something of a nonentity. His barefootedness is presumably in imitation of S., whose close follower he is (so close that, when Agathon sees him, his first question is why S. isn't with him: 174e); his small size also makes him physically distinctive, as S. is. He generally appears out of place in the aristocratic context of Agathon's party (see esp. 174b3-c5n., e7-8n., 175a6n., 185d4-5n., 193e1-2n.) – but then so, in a different way, is S.

b4 **'he was a lover of S.':** lit. '(he had been at the gathering,) being a lover of S.', which perhaps implies what is true in any case, that his presence at the party is explained by his love for S. (despite Agathon's polite protestations at 174e, he would not have been a natural person to invite). He is not being described as S.'s 'lover' in the sense of being his sexual partner; rather his passion *resembles* that of a lover for his beloved (an idea which foreshadows a number of themes introduced later in *Symp.*). By contrast, Apollodorus is merely S.'s 'friend', *hetairos*, 172b7. – **'as much as anyone of those who were around at that time':** lit. 'among those most (sc. his lovers) of those then'. But expressions of this sort seem to be as capable of meaning '*more than* anyone' (cf. Adam on *Crito* 43c) – as indeed, in a conversational context, might 'as much as anyone' in English, said in the right tone of voice.

b5-6 **'I did also later ask S. himself ... Aristodemus' account':** so the account we're to hear is (a) true (verified by S. himself), (b) Aristodemus' account, (c) Apollodorus' (insofar as he has 'rehearsed' it); and (d) no one else's. None of (a) - (d) is true.

b9   **'had our talk':** lit. 'conducted the/our *logoi*', i.e. the ones previously mentioned (mainly, presumably, Apollodorus' account of the party).

c2   **'you people too':** Apollodorus' 'if I *must*' is playful; as a 'friend' of S.'s, and a devotee of philosophical talk, he is more than happy to give his performance (c2-5).

c3   **'talking ... about philosophy':** so Apollodorus, at any rate, thinks of what he is going to report as 'philosophical'. Many modern commentators think differently, but maybe they should listen to Apollodorus.

c6   **'your rich businessmen's talk':** lit. 'your (talk), the (talk) of the rich and occupied with money-making'. Should we perhaps then infer that the dialogue is philosophical, but intended for non-philosophers? Certainly the main lesson of S.'s contribution to the feast, about the need to re-direct one's attitudes and concerns (by doing some philosophy), will apply mainly to the non-philosophical. The presence at the party of the glittering Agathon and the wealthy, aristocratic, and notorious Alcibiades, along with S., might be enough to arouse the curiosity even of the least intellectually committed person; and if these businessmen have a lot of money, they will presumably have spent a lot of their time getting it.

d1   **'in a wretched state':** *kakodaimôn* (the opposite of *eudaimôn*, usually translated as 'happy': roughly, 'having what is desirable in life'), which is more or less equivalent to *athlios*, 'miserable', in a1.

d2   **'and I think what you think is true':** that is, presumably, from a *Socratic* point of view; Apollodorus apparently admits the superficiality of his engagement with philosophy (but, as Dover says, the tone is one of 'banter, not preaching').

d7-8   **'that nickname of yours, "Softy"':** an alternative manuscript reading (*manikos*) would give 'crazy' instead of 'soft' (*malakos*), which would not make much sense of what immediately follows ('you're always savaging everyone'). 'I'm mad, off my head, am I?' in e1-2 sarcastically picks up the general implications of what the Friend has said – but is probably what misled the copyist(s) to think of *manikos* here.

e3   **'It's not worth quarrelling about these things now, Apollodorus':** but it is on such issues about values that the 'talk' that he is so anxious to hear will, in the end, turn.

e6   **'Well, it was something like this. Or rather ...':** on second thoughts, Apollodorus decides to include an account of events before the talking began.

174a2 **'What he said was that ...':** Aristodemus' report will be given mainly in a mixture of three different styles. There is (i) reported speech proper, as in 'he said that ...', with the 'he/Aristodemus said' usually left to be understood. Then there is (ii) what may be called reported direct speech, as in '(He said that) S. said "To dinner at Agathon's"' (a5, where the direct speech is introduced, as it sometimes is, by an apparently redundant *hoti*, 'that'). Alternatively, (iii) Apollodorus misses out Aristodemus, as in a8 and b3, where the 'he' in 'he said' in the Greek refers to S. (supplied, in the second case, in the translation). Even where, in the case of (i), 'he said' is unexpressed, the construction serves to remind the reader of the Greek that it *is* a report; we are thus kept in the time of its narration to the audience of businessmen, rather than being allowed – except temporarily, in long passages of mode (ii), like the speeches on love which begin in 178a – to go back to the time of the 'real' events themselves. This feature, whatever its purpose (see Introduction, §5), is impossible to reproduce in English without the repeated introduction of 'he said', which if not actually distorting would soon begin to grate. The present translation aims for a compromise, supplying a 'he said' wherever the presence of the narrator, and by implication his audience, seems in danger of being forgotten.

a3   **'both things he rarely did':** i.e. full washing/bathing, and wearing fine sandals (though it was evidently also rare for him to have anything on his feet (cf. 220b). As Dover argues, we need not go so far as to suggest that S. rarely even *washed* at all; his morning wash at the end of the dialogue (223d) seems to be part of a regular routine, since the whole emphasis there is on how even after a whole night of drinking and talking, he carries on as normal.

a4 **'to have made himself so beautiful'**: particularly unlikely, in S.'s case, given his notorious ugliness – that is, physical ugliness; beauty and ugliness, and their various forms, will figure prominently in the later speeches on love.

a6 **'I was afraid of the crowds'**: hardly, perhaps, to be taken at face value, given the description Alcibiades will give of his courage; if P.'s S. avoids crowds, it is more likely to be because philosophy and large numbers do not mix (see Introduction, §§3.4-6).

a8 **'so that my beauty matches his'**: lit. 'in order that I may go, a beautiful person, to a beautiful person'. Agathon is as vain about his good looks as S. is unconcerned about his own lack of them (see 194e4-197e8n.).

b3-c5 The logic of the whole passage ('we'll make a mess of the proverb by changing it to "good men go to good men's feasts of their own accord"; Homer did even worse to it by having an inferior person go to a good man's feast') suggests that the proverb in question ought to be of the form 'good men go to inferior men's feasts of their own accord'. The commoner form is actually more like what S. has (good men/good men), which has led some commentators to write ᾿Αγάθων᾽ – 'to Agathon('s)' – in place of ἀγαθῶν ('good men's'), so that the whole point is the pun on Agathon's name. The pun is certainly there, but it hardly even 'changes' (b4), let alone 'makes a mess of', the good-good form. If the other (good-inferior) form, which we find in a fragment of Eupolis, a comic playwright contemporary with Aristophanes (fr. 289 Kock), is actually already a play on the other (cf. Bury), then that too may be part of the point. S. is trying to encourage Aristodemus to go with him to the party uninvited, so he says 'good men (we know) go to good men's/Agathon's feast(s) without waiting for an invitation'. But now *agathos* has at least two sets of (not necessarily mutually exclusive) connotations, one associated with high social status, the other with what we should call 'moral qualities' ('virtue'): while Agathon is *agathos* in the first sense, whether he is in the second will eventually be called into question; Aristodemus, on the other hand, is fairly clearly not *agathos* in the first. See 173b2-3n. The next part of the conceit, which playfully criticizes Homer, certainly flatters the diminutive Aristodemus; indeed the very incongruity of the implicit comparison of him with Menelaus might itself raise the question about what he would be doing in the company of such 'good men' – a point which Aristodemus himself at once quietly makes in c6-8. The relevant passages here are *Iliad* 17.587-8, 2.408: in fact Menelaus is a stout fighter, and is only *called* a 'soft spearfighter' (Lattimore's translation), by Apollo (in a particular context, to Hector).

b6 **'criminal damage'**: the verb *hubrizein*, 'to commit *hubris*', is virtually impossible to translate, but its flavour (when used in earnest) is given by Dover's note on 175e8 – a *hubristês*, committer of *hubris*, is 'someone who treats others with contempt, ridicule or violence, as if they had no rights' (i.e. of the sort implicitly attributed to them by law and custom).

c8 **'a man of accomplishment'**: the adjective *sophos* frequently requires translation as 'wise' (cf. *philo-sophia*, 'love of/pursuit of wisdom'), but as applied to a poet it will suggest accomplishment – which may, of course, also include wisdom. Cf. 196d5-6n.

d3 **'"As we two go together further along the way"'**: *Iliad* 10.224, 'deliberately misquoted' (Dover, because the line is quoted correctly in *Protagoras* 348d), with the substitution of *pro hodou* ('further on the way'), from 4.382, for the original *pro ho tou* (*enoêsen*) ('one (sees) before the other); the change neatly provides for the new verb.

d5 **'this sort of conversation'**: we should probably note this first innocuous use of the verb *dialegesthai*, which in its semi-technical sense in P. stands for a special sort of conversation, i.e. philosophical, or 'dialectical' (cf. esp. 194d-e). According to the Platonic conception real philosophical progress itself depends on the give and take of verbal exchange – though as is shown by the following episode, and by Alcibiades' later description of S.'s behaviour at Potidaea (220b-d), this does not preclude the philosopher from thinking things through by himself. It would be surprising if it did; however what conversation with others seems to be thought of as providing is (above all) some kind of check on the validity and usefulness of provisional conclusions reached.

d6   'wrapped up somehow in his own thoughts': more literally 'applying his mind (*nous*) somehow to himself'.

d8   'When he arrived': the accusative and infinitive construction here percolates into the subordinate clause (so too in e4-5).

e1-2   'an amusing situation': 'amusing' is *geloion*, which derives from *gelôs*, 'laughter' (so: 'of the sort to laugh at', 'laughable'). There is a good deal of laughter in *Symp.*, even if what is laughed it usually turns out somehow to have a serious side.

e7-8   'because just yesterday ...': the excuse is presumably meant to be transparent, given what we know about Aristodemus' closeness to S. – as Agathon's immediate question shows ('but where's S.?'), thinking of Aristodemus means thinking of S.; if S. got his invitation, Aristodemus should have got his. Although the host gives him a polite welcome, he remains an outsider at the party, and a spectator: see 173b2-3n., 185d4-5n.

175a3 'slave': on the possible reasons why one of the words for 'slave' (*pais*) is the same as the standard word for a child (or, relevantly, 'boy'), see Golden 1985.

a4-5   'Aristodemus, recline beside Eryximachus': probably to Eryximachus' left, next to Aristophanes – and so in the very middle, as it turns out, of those speakers whose contributions he reported to Apollodorus. 'Reclining' (on a couch) would be the ancient Greek equivalent of taking a seat.

a6   'He said the slave then washed him, so that he could take his place on the couch': interestingly, the (freshly bathed) S. doesn't get a wash; but after all Aristodemus has literally just come in off the street, and has nothing on his feet. Once again he is marked off from the rest – except for S. (who has merely 'beautified himself' for the occasion). ('The slave' is presumably the one on washing-duty; Agathon's is no mean establishment.)

a10   'a pretty strange thing': 'strange' is *atopos*, 'odd', 'out of place'; what S. is doing is not what people like Agathon go in for.

b1   'said he intervened': lit. 'said he said', but the Greek is able to vary the word for 'said' (even if a Greek writer is likely to be less concerned about verbal repetition than an English one)..

b4   'if you say so': lit. 'if it seems (so, or right) to you'.

b6-c2 'In any case   ... so we can applaud you': Dover is probably right in saying that Agathon is here simultaneously complaining and boasting about the quality of his slaves; is he perhaps also delicately signalling his abdication of the control of the proceedings that might naturally belong to the host ('I expect to be treated just like the rest of you')?

c5-6   'Well, not long afterwards ... in his usual way': lit. 'having spent not much time in the way (i.e doing what) he was accustomed (to do – i.e. standing wrapped in thought)'.

c7   'At that point': οὖν here simply marks the next thing that happened; similarly in c5 ('Well, ..), and frequently.

c7-8   'who as it happened was in last position on a couch by himself': the host presumably chooses where to place himself; 'last' position is last (notionally) in importance, because last served (but if occupied by the host, presumably also, in a different way, first in importance), so furthest 'to the right', with the serving of food as well as the circulation of drink going *epidexia*, from left to right.

d1   **'that bit of wisdom of yours ...':** 'that bit of wisdom' is literally 'the wise (thing)', where 'wise' is *sophos* (see 174c8n.). Agathon takes it for granted that S. has added to his total sum of wisdom; S. responds with an elegant version of his usual disavowal of knowledge (but there will turn out to be *one* area in which he is an expert, namely 'things to do with love': 177d7-e1). See Introduction, §§2.3-4.

d3   **'you wouldn't have come away before you had':** S. neither confirms nor denies this idea; but the picture of philosophy that gradually emerges will suggest that doing it is a rather more difficult matter than Agathon supposes.

d4   **'S. sat himself down':** he reclines, and so in a sense fully joins the party, only at 176a1, after his disclaimer of wisdom (cf. d1n.).

d5:   φάναι represents the ἔφη we should expect if we we had a simple report of direct speech ('It would be a good thing, Agathon,' he said, 'if ...'); such redundancy – after *eipein* in the previous line – is not uncommon in *Symp*. To put it in the translation would be merely irritating; in Greek the redundancy is apparently less awkward.

d6   **'what is emptier':** P. could easily have written 'from the fuller of us into the emptier', but if the mss. are to be believed, he used the neuter instead (lit. 'what is fuller ... emptier of us').

d7   **'through the thread of wool':** according to Dover, this 'is slow, but it works'.

e1   **'I put a high value on reclining beside you':** see 213c for a different view of why S. values sharing a couch with Agathon.

e3-4 **'an inferior sort of wisdom, or even a debatable one ...':** according to S. at *Apology* 23a-b, he has a *name* for wisdom, but really – so he interprets the Delphic oracle's response – only gods are wise, and he has wisdom just to the extent that he recognizes that 'he is in truth worth nothing when it comes to wisdom'. What he says here in *Symp*. makes sense in the context without this complex set of ideas from the *Apology*; but what the two works share is a predominant sense of S. as a *searcher* for truth – which according to 204a will itself imply that he does not presently possess it. Agathon takes S. to be merely pretending, but there is no reason to suppose him not to be serious: P.'s S. *is* a searcher, and insofar as he has not yet reached his destination (even though he may have been told about it by Diotima), he *is* still ignorant, even if not as quite as ignorant as Agathon. (Cf. his conclusion about the poets at *Apology* 22a-c.)

e6-7 **'with more than thirty thousand Greeks as witnesses':** an overstatement even for the City Dionysia. Sider (1980: 45) thinks that if S. were meant to be referring to the Lenaea (cf. 173a5-6n.), what he says here would be 'less bantering than snide' (so too, according to Sider, the reference to *Greeks* is meant to point us away from the Lenaea, where only Athenians would tend to be present).

e8   **'You're a downright criminal':** i.e. a *hubristês* (cf. 174b6n.). Such humorous uses, according to Murray, 'retain an edge inconsistent with light-hearted parody: they involve insulting, scoffing, or jeering at the person or institution concerned, which can itself be seen as a sign of disrespect or disbelief' ('The affair of the mysteries ...', in Murray 1990: 156 n.21, with reference to the present passage – though I for one do not find much 'edge' here).

e9-10 **'we'll take our rival claims to wisdom to court a bit later on, with Dionysus as judge':** see esp. 201b-c, 213d-e (Alcibiades' crowning of S., after Agathon, but as more worthy), and perhaps also 219c – where it is the others present who become the 'judges' (*Dionysus* is here of course the god of wine: he will 'preside' over the talk or other entertainment following the meal itself in the sense that it will be under his/its influence). A 'dikast' is not strictly a judge, or a member of the jury; both roles are combined in an Athenian court.

176a3 'and the other usual things': with τἆλλα τὰ νομιζόμενα understand ποιησαμένοις.

a4   'Pausanias': also appears in the *Protagoras* (315d), and in Xenophon's *Symp.*, but we have no information about such a person beyond what we might be able to gather from these literary contexts. In Xenophon's *Symp.*, as in P.'s (193b; cf. 177e1-2n.), he is Agathon's lover; but Xenophon's picture of him and his attitudes ('defending those who wallow together in losing control of themselves', put into S.'s mouth at 8.32 in apparent reference to Pausanias' speech in P.'s *Symp.*) is evidently rather less sympathetic than P.'s.

b4-5 'going a bit easy on the drinking ...': lit. '(you're absolutely right about this, namely) the providing in every/any way of some ease of drinking' (construction with neuter of def. art. + inf.).

b5   'got thoroughly soaked': more literally, 'got in deep'; *baptizesthai* is to 'plunge oneself in', 'submerge' (a rather more extravagant way of putting the idea than Pausanias').

b6   'Eryximachus, son of Acumenus': a doctor (see e.g. 176d); apparently a friend of Phaedrus' (177a-d, and 223b, where he seems to leave with him; cf. also *Protagoras* 315c). The real Eryximachus was denounced with Phaedrus for the mutilation of the herms in 415 (Andocides 1.15, 35); an Acumenus was one of those denounced for profaning the mysteries (Andocides 1.18), and is mentioned as a doctor and friend (*hetairos*) of both Phaedrus and S. in the *Phaedrus* (227a).

b7-8 'And there's one more of you ...': with Vahlen's conjecture, Ἀγάθων<ος>, in b8, the sense will be 'I want to hear from one of you , namely Agathon, how he feels ...'; without the colon after *akousai*, and the question mark at the end, the unemended text will give 'I still want to hear from one of you in what state Agathon is ...'. But Agathon is the other side of Eryximachus from Pausanias and Aristophanes (cf. 185c-e); why shouldn't he ask his question before he looks in Agathon's direction, or as he looks towards him? – **'how is Agathon? Is he feeling strong enough ...?** Lit. 'in what condition is Agathon with respect to feeling strong enough to drink?'

b9   'Certainly not': lit. 'in no way (sc. am I strong enough)'.

c1-2 'me, and Aristodemus, and Phaedrus, and these people here': when the party finally descends into chaotic and excessive drinking at 223b, 'Eryximachus and Phaedrus and some others' (the moderate drinkers) leave. Aristodemus is not a big drinker – perhaps – because like S. he is no great frequenter of drinking-parties. (If he stays at the end, that is because S. is still there, talking – and drinking, but then, as we are about to be told, drinking doesn't affect *him*.)

c2-3 'the best drinkers among us': as if the ability to go on drinking and drinking without passing out were a real competitive skill; no doubt an idea that was taken more than half-seriously by some dedicated symposiasts (cf. the case of Alcibiades at the end of the dialogue: esp. 213e-214a). But in any case e1-5 makes it look as if heavy drinking, up to the point of drunkenness, would have been the norm, enforced by social pressures (cf. also c5-d1).

c4   'actually he can manage either way': the 'actually' is intended to convey the force of καί, emphasizing ἀμφότερα.

d1-3 'What I believe I have discovered from my own practice as a doctor ...': Eryximachus asserts on his authority as a doctor what everyone – including a poet like Theognis (211), or Aristophanes himself (*Wasps* 1253: passages quoted by Bury), and no doubt plenty of others – knows perfectly well. The usual judgement, that the good doctor is a pedant, seems inescapable; Phaedrus' reply (d6-e1), and everyone's else's ready agreement that they should listen to the expert (e1-3), are then easily taken as mock-serious.

d6-7 'Phaedrus of Myrrhinus': presumably the same Phaedrus after whom the *Phaedrus* is named; his speech – the first of the series in *Symp.* – certainly seems to suggest the same amateur interest in rhetoric that forms the starting-point of the *Phaedrus*. On the chronological relationship between the two dialogues, see Introduction, §5.

e6-7 **'the *aulos*-girl'**: *aulos* tends to be translated as 'flute', and *aulêtris* as 'flute-girl', but this is now liable to suggest the transverse flute, which it is not; Waterfield prefers 'pipe' or 'reed-pipe' (so at 215b2, contrasting with the 'wind-pipe'), but 'pipe-girl' might suggest 'girl-pipers', and so bagpipes. ('[M]ore like recorders', Dover; and either single or double.) '*Aulos*-girl' ought at least to confuse no one.

e8 **'to the women in their quarters'**: lit. 'the women inside'. The *aulos*-girl will have been a slave, available – probably – for the purposes of sexual as well as musical entertainment; her banishment to the women's quarters leaves the men entirely to their own company.

e8-9 **'entertain each other with talk'**: the verb *suneinai*, in the right context, can refer to sexual intercourse (as the cognate noun *sunousia* does at 206c5-6); here, presumably, it mainly looks back to Phaedrus' *poiêsasthai tên ... sunousian* ('carry on the party': cf. 172b1-3n.) in e2, but coming after the reference to the girl the whole phrase may have something of the flavour of 'have intercourse with each other through talk' (*logoi* again).

177a1-2 **'not only wanted him to make his proposal, but ...'**: lit. '(Aristodemus said) that they all said they both wanted and ordered him to introduce (it).'

a3-4 **'"The tale is not mine"'**: 'but from my mother' is the rest of the first line of a fragment (488 Nauck²) from the tragedy *Melanippe the Wise*.

b1 **'despite his venerable age and greatness'**: these are the themes with which Phaedrus will begin and end. It looks as if the 'favour' Eryximachus is doing Phaedrus (c5-6) includes setting things up so that he can give a speech he has prepared (the beginning of the *Phaedrus*, too, has Phaedrus anxious to show off his rhetorical skills).

b1-2 **'not a single one of all the many poets there have been ...'**: in fact we have a fragment of Alcaeus which seems to come from a hymn to Love (Alcaeus fr. 327 Voigt; cf. Burnett 1983: 130, and West 1993:51) – 'most dreaded (*deinos*) of the gods, / whom fair-shod Iris bore, having mixed /in love [where 'mixed in love' renders a simple 'mixed' in the Greek] with golden-haired Zephyrus' (translation from Burnett); contrast Hesiod's account of Love's origins, as quoted by Phaedrus at 178b. Maybe Alcaeus' poem did not match up to the description of an 'encomium'; but Phaedrus was at least over-egging his pudding. The implication will be that he is the first person to do justice to Love, whether in poetry, or in prose (b2-c1); see esp. c2-3 ('no one ... to this very, *tautêni*, day'). Cf. Lasserre 1944:176.

b2-3 **'if you like, consider the case of the sophists, I mean the respectable ones'**: P.'s dialogues regularly reflect the use of the term 'sophist' ('wise person', 'expert', 'intellectual' (?), usually but not necessarily associated with expertise in rhetoric), as a term of abuse; Aristophanes' *Clouds* probably illustrates the popular case against them (as atheists, tricksy lawyers, and so on), and incidentally treats S. as one of them. (After all, who can tell one intellectual from another?) See further 208c1n. By the end of the fourth century, the older sophists like Gorgias, Protagoras and Prodicus (b4-5) may well have come to be contrasted, at least in educated circles, with newer ones of the sort illustrated e.g. by the logic-chopping brothers Euthydemus and Dionysodorus in P.'s *Euthydemus*; and there is some evidence for this in the *Sophist*. See also b6n., on Polycrates. (Interestingly, Critias – a relative of P.'s, a member of the notorious regime of the Thirty Tyrants, perhaps a poet as well as a prose writer, and himself sometimes counted as a 'sophist' – seems to have written a work called *On the Nature of Love or (the) Virtues*: see (Critias) fr. 42 Diels-Kranz. According to Lasserre 1944:177, fr. 48 may also belong to the same work: '(Critias said) the most beautiful shape (*eidos*) among males was the feminine, and that the converse held among females.')

b5   **'Prodicus'**: the work in question, summarized by Xenophon in his *Memoirs of S.* (2.1.21-34), showed Heracles confronted by a choice between the path to virtue and the path to vice, and choosing virtue (what could be more 'respectable'?). The same Prodicus, from Ceos, is one of the distinguished visitors present – and caricatured – in the *Protagoras* (315c-d).

b6   **'a clever man'**: or a 'wise' (*sophos*) one, but here *sophos* has an ironic tone to it, as it commonly does in P.. – **'salt'**: Isocrates, in his *Helen* (ch.12), similarly refers to those who set out to praise 'bumble-bees (*bombulious*), salt, and things like that'; P. may well have had in mind people like Polycrates, a fourth-century 'sophist' who wrote against S. after his death, and who is said to have written on 'similar paltry subjects' (Bury, xxi).

c6   **'do a favour for him'**: cf. b1n.

d4-5   **'since he's both reclining in first position, and is also the person who conceived the whole subject'**: so perhaps Phaedrus needn't have gone first (and the more pedantic reader can dispense with asking how he came so conveniently to be sitting in 'first position'). The metaphor of 'conception' (literally, Phaedrus is said to be 'father of the *logos*'), in relation to *logoi* ('speeches', 'talk'), will become central in Diotima's speech; but actually the idea of invention as 'fathering' appears to have been a fairly common one.

d7-e1   **'I claim not to know about anything *except* things erotic'**: as we shall discover, S. knows about 'things erotic' (*ta erôtika*: 'erotics', Bury; 'things to do with *erôs*') in either, or both, of two senses. Firstly, Diotima, an expert, *taught* him about the subject; but secondly, and more subtly, love turns out to be – according to Diotima – desire for what we lack, including (especially) knowledge. Love himself, too, turns out to be a philosopher, with a remarkable resemblance to S. (Quite what all this means remains to be established; for the moment what is important is that this proclaimed exception to the rule of Socratic ignorance will be found not to be an exception at all.) Cf. Roochnik 1987.

e1-2   **'or, I imagine, that Agathon and Pausanias would'**: that is, because Pausanias is Agathon's lover (cf. 176a4n, though the fact is not confirmed until 193b-c).

e2-3   **'nor indeed Aristophanes, since his whole business is with Dionysus and Aphrodite'**: there is a tradition of interpretation, going back at least to Wilamowitz, that this remark is neutral and descriptive, with no hint of criticism; after all, Dionysus is god of the theatre, Aphrodite an honoured member of the pantheon, and so on. However if the question is why Aristophanes' total preoccupation with these two gods should cause him not to resist Phaedrus' proposal, the answer can surely only be because it indicates his total preoccupation with drink and sex: wine, another of Dionysus' responsibilities, is connected – particularly *via* the institution of the symposium – with sex, and sex is regularly referred to as 'Aphrodite's things'. It is a joke, undoubtedly (like the point following: 'I don't see anyone else here either who'll object', sc. because love/sex is something you're always ready to talk about), but a joke with an edge.

e5-6   **'it'll be enough for us if those before us give an adequate speech, or indeed a good one'**: the others clearly see it as a *competition*; what S. is interested in is the truth. See 198b-199b. (For καί linking alternatives, see Denniston, *GP* 292 (8).)

178a1-4   **'Aristodemus, I have to say, didn't remember everything ... the speech each of these gave'**: all of this seems consistent with the idea (fictional, of course) that each speech that will be included will be reported at least reasonably accurately. In the event, the only place where speeches will be said to have been left out is between Phaedrus' and Pausanias' (180c); if they were discarded because they were unmemorable, it is probably fair to say that Phaedrus' can barely have escaped the cut (see following n.) – but since he is 'father of the *logos*', his own 'offspring' can scarcely be left out. The only place where Apollodorus clearly leaves out anything from a speech he includes is at the beginning of Phaedrus', where he paraphrases for a brief moment before switching to what claims to be the full version, though he uses almost exactly the same form of words – 'starting from this sort of point', 178a5-6 – in introducing S.'s rather different sort of contribution at 199c (cf. also 180c1 'Phaedrus gave a speech something like this').

178a5-180b9: Phaedrus' speech. The main characteristic of Phaedrus' contribution is perhaps the way it tries to be clever, without quite pulling it off. Agathon's speech – which may be more like Phaedrus' than any of the others', at least in the degree that it lacks a precise argument – is cleverer, and in a different, more brilliant mode: if Agathon is an orator in Gorgias' mould, Phaedrus is in the less ornate tradition of an Isocrates, or a Lysias (cf. *Phaedrus*). His basic themes are that Love is (a) among the oldest of the gods (or oldest), and (b) responsible for very great, or the greatest, blessings (the speech thus combines 'certain ingredients of standard encomia: nobility of lineage and responsibility for good consequences', Dover). The connection between (a) and (b), if any, is not made explicit (see 178c2-3n.); it seems likely that Phaedrus' chief priority is to look for superlatives (cf. S.'s criticism at 198d-e of all the speeches preceding his). The underlying theme, as – I believe – of all the first five speeches, is that it is a good thing for the 'beloved' (see 178c4n.) to 'grant (sexual) favours' (*charizesthai*), under the right circumstances (when lover and beloved are of the right sort, and rightly motivated), to the lover. True, Phaedrus talks of the benefits accruing on *both* sides; however it is the younger partner who needs persuasion, and the lover needs no encouragement. Cf. Lasserre 1944:172; and Introduction, §4.6.

178b1-2 'among the oldest': the Greek expression is as at 173b4; see n. Phaedrus surely must mean to say '*among* the oldest', since that is all that most of his 'evidence' supports. However by 180b7, he is happily saying that Love is 'oldest of gods'.

b3-4 'Love neither has any parents, nor is he said by anyone ... to have them': if Love – at his most basic, representing sexual desire – is responsible for sexual coupling, then presumably he ought not to have any birth-parents, nor *ought* he be said to have any. Phaedrus can quote some impressive authorities for his view, but in fact not everyone chose to be so logical: see e.g. the Alcaeus fragment cited in 177b1-2n. (in the fragment, Love's parents indicate his own attributes; Diotima's own story of his birth, at *Symp.* 203b ff., uses the same conceit but a different couple).

b4-5 'Hesiod says': *Theogony* 116, 117, and 120 (omitting a line which specifies that the 'all' in 117 are actually gods).

b9-11 as it is printed ('Acusilaus ... the origin of love') has been heavily reconstructed by editors. The text of the mss. would give 'he [sc. Hesiod] says that these two came into being after Chaos, Earth and Love. Parmenides says ... "First was devised Love, of all gods". And Acusilaus agrees with Hesiod. Thus ...' This has some odd features; if it is not (in my view) entirely impossible, it hardly seems worth defending, since the sense is not changed in the least.

b9 'Acusilaus': of Argos, fifth-century; he apparently specialized in genealogies, on the Hesiodic model.

b10-11 'Parmenides says': we do not know the context of the line attributed to him (= fr.12 Diels-Kranz); who or what 'devised' (*mêtisato*) Love is unclear.

c2-3 'And being very old, he is cause of very great goods for us human beings': the form of the sentence suggests a connection between these goods and his age; is the point perhaps that if all gods bring benefits to us, then Love, having had more time, must have brought an especially large number?

c4 '... than a lover of a respectable sort, and for a lover, a beloved of the same sort': 'of the same sort' is left implied – but it is clear from the sequel that both lover and beloved must be rightly motivated. ('Beloved' will be used as the standard translation of *paidika*, the term mainly used – along with *ho erômenos*, 'the one loved' (e2) – to refer to the object of the lover's passions: usually younger, and male.) Since the chief benefit Phaedrus identifies as coming from Love is improved, even heroic, standards of behaviour, it will hardly help his argument if, as seems to be the case, lover and beloved must *already* be 'respectable', or 'of the right sort' (or simply 'good', 'of the sort we all approve of': *chrêstos*, as in 177b3); though at 179a7-b1 Phaedrus tells us that love can make even the coward brave, the same passage shows that he generally supposes our moral character to be something we are born with. However, on his account, as we discover next, a person 'of the right sort' may still need to be shamed into refraining from wrong actions, and does the right thing out of a desire for approval by others.

c6-d1 **'not kinship, or public honours, or wealth, or anything else'**: the list suggests a broadly aristocratic set of values (high birth, high political office and wealth would not be an unusual combination even in democratic Athens).

d5-e1 **'I declare, then ... as he would if seen by a beloved'**: Books II-X of the *Republic* include an extended critique of a system of values which depends on what one is *seen* doing (which seems to allow one to do anything provided it goes undetected).

e2 **'a beloved'**: here *erômenos* (c4n.).

e2-3 **'has a particular sense of shame towards a lover'**: i.e. is particularly concerned to avoid incurring his disapproval (the plural 'lovers' in the Greek is clearly a generalizing plural; the idea of promiscuity would be irrelevant here).

e4-5 **'a city or an army of lovers and their beloveds'**: 'an army of lovers' is usually taken as a covert, anachronistic, reference to the Theban 'sacred band', formed on just such a basis in the early 380s; but the combination '*city or* army' might more readily have recalled the Spartan example – itself partly reflected in the army regulations of the best city at *Republic* 468b-c. Cf. Schofield 1991:35-46 (in a chapter on a Stoic notion of a 'city of lovers').

e5-6 **'there is nothing that would enable them to govern their country better than their abstention ...'**: more literally 'there is no way in which they would govern their country [τὴν ἑαυτῶν, sc. γῆν] better than by abstaining ...'; omitting the ἤ ('than') at the end of the line, as proposed by more than one editor, might allow us to get much the same sense ('they would govern their country best, because they would ...') slightly more easily.

179a1 **'their rivalry with each other'**: showing *philotimia* (*philotimoumenoi*), 'love of honour' (as in 178d3) towards each other.

a6-7 **'as for abandoning his beloved, or not going to his aid when he was in danger'**: cf. 220d-e (involving a rather special instance of 'lover' and 'beloved').

a8 **'give him a courage that was inspired'**: 'make him *entheos* with respect to *aretê*. To be *entheos* is literally to have a god in oneself, to be 'possessed by' a god (cf. 180b4n.); *aretê* and its opposite, *kakia*, are both 'virtue' and 'vice', generally (or, more broadly still, 'excellence' and its lack), and also, in the right context, 'courage' and 'cowardice' (with no implication, of course, that courage is the *only* virtue). The corresponding adjectives, *agathos* and *kakos* can behave in a similar way: so 'most courageous' in b1 = 'most *agathos*'.

b1-2 **'when he has the god "breathing might" into some of the heroes'**: different gods in different contexts (but not Love).

b2-3 **'this is what Love himself causes to happen to those in love'**: lit. 'this Love offers to those in love (as something) coming about from himself'.

b4 **'Moreover, when it comes to dying for others, only those who are in love are willing to do it'**: most of the rest of the speech formally sets out to provide 'evidence' for this principle (cf. b5-7), but by the end Phaedrus has not succeeded – if he means to succeed – in providing even one clear example of a lover dying for someone else.

b5-6 '**Alcestis, daughter of Pelias**': Alcestis provides the most obvious example of someone's being the only one willing to die for someone else; in her case, her husband Admetus, who was allowed the privilege of putting off his early death if he could find someone to go in his place, but failed to persuade his elderly parents to do so. However she is a rather less obvious instance of 'someone who is in love' (is experiencing *erôs*, b4), i.e. – to judge from the general context of *Symp.* so far – someone who wants sexual satisfaction as at least part of the deal (cf. 180d3-4n.). When Phaedrus claims this for her (c1: she 'so exceeded [Admetus' parents] in affection because of her love', i.e. her *erôs*), there must be more than half a suspicion that she has to be in this state just because of the principle in b4: only *hoi erôntes* die for others; Alcestis was the only one willing to die for Admetus; so she must have felt *erôs* for him. If so, then Alcestis' case represents an application of the principle rather than being evidence for it. But Phaedrus' other examples probably show in any case that he is only playing with the idea of proof. (Euripides' Alcestis, in his *Alcestis*, certainly seems to act more from extreme marital fidelity than from sexual passion – though of course Phaedrus need not be meant to be referring to Euripides. Cf. d2n.)

c6: changing ἀνεῖναι to ἀνιέναι (see app. crit.) would give the sense 'having their souls *come up* again ...'; the suggestion is that a copyist's eye may have been taken by ἀνεῖσαν in the next line.

d2 '**Orpheus, son of Oeagrus**': in his version of this story, Phaedrus is surely doing what the playwrights and other poets regularly did too – modelling the story to fit his purposes (no other version has Orpheus failing to rescue Eurydice because he was a cithara-player, presumably meant to be a little joke of Phaedrus' own invention).

d5 '**not to be brave enough to die for the sake of his love**': so Orpheus was in love, but *didn't* die for someone else's sake; once again (cf. 178c4n.) love seems to have less effect than a person's pre-existing character.

e2 '**the isles of the blest**': i.e. the isles of the more favoured dead – cf. Hesiod, *Works and Days* 141, 171; Homer has 'Elysian fields' for the same purpose (*Odyssey* 4.563).

e5 '**to go to his lover Patroclus' aid**': on whether Achilles and Patroclus had a sexual relationship, see Clarke 1978; they certainly do in tragedy, but not so certainly in Homer (Clarke is an exception in thinking so).

180a1 '**not merely to die for him but to add his own death to his**': dying in order to avenge someone already dead is not perhaps the most obvious case of dying 'for' someone; still, if Achilles really had been Patroclus' lover, then he could certainly be said to have died for that love. However Phaedrus now introduces a further subtlety: Achilles was *not* Patroclus' lover ...

a4 '**Aeschylus is talking nonsense ...**': the extant fragmentary evidence suggests that the reference is to the lost play *Myrmidons*.

a5 '**but in fact**': Denniston *GP* gives no other example of ἄρα quite like this.

a6-7 '**and also much younger**': *Iliad* 11.787 makes Achilles younger, not 'much' younger (for Achilles' outstanding beauty, see 2.673-4).

a7-b4 '**In any case it is really true ... when the lover shows it for his beloved**': despite what Bury says, with a remark that now seems as curious as it is objectionable ('This savours of a Hibernicism'), the logic here is more or less intelligible – the gods love most 'this courage, the kind that relates to love', that is, all such courage, but of such courage they give more respect to Achilles' sort. The only problem is whether, if Achilles was Patroclus' *beloved*, he counts any more as evidence in favour of the principle at 179b4 than did Alcestis and Orpheus. That principle was that only those *in love* die for others, and Phaedrus has in effect denied that Achilles was in love with Patroclus. The word he uses (b3) is *agapan*; and though – as Dover:2 n.1) suggests – this can include sexual love, it will still be Patroclus, as lover or *erastês*, who is in love, *erai*. (The relationship between lover and beloved, as the terms themselves suggest, is an asymmetric one: see Introduction, §3.) More than likely, however, Phaedrus is meant to be taken as being *deliberately* perverse (again see S.'s judgement, on all the preceding speeches, at 198b–199b).

b4   **'For a lover is something more divine than a beloved; after all, he is possessed by a god':** which makes him, in effect, more than human, so that the task of the beloved, as merely human, is greater. 'Possessed by a god' (*entheos*: cf. 179a8n.) – in this case, of course, by, Love; further confirmation that Achilles, as beloved, is not 'in love'.

b7   **'I declare Eros oldest of gods':** but earlier he was only among the oldest (for confirmation, if it were needed, that superlative + genitive *means* 'most ...', see *Gorgias* 509b).

b8-9   **'the acquisition of virtue and happiness':** given that Phaedrus is summing up, or claims to be, *aretê* here must mean not just 'courage' but 'virtue' (cf. 179a8n.); cf. 178d2-4 (presumably the 'fine actions' referred to there extend beyond courageous ones, though the latter are the only ones illustrated). 'Happiness', *eudaimonia*, is a matter of possessing whatever is thought to be most worth having (cf. 173d1n.), and at least some of that can be retained after death (i.e. one's reputation in the minds of others: hence 'both in life and after they have ended it', b9); this will become a major theme in Diotima's account of love.

180c4-185c4: Pausanias' speech. Insofar as Phaedrus made Love himself the cause of virtuous behaviour, and capable of affecting even the coward, all love is good, and all lovers to be welcomed (the qualified statement at 178c4 that *respectable* lovers and beloveds bring benefit to each other probably refers primarily to good breeding: see n.). Pausanias, by contrast, begins from a distinction between good love and bad love, though he manages to avoid the appearance of criticizing Phaedrus directly. There are two Loves, one heavenly, one common or vulgar; both are divine, and one must of course praise all gods, but in fact only the heavenly Love deserves to be the object of encomium, namely the one who urges us to love rightly. At 181a8, Pausanias then begins a description of the two kinds of love, which he follows (182a8 ff.) with an explanation of the different laws and customs 'relating to love' (i.e., as before, between older and younger males), and of how these are compatible with his general thesis about the difference between good and bad loves. He ends with the claim (185b4-5) that '... all granting of [sexual] favours, under all circumstances, is a fine thing, if only it is for the sake of excellence'. Hamilton's suggestion that 'it is possible to see in Pausanias a clever pleader for homosexual licence, who employs high-sounding but sophistical reasoning to justify the satisfaction of physical desire' (Hamilton:15), even if true (it is *possible* to see that in Pausanias: cf. Xenophon's S.'s judgement, quoted at 176a4n.), is unhelpful. We have to take into account that everyone present at the party, with the exception of S. (and possibly Aristodemus, as his follower), is likely to accept something like Pausanias' position, and that Athenian law and custom is on balance not against it. Thus the idea that he is 'pleading for homosexual licence' is to get the matter precisely upside down: it is S. (and P.) who must plead, if he disagrees with Pausanias' position, to an audience which will not be easily persuaded. Nor, I believe, is Pausanias' reasoning – which is considerably tighter than Phaedrus', and as a rule quite careful – particularly 'sophistical'. (Allen is especially dismissive.) Hamilton's 'sophistry', I propose, should rather be interpreted as *wit*. In general, what Pausanias presents is roughly the best case for the kind of love, albeit described in an idealized form, that the symposiasts would recognize and approve of. That he has a vested interest, in the shape of his relationship with Agathon, is neither here nor there; so too, at least in principle, does everyone else (except S., although even he plays continuously on his fascination with beautiful young men). What is more relevant is that because of his faithfulness to Agathon, Pausanias can plausibly put the case for the 'better' kind of love: *his* choices are plainly not determined by mere passing lust (see 181a8-182a7). See Introduction, §4.6.

c5-6   **'If Love were such that there were just one of him':** lit. 'if Love were one', the meaning of which is indicated by what follows ('but in fact ...': for the γάρ, see Denniston, *GP* 69-71).

d3-4   **'there is no Aphrodite without Love':** because there is no sex (cf. 177e2-3n.) without (sexual) desire – this is what the audience can all reasonably be expected to know ('we all know ...'). Alternatively (Dover) what they all know is that the god of Love 'is an agent inseparable from Aphrodite and always at her service'. However I believe it misleading to suggest (as Dover does) that Love here stands for 'being in love' as distinct from feeling desire for sex; the term *erôs*, in Pausanias' speech as much as in Phaedrus' (cf. 179b5-6n.), includes desire for sex within its range, and must refer at least as much to that as to whatever is left of 'being in love' when the latter is distinguished from it (i.e. in English). If it does not, it will be hard to see what 'favours' the lover is supposed to want from the beloved, and what exactly the beloved is supposed to grant or not to grant.

d6-e1   **'One, I imagine, is older ... the one we call Common':** Pausanias constructs the theology he needs, using two separate accounts of the birth of Aphrodite, one in Hesiod (*Theogony* 188-202: within the foam caused by the genitals of *Ouranos* = Uranus, 'Heaven', splashing into the sea after they had been cut off by his son Cronus), and the other in the *Iliad* (5.370-430: born more conventionally from Zeus and Dione), together with two epithets belonging both to Aphrodite and to other gods – Ouranios/a, not exclusively indicating (any kind of) descent from Uranus, and Pandemos, probably in the sense of 'belonging to the whole people' ('*sc.* and not simply [to] particular families or [to] particular localities', Dover). (Pausanias' namesake, the 2nd century A.D. travel-writer, saw a temple to Aphrodite Ourania at Athens, and connects Aphrodite Pandemos with the 'bringing of the Athenians from their demes into one city': 1.14.7, 22.3.) In its general use the adjective *pandêmos* comes to mean 'vulgar', so that Pausanias' move from Aphrodite Pandemos, to her co-worker Eros Pandemos (e2-3), to Eros Pandemos standing for *erôs pandêmos*, 'vulgar love' (181a8), is an easy if strictly illegitimate one.

e3-4   **'Now one should praise all gods ...':** '[t]his is merely a formal saving clause, to avert possible Nemesis ... The laudation of base gods [Pausanias will, of course, criticize Eros Pandemos along with bad, vulgar love] would sound less strange in ancient than in modern ears' (Bury). (Waterfield talks of a 'rather blatant contradiction' with 181a6-7.) Pausanias in principle has a kind of let-out clause available, in the shape of his general claim that 'no action is good or bad in itself, but only in relation to the way it is done' (181a1-5), since that would allow him to say that loving is itself neutral, and good or bad depending on the way it is done; but of course he could not then *praise* Love, which is the task confronting him.

e4   **'but for now what matters ...':** for δ' οὖν here, see Denniston, *GP* 461.

181a2-3 **'whether we drink, or sing, or talk to each other':** the proposed principle works well in these cases, but in general it will only work, if at all, with a careful specification of what is to count as an 'action' (so e.g. stringing things up in trees might be neutral, but stringing up the neighbour's cat in a tree is unlikely to be). Nevertheless, it is surely neither silly, nor 'sophistical', and may even have some application in the case in question (love and sex). ('Talk to each other' is *dialegesthai* again: cf. 174d5n.)

b2-3 **'people like this love women no less than boys':** this idea in particular may reflect Pausanias' own situation (cf. Dover:96); there is no hint of levity in the absoluteness with which he excludes women as possible objects of the better kind of *erôs*. Yet at the same time his attitude is in itself something of a caricature of the all-male ambience of the institution of the symposium. Careful questions also need to be asked about Diotima's purposes when she (more or less) echoes Pausanias' sentiments at 208e.

b4 **'souls':** *psuchai* here might easily be translated as 'minds', but *psuchê* and mind are only partly overlapping concepts, and the contrast *psuchê/sôma* is far from identical to our normal understanding of the contrast between mind and body. The 'soul' in the present context stands in large part for what we should call the 'moral' aspect of a person, which in the ordinary Greek context consists primarily in the presence or absence of the recognized virtues.

b5-6 **'they have their eye simply on achieving what they want':** i.e. sexual satisfaction. The 'simply' (*monon*) is important; Pausanias' good love also includes the same aim.

c1-2 **'the goddess who not only is much younger than the other':** as great-granddaughter of the other's 'father' Uranus.

c2-3 **'by reason of her birth shares in both the female and the male':** lit. 'in her birth ...'. Her origin from a coupling of male and female is here meant to explain the lack of discrimination between women and boys shown by her Love (which might suggest that since all of us too have both fathers and mothers, we all ought to be equally indiscriminate – not an implication, presumably, that Pausanias would welcome).

c4-5 **'and this love is accordingly the love of boys':** it is easy to sympathize with Bury and other editors when they bracket these words, which may seem to anticipate 'it is for this reason that ...' in c5-6, and grate with d1 'they do not love boys'. But on the latter objection, see d1-3n., and the former misses the point that there are two separate arguments: 1. (c3-5) this Love/love is of boys/males (and not also of females), because its Aphrodite only 'shares in' the male; 2. (c5-7) this Love/love is of the male because its Aphrodite is older and (therefore) 'with no portion of lawlessness', and the male has that greater strength and intelligence which goes with greater maturity (contrast the way the other love is said to go for 'the least intelligent': b4-5).

c5 **'no portion of lawlessness':** *hubris* again (see 175e8n.), particularly associated with youth (or rather, young males); see references in Bury.

c6 **'those whose inspiration comes from this Love':** 'inspiration' is here the – more or less – literal translation ('those who are *epipnoi*', 'breathed on').

c7 **'feeling the attraction of':** *agapôntes*; cf. 180a7-b4n.

d1-3 **'they do not love boys ... their beard starts growing':** lit. 'they do not love boys, but when they (sc. boys) are already beginning ...'. 'Boy' (*pais*) is in fact still an appropriate description of someone of the age in question (and after all the whole context is one of *paiderastia*, 'boy-loving': c8), but Pausanias' meaning is perfectly clear (not 'young children', as *pais* might also suggest).

d4 **'are ready to be with them for their whole lives':** as he is with Agathon?

d7 **'a law against loving boys':** i.e. those below the age specified in d2-3.

e4-5 **'those vulgar lovers too':** οὗτος here is tinged with contempt (cf. Bury, and *LSJ* s.v. C.3).

181e5-182a2 **'just as we impose a rule on them, so far as we can, not to love free women':** 'free' women, i.e. citizen ones, would be given in marriage by their nearest male relative, who would hardly welcome dalliances unsanctioned by them. 'So far as we can': the qualification perhaps most naturally refers to the inefficacy of the 'rule'; but it might (also?) refer to the ambiguity of *eran* – not just to 'have an affair (with)' (Waterfield) but 'to feel *erôs* (for)'. There could scarcely be an effective rule against *eran* in the second sense.

182a3-4 'to go so far as to say that it is shameful to grant favours to lovers': as certainly none of those present would (unless perhaps it was their own son that was involved); even for (P.'s) S., the achievement of sexual satisfaction is – as we discover – simply not part of the overall good.

a5   **'their inopportuneness and their injustice':** *'akairia* is doing things at the wrong time, to the wrong extent, and in the wrong way' (Dover); the injustice lies, presumably, in the one-sidedness of any encounter of the sort in question (the lover simply 'achieves what *he* wants', 181b5).

a8   **'the way things are laid down':** 'way things are laid down' represents the single word *nomos* – 'law' at 181e3, but now, as the sequel shows, including what can be called 'unwritten law', i.e. custom/inherited tradition, as well as its formal written counterpart.

a9-b1 **'here, and in Sparta, it is complex':** editors have tended either to bracket 'and in Sparta' (καὶ ἐν Λακεδαίμονι), or to propose reading it after 'In Elis' in the next sentence – because the Spartans were notoriously 'not expert at speaking' (b2). But this is probably to misunderstand Pausanias' methodology. He is not giving an accurate historical account of the facts, but making up an explanation of them; and if the Spartans end up being implied to be *good* at talking, that is consistent with the general lightness of tone of the whole passage (also detectable, of course, in Pausanias' theological excursions in the last paragraph). See also Dover: 'the Spartan attitude to homosexuality was indeed ... "complicated" ...., as described by Xen. [*Constitution of the Spartans*] 1.12 ff.; Xenophon there contrasts Sparta with Boeotia and Elis.'

b4-5   **'spare themselves the trouble of trying to persuade the young by speaking to them':** Dover comments '[i]nability to persuade by words could as well have had the opposite consequence; but many an argument of Pausanias *non sequitur*'; I should add, 'and neither are many of them intended to'. The present 'argument' is surely intended to be a joke (and not a bad one?).

b5-7   **'in Ionia and in many places ... under the rule of non-Greeks':** the Ionians, in the eastern Aegean and on the mainland opposite, were not under non-Greek (Persian) rule in 416 B.C., but those on the mainland were after the 'King's Peace' of 387/6, i.e. at around the time when *Symp.* is often supposed to have been written (see Introduction, §5). On the other hand, someone who – like Apollodorus' friends in (?) 404 – knew that Ionia wasn't currently ruled by non-Greeks might perhaps be expected not to hear the sentence as implying it (the Ionians' attitude, maybe, was the result of the fact that they *had been* under Persian rule ...?).

b8   **'love of intellectual and physical excellence':** 'love of intellectual excellence' is *philosophia*, 'love of wisdom' (cf. 174c8n.); 'love of physical excellence' (*philogumnastia*) is more immediately devotion to physical exercise or training.

c3   **'all the other things':** i.e. 'love of intellectual and physical excellence'?

c4-5   **'Aristogeiton's love for Harmodius, and Harmodius' affection for him':** the two famous tyrant-slayers of the late 6th century, who in fact only killed the tyrant Hippias' brother, evidently for trying to seduce Harmodius. That Aristogeiton is said to feel *erôs* for Harmodius, and Harmodius *philia* ('friendly affection') for Aristogeiton, is the clearest indication yet of the expected asymmetry of the relationship between lover and beloved (cf. 180a7-b4n.).

c7   **'the failings':** or 'the vice' (*kakia*).

d2   **'a fine thing':** i.e. *kalon* ('noble', 'admirable', 'beautiful').

d2-3   **'because of the mental laziness of those who laid it down':** 'mental' here represents 'of the soul' (despite what was said at 181b4n.); 'laziness of the soul' sounds merely odd).

The sentence as a whole, which sums up practice outside Athens, is deliberately but unobtrusively balanced.

182d4-183b3: this ungainly sentence (left ungainly in the translation) strikingly contrasts with the neatness e.g. of 182c6-d3; is it perhaps designed to echo the 'complexity' of its subject (b1)? For the structure, see Dover.

182d6 'even if they are not as beautiful as others': Pausanias perhaps adds the clause to make clear that he is still keeping to his distinction between good and bad love – if the laws and customs at Athens are better than elsewhere (d3), then clearly it is the good sort of lovers that they ought to encourage, and one could simply lust after the noble and good for their beauty.

e2-3 'our customary rules': again, the Greek has just *ho nomos* (see 182a8n.; but 'customary' perhaps also helps to convey the perfect tense *dedōke*, lit. 'has/have given').

183a1 'to achieve': *diapraxasthai*, as at 181b5. – Allen proposes to keep φιλοσοφίας, (generally excised by editors), on the basis of supposed connections with 184c7-d3 and 182b8. He translates 'deeds which ... would issue in the greatest blame for philosophy', apparently excusing the lack of any obvious sense on the grounds that 'the speakers are sometimes drunk not only on wine but on their own rhetoric, and this is specifically true of Pausanias'. But there is no evidence that Pausanias is drunk on wine, and his rhetoric too seems to me rather carefully controlled. The offending word may perhaps in origin have been a mistaken gloss on τοῦτο (πλήν may also be a preposition taking the gen.).

b3 'being ashamed on his behalf': the manuscripts have αὐτῶν; I follow one or two editors in emending to αὐτοῦ (supposing a copyist to have had his eye on the preceding three endings in -ων).

b4-5 'the rules': once more, *ho nomos*.

b6 'though here I only report what most people say': Pausanias carefully attempts to distance himself from an aspect of approved practice which might not reflect well on it; and indeed he has already made the implicit claim that the good lover will not deceive his beloved (181d5).

b8 'because, they say, an oath prompted by Aphrodite is no oath': it seems simplest to understand ὅρκον after εἶναι ('they', I take it, are still 'most people').

c1-2 'according to what the rules here in Athens say': Waterfield (n. on 183a), referring to Dover 1964 and 1978, claims that '[Athenian society as a whole] condoned [homosexuality], but it was only actually encouraged in the upper-class circles in which P.'s characters moved. Pausanias' description of Athenian ambivalence, then, is a fiction designed to support his division of Love into good and bad.' This seems broadly right (cf. 180c4-185c4n.), except insofar as it misses out the point that Pausanias must be assumed to *know* just to what extent his account is fictional; in any case, if he gave a full and accurate description of Athenian attitudes, it is hard to see exactly how he could turn it into an encomium (cf. 180e3-4n.).

c3-4 'both being in love and giving affection to lovers': cf. 182c4-5n. ('giving affection to': (?) lit. 'becoming friends/friendly with').

d4-5 'It is not a simple matter: as I said at the beginning, in and by itself ...': I (hesitantly) take the construction to be 'it [love, but especially the matter of granting favours to a lover] is not a simple thing, the very thing (ὅπερ) that was said at the beginning, (namely when I said) that ...'; the Greek is difficult however one takes it.

d8 'granting favours to a person of the right sort and in a fine way': but favours *will* be granted; that is part of the deal ('of the right sort ': *chrēstos*, as at 178c4).

e1 'that vulgar one': i.e. that *pandēmos*, 'common' one.

e1-2 'the one who is in love with the body more than with the soul; for he is not a lasting lover either': so too earlier, Pausanias connected fickleness in the lover with mere physical lust (181b5-6, d5-7).

e4 'he "takes to his wings and is gone"': as if he were a dream (*Iliad* 2.71).

e5 'the lover of the character which is of the right sort': once again, Pausanias is precise (in principle, after all, it would be possible to fall for someone because he had the *wrong* sort of character).

e6 'insofar as he is fused together with something lasting': if we wish, we may see Aristophanes' speech as picking up and developing this idea (see 192e1).

183e6-184a2 'It is these two sorts of lovers ... get away from the other': the translation here (and also in the next sentence) fills out a rather sparer Greek (lit. 'These our law means to test well and finely, and (beloveds) to grant favours to these, but get away from those'). (For similar language, applied differently – 'test with due care, and if it's a bad thing, turn people away, but if it's good ...' – see the last lines of the *Euthydemus*, where the thing to be tested is philosophy itself.)

184a4-5 'and to which the one who is loved belongs': cf. 183d7-8.

b2 'gives in without resistance': lit. 'cowers (with fear)'.

b4-5 'none of these things seems either reliable or lasting': quite why is Pausanias so concerned that affairs should *last*? Perhaps here too he is reflecting his own personal situation, i.e. his long-standing relationship with Agathon (Dover). But again I believe we should (also) be prepared to take Pausanias' *argument* seriously: he has just claimed that time will sort out both lovers and beloveds – that is, if they stay, then we may suppose that they have the right motives; but money and political influence seem to be ephemeral things; therefore if anyone gives in to a lover for the sake of these, we shall soon know that he is not of the right sort. This is hardly reasoning of a high order, but it is more than a mere assertion of personal preferences, or mere disguised self-praise.

b5-6 'a noble affection cannot possibly arise from such sources': i.e. for people of quality, a friendship ('affection' again = *philia*) must rest on more than material advantage.

c3 'slavery that relates to excellence': *aretê* here includes 'virtue', but also any sort of beneficial wisdom or knowledge (c5); hence 'excellence' (cf. 179a8n.).

c3-4 'For it is our considered view': *nenomistai ... hêmin* is here equivalent to/a variant of *esti ... hêmin nomos* ('our rule is') in b7.

c5-6 'as measured by some kind of wisdom, or by any other part of excellence whatever': Pausanias makes clear that he is enunciating another general principle, and Dover is probably right in saying that he will have in mind both apprentices in the ordinary sense, and the disciples of a philosopher; *philosophia* in d2 will mean 'pursuit of wisdom' generally (cf. 182b8n.). Given the range of meaning of *sophia* (see 196d5-6n.), we probably need to beware of tying *philosophia* too tightly to the Socratic-Platonic idea of 'philosophy', except where S. himself is speaking.

d7 'he would be justified in that': ὑπουργεῖν (inf.) can easily be understood after ὑπουργῶν, after the model of ὑπηρετῶν ... ὑπηρετεῖν (d5-6); omitting the inf. adds to the variation between the two balancing parts of the sentence. (The alternative reading, ὑπουργεῖν, found in some mss., would of course achieve the same effect.)

e1 'understanding': *phronêsis* seems here to be a variant for *sophia* ('wisdom').

e6 'it brings shame': 'it' is presumably 'granting (sexual) favours'.

185a3-4 'his own character': more literally 'what belongs to himself' (with emphatic γε).

b3-4 'he would be eager to do anything for anybody': 'here, as in b[4-5] *pan pantôs* ['all ..., under all circumstances'], Pausanias' fervency in advocating homosexual eros shows through' (Dover). However if one takes into account the qualifying 'if it is for the sake of excellence, and of becoming a better person', things are not so clear. Being prepared to do literally *anything* for a person would hardly be consistent with any ordinary notion of excellence, and if the lover is going to put up a decent show of being an excellent sort of person, there are plenty of things he had better not demand. On Dover's reading, Pausanias will in fact be arguing for licence in the promotion of virtue; I suggest rather that he is playfully suggesting that idea, especially in b4-5, and leaving us to see the contradiction, and the point, which he then drives home in b7-c1 – that love 'compels' both lover and beloved to pay great attention to excellence.

b4   **'and *that* is the finest thing of all'**: the αὖ marks the contrast with a5 'and that is not a fine thing' (see also b2 with a3-4).

b4-5   **'so that all granting of favours, under all circumstances, is a fine thing, if only it is for the sake of excellence'**: if it is the finest thing to do anything for anybody for the sake of excellence, then it must be a fine thing under all circumstances for the beloved to grant favours, for the sake of excellence (but see preceding n.).

b5-6   **'This is the love that belongs to the heavenly goddess, heavenly itself'**: but still involving sexual gratification – the starting-point, after all, is not *whether* it's a good thing for a beloved to 'grant favours to' a lover, but *when*.

c2   **'all the other loves'**: the plural presumably reflects the multiplicity of the other objects that drive *erôs*, or are involved in erotic affairs, apart from 'excellence'. But it looks as if no single account can in fact be given of the motivation of the 'heavenly' lover: he loves the beloved's character, 'takes great care of himself with respect to excellence', and at the same time wants sexual satisfaction. Diotima's ideal lover will lack this complexity; but then he is no ordinary lover.

c3   **'just on the spot'**: we are, presumably, meant to believe him (there is no reason to suppose that *he* has prepared anything in advance, whatever may be true of Phaedrus).

c5-6   **'When Pausanias came to a pause (the experts teach me to balance things like this)'**: 'me', of course, is Apollodorus, in whose voice everything from 174a is. This is simple banter, taking the fairly obvious opportunity provided by Pausanias' name for gentle caricature of Pausanias' rhetoric (without necessarily devaluing it); the 'balance' illustrated by the clause in the Greek – *Pausaniou de pausamenou*, 'involving ... assonance as well as symmetry', Dover – is probably more extravagant than anything in the speech itself.

c7-8   **'he happened to be having a fit of the hiccups, brought on either by overeating, or by some other cause'**: P. could, of course, have had it happen to any one of those present, or none; why did he choose Aristophanes? Because '[m]uch humour in Old Comedy is founded on bodily processes' (Dover); but of more immediate importance is that the episode is also consistent with the characterization of Aristophanes begun at 176b5 and – especially – 177e2-3 (see n.: it is the *physical* aspects of life that concern him). From a dramatic point of view, the episode also has the advantage of leaving the speech of the comic poet Aristophanes, as if by accident, next to that of the tragedian Agathon. See also d4-5n., 187a1-3n.

d1-2   **'the doctor Eryximachus was reclining on the couch next down from him'**: with Aristodemus (175a).

d4-5   **'I'll speak in your place, and when you stop, you speak in mine'**: and so it is that Aristodemus, unobtrusively, is left out. He neither gives a speech, nor is one from him missed (no one says 'what about Aristodemus?'); either P. has forgotten about him – or he is sitting between Aristophanes and Eryximachus. Their present exchange takes place over his head, and by the time both Eryximachus and Aristophanes have given their speeches, the speaker's baton (as it were) has passed beyond him. So he remains the outsider: a little man, not properly dressed, probably out of his league, and ignored (but observing everything). Or, for a slightly more specific suggestion, see 193e1-2n.

e3-4 'Start speaking at once': sc. so I can start doing something about these hiccups?

185e6-188e5: Eryximachus' speech. Hamilton is expressing a common view when he declares that this contribution is 'poor stuff and meant to be so' (Hamilton:15); however that may be, the speech will turn out to have an important place in the economy of the dialogue. In very bare outline, it runs as follows: 'Pausanias was right to talk about two Loves, but the operation of these is not restricted to the human sphere; they are at work in the universe as a whole. This I have observed as a doctor, and I shall begin from medicine: medicine is in fact a matter of knowing about bodily erotics, gratifying what is healthy and refusing what is diseased, and reconciling opposites ... Medicine is wholly governed by Love, as is the expertise of the trainer, the farmer and the musician. Music, like the body, brings together opposite things; skill is needed in applying it to humans in order to encourage the right desires/loves. So in everything one must look out for the two Loves: thus when the bad, excessive Love predominates in relation to the seasons, plagues and disease result, and here the relevant skill is astronomy. The priest and seer also watch out for the kind of desire/love that leads to impiety. Such is the power of Love ...' There are many different elements in the speech, including – perhaps – continuing characterization of Eryximachus as a pedant who likes the sound of his own voice, and is inordinately proud of his medical expertise, as at 176c-d (though he is also capable of a fair degree of self-parody: cf. Edelstein 1945:89); a caricature of 'the tendency of scientific theorists to formulate excessively general laws governing the phenomena of the universe' (Dover, with references to [Hippocrates] *On Regimen* 1.3-10, *On Breaths* 1-5; and to *On Ancient Medicine* 13-16 and *On Regimen* 2.39, where the medical writers themselves criticize the same tendency); an underlying reference to Empedocles' theory of the universe as ruled by twin principles (in his case Love and Strife); and a curious critique of Heraclitus. There are also some other striking features, for example the fact that the treatment of music actually takes up more space than that of medicine, and that there is apparently so little reference to *human* sexuality, and indeed to sexuality at all. What is it all *for*? (Why did P. write it, and just in this form?) This question can only be answered, if at all, on the basis of a detailed reading of the whole speech. (For other treatments of Eryximachus' speech, see esp. Edelstein 1945 and Konstan and Young-Bruehl 1982; Rowe, 'The speech of Eryximachus ...' is a fuller version of the interpretation proposed in the notes following.)

186a5-6 'but also in relation to many other things and in other things': i.e. not just in human souls in relation to other humans, but in lots of other things, and (so) in relation to many other things; 'in other things' is delayed at least partly because Eryximachus is going to give some examples of the things in question. (He says 'in *the* other things', which strictly ought to mean literally 'everything else'; but 'the rest' can be used loosely, and the fact that he goes on to say 'and (in) practically everything that exists' suggests that it is so used here.)

a8-b1 'my own expert knowledge as a doctor': lit. 'medicine, our/my expertise/skill'.

b3 'in order that we may also give a special place to that branch of knowledge': he has already given one reason for starting from medicine, namely that it is the source of his observations.

b6 'desires and loves': if 'love', i.e. *erôs*, is (a kind of) desire, one might still wonder whether the kinds of phenomena in question ought even to count as desires (i.e. let alone cases of 'love'). However a *cosmic* theory of Love – like Eryximachus', and like Empedocles' – will inevitably take what we would be likely to call unconscious processes as the starting-point, and assimilate human *erôs* to them.

c1 'immoral': *akolastos*; see 187e3n.

c6-8 **'Medical expertise ... is knowledge of the erotic affairs of the body in relation to filling up and emptying'**: i.e., roughly, of what the body needs to take in and what it needs to evacuate. So far, it might be said, the speech has not looked promising. Eryximachus has pointed out what looks like a wholly superficial resemblance between the doctor's treatment of 'healthy and diseased things' (and their 'desires') in the body and the beloved's treatment of lovers; he has now laid claim on this basis to expertise in 'erotics of the body', a claim which looks even odder than S.'s suggestion at 177d-e that *he* was an erotic expert. But before we pass judgement, we need to see the use Eryximachus will make of these ideas.

d3-4 **'how to produce love in those in whom it does not exist, but should, and remove it when it is present'**: i.e. the 'fine'/good 'love' and the 'shameful'/bad respectively.

d4-5 **'will be a good practitioner'**: there is not meant to be a difference between the possession of medical expertise (being *iatrikos*, d1), and the ability to produce results, like any other craftsman (*dêmiourgos*, d5: 'practitioner' in the translation); the 'while' at d1 represents a simple 'and' (*kai*) in the Greek.

d5-6 **'For what is needed is the ability to make the things in the body that are most hostile to each other into friends, and make them love one another'**: given the 'for' (*gar*), this idea ought at least to be consistent with the preceding one. In that case, the 'things in the body' here (which turn out to be the opposites: cold, hot, etc., d6-e1) should be the same as the 'things in the body' referred to in b4-5 ('what is healthy and what is diseased in a body'), b7-8 ('the healthy' and 'the diseased'), and c2-5 ('the good and healthy things in each body', 'the bad and diseased things'); and it should be the doctor's business to make these love each other, and so love the same, or 'like' things, rather than 'unlike' things (b6). 'Bad love' on the part of one of a pair of opposites will lead to 'hostility' with the other because it will be desire for excess, or over-filling (cf. c7-8), which if satisfied will lead to imbalance and disorder (188b3-5). Evidently the 'erotics of the body' are a complex matter. The idea of material things in general as consisting of opposites in combination, often represented in medical theory in the doctrine of the 'humours', is fundamental to ancient science; the idea of the opposites 'loving' one another looks rather more specialized, and is perhaps an invention of Eryximachus' (i.e. of P. for E.), after Empedocles, for the sake of the theme of the party. S. refers to some unnamed individual as advancing a remarkably similar-sounding set of ideas at *Lysis* 215d-216a ('the dry desires the wet, the cold the hot ...'); but there too they are likely to be an *ad hoc* conceit, again with an underlying reference to Empedocles. For the close connections between *Symp.* and *Lysis*, see Introduction, §5.

e2-3 **'our ancestor Asclepius -- as these poets here tell us, and I believe them'**: Asclepius is the mythical founder of medicine, according to Hesiod (fr. 51) a son of Apollo; any doctor may be metaphorically his 'descendant', reflecting the tendency for medical knowledge to be handed down within particular families. Cf. Dover. – 'As these poets here tell us', i.e. poets like Agathon and Aristophanes; poets especially 'record' the mythical past ('and I believe them' is a somewhat back-handed compliment, raising the possibility that one might not).

186e3-187a1 **'both the whole of medicine, as I say, is governed through the agency of this god, and ... also gymnastic and agriculture'**: insofar as 'love' is involved, of course, so is Love. The move to other areas of expertise has been prepared for by 186a ('Love is there ... in ... practically everything that exists').

187a1-3 **'it is clear to anyone who pays even small attention to the matter that music is in the same position'**: it is uncertain whether *mousikê*, 'music', here means music (in our sense, usually without words), or music and poetry (as in 196e); it could in principle mean either, and while most of what follows seems to suggest the first, c7-d4 either does not definitely exclude, or positively includes, poetry (see d2n.). In either case, Eryximachus is trespassing on territory that belongs to Agathon and Aristophanes, since both certainly 'use' music (d1-2, 2-3), and everything that is said in d5-e5 about those who do has a ready application to them as poets. 'It is clear to anyone ...' perhaps throws down a lighthearted challenge to 'these poets here' (186e2): 'having dealt with my own subject of medicine, I'm now going to tell you all about yours'.

a4   **'though so far as his actual wording goes he doesn't say it very well':** Heraclitus was notoriously obscure, apparently expressing himself in disconnected sentences (so that in a way, if one wanted to put it like that, he doesn't say much 'very well': see a8n., on Eryximachus' tone).

a4-6   **'the one "being at variance with itself is in agreement, like a harmony of bow or lyre"':** Eryximachus seems slightly to misquote Heraclitus, and supplies a subject ('the text preserved elsewhere runs 'They do not understand that it [sc. what there is?], being at variance, is in agreement; a backward-stretching [or 'backward-turning'] harmony [*harmonia*, 'fitting-together'], like that of a bow or a lyre': fr. 51 Diels-Kranz).

a6-7   **'But it is quite illogical to say that a harmony is at variance':** 'harmony' (*harmonia*) here and in the remainder of the passage I take to stand for the collection of notes which constitute any given mode; it will be the harmony 'of a lyre' in the sense that it is that set of sounds which a lyre would produce if tuned to produce those notes. (If this means that Eryximachus is using the term in a different sense from Heraclitus, that hardly matters, since he is already reading what Heraclitus said in a fairly radical way, as well as – probably – misquoting it.) Here I follow a line suggested by Dover's comments on b4 *sumphônia* ('concord'), which (unlike Dover) I treat as intended as a synonym of *harmonia* as defined above. The other part of the key to the passage is provided by Bury (on 187c): 'Eryximachus analyses Music into Theory (*autê hê sustasis* [c5, 'the structure itself', sc. of harmony and rhythm]) and Practice (*katachrêsthai* ... [d1, i.e. deploying them]) ...' What is being talked about up until c7 is *theoretical* 'harmonies' and *theoretical* rhythms (i.e. types of harmony and rhythm), as distinguished by the expert musician.

a8   **'Perhaps what he meant to say':** it is not easy to believe that Eryximachus is supposed to be serious here (*of course* something can be simultaneously in disagreement and in agreement, if what's meant is something like a bow or a lyre: both exhibit an organized structure based on tension in two opposite directions). What one can say is that the correction of Heraclitus – or 'correction': S. started the vogue at 174b-c – provides a convenient launching-point for his next new idea (c5-7), that 'harmonies' and rhythms, as put together by the musician, in fact already illustrate the kind of friendship and unanimity that it requires work to achieve in the body (what else would one expect from harmonies?); where the two kinds of love, good and bad, come in, with music, is 'when one needs to deploy rhythm and harmony in relation to human beings' (c7-d2) – and *that*'s where one really needs skill from the practitioner ...

b1-2   **'from the high and the low, which were previously at variance, but which then later struck an agreement':** we do not need to ask whether 'the high and the low' are the sorts of things that could 'strike an agreement'; who would seriously disagree that a 'harmony', in the sense defined (see a6-7n.) represents (some sort of) concord between high and low?

c5-6   **'in the structure itself of harmony and rhythm':** i.e. in harmonies and rhythms as dependent on the peace-making function of music.

c7   **'nor is the double love yet present here':** Dover's comment that 'it comes as a surprise, after reading c3-5 with 186c[6]-e3 in mind, to hear now that there is no bad eros in mode and rhythm' spoils Eryximachus' legitimate if fairly laboured point. When he says it is easy to see 'what belongs to love in the structure itself of harmony and rhythm', he means just that harmony and rhythm themselves depend on the 'reconciliation' of the opposing elements out of which they are constructed; without it they would not exist (whereas a body in which the elements are 'at war' is still a body). (The mss. reading πῶς is meaningless; Konstan and Young-Bruehl's attempt to defend a πως looks unsuccessful.)

d2   '**whether one is composing, which they call musical composition':** *melopoiia can* in principle refer to the writing of lyric poetry, and similarly *melesi te kai metrois* ('melodies and measures') in d3 *could*, in principle, mean 'songs and measures' (*melos* is also the standard term for a lyric poem or song). The argument so far has referred to music without words, and that is how d1-4 must primarily be taken. Nevertheless lyric poets (who will include comic and tragic playwrights, insofar as comedies and tragedies both include lyric elements) themselves 'deploy rhythm and harmony', and a Greek listener or reader for whom the term *melos* was ambiguous would therefore not have had to make a clear choice between its different applications. Moreover, as Books II-III of the *Republic* amply testify, 'education' ('making correct use of melodies and measures once composed, which is called education', d3-4) would certainly have been conceived as including poetry as well as music. In short, d1-4 at the very least does not exclude, and should probably be taken as positively including, reference to poets – as should what follows: the Muses (d8-e1) are nothing if not patronesses of poetry. (The question underlying this n., of course, is why Eryximachus should spend so much time talking about *music*: cf. 185e6-188e5n. The answer I propose is that he is speaking with his eyes on Agathon and Aristophanes, whose speeches are yet to come – but especially on Aristophanes, in whose place he is speaking. See e1-2n.)

d3-4   '**which is called education':** the repeated use of this formula – what (*ho dê*) is called/they call (d2) *x'* – is no doubt partly for the sake of balance (echoing Pausanias at 180d6-e1); but Eryximachus' particular use of it perhaps also illustrates his fondness for (a kind of) precision, and a not unrelated habit of treating the familiar as if it were novel.

d4   '**here there really is something difficult, and which calls for a good practitioner':** i.e. a good musician (/poet), who will share the same general function as the good doctor, namely of distinguishing between good and bad 'loves', and acting accordingly ...

d5-7   '**The same theme as before comes back again ... it is these people's love that should be cherished':** 'the same theme as before' is Pausanias', cited at 186b8-c2, to the effect that 'it is a fine thing to grant favours to those people who are good, and shameful to gratify those who are immoral'. Now it is already reasonably clear that the good love that is to be cherished (by the musician/poet) is that of the people 'in relation to' whom music/poetry is to be 'deployed' (d1); and one might reasonably ask what on earth that has to do with *Pausanias'* idea, which relates to the beloved's 'gratifying' of a lover. The usual response is to say 'nothing', and to mount an explanation in terms of Eryximachus' intellectual limitations. But I suspect this to be too hasty a judgement. We have already been informed that doctors are among those who make people 'more orderly' – or at any rate their bodies (but e3-5 will also hint that medicine has a role to play in preventing 'immorality', by discouraging over-indulgence); if so, then d5-7 potentially has a double meaning – (1) 'one must gratify the orderly' (that is, musicians/poets must), and (2) 'the orderly ought to be gratified' (by the objects of their love), i.e. orderly people like doctors (and medicine is *my* trade). This playful ambiguity is, I propose, an important part of the reason for all the unconvincing rigmarole about the doctor as an expert in the 'erotics of the body' (though no doubt it does also target the 'philosophical' doctors for their airy theorizing, and play on Empedoclean theory). The overall thesis of the speech now becomes: 'doctors, gymnastic trainers, farmers, musicians(/poets), all experts (186a7, b1-2, 187e6-7) have it as their business to increase the amount of order in the world by 'gratifying/implanting the good love' – and by the way, as orderly ourselves (and as experts: see Pausanias at 184c ff.?), 'one should gratify', i.e. those we love should gratify (*dei charizesthai*, d7), us, on the basis that we improve them. ('Cherish' in d7 is *phulattein*. Its positive sense – 'guard' – here is guaranteed by its juxtaposition to *charizesthai*, 'gratify'; but in 188a1 it will mean 'watch out for'.)

d7-8 **'this is the beautiful Love, the heavenly one, the one who belongs to the Heavenly Muse':** if the suggestion in the preceding n. is right, Eryximachus has in a way genuinely returned to Pausanias' 'heavenly Love', who operates through the exchange of sexual favours for personal improvement; but now he adds a flourish of his own, with the unexpected substitution of 'muse' for Aphrodite. If Love really does operate in the musical sphere, then the substitution (and that of the Muse Polymnia for Aphrodite Pandemos, d8-e1) is far from 'pointless' (Allen); poets and musicians belong to the Muses, and so if they fall into good and bad (depending on whether they address the good and bad loves correctly or not), so will their presiding Muses. Eryximachus, no doubt, would have been rather pleased with his invention here. Urania ('Heavenly') and Polymnia (see following n.) happen to be two of the names of the Muses (see Hesiod, *Theogony* 75-9), but there is not the slightest suggestion that they would normally have been distinguished along the lines of Pausanias' Heavenly and Common Aphrodite.

d8-e1 **'the other one, the common one, belongs to Polymnia':** Polymnia is chosen presumably because her name ('she of the many hymns'; Allen has 'many-tuned') suggests, even if vaguely, '(the) many', 'the vulgar crowd'.

e1-2 **'and he must be applied with caution to those to whom one applies him':** if it is true that the present passage is (partly) addressed to the poets present, then it is plainly Aristophanes who is singled out here; it is the Muse of comedy, not of tragedy, that ought to be the 'vulgar' one. In ever so gently, and good-humoured, a way, Eryximachus is preaching to his neighbour. (For the larger implications of this reading of his speech, see Introduction, §4.5.) Pausanias had wanted to ban the 'bad' Love entirely; Eryximachus can hardly propose banning the vulgar Muse and her vulgar Love, suggesting instead that he be 'applied' (a good medical term) with caution – after all, he brings pleasure (e2). 'Applying him' must apparently be a matter of stimulating/gratifying that love in the hearer that belongs to Polymnia's Love; thus desire for excess – which is Eryximachus' conception of 'bad' love: see 188b4-5n., 186d5-6n. – will after all in this case be acceptable, within limits. But of course the musical practitioners' *own erôs* will also need to be 'applied with caution', in the sense that their beloveds will need to be wary of the attention of experts of such a dangerous kind (so: I'm an ideal lover, but watch out for Aristophanes?) – and this is perhaps the explanation of the otherwise rather peculiar notion of the *application* of (Polymnia's) Love.

e3 **'but that he may implant no tendency to immorality':** 'tendency to immorality' renders the single word *akolasia* (cf. 186c1), which used to be translated e.g. as 'licentiousness'; 'immorality' is less than satisfactory, insofar as the category of the 'moral' sits less than easily in the (ancient) Greek context, but English is short of general terms of moral approval and disapproval.

e4 **'desires relating to the expertise of the cook':** that is, in the language of the theory in play, 'love(s) ...'.

187e6-188a1 **'... and in everything else ... one much watch out ... for each of the two kinds of Love, for both are there':** Eryximachus now goes back to the idea – so far only broadly suggested – of love as working on a cosmic scale, by reference to other branches of expertise ('knowledge of these [the opposites], relating to movements of the heavenly bodies and seasons of the year, is called astronomy', b5-6, followed by a passage on the art(s) of the priest and the seer).

a2 'constitution': the same word that was translated as 'structure' in 187c5 (*sustasis*).

a3-4 'the things I was talking of just now': 186d6-e1.

a5 'find a controlled harmony and mixture': 'controlled' is *sôphrôn*, in P. most often used of self-control in human character and action; 'harmony' is somewhere between 'agreement' and 'fitting-together' (the root meaning of the word *harmonia*: cf. 187a4-6n., 6-7n.).

a7-8 'the lawless sort of Love': 'lawless' is 'with *hubris*'.

b2 'many other diseases of different kinds': 'of different kinds' is *anomoia* (lit. 'unlike', 'dissimilar'). Bury compares Aristotle, *Poetics* 1459b30 ('with episodes that are unlike', sc. each other). The unexpected word might perhaps be meant to suggest *anomos* (lit. 'law-less'); or – a more attractive suggestion? – it continues the punning we may want to discover in *anomoia* at 186b6 ('unlikes') and *homonoia* ('unanimity') at 186e1 and 187c3. (Dover has 'abnormal', Allen 'unusual'; at present I can find no parallel for such a sense, but that is hardly decisive.)

b4-5 'excess and disorder of such things in relation to each other – erotic things': 'such things' in b2 meant something like 'events arising out of the domination of the "lawless" Love'; here it must be the 'opposites', i.e. hot, cold etc. (a3-5). The surprising adjective *erôtikôn*, 'erotic', 'feeling desire' (as applied to people, it would mean 'amorous'), seems to be delayed for effect; its purpose is clearly to remind us that astronomy too, like medicine and music, is a branch of 'erotics'.

b6-c3 'Then again, all sacrifices ... cherishing or curing Love': religious practice generally will be concerned with human desires; sacrifices (which presumably bring in the category of priests) are ways of trying to ensure normal traffic – succinctly described by Diotima at 202e – between gods and men, while the seer will perhaps be occupied particularly with discovering what has gone wrong with divine-human relations. Once he has established that all impiety results from 'not gratifying the orderly Love, ... but the other one' (c3-5), Eryximachus tells us that the seer specializes in 'examining those who are in love' for signs of the bad love, and curing it. It is not easy to think of things real seers might do that resemble this; but if seers are concerned with the causes of impiety, and impiety has its origins in people's desires, then seers *ought* to be involved in examining them. In other words, perhaps this is another instance of Eryximachean invention – and identifying our innermost desires might well be thought to require the powers of a seer. In any case Eryximachus turns out to be a bit of a prophet himself: after all, it is Diotima, the woman from Mantinea, herself apparently a seer or *mantis*, who will turn out to 'know about matters of human love, that is, those that aim at right and piety' (d123). – ('Cherishing': *phulattein* (*phulakên*) as at 187d7.)

c3-4 'For all impiety tends to arise when one does not gratify the orderly Love ...': is it too fanciful to think here of Alcibiades, profaner of the Mysteries, and himself a lover of excess, failing to honour 'the orderly Love'? (No such example, of course, can be in *Eryximachus*' mind.)

d3 'right and piety': the mss. have ἀσέβειαν, 'impiety', instead of 'piety' (εὐσέβειαν), which is restored from Stobaeus; 'impiety' would work perfectly well (since the knowledge will be of both good and bad love), but 'piety' reads more naturally.

d4-5 'Love taken together as a whole has all power': that is, between them, good and bad Love (again, recalling Empedocles' Love and Strife) move everything.

d6-7 'both among us and among the gods': a 'polar' expression, giving the sense 'everywhere', 'in everything'.

d8-e1 'enabling us to to associate and be friends both with each other and with the gods': i.e. 'insofar as we are able to associate ...'? (P. writes δυναμένους as if he had written e.g.

πάντως ἡμᾶς ποιεῖ εὐδαιμονεῖν, 'makes us happy in every way' – sc. in every way that we *are* happy?.)

189a4 'the sort of noise and tickling that sneezing really is': Aristophanes perhaps caricatures the style as well as the content of Eryximachus' speech (cf. 187d3-4n., e1-2n.).

b1   'funny': *geloion* (see 174e1-2n.).

b6-7 'in the province of my Muse': i.e. of comedy. Rettig (ap. Bury) notices the connection with Eryximachus' references to the Muses Urania and Polymnia; the terms of Aristophanes' appeal (or pretended appeal) for sympathy (see following n.) half-suggest that 'his' muse is the 'heavenly' one.

b7   'things that people will laugh out of court': *katagelasta*. Dover proposes to translate 'contemptible' ('a quite strongly derogatory word'), but that may suggest slightly the wrong tone; rather 'things people will (simply) mock / treat with derision / fail to treat with any seriousness'. Aristophanes wants people to laugh at what he says, but not to behave as if he were just a buffoon – there will (or so he claims) be a serious point to what he has to say.

189c3-193e3: Aristophanes' speech. Since this mostly consists of a fairly straightforward, linear narrative, there is little point in attempting to summarize it. It is a story that attempts to 'explain' the passion that attaches to our sexual drives, and ends with a moral. (For detailed discussion of the *genre* it belongs to, see Dover 1966.)

189c3-4 'indeed I do mean to give a different kind of speech from the ones you and Pausanias have given': cf. 188e4-5. In fact he starts off in what looks like a rather similar vein; but that only serves to make what follows even more startling. Aristophanes' pairing of Eryximachus' and Pausanias' speeches reflects the fact that the former was explicitly designed to 'round off' the latter (186a1-3); by contrast, he will make a new start.

c5-6 'It seems to me that people have completely failed to recognize the power of Love': the way Aristophanes seems to pick up from Eryximachus' peroration ('... has the greatest power ...', 188d7), together with the *gar* introducing the sentence, perhaps suggests that 'people' here are meant to include Eryximachus and Pausanias (though the *gar* could be, not explanatory, but simply the sort of *gar* that introduces the fulfilment of a promise: 'I'm going to tell you a story: ... *gar* ...'). 'Recognizing Love's power', as it will turn out, means not just recognizing how powerful he is, but also, and especially, what *kind* of power it is. (Editors of the Greek text tend to print *erôs* here with a lower-case initial letter, while translators tend to translate 'Love'; the translators are surely right. P.'s original text, of course, would have made no such distinctions.)

c8   'whereas, as things are now, none of these things happens': Aristophanes here offers a variation on Phaedrus' original point (177a-c); the necessity for proper behaviour towards the gods provides a *leitmotiv* for his whole speech. (Dover's explanation of the construction of the Greek here seems to me helpful: 'not in the way in which, as things are now, ...'.)

d1-3 'helper of humankind and doctor of those ills the cure of which would bring happiness to the human race on the largest scale': Aristophanes picks up another part of Eryximachus' peroration (188d7-8), and reinforces his rejection of the doctor's account, while at the same time cheekily making Love himself a doctor; see also 191d3, 193d5. There will definitely be no 'filling in gaps' (188e4) here, only pure original invention.

d3-4 'So I shall try to explain his power to you, and you will teach other people': Aristophanes makes a playful claim to authority; compare Diotima's role as the (?) real (?) teacher of S. ('All these things she taught me', 207a4). But we should remember

189b5-7: Aristophanes still thinks he has something serious to contribute – or does he? The *style* of his narrative throughout, of course, is mock-serious.

e3   **'one of the kinds was androgynous'**: it may or may not be relevant to this part of Aristophanes' story that we evidently find an *Eros* with two genders and two or more of other things in Orphism – an Eros-Phanes 'described in the fragments as simultaneously male and female, with two pairs of eyes allowing him to see on all sides, two sets of genitals placed above his buttocks, and many heads' (Vernant 1989: 468); or that it has been suggested that the kind of cosmogony in which this strange figure appeared is actually parodied in Aristophanes' own *Birds* (see e.g. Calame 1996: 219-225). But for the difficulties even of dating the material in question, see esp. West 1983.

e5-7   **'the shape of each human being was entirely round, with back and sides making a circle'**: 'entirely round', I take it, is opposed to 'partly round' (like any ordinary middle-aged British male), and consistent with the possession of limbs; the reference to back and sides makes it clear that the trunk is meant. The idea as a whole may well allude both to Empedocles' 'whole-natured forms' (fr. 62 Diels-Kranz) and to his two-faced, two-chested monsters (fr. 61, which also refers to the mixing of male and female); given the tone of the whole, the allusion will merely be given an extra angle by the fact that Aristophanes' original humans actually *lack* chests, or fronts (fronts come later). *Pace* Waterfield, it will do no harm for the picture to include 'grotesque' (monstrous) elements, if we remember who the author is supposed to be.

e7-8   **'an equal number of legs'**: lit. (perhaps) 'as for legs, the same number as hands'.

190a4   **'in whichever of the two directions it wished'**: i.e. whichever of the two in which it faced; talk of 'forwards' and 'backwards' of course does not any longer (or rather yet) make sense.

a6-7   **'well, they used ...'**: at this point, influenced by the analogy, Aristophanes switches from singular (early humans visualized in terms of a single example) to plural, and also forgets the way he started the sentence – or so I suppose (other editors punctuate differently, in a way that seems to ignore the first *kai* in a4: '*both* in an upright position ...').

b2-3   **'and what shared in both male and female from the moon, because the moon too shares in both'**: that the moon is also double-gendered in some later texts (Bury) might suggest that it was a common notion; but it is just as likely that Aristophanes has invented it – the sun is irreversibly male, earth irreversibly female, so the moon has to be male-female (despite the fact that its name, *selênê*, is feminine, and that it is regularly identified with goddesses).

b6   **'their ambitions were on a large scale'**: 'the thoughts they had were big'.

b7-8   **'and what Homer says about Ephialtes and Otus is said about them'**: it is a regular part of P.'s methods in constructing stories/'myths' to say '*x*, which is said to have been about *y*, is really about *z*' (for a series of examples, see *Politicus* 268e ff.), and this is probably the point here. But Aristophanes could just mean 'what Homer says about Otus and Ephialtes is (also) said about these original human beings'. The reference is to *Odyssey* 11.305-20 (the pair plotted to pile Ossa on Olympus, and Pelion on Ossa ...; cf. also their imprisonment of Ares, *Iliad* 5.385-91). Homer plainly understands Otus and Ephialtes as human; their mother *claimed* that she conceived them from Poseidon, but even if she was telling the truth, that would not have been enough to make them divine.

c3   **'the giants'**: perhaps Otus and Ephialtes; but 'the giants' in principle represents a large and flexible category, including Hesiod's primordial creatures, sons of Earth (*Theogony* 185), one of whom, the monstrous Typhon, lies imprisoned beneath Mount Etna in Pindar, *Pythians* I ('wiping out' translates *aphanizein*, lit. 'remove from sight').

d1   **'immoral behaviour'**: *akolasia* again (cf. 187e3n.).

d4-5 'and they'll move upright on two legs': i.e. now they'll have just one way of moving about (called 'walking').

d8-e1 'like people who cut up sorb-apples before they preserve them, or like people cutting eggs with hairs': from *oa* (admittedly restored by editors using evidence from late lexicographers), 'sorb-apples', we move, perhaps (as if?) by sound-association, to *ôia*, 'eggs'. Dover and Waterfield both report having managed to cut a hard-boiled egg (shelled, of course) with a hair. Older editors tended to want to bracket the words 'or ... hairs', but Dover neatly explains it: 'Plutarch *Moralia* 770b mentions "dividing an egg with a hair" as a proverbial expression used jokingly of the ease with which lovers, apparently so firmly united, can fall out over a triviality. The point of the comparison here is the ease with which Zeus halved individuals who had taken their own physical integrity for granted.' One might add that any pair of halves will turn out to treat their original undivided state as something that would be the ideal consummation of their passion for each other – so that in retrospect Zeus *was*, in a sense, dividing lovers. If so, we might see the first comparison as a kind of cover for the second, suggesting just another reference to the ordinary business of life.

e2 'Apollo': as healer (and doctor), presumably (see e4, 186e2n., 197a7).

e8 'which is what they call the navel': here Aristophanes uses exactly Eryximachus' formula, and in just Eryximachus' way (see 187d3-4n., 189a4n.).

191a7 'locked themselves together': the transitive form of the verb means 'weave together', 'entwine' (also in b4).

b4-5 'whether it was a whole woman's half it encountered, what we now call a woman, or a whole man's': we might have expected a reference to the third, androgynous, gender here; but the point may in any case just be that the bereaved half is flailing about, desperately looking for any other half (no matter what it was half of). No doubt Aristophanes also wanted to get in the 'what we now call ...' formula, and he has already dealt with the name of the androgyne (189e1-5).

c1-2 'but in the ground, like cicadas': on how cicadas actually reproduce, see Dover. Athenians regularly understood, or expressed, their sense of autochthony in terms of their original ancestors' birth from the ground of Attica: see Loraux 1986 (esp. 148-50).

c5 'if a man encountered a woman': all halves are apparently now wandering around alone, looking for their matching halves (see d3-6), but the present description covers only those cases where they have intercourse not with their own halves; see c6-8, which suggests a kind of recreational sex that falls rather short of the total commitment involved when halves succeed in finding their own proper partners (192b5 ff.). In c8-d3, the picture switches to the present, when one of the main effects of our desire for our 'other half', until we find him/her (if we do), seems – to judge from the description in c4-8, and also from d6-e6 – to be sexual promiscuity. (We need not ask how the idea of 'other halves' can still apply to generations who have been born in the ordinary way, and are not the direct product of cutting in half; or if we do ask it, there is no answer.) In this sense at least, Aristophanes' theme has rather less in common with romantic ideas of love than is sometimes supposed (see also 192b5-c1n., e6-9n., e9-10n.).

c5-6 'they would breed and the race be reproduced': i.e. the human race (cf. 190c2-5).

c6 'satisfaction': lit. a 'filling-up' (cf. Eryximachus' description of medicine as 'knowledge of the erotic affairs of the body in relation to filling up and emptying' (186c7-8).

d2 'a restorer': lit. 'a bringer-together', 'assembler'.

d4 'a tally of a human being': '[i]f an object is cut in half and given half each to *A* in one part of the world and *B* in another, *A* and *B* can prove their identity to one another for any personal, commercial or political purpose' (Dover).

d4-5 'sliced like a flatfish': the point (Stallbaum) is that when one slices a flatfish, one slice at least has a complete 'face'.

d6-e3 'Those men who are cut ... come about from this kind': adulterers/ adulteresses, because they are always on the lookout for their half, and have not married her/him. The repetitiveness of '... have their origin in this kind ... come about from this kind' (with 'come about from this kind' again in e6) is awkward, and unparalleled elsewhere in the speech, though it just about fits as a kind of pseudo-scientific listing. If we followed some editors and omitted the last five words of the sentence, the result would be 'and those women (sc. who are cut from the combined kind) are attracted to men, and are adulteresses'.

e4 'do not pay very much attention to men': i.e. do not pay any (litotes)?

e6 '*hetairistriai*': the passage from Lucian cited s.v. in *LSJ*, and the lexicographers, suggest that the term tends to refer generically to 'women of Lesbos' (Lucian), but it looks as if here in *Symp.* it ought to be more specific, picking out a sub-class of women with the characteristics just described (not paying attention to men, inclined towards women) – somehow indicating *promiscuousness*, like 'adulterers' in d7-e1 and (by implication) 'adulteresses' in e2. The form of the word, apparently used only here in classical Greek literature, connects it with *hetairizô*, 'choose as one's *hetairos*', i.e. as 'friend, 'companion', 'member of *hetaireia*' [private, often political, grouping]', 'play the *hetaira*', or, apparently, 'associate with *hetairai*' (*LSJ* s.v.); it might then be reasonable to suppose that *hetairistria* could have the specialized sense of (e.g., a type that appears at least in Lucian) a 'respectable' woman who preferred the company of, and sex with, *hetairai*. On the term *hetaira*, usually translated 'courtesan' or 'prostitute', see esp. Kurke 1997, which among other things discusses the relationship of *hetairai* to the institution of the symposium.

191e8-192a3 'they show affection for men ... insofar as they are most manly by nature': the last clause gives the game away – that is how they *should* feel, and what they *should* enjoy, given their origin; but then their origins are fictional, and so too are the attitudes described (that is, insofar as they are ascribed to a particular group: see 192a7-8n.). That Aristophanes is up to something here is also surely suggested by the fact that those who would in effect take the *female* role, submitting themselves to the advances of their older lovers, are 'the most manly'; if they are 'all man' in one sense, they are hardly so in another (*andreios*, here 'manly', and deriving from *anêr*, 'man', is normally 'courageous'; a courageous woman is *ipso facto* a manly one). In short, Aristophanes is *joking*, something that should hardly come as a surprise; the passage, and indeed the context, as a whole teaches us practically nothing about fifth/fourth century Athenian mores. But the real pay-off is still to come ...

192a3-4 'It is a lie to say, as some people say, that they are shameless': the evidence suggests that most people would have believed in this 'lie', i.e. in the case of anyone who did behave in the way just described (Dover 1978:81-109); and of course if all Aristophanes has on hand to rebut it is his story of the three genders, they are likely to go on believing it – as he means them to do.

a7-8 'such people the only ones who as adults turn out to be real men in the political sphere': not 'these are the only kind of boys who grow up to be politicians', which omits *andres* (Nehamas/Woodruff), or 'it is only men of this sort who, when they grow up, enter on political affairs', which translates *andres* as if it were in a different place (Allen; similarly Waterfield). So: the real men among politicians are the ones who in their youth showed themselves not to be, though of course in the terms of the story these *were*, and *are*, the only ones with a truly masculine nature; Aristophanes offers a subtle version of the 'taunt in Old Comedy (e.g. Ar. *Knights* 875-80, Plato Comicus fr. 186) that eminent politicians in their youth submitted shamelessly (or for money) to homosexual importunities' (Dover).

b2   **'the rules of custom':** *nomos* again (see 182a8n.).

b3-4 **'it's enough for them to live with each other without getting married':** that is, presumably, for as long as their affair lasts; those who 'stay with each other throughout life' are the ones who have met their very own other halves, a class which is about to be, but has not yet been, introduced.

b   **'So there are no two ways about it':** or 'Absolutely, then ...'; πάντως, 'in every way', apparently reinforced by μέν, with οὖν functioning as connective. Cf. Denniston, *GP* 470: '... μέν may be either prospective, adversative (possibly) or affirmative: while οὖν may be either retrospective, logical-progressive, or ancillary and emphatic. Hence the combination of the particles presents a considerable diversity of usage.' Denniston does not discuss the present passage, and I have not been able to discover a precise parallel – unless it is in the next sentence, where again we have no use for a prospective μέν (the sentence marks the beginning of the climax of the whole story, and there is not even an implied contrast involved), and we do seem to need a 'logical-progressive' οὖν.

b4-5 **'such a person becomes ... someone who shows affection to lovers':** i.e. someone who shows/feels *philia* for lovers; S. will teasingly claim at 213d that Alcibiades has a manic version of *philerastia*, and indeed the description in 191e7 ff., to which 'such a person' refers, does not fit (the politician) Alcibiades at all badly, at least in his relationship – as he will describe it – with S.

b5-c1 **'whenever the lover of boys, or anyone else, encounters that half which belongs to him':** we now come to the climax of the story (192b5-193d6), the part to which the rest has been leading – and in which, perhaps, we might hope to find the substance and seriousness which Aristophanes seemed to promise at 189b (and which has so far hardly been in evidence). Dover:113 expresses a view which is probably representative, at least in tone, of modern readings of the passage: 'Aristophanes, unlike all the other speakers in *Smp.*, recognises that when you fall in love you see in another individual a special and peculiar "complement" to yourself; for you, union with that individual is an end, most certainly not a means, not a step towards some "higher" and more abstract plane, and very often you continue to love and desire that person even when much more powerful sensory or intellectual stimuli impinge upon you from alternative sources. Having composed for Aristophanes the only speech in *Smp.* which strikes a modern reader as founded on observable realities, P. later makes Diotima reject and condemn its central theme (205de, cf. 212c).' On this view, P. has in effect given Aristophanes an understanding of human love superior to his own – if that is represented by Diotima – and then proposed to throw it away. However there is an important question that needs to be asked. To what extent is Aristophanes starting from ordinary experience, and trying to 'explain' (or describe) that, and to what extent is it *the story itself* that is the point? This is a question that matters, because a considerable generosity is needed to discover in the detail of the passage what Dover and others have found in it, and it will only make sense to accord it that generosity if a case can be made for finding in (P.'s) Aristophanes a sympathetic and insightful commentator on the human condition rather than just, or mainly, a story-teller who takes his chances, especially for deploying his wit, where he finds them. So, for example, Dover says 'very often [when you have fallen in love] you continue to love and desire that person ...', but according to the requirements of the story, if you have really 'fallen in love', i.e. found your matching half, there is no possibility of ceasing to 'love and desire' the other person. Is Aristophanes then talking about the kind of love we might wish to idealize, or the kind of love which is described in his story – an urge towards 'union' which is more akin to unconscious biological processes (indeed *is* an unconscious biological process: cf. 192e9-10n.)? See further e6-9n.; and, for the larger issues involved here, Introduction, §4.4.

c2   'belonging': or 'relatedness' (*oikeiotês*); 'affection' is, as usual, *philia*.

c2-3   'they practically refuse to separated from each other, even for a short time': compare the behaviour of the just separated halves at 191a-b.

c4-5   'though they wouldn't even be able to say what they want ...': lit. '(people) who wouldn't even be able to say ...', sc. which makes their behaviour odd – in that case, why should they want to stay together? (Well, of course, my – Aristophanes' – account explains it.)

c7   'that it is for the sake of *this* ...': the ἄρα is what provides the sceptical tone (Denniston, *GP* 38).

c8-d1   'it is something else that the soul of each manifestly wants': Aristophanes is apparently working here with some vaguely defined soul/body (mind/body?) distinction – sex answers the body's need for filling up (cf. 191c6n.), but still we (our soul) can see, however dimly, that there is something more. See d7-e4n.

d3   'with his tools in his hands': i.e. his smith's tools.

d6   'to be together': lit. 'to be in the same (sc. location?)'.

d7-e4   'If this is what you desire ... having shared a common death': the idea of 'sharing a common death' looks initially like support for the romantic reading of the speech, and a corrective to the grossly physical language of the rest of the passage. However if Aristophanes' view of death and of Hades is anything like the traditional (Homeric) one – and we have no reason to suppose otherwise – it is anything but romantic. There is no afterlife; the dead, in Hades, are *dead*, mere shadowy phantoms of their former selves, quasi-physical entities robbed of their wits (*phrenes*). (See esp. *Odyssey* Book 11, and the beginning of Book 24.)

e1   'I am willing': since it is a god speaking, it seems appropriate to keep the shortened form of the verb (θέλω, as opposed to ἐθέλω) – as I take it, a witty gesture in the direction of expressions of the type 'if god wills' (part of the ms. tradition has θέλω, part ἐθέλω).

e6-9   'We know that there is not a single person ... and so from two become one': well, that's what Aristophanes claims, but it is not at all clear that anyone *would* want what has been described, insofar as it seems to involve the complete loss of separate identity. The other person would no longer be other at all, or a 'complement' (cf. b5-c1n.), or even a 'part of oneself', since 'oneself' would no longer have any reference. This is hardly likely to be what the modern reader will want from 'union' with someone else. (Why – unless we are mystics? – should we yearn for a state in which we no longer exist to experience its bliss?) The only way in which the whole image can be rendered acceptable is perhaps by smuggling in a continuing reference to the idea of two individuals even after the imagined welding process has taken place – despite Aristophanes' continued and emphatic insistence that two will now have become *one*. But why does he insist on this? I suggest that the idea of the original whole beings is primarily a (comic writer's) attempt to describe the origins of the phenomenon, not of what we call 'love', but specifically of sexual intercourse (we should keep in mind, as always, that 'love' is itself a makeshift translation of *erôs*; and that the basic connotation of *erôs*, in *Symp.* at least, is *sexual* passion). Just why is it that we are so eager to 'lock ourselves in embrace' with someone, and make Shakespeare's 'beast with two backs'? Answer: because originally we *had* two backs ... See following n.

e7-8   'what it was after all that he desired all that time': the question of what one's desires are *really* for will be central to what S. learned from Diotima – and will receive a wholly different answer; Aristophanes' view will be directly rejected (see 205d10-e3, which connects with 192e10-193a1), though not on the grounds suggested in the preceding n. (i.e. because it would entail a loss of identity).

192e9-10 'The cause is as I have said, that this was our original nature, and that we were wholes': separateness, then, is simply something to be regretted, and to be 'cured' (193d5). In terms of the latter image, the love of the two matching halves begins to look just like the process that drives the healing of a wound: the Hephaestus solution *is* the healing of a wound. Sexual intercourse is a kind of sticking plaster, whereas Hephaestus' tools would do the proper job. But this, after all, might be the kind of perspective we should expect from someone whose whole business is with drink and sex – or so S. said (177d-e). We must not, of course, forget that P. is writing Aristophanes' speech, and so in principle – provided it looks broadly Aristophanic, as it does – can do what he likes with it.

192e10-193a1 'the name "love" belongs to the desire and pursuit of the whole': cf. 192e7-8n. It is – I suggest – on this fine-sounding generalization, to which his whole story has in a way been leading, that any pretensions to seriousness on Aristophanes' part are likely to depend.

a2   'our crime': as described at 190b-c.

a2-3 'as the Arcadians were by the Spartans': often taken as an anachronistic reference to the destruction of Mantinea, and the dispersal of its population, in 385; but some voices argue that the passage could equally refer to Spartan action in the area in 418 (see Mattingly 1958). One possible view is that in dramatic terms the reference is to 418, but that any contemporary reader/listener after 385 might take it as covertly referring to 385. (Mattingly raises the intriguing possibility that Aristophanes himself might have served in the Athenian army in Arcadia around 418, which would provide an immediate motive for mentioning the area.)

a7   'becoming like dice-tallies': cf. 191d4n. The relevant point about a die cut in half is presumably that it is useless without the other half.

a7-b1 'This is why everyone must urge pious behaviour in relation to the gods in everything': sc. because even if only one or two of us step out of line (like Otus and Ephialtes), we shall all suffer?

b2-3 'and achieve the other, as Love guides and commands us': i.e. achieve reunion with our other halves, which Love prompts to us to seek throughout our lives ...

b3-4 'and he acts contrary to gods who is hated by them': this has the ring of verse (cf. Bury). The translation supplies 'to gods', as the Greek would allow (lit. 'he acts contrary who by gods is hated'), and as seems required by the logic of the sentence, such as it is. (Not: 'whoever acts to the contrary is hated by the gods', Allen, or 'Whoever opposes Love is hateful to the gods', Nehamas/Woodruff.)

b4   'if we become friends': sc. with the god. The general moral seems to be: go with the flow, don't resist Love, and be pious to the gods (where piety is implied to include not resisting Love).

b5-6 'we shall find and meet the beloved who belongs to ourselves': as shown by what follows, 'the beloved' here refers to other halves in general; all of us, as halves, will be like lovers to the other half of us.

b6   'which few people nowadays do': so that the vast majority of us are doomed to disappointment or promiscuity, or both (and even those who do find their other halves will still, in their deepest selves, remain frustrated: c3-5n.).

b7-8 'turn my speech into a comedy, by saying that I'm talking about Pausanias and Agathon': *kômôidein* must here mean 'treat me as saying something (merely) funny' – which would be a case of mocking him, because he is (supposedly) *trying* to say something serious (cf. Dover). But again we are entitled to ask just how serious he has really succeeded in being; the denial that he is referring to Pausanias and Agathon, that faithful pair, itself looks transparently disingenuous, although of course he can claim not *only* to be referring to them.

c3-5 'if our love were to run its full course ... returning to our original nature': Waterfield fills out 'and *thereby* recover our original nature' (my italics); in fact, of course, Hephaestus is not going to appear with his tools, so that the very best we can really hope for is just to *find* our other half – and even that, as we already know from b6, and are about to be reminded (c5-d1), is likely to be more than most of us can ever achieve. But according to what was said earlier, even those lovers who are perfectly matched are still dissatisfied (192c-d): sex isn't enough, nor apparently is each other's company. Thus what Aristophanes ought to be saying now is that true happiness lies in actually returning to our original condition; and c4-6 could in fact also be taken (without Waterfield's supplement) in that way. A little ambiguity, here and in d1-6, is in Aristophanes' interests. However if this is right, then the net outcome is that he himself will have admitted the essentially unsatisfactory nature of the best kind of life he recognizes – something that will entirely suit P.'s own purposes.

c7-d1 'this is to find a beloved with a nature congenial to oneself': sc. with whom to spend time and enjoy sex (if the story means anything at all), but probably not on a permanent basis – which is after all meant to be one of the main distinguishing features of lovers in the preceding category. (*They* live permanently together, of course, because they have found their matching tally.)

d5-6 'he will establish us in our original condition and, by healing us, make us blessed and happy': on the likely ambiguity of this, see c3-5n.

d7-e1 'as I asked, don't make a comedy out of it, because ...': i.e. don't take up time picking out things to laugh at. ('As I asked': b7-8.)

e1-2 'what the people who are left will each say – or rather what each of the two of them will say': 'a precision worthy of Prodicus', says Bury (i.e. because a different term in Greek is more appropriate if there are two people involved: cf. 194d8-9), but it may be more interesting than that. The move from 'each' to 'each of the two of them' has the specific effect of excluding Aristodemus, who is sitting between Aristophanes and Eryximachus (cf. 185d4-5n.); either, perhaps, Aristophanes is actually proposing to pass over him, or he is represented as particularly anxious to hear what Agathon and S. will say – as well he might be (for his interest in S.'s reaction to his speech, see 212c).

e4 'according to Aristodemus': in fact, the Greek just has the normal 'he said'; P. does not here draw any more attention than this to Aristodemus' presence (see preceding n.).

e7-8 'because of the many and varied things that have already been said' continues the mild compliment to Aristophanes, simultaneously putting his speech on a par with the others. So nothing special there, at any rate so far as Eryximachus is concerned (nor, evidently, was there anything worth reporting about the general reaction to Aristophanes' speech).

194a1 'you've already made a fine showing in the competition': in talking of it as a competition, or *agôn*, S. here acknowledges something that the speakers themselves have in any case taken for granted (see e4-5n.); Agathon follows up by comparing it to a *theatrical* competition (a 5-7).

a8 'I'd be pretty forgetful': μεντἄν = μέντοι ἄν, with μέντοι emphasizing ἐπιλήσμων (also in c1).

b1-2 'as you mounted the platform with your actors': S. appropriately refers to the *proagôn*, an occasion in advance of a dramatic festival when publicity about the plays could be presented ('but there is no evidence that there was ever a proagon at the Lenaia', Sider 1980:46 – apart from the present passage?).

b3-4 **'compositions of your own'**: *logoi*, which of course can also mean 'speeches'.

c3 **'you thought to be clever'**: 'clever' is *sophos* again ('ordinary people': *hoi polloi*, 'the many', 'the majority').

c4-5 **'Now maybe we're not the ones ... part of the mass'**: a deliberately appalling, provocative argument, giving another variation on the familiar theme of Socratic ignorance.

d1-2 **'And towards ordinary people you wouldn't feel ashamed ...?'** Is there the faintest of suggestions that Agathon *was* doing something shameful in presenting his compositions to the public? (Certainly, by the end of the dialogue it will have become perfectly clear that S. has no high opinion of Agathon's qualities, either as intellectual or as poet.) If so, Phaedrus' sudden intervention (d3) is timely.

d5-6 **'so long as he has someone to converse with, especially someone beautiful'**: 'converse with' is *dialegesthai*, here for the first time with reference to that special kind of *Socratic conversation* (see Introduction, §§3.4-6). Talking to other people (especially beautiful ones: quite what philosophy has to do with beauty may become clearer later), in the style in which he has just been talking to Agathon, is what S. most likes doing; and as if to drive home the point the same verb, *dialegesthai*, is repeated three times in the next six lines. But whatever S. would prefer to be doing, speech-making is the present business.

e2-3 **'S. will have other plenty of other opportunities for conversation'**: as if philosophy were just another thing to do (as it is, apparently, for Agathon – and for Phaedrus: d6-7).

194e4-197e8: Agathon's speech. 'An encomium calls for the right kind of method: first one must say what the subject's qualities are, then say what benefits he brings. Well, Love is happiest of the gods, because he is most beautiful and best. He is most beautiful, because he is youngest, not oldest, and indeed has nothing to do with old age, and because he is most delicate, most supple, and has the finest of complexions. He is also just, moderate [i.e. 'self-controlled', *sôphrôn*], courageous – and wise, being not only a poet, of a wisdom sufficient to make others into poets, but also creator of other things [i.e. living ones]; he is responsible, too, both for excellence in all sorts of expertise and for the bringing into being of that expertise. Before Love – clearly, of beauty – was born, Necessity ruled; after his birth, order supervened and everything good came about for both gods and men ...' The last part of the speech (197c-e), which enumerates the goods in question, is a particularly exaggerated display of rhetoric at its most ornamental, and 'Gorgianic' (as S. will suggest at 197b-c). On the extent of the connections with Gorgias, see Dover:123-4; just as striking, as Dover shows, is the extent to which Agathon's peroration exhibits poetic rhythms. (The few fragments of Agathon's tragedy that remain – see Nauck 1889 – are probably enough to confirm the accuracy of P.'s parody of him.) One of the other main features of the speech is the extent to which, implicitly, it is about the speaker himself, not only through the conceit of Love as poet and maker of poets (in a speech which, in addition to its poetic diction and rhythms, actually breaks into verse at one point), but no doubt also through the emphasis on Love's youthful beauty; almost the first thing we were told about Agathon was that he is *beautiful* (174a8), and there is little doubt about his awareness of the fact (but see 195b3n.). According to von Blanckenhagen 1993 we are meant to think of Agathon's claim to being young and beautiful as inappropriate, even grotesque, and to find 'a tinge of malice' (66) in S.'s describing him at 223a1 as a 'boy', or 'young lad' (*meirakion*). However this interpretation probably depends too heavily on Aristophanes' portrait of Agathon – as effeminate, clean-shaven and 'wide-arsed' – in *Thesmophoriazusae* (191-2, 200 ff.). There is no clear trace of any negativeness of attitude on the part of the other symposiasts towards either Agathon or his view of himself, and indeed, since they are his guests, there could hardly be. In any case we can only guess at what Agathon's age would have been at the dramatic date of *Symp.*; he could still have been in his twenties, if he was around puberty at the dramatic date of the *Protagoras*, i.e. about 430 (see *Protagoras* 315d-e, where he appears as *neon ti eti meirakion*, i.e. 'still pretty much a young lad', and already Pausanias' beloved). Then again, we may reasonably ask how precise P. is, or needs to be, about such details. But suppose Agathon to be about thirty: even then he surely could have been described, with the kind of seriousness appropriate to the context, as a beautiful 'boy', especially by someone more than twenty years older (S.). After all, Apollodorus (or Aristodemus) himself describes Agathon, in an apparently matter-of-fact, or even affectionate, way, as *neaniskos* ('young man'), a term sometimes associated with *meirakion* (see *LSJ* s.v.): 198a2. If our own attitudes, if we had been present, might have been different, that is of questionable relevance; our starting-point, at least, must be what those who *are* present think, not least because that will – presumably – determine what they say and do (nor, again, is there anything in that to suggest that they are laughing silently at Agathon). S. will have other, and more important, criticisms to make of Agathon, and although these are not unconnected with his vanity, the latter as such is merely allowed to surface without itself becoming an issue. (But see 195b3n., 213a1n.)

e4-5 **'What *I* mean to do is first to say how I must say what I say, then to say it':** the repetition of 'say' (*eipein*: actually only three times in the Greek) is of course deliberate. The stress in 'what *I* mean to do' (*egô men dê*) immediately signals Agathon's consciousness of the competitive context – 'none of the others has done it [cf. e5-7], as they should have; I shall'. Cf. (a1n., and) Pausanias at 180c-d, Eryximachus at 185e-186a, and 189c3-4n.

e5-7 **'For all those who have spoken before me ... the goods the god is responsible for giving them':** it is perfectly true that no one else has said much about the god himself, which one might expect to have been unusual in encomia (cf. Dover:12; 'eulogizing' in e6 = *enkômiazein*, 'giving an encomium to'). The data available, one might say, would have been somewhat sparse, apart from poetic and artistic representations; however Agathon will make up his own data by means of a kind of 'argument' from 'evidence' which is by now familiar.

e6 **'congratulating':** lit. 'calling happy', *eudaimôn* (for the connection between 'happiness' and goods, cf. Diotima at 205a1).

195a2-3 **'namely to describe in speech what sort of character whoever is the subject ...':** i.e. 'the nature of the subject of the speech and the nature of that for which he is responsible' (Dover), but with the emphasis falling on the first.

a6 **'if it is permitted and will not cause divine anger to say it ':** perhaps a slightly more successful formula than Pausanias' at 180e3-4.

b1 **'First, he is youngest of the gods, Phaedrus':** i.e. not the oldest, as you said.

b2 **'flitting as he does in flight':** both words in Greek derive from the same root, and their juxtaposition is unexpected. Bury calls it a 'poetic mode of giving emphasis' – though in fact the only two classical parallels he gives are both from prose: in the possibly inauthentic (Platonic) *Letter* VIII (354c), and the certainly inauthentic *Epinomis* (974b).

b3 **'at any rate it comes to us more quickly than it ought':** might this idea – which looks extraneous to the argument – perhaps be a wry comment on his own situation (cf. 194e4-197e8n.)?

b5 **'and he *is* young':** 'young' is supplied in the translation, as it must be. – **'the old saying':** see *Odyssey* 17.218.

b7-c1 **'more ancient than Cronus and Iapetus':** calling someone by either of these names is a way of saying that they are out-of-date (so with Cronus e.g. at *Euthydemus* 287b). Cronus took over kingship of the gods by castrating his father Uranus, Zeus by imprisoning Cronus (cf. c4-5); Iapetus is Cronus' brother, another Titan, imprisoned with him – and also father of Prometheus, another benefactor of mankind, rather better-known in that role than Love.

c2-3 **'those old happenings that Hesiod and Parmenides report in relation to the gods'**: if 'those old happenings' already refers to things like castration and imprisonment (c4-5), then apparently there was a description of such things in Parmenides to parallel that in Hesiod's *Theogony*. But that would scarcely be in tune with our other evidence about Parmenides' concerns, and in fact the reference need only be to 'old happenings' in general, i.e. anything that happened before (on Agathon's account) Love was born. Phaedrus quoted Parmenides as making Love first of the gods (178b12), and Hesiod as making him one of the first: no, says Agathon, it must have been Necessity (here associated with violence: c5) that operated then – and in fact, one of Parmenides' fragments has 'strong Necessity' (*kraterê ... Anankê*) 'holding [sc. what there is] in the bonds [*desmoi*, as here in c5] of limit, which pens it in all around!' (fr. 8.30-1 Diels-Kranz). Agathon might, then, be indulging in a playful correction of Parmenides, paralleling Eryximachus' of Heraclitus, but perhaps that is not his style, and in any case there is nothing to show that *he* – as opposed to the author, P. – knows anything much about Parmenides; he behaves, perhaps, as if Parmenides is just another poet telling of the birth of the gods.

c4 **'if they were actually reporting the truth'**: whether Agathon has any interest at all in 'truth' must at best be an open question (cf. S. at 198d-e).

c6 **'affection'**: or 'friendship' (*philia* again).

c6-7 **'since Love has been king of the gods'**: a deliberately extravagant way of putting the idea that the gods' affairs are 'governed' by friendly affection (who doesn't know that Zeus is king?).

d1-2 **'he lacks a poet of Homer's quality ...'**: a deficiency, of course, which Agathon will supply, in part building on Homeric resources (d2-e4). We need not suppose that the implicit comparison of himself with the greatest of poets is anything (or much) more than humorous.

d2-6 **'For Homer is declaring ...'**: the quotation is from *Iliad* 19.92-3; Atê is the goddess who takes away men's wits, and causes them to make stupid decisions (as Agamemnon is claiming she did him, when he slighted Achilles).

e8 **'both with his feet and all over'**: this kind of artful precision ('I started with Love's feet; now I'm moving on from there'), different from Eryximachus', is typical of Agathon's style.

196b6 **'Love neither wrongs nor is wronged'**: 'a somewhat reckless statement, considering the importance of eros as a motive of violence and fraud in myth, history and everyday life' (Dover); but such 'reckless', or deliberately paradoxical, claims are fundamental to Agathon's speech as a whole (see already 195c6-7n., and there is much more to come), and are typical of the kind of display oratory it represents – i.e. the kind that is primarily designed to demonstrate the virtuosity of the speaker. Gorgias' own *Encomium of Helen* is of this type: even (Homer's) Helen herself did not think she was *completely* innocent, but Gorgias claims to be able to show it, as Agathon will pretend to demonstrate the truth of *his* claim (unless 'pretend' suggests a sharper awareness of the line between truth and falsehood than P. wishes to attribute to him).

b7-c3 **'For neither does Love himself have things done to him by force, ... nor ... does he do things by force ...'**: both arguments are (again) entirely verbal. If it means anything to say that 'force does not touch Love' (or love), it means e.g. that the presence of Love implies that of 'affection (friendship) and peace' (195c6); but Agathon chooses to take 'touch' in the sense of 'lay hands on'. Similarly, 'everyone serves Love willingly in everything' makes sense as a description of the willingness of lovers to undertake any form of slavery to achieve their ends (cf. e.g. Pausanias at 183a), but Agathon understands it instead as meaning that all the effects of Love are willed by those subject to him (and therefore not forced, therefore not unjust), which is at best a more doubtful proposition, at least within the Greek literary tradition (cf. Dover). The idea of laws as 'kings of cities', according to Aristotle (*Rhetoric* 1406a18-23), is taken from the fourth-century rhetorician Alcidamas, himself apparently a pupil of Gorgias.

c3-8 **'As well as justice, he shares most fully in moderation. For it is agreed ...':** more verbal play, this time on the idea of 'mastery' (*kratein*: 'to control', 'to be stronger/better than') – no pleasure is stronger than Love (we get no greater pleasure from anything than we do from *erôs*); if they are weaker than him, (other) pleasures and desires are mastered by him; but moderation (= 'self-control', 'self-mastery') is agreed to be mastery over pleasures and desires; therefore Love is superlatively moderate.

d1 **'"not even Ares stands up to" Love':** Agathon quotes from a line of Sophocles (fr. 235 Nauck[2], from the lost play *Thyestes*), substituting 'Love' for the original 'necessity'.

d2 **'for Aphrodite, so they say':** see *Odyssey* 8.266-366.

d2-4 **'and the possessor is stronger than the one possessed; but if ...':** Agathon seems to continue the play on *kratein* (and *kreittôn* 'stronger', or 'better') – if Love masters/is superior to the most courageous of the others, he must therefore himself be the most courageous of all (but of course Love's 'superiority' is not in courage).

d5-6 **'it remains to speak about his wisdom; so one must try so far as possible not to fall short':** 'wisdom' is *sophia*, giving us the list of four main virtues which – sometimes with the addition of 'piety' – features regularly in P.'s dialogues (most famously in Book IV of the *Republic*), although it probably would not have struck any contemporary Athenian as strange or novel. But Agathon's 'wisdom' is no more Platonic wisdom (or wisdom as understood by P.'s S.: i.e., roughly, knowledge of what is good and bad for us): than his 'justice', 'moderation' or 'courage' are their Platonic counterparts; it turns out to include any technical expertise, from poetry to metal-working, and from weaving to politics. Cf. Pausanias at 184c-d, and esp. 184c5-6n. Agathon starts from poetry, identified as 'my own expertise' (d7); he too, then, is 'wise', in this respect (cf. 174c8n.) – and when he says 'so one must try so far as possible not to fall short' in talking about the god's wisdom, he presumably means just that he shouldn't fall short *in wisdom*. ('Skill' increasingly looks closer to the sense of *sophia* in this context, but this translation would of course hide the connection, and contrast, with Socratic-Platonic 'wisdom'.)

e1 **'as Eryximachus honoured his':** 186b-e.

e2-3 **'certainly everyone who is touched by Love turns into a poet ...':** on the likely quality of such 'poetry', see *Lysis* 204d. The idea, or at least the quotation ('even if he is unmusical before'), is from Euripides' lost *Sthenoboea* (fr. 666 Nauck[2]).

e4-5 **'a poet skilled in all kinds of creation in the sphere of music':** 'creation' here translates the usual word for 'poetry', *poiêsis*, lit. 'making' (cf. 205b-c); 'in the sphere of music' (for this sense of *mousikê*, including both music in our sense and poetry, see 187a1-3n.) prepares for the introduction of Love as creator on a rather larger scale (197a1-4) – i.e. as creator of living creatures. That this rather more obvious role of Love should be introduced in passing (197a4 ff. picks up again from 196e5-197a1), and on the back of the idea of Love as poet, is itself no doubt meant (by Agathon) as witty, and (by P.) to illustrate the nature of Agathon's 'wisdom' or 'skill'. 'Skilled in' is 'good at' (*agathos*, the adjective corresponding to *aretê*, 'virtue' or 'excellence', + accusative).

197a1-4 **'And then again, ... who will refuse to accept ...?'** Well, many might jib – as of course Agathon knows perfectly well – at the idea that it is Love's *wisdom*, exactly, that is responsible for procreation. (But on Diotima's account, Love will at any rate turn out to be a philosopher.)

a4-6 'But with the craftsmanship that belongs to the various skills ...': Agathon here seems to embellish and generalize the idea in 196d6-197a1, perhaps partly as a bridge to a7 ff. (Apollo and archery, etc.). But 'craftsmanship' (cf. 205c2) and 'skills' are wide enough to include poetry itself; presumably Agathon would like to be thought of as having been taught by Love (and 'felt his touch') to greater effect than the ordinary lover (cf. 196e2-3n.), and his prize at the dramatic festival means that he is, for the moment at least, anything but 'obscure' (a6). 'Being taught/touched by Love' seems to mean being motivated by a love of beauty (see b4-5); at the same time achieving excellence in the skills will mean acquiring 'wisdom', which is part of virtue, or goodness (his possession of supreme virtue is what makes Love himself best, most good: 195a, 196b). By implication, great and famous artists (and poets) will be driven by love/desire (a8) of both the beautiful and the good, as exemplified in the person of Love.

a7-b3 'Archery, furthermore, medicine ...': having made Love a musician and poet, and responsible for excellence in all spheres of expertise, Agathon now claims, or half-claims, that the divine inventors of all of these actually learned them from Love; after all, must their achievements not have been driven by 'desire and love' – for beauty (b4)? The pairing 'desire (*epithumia*) and love' is presumably necessary because whatever caused Apollo e.g. to invent archery, it was not *sexual* desire, even if it was desire for something beautiful (and good: see preceding n.), and even if Diotima will play with such an idea (see esp. 208c1 ff.). But then if that cause was Love, as Agathon claims, then Love simply is desire for the beautiful, and in relation to beauty 'love' and 'desire' are interchangeable. Some such broadening of the scope of *erôs* will later turn out to be built into the foundation of S.'s account of the subject. (γε μήν = 'furthermore': see Denniston, *GP* 349.)

b2-3 'in "the government of gods and men"': the metaphor ('government' is literally 'steering', *kubernan*, Lat. *gubernare*), and the unusual genitive that follows it, make it attractive to treat the words as a poetic quotation; and *Euthydemus* 291d at least indicates that the metaphor was alive and kicking in Aeschylus. Cf. Renehan 1990. We should not of course forget (and have not been given much chance to forget) that Agathon is himself a poet; but he seems to save composing, or quoting from himself, till a bit later (c6-7).

b4-5 'of beauty, clearly, since there is no love for ugliness': at 206e2-3 Diotima will claim, somewhat surprisingly, that love is not of 'the beautiful' (or what is beautiful: *tou kalou*; cf. *tôn kalôn*, 'the beautiful', lit. 'those things/people (?) that are beautiful', in b7-c1 below), but see the detail of the n. on 206e2-3. The question of what love (*erôs*) is truly of will be one of Diotima's main preoccupations; Agathon typically deals with it in a mere parenthesis. It will also become clear that *erôs* can be felt for ugliness, or at least for the ugly: Alcibiades, after all, feels it for S. But counter-examples are likely to be of as little concern to Agathon as counter-arguments will be (see 201b-c).

b5 'just as I said at the beginning': so Agathon neatly closes the circle.

b7-c1 'from the love of the beautiful all good things came about for both gods and men': the ambiguity of the plural *tôn kalôn* (see b4-5n.: neuter, or masculine?) has a point; after all, whatever may be true of the gods, or of other craftsmen/experts, Love's connection with *poets* was by way of his habit of inspiring lovers. In this case, then, which matters particularly to Agathon, good things – poetry, but also presumably other things too (e.g. sex) – do come about from loving beautiful *people*.

c2-4 'being himself first most beautiful and best', is then responsible ...': i.e., as I take it, other things are still allowed to be 'most beautiful and best' (of their kind, maybe), but his possession of these qualities, as cause of them in others, is prior.

c6-7 **'"peace among men, on the sea calm,/ without wind, bedding of winds and sleep amidst grief"'**: the deliberately clever transition back from metaphor to original idea in *nênemian / anemôn / koitên / hupnon* ('without wind' / 'of winds' / 'bedding' / 'sleep') suggests parody (i.e. by P.), but who can tell? (An alternative punctuation, with the comma after *anemôn* rather than after *nênemian* – giving 'windless of winds, bedding and sleep' – would probably not help.) Bury points out the echo of *Odyssey* 5.391-2/12.168-9, where however a similar repetition is less obtrusive.

d3 **'in festivals, when choruses perform, at sacrifices'** partly continues the reference to the present occasion (for the sacrificial element, see 173a6).

d6 **'a spectacle for the wise'**: or 'a wonder to the wise', but *theatos* (given Agathon's association of himself with Love) may be meant to suggest *theatron*, 'theatre' (cf. the play between S. and Agathon at 194a-c on the theme of theatres and the wise).

d8 **'caring for good, uncaring of bad'**: i.e. caring for *agathôn* ...; it would surely be entirely in tune with Agathon's speech if we detected here another pun on his name (cf. 174b).

e1 **'in speaking, a steersman ...'**: as he has been 'steering' Agathon in his speech ... 'Defender' ('steersman, defender ...') is Dover's rendering of *epibatês*, formed from *epi* + *bainein* ('go/walk on'), and normally used of a soldier on board ship to defend the rowers. The choice of word is puzzling until we recall the idea of Love as walking (*bainein*) not on (*epi*) earth, or on skulls, but ... (195e2-4); its effect is to confirm the self-reference – which may also perhaps underlie 'in trouble, in fear, in longing' as well as 'in speaking' (Agathon is after all labouring, fearful of what his audience will think, longing for victory?).

e3-5 **'whom everyone must follow, hymning him beautifully, sharing in the song he sings ...'**: here Agathon's identification of himself with the poet Love is perhaps at its most open; given the nature of the connection between Love and poetry (196d6-197a1), 'following' Love may also be meant to include pursuing beautiful young men (cf. 197b7-c1n). See 204c1-2n. Is the implication that Agathon did not necessarily match Pausanias' fidelity to him? Or is he just teasing, and/or falling in with the mood of the occasion?

e7-8 **'sharing as it does partly in play, partly in a modest seriousness, to the best of my personal ability'**: 'to the best of my personal ability' probably explains the 'modest' ('moderate', *metrios*). The upshot is probably that Agathon *is* in fact claiming to have been partly serious – in contrast to his model, Gorgias, who seems content to write off his *Encomium of Helen* as a *'paignion* ['plaything' or 'trifle'] of mine' (fr. 11.21: ... *Helenês men enkômion, emon de paignion*): '(Gorgias) reveals in the very last word that he regards the whole paradoxical composition as a game', MacDowell 1982:43). It is not clear where exactly the seriousness of Agathon's speech is supposed to lie; but then P. clearly wishes to leave us with a picture of someone who has a distinctly uncertain relationship with anything resembling the truth.

198a1-199c4 represents a short interlude, in the course of which S. states the terms on which he will make his contribution (namely that he be allowed to tell the truth, 'with whatever terms and arrangement of expressions happen to occur to me': 199b4-5); he then starts by getting Phaedrus' permission 'just to put a few more little questions to Agathon, and then after I've got his agreement on these I'll speak my piece' (199b8-c2). In fact, the question and answer session extends at least up to 204c8, but with a change of personnel in the middle: at 201d1 ff. S. introduces his report of conversations he had with a Mantinean woman of unusual powers, Diotima, in which she corrected him for making – as it happens – just the sort of mistakes that Agathon has made. She herself is an expert on things erotic, and at 204d1 S. launches into the positive part of her account; but it is still in the form of responses to S., so that in effect, although the final part is a long piece of monologue in reply to the briefest of questions (208b7-9), there is strictly speaking nothing by way of a continuous speech to match the others, and in any case strictly nothing (if we believe S.; but should we?) that he did not get from someone else. In short, he 'speaks his piece' in a rather special way, which has more in common with his preferred method of conversation (*dialegesthai*: see esp. 194d5-6n.) than with the set speeches of the other contributors, even if it reaches what is certainly, in retrospect (and must in any case be) a predetermined conclusion.

198a2-3 **'at the appropriateness of the young man's speech both to himself and to the god'**: i.e. Agathon has served the god well, as we should have expected from someone of his brilliance (but is there perhaps also, at another level, a reference to the way Agathon has continually contrived to associate Love with himself?).

a5 **'I was foolish to feel the fear I felt before'**: the translation, borrowed from Nehamas and Woodruff, perhaps gets close to the feel of the Greek *adees ... deos dedienai*, lit. 'to have feared a fearless fear'; 'in caricature of Agathon's style', Bury (who offers parallels from Euripides: 'marriage that is no marriage', and so on), and preparing us for the sharp irony of what S. will go on to say in b1 ff.

a6 **'just now'**: 194a2-4.

c3 **'I found myself exactly in the position Homer describes'**: *Odyssey* 11.633-5, of which there are several direct echoes in c4-6; the *Odyssey* passage does not include a reference to the peculiar effect of seeing Medusa's head, but it does have Odysseus leaving (Hades) in a hurry in case he encounters it.

c4-5 **'by sending a terrifying Gorgias' head of eloquence in his speech against *my* speech'**: lit. 'by sending a head of a Gorgias clever [*deinos*, recalling Homer's different *deinos*, of the 'terrible', 'awesome', monster] at speaking, in his speech, against my speech'; the repetition (which itself seems art*less*) is hard to reproduce in English, in what is already a complex sentence.

c6 **'as I hadn't before'**: ἄρα (as in d2: 'after all' – and again in d7, 199a4).

c7 **'was behaving ridiculously'**: *katagelastos ôn* (cf.189b7n.).

d1-2 **'declared that I was an expert in things erotic'**: 177d7-e1n. ('expert' is *deinos*, as in c5).

d2-3 **'when after all I knew nothing about the matter – I mean, how one should go about composing an encomium on anything'**: it looked for a moment as if S. was withdrawing his claim to know about love-matters, but after all he was not; and since he is about to insist on telling the truth about them, he had better not.

e4-5 **'For it seems that what was proposed ... not that we should actually offer him one'**: sc. because if what was said was not true of him, then it was not an encomium *of him* at all?

198e5-199a1 **'It's for that reason ... that you rake up everything you can think of saying, declaring him of such a character and responsible for so many things'**: the 'you' here is plural, but the phrasing 'of such a character ...' seems to refer specifically to Agathon's speech (see esp. 194e7-195a3), and it is doubtful how far S.'s criticisms would in fact touch e.g. Aristophanes' speech. It looks as if he is actually still talking about Agathon's performance, but associating the others with it, which is after all not unreasonable, given the rapturous reception they all gave it (198a1-3). S.'s applause ('*everyone* present burst into applause') will presumably have been ironic. 'You rake up everything you can think of saying': 'rake up' is borrowed from Bury (lit. 'set in motion', *kinein*); 'everything you can think of saying' is just 'every *logos*', 'every thing to say'.

199a4 **'But the truth is ...'**: for this use of ἀλλὰ γάρ, see Denniston, *GP* 101-2. The ἄρα ('I see it now') is almost a reflex after 198c6 (see n.), d2, d7.

a6-7 **'"It was my tongue", then, that promised, "and my mind" didn't':** 'it is my tongue that has sworn, but my mind is unsworn', Euripides, *Hippolytus* 612.

a7-8 **'I'm not prepared to give another encomium in that way':** i.e. I'm not going to follow you others in giving that kind of encomium ('[i]n animated language the present often refers to the future, to express *likelihood, intention*, or *danger*': Goodwin, *MT* 32, with parallels, e.g. from Thucydides 6.77). A rather more obvious translation, 'I no longer give encomia in that way', would give a surprising thing to S. to say – why should he ever have given encomia of the Agathonian type? It might perhaps just be a piece of politeness on S.'s part, to soften his criticisms of his host; but then the following 'I wouldn't have the capacity to do it' fails to fit. (With 'I'm not prepared ...', S. perhaps means both 'I don't have the technical capacity', and 'I couldn't bring myself to do it', the first being said ironically.)

b1-2 **'not on those of your speeches, because by your standards I'd be a laughing-stock':** more literally, 'not by reference to your speeches, in order that I may not become an object of laughter'.

b2 **'So, Phaedrus, see ...':** S. turns to Phaedrus as 'the person who conceived the whole subject' (*patêr tou logou*, 177d5; cf. 198e4-5).

b4-5 **'with whatever terms and arrangement of expressions happen to occur to me':** if this is likely to look (at best) disingenuous, it is at least true that S.'s language will for the most part be strictly functional, and without ornament.

b6-7 **'in whatever way he decided for himself that it should be done':** so everyone misses the point (it isn't just a matter of *choice*, for S., whether or not one goes for the truth).

c2 **'I'll speak my piece':** see 198a1-199c4n.

199c5-204c8: S. clears away Agathon's misunderstandings – just as Diotima had earlier cleared away his own (which were identical, or similar: 201e). The whole passage, but especially the first part, down to 201c9, when Agathon drops out, resembles the kind of Socratic examination or testing (*elenchus*: cf. *elenchein*, the cognate verb, at 201e5) of other people's views which occurs in many of P.'s shorter dialogues (e.g. *Euthyphro*, *Laches*), ending with apparent confusion or *aporia* on both sides. The difference here is that, thanks to Diotima's superior knowledge, we gradually advance, after 201c, and then, after 204c, rather less gradually, to a positive account of the subject in hand (though some of the basic premisses for that are beginning to be assembled in the initial session with Agathon, and indeed even before then). That Agathon is allowed to drop out (at 201d1) is no doubt partly because of this positive turn in the discussion. It seems to be P.'s intention to paint him as someone who has no interest in the truth (see esp. 201c); but in any case it would be highly implausible to have someone apparently so philosophically unsophisticated being led up into the thickets of Platonic metaphysics. Or, to put the matter more positively: S. provides the example that Agathon fails to provide, of what a philosophical partner ought to be.

199c5-201c9: S. questions Agathon. He begins with the question which, as it will turn out, matters most to him: what is Love love *of* – or rather, since 'love' will become increasingly less appropriate as a translation of *erôs*, what is *Erôs erôs* of? (As before, we may treat the god as a personification of the phenomenon, provided only that we do not assume that, for all or any of the speakers, god is always and necessarily reducible to phenomenon.) With Agathon, he gets as far as establishing that *Erôs* loves/desires what he does not (yet) possess; if, then, as Agathon claims, he is of 'the beautiful' (see esp. 197b4, 200a3-4n.), Love/*Erôs* cannot after all be beautiful – or good either, if good things are also beautiful (201c1-2n., 197a4-6n.). After what S. has said about his intention to tell the truth, we must surely suppose that, in principle, he (and P.) is in earnest. Dover claims that S. 'forc[es] fallacious inferences and assumptions on

[Agathon]' (Dover:133). In fact, I suggest, Agathon is not 'forced' to agree to any assumption to which his speech has not already committed him, and while S. may come close to bullying him into accepting certain moves, there is no single move which we have reason to think that S. would not (reasonably) have expected him to accept (see esp. 200b3n.). Nor – to take up another of Dover's points – is Agathon there simply to preserve the appearance of a conversation. Rather, he is there because he got things wrong, and can be persuaded – up to a point – to see that he did. Whether, or to what extent, S. himself accepts Agathon's assumptions must be a separate question (in fact, he will reject the view that Love (or love) is of the beautiful, but accept that the good is also beautiful). On the issues here, see ch.3 of Stokes 1986, 'S. and a tragic poet', which includes a challenging commentary on S.'s conversations with Agathon and Diotima; despite the fact that I frequently disagree with Stokes's handling of the argument, and reject a large part of his conclusions, my own treatment has a good deal in common with his general approach.

199c8 **'So then, on the subject of Love'**: i.e. so let's start with Love's character.

d1 **'magnificently attractive'**: *kalôs kai megaloprepôs*; cf. a3-4 *kalôs ... kai semnôs* ('... attractive enough, even impressive').

d3-5 **'My question is not whether he is of some mother or father (for it would be ridiculous to ask whether Love *is love of* mother or father)'**: commentators have expended much ink on this, but it seems to give a perfectly straightforward sense, i.e. 'I'm not asking whether he has a mother or father, because – note – my question was "is Love *love* of something?", and it would be absurd to ask that if my question were about Love's origins; of course Love isn't *love* of mother or father'. The point would be clearer if we were not stuck with 'love' for *erôs*: *erôs*, in normal usage, is (again) primarily *sexual* passion, which isn't what one feels for one's parents – unless one is Oedipus (does the fact that 'mother' is mentioned before 'father' suggest a reference to this best-known case of *erôs* directed towards parent?). In sum, S. is making a somewhat laboured point, but with a touch of humour; Agathon surely needs his help.

200a1 **'Yes, he is; certainly:'** Dover claims that it is possible to experience desire 'without forming any idea of what it is one desires ..., especially in dreams' (Dover:134), but Diotima's treatment of desire in animals at 207a ff. suggests that desire can be 'of' something independently of the formation of ideas (see esp. 207b7-c1); and it would surely be a peculiar kind of desire (like one experienced in a dream?) that was not somehow of *something*.

a2-3 **'Well then ... keep this result by you, remembering all the time *what* it is love of'**: lit. '... guard this by you remembering what (sc. Love is love) of', which I take to mean 'store up the point we've just established (that Love/love is of something), and remember what you say that something is' (cf. 201a2-3 'remember what things you said in your speech Love is of'). Translators take a different line (so e.g. Allen, sparingly: 'Keep in mind what that something is'), probably interpreting the passage along Dover's lines: 'Agathon's emphatic reply suggests that he knows what the object of eros is; S. is therefore saying "don't tell me yet! Remember it, but keep it to yourself."' This may be right, although it is not easy to see how 'this' (*touto*) and 'what of' (*hotou*) can have the same reference; and n.b. 200e8-9 (preceding the direct reference back to Agathon's view on the object of love) '... let's reckon up together what's been said. Am I right in saying that Love is firstly of certain things ...?' But the important point, I think, is to see that there is already, here in a2-3, an implicit reference back to Agathon's account of what Love is love of (as 201a2-3 in any case surely confirms).

a3-4 **'Now tell me this – does Love desire the thing he is love of, or not?'** Anyone would give a positive answer to this question (if it means something like 'if we feel *erôs* for something, do we desire it?'), but in effect S. is doing no more than picking up Agathon's pairing of desire and love, and his identification of love as desire for the beautiful, at 197a7 ff.; Agathon, remembering as he has been told to do (see preceding n.), answers S. readily, as he does the next question, because he feels himself on familiar territory. Dover, on a5-6, talks of 'the equation of *epithumein* ['desiring'] with *eran* ['loving']' in the present section, but since S. (through Diotima) will take considerable care to introduce this equation later on, at 204d ff., it would be disturbing to find him already taking it for granted. The present section in fact works well enough on the basis that S.'s argument against Agathon is *ad hominem*: 'if you say, Agathon, that love is desire for the beautiful, then this has the following consequences ...'. Neither Agathon nor S.'s argument assumes that 'love' includes *all* desires (although it does include desire for the good: see d7-e1n.); if b9-d6 talks about wanting/wishing, apparently in a quite general way, that is simply in order to illustrate the structure of desire (which will be shared by the specific desire which is *erôs*). After d6 we immediately return to *erôs* (d7-e1), and desire and *erôs* as a pair (e3), and finally Agathon's identification of the object of love surfaces explicitly (201a2-5).

a6-7 **'Does he desire and love the very thing he desires and loves as a consequence of having it, or of not having it?'** Lit. 'Is it the case that having the very thing he desires and loves, he then desires and loves (it), or not having (it)?' The 'then' (*eita*) can in principle mark either time or consequence, but presumably only the latter will work here.

a10-b1 **'what desires desires what it lacks, or, if it doesn't lack it, it doesn't desire it':** i.e. lack is a necessary condition of desiring – either there is lack, in which case there may be desire; or there is no lack, in which case there is no desire. It is a standard Platonic idea that desire implies lack (see esp. the discussion of true and false pleasures in *Republic* IX, and Aristophanes' speech in *Symp.* itself, which P. constructs specifically around the idea of sexual desire as lack – of part of oneself), and the idea probably does no significant damage to the logic either of the English ideas of 'desiring', 'wanting' or 'wishing', or of the Greek *epithumein* ('desiring') or *boulesthai* ('wishing': cf. b4, etc.). But what use S. means to make use of it still remains to be seen. – Halperin 1985:161-2 gives a vivid description of how the idea in question first demonstrated to him that 'P. ... was not discussing love at all but rather *eros* ..., or passionate sexual desire'. But in fact, as has been pointed out to me, there may always be a question about the extent to which one 'has' the object of one's love, even in a stable relationship.

b3 **'It looks so to me too':** it is hard to escape the conclusion that Agathon has been bludgeoned into this admission; but if he ought to have made it in any case (see preceding n.), S. might well suppose his behaviour justified. If it hardly matches up to what might be expected of a philosophical 'conversation', the success of such a process will partly depend on the ability of the collaborator to see a point when it is put to him. Cf. 199c5-204c8n. above.

b6 **'From what we've agreed':** i.e. in a6-b3.

b9-10 **'For if he did wish to be strong even when he was strong ...':** it seems to emerge that S. is referring to the case where someone *says* he wishes to be strong when he actually is, and so on (see c5 ff.); quite how he would have completed the sentence, i.e. if he hadn't broken off in b10, is anybody's guess (perhaps 'then he would be wishing for something he has whether he wishes it or not, which makes no sense'?). The style is that of someone trying to decide how best to explain a difficult point, gently (i.e. more gently, this time).

c5 **'and surely no one could desire *that*?'** The point seems to be as in Nehamas and Woodruff's translation: 'who would ever bother to desire what's necessary in any event?'

d3-5 **'"I desire the things I have" ..."I wish to have the things I have now ..."'**: lit. 'I desire the things present to me', 'I wish the things now present to me to be present to me in the future too'.

d7-e1 **'So this is in fact a matter of his loving what is not yet available to him ... these things in the future'**: 'this', as S.' next contribution shows, must – *pace* Dover, and Nehamas and Woodruff – refer back to the case just mentioned, of someone's desiring the continuing possession of good things (so Waterfield: 'the preservation ...' is in apposition to, and explains, 'what is not yet available ... to him'). *Loving* comes back in here (cf. a3-4n.) because it is Love, and what Agathon claimed about Love, that the present discussion is about (see 199c8, (200)e8 ff.). True, he only talked about love being of beauty, or *the beautiful* (197b4, b7-c1, 201a2-5), not the good, but he also made an implicit connection between love and at least some goods (197a4-6n.), and he is about to agree that good things are also beautiful (201c2-3) – from which it follows, if all beautiful things are loved, that all good things are loved too. The upshot is that the lesson of 200b9-d6 applies to loving, as a species (however extensive: cf. a3-4n.) of desiring (cf. e3-4 'he [the one who loves] and everyone else who desires ...'), and that this removes the obstacle (i.e. that people *say* they desire what they already have) to the principle that love is of what one lacks (a6-b3, e3-6); this principle is then formally announced in e8-10 as the outcome of the discussion so far, along with the principle that 'Love is ... of certain things'.

e3-4 **'In that case both he and everyone else who desires, desires something not available ...'**: i.e. it is a general rule that applies to the person who loves as much as to anyone else who desires ... Dover objects: '[a] real interlocutor might say, "I am wise/rich/strong in many ways or to a great extent, but I wish to be wise (etc.) in more ways or to a greater extent."' But S.'s thesis could accommodate this case with only marginal rephrasing; after all, this real interlocutor is not yet wiser, etc. than he presently is.

e10 **'of those things of which he has a lack, whatever they may be'**: more literally, 'of those (things), whichever may be lacking to him' ('of whichever a lack may be present to him'), i.e. to Love, standing for the lover. S. plainly does not mean to imply that one necessarily desires anything one lacks, only to indicate that things desired must be lacked.

201a3-5 **'I think you said ...'**: i.e. at 197b3-c1. 'Beautiful things' (*kalôn*) picks up *tôn kalôn* at 197b7-c1; the absence of the definite article evidently makes no difference (we have *tôn kalôn* again at 201c4).

a11-b1 **'Now then, we've agreed that he loves what he lacks and does not possess?'** Dover considers two candidates for the subject of 'loves' here, 'he who loves' (the lover) and *erôs*, concluding that in the first case the argument will not work, while in the second the claim about what 'we've agreed' would be false; 'therefore P. prudently leaves the subject unspecified'. However there is a third candidate, namely Love, who is in any case naturally supplied from the preceding sentence, and with him everything works smoothly enough (as Dover recognizes in his n. on b4 = his b5). The whole argument is actually about the god, and while language about him is sometimes translatable into propositions about love and lovers, it is not always so: see 199c5-201c9n., and b5n. – N.b. (generic) μή – so, 'the kind of thing he lacks and does not possess'.

b5 **'does not possess it in any way'**: 'in any way' is a fair addition, if Love is of beauty as a whole (as Agathon suggested: cf. 197a7-b3n.); here is one case where what is being said has rather little *literal* sense (see preceding n.) – but then it was Agathon who started it all, and it is his claims that are being investigated. (So *he* said that Love – not love – was of beauty, 197b4: so Dover's complaint, that it is not Love who loves but the lover, ought to be directed against Agathon, not P., or S. If Agathon makes mistakes, that will of course also be P.'s fault; but then he has S. try to show him that he has.)

b10-11 **'And Agathon said "It looks very much, S., as if I didn't know the slightest thing about what I said then"'**: if Love is not beautiful at all, S. has destroyed one of Agathon's main claims (that Love is the most beautiful of the gods); he is about to destroy the other (that he is best of gods).

c1-2 **'"And yet you said it so beautifully ... don't you think that what is good is also beautiful?" "I do".'** If Agathon has spoken *beautifully*, but ignorantly (therefore not wisely, and therefore not well, on his own assumptions), then it will be possible for something to be beautiful without being good. Even if it is not very likely that S. is genuinely complimenting Agathon, this is enough to account for his asking whether good things are also beautiful rather than, as we might expect, the other way round. That what is good is also beautiful could plausibly be supplied as a missing premiss in Agathon's argument, to allow his move from 'Love is of beauty' to 'Love is of wisdom/excellence in any skill' (see 197a4-6n.). But it is in itself hardly likely to have been a controversial idea, given the range of meaning of *kalon* (from 'beautiful', which is generally the most appropriate translation in *Symp.*, to 'fine', 'admirable', ...), and indeed the fuzziness of both *kalon* and *agathon* ('good', 'fine' from whose point of view?). Insofar as he is presently occupied in an *ad hominem* refutation, there can be no presumption that S. himself is endorsing the proposition in question, and indeed there is what might look like good evidence that he shouldn't be: Diotima has taught him (a) that people love nothing except the good (206a1-2), but (b) that love is not of the beautiful (206e2-3). On the other hand, 204e ff. apparently shows her, and S., happily behaving as if 'good' can readily be substituted for 'beautiful' in any context. The question here is, then, scarcely a 'little' one. See further 204e1-2n., 206a1-2n., 206e2-3n.

c4-5 **'what is beautiful ... what is good ... what is good'**: 'what is ...' in each case here represents definite article + adjective in the neuter plural – so 'beautiful/good (things)'.

c8-9 **'No, it's rather the truth, beloved Agathon, ... that you can't argue with ...'**: if S. has not been allowed (as Dover proposes) to be straight with Agathon, this claim will be so much hot air. But if S. really has no more concern with the truth than Agathon, one of the main theses of *Symp.*, about the difference between poetry and rhetoric and (Socratic, and by implication Platonic) philosophy, will have been put in jeopardy by its proposer, i.e. P., himself. Whether or not we like the sound of this outcome, the only question is what the quality of the argument is, and (in case this is different) what quality P. means it to have – and so far, at least, I see no evidence for answering anything other than 'pretty high' in both cases. Agathon recognizes that he didn't know what he was talking about, but still seems to think that the real problem is that S. is a more skilful debater than he is; S. says, and means, that he (S.) simply represents the cause of impersonal truth – 'if *this* is true, then as a plain matter of fact *that* cannot be'. 'This', of course, is Agathon's assumption that Love is of beauty (and goodness), 'that' his view of Love as beautiful and good (but that Love/love is of beauty, S. will reject, while still retaining the picture of Love that has been built on it, i.e. as neither beautiful nor good, for just so long as it suits him). – 'Beloved Agathon': as Dover points out, this form of address (*ô philoumene*) has no precise parallel anywhere. But it has a certain appropriateness: if Agathon is 'beloved', i.e. someone who is loved (as he is by Pausanias, and no doubt by others – including S., in his way), then at any rate *he* won't lack beauty and goodness, whatever may be true of Love (whom he so closely associated with himself). On this reading S. will be paying Agathon an inconspicuous parting compliment, as compensation for his discomfiture in the argument. (If the papyrus reading, the standard *ô phile*, were right, it would be hard to understand how the unusual *ô philoumene* entered the tradition. On the other hand, given that the papyrus is by far the oldest evidence we have, the present case serves as a sobering reminder that we *might* be discussing the finer details of a mangled text.)

201d1–204c8: Diotima takes S.'s place as questioner, and (so it seems) as representative of truth, while S. takes Agathon's as ignorant respondent; evidently S. had said the same sorts of things to her about Love as Agathon said in his speech, and she had similarly shown him that, even on his own account, Love was in fact neither beautiful nor good (201e3-7). Now in effect she completes S.'s criticisms of Agathon's speech, the last explicit reference to which is in 204b-c (in the guise, of course, of what S. said, along the same lines, to her), while at the same time developing a rival description of Love (not beautiful, but not ugly either, neither good nor bad, neither man nor god – always in between, a *daimôn*, acting as messenger; son of Poverty and Resource; a philosopher ...). For one explanation of these substitutions among the *dramatis personae*, see 199c5-204c8n.; another will emerge in relation to 203b1-204a6 (see 203d3-4n.; cf. also 205d9n.). Some have held that Diotima was a real person: so one scholar cited in Levin 1975 identifies an uninscribed statue at Mantinea with her, while another claims that there were a number of women at Mantinea with a similar mystical bent. However the very manner of her introduction, and especially the exact and convenient way in which her interrogation of S. dovetails with his of Agathon, seem to demonstrate beyond any reasonable doubt – quite apart from any question about the (Platonic) content of what is attributed to her – that she is meant to be a fiction (as Aristophanes tacitly assumes her to be at 212c5-6). Commentators regularly refer to her as a 'priestess', as she no doubt is, though she is never explicitly given this title (see further 202e7-203a1n.); she is rather referred to as *xenê*, i.e. 'visitor', 'guest' (see e.g. 201e2, and 204c7, where S. addresses her like this), which recalls e.g. the role of the 'visitor from Elea' in the *Sophist* and the *Politicus*. (P.'s S. never goes outside Athens except when absolutely necessary, so that if he is to meet anyone new, they have to come to him.) She has powers of intervention with the gods (201d3-5), which immediately connects her with several groups of people she describes in 202e7-203a1 ('the whole expertise of the seer ..., and that of priests, and of those concerned with sacrifices, rites, spells, and the whole realm of the seer and of magic'); that she is a 'Mantinean' is usually taken – by those who treat her as a fiction – to be intended to suggest a particular connection with seers (*manteis*, sing. *mantis*). The traditional role of the seer is to have an understanding of things, past and present as well as future, which is superior to that possessed by ordinary human beings, and Diotima certainly has that. On why Plato chooses a woman for the role, see Halperin 1990 (though the question turns out to be more interesting than the answer, and indeed 'ultimately *has* no answer': 151, my italics); the form of the name 'Diotima' suggests 'honouring / honoured by / privileged by Zeus'.

201d1-2 'the account of Love that I once heard': this will take us down to 212a7. S. himself, by implication, treats the present section as part of Diotima's positive treatment rather than as part of any 'examination' or *elenchus* (see e5, and 199c5-204c8n.), but the latter perspective probably throws more light on its place within the actual structure of S.'s contribution as a whole. There is in any case a clear break in the structure of the argument at 204d1: not only is there no more reference to Agathon's speech as such (however indirectly achieved before that), but the figure of Love himself virtually disappears, to be replaced by talk exclusively about love, desire, and the ends of human life. (Or, if he is still present and presiding, he is so in his new guise as *daimôn* and seer – and also as philosopher: see 203d ff.) S. himself refers to this division in Agathon's terms: first, Love's 'character'; then his *erga*, 'what he does' (d7-e1).

d3-5 **'once, before the plague, brought about a ten-year postponement ..':** for the general idea, see the story of Epimenides the Cretan at *Laws* 642d. It is presumably meant to indicate the genuineness of her credentials as well as the peculiar nature of her powers; it also conveniently provides a context in which S. could have got to know her (cf. Levin 1975). Commentators generally are probably too circumspect on the question of the status of this supposed event – if anything like it really happened, why does S. describe it as if his hearers hadn't heard about it?

d5 **'she's the very person who taught me too about erotics':** i.e. she's the one who taught me, so that I know about them too (sc. you others here do?). 'Erotics' = 'things erotic', (*ta erôtika*, 'things to do with love'), as at 177e1, etc.

d7 **'in whatever way I can manage it':** cf. 199b (but now the idea has a new twist: S. is going to have to take on the work of two).

d7-e1 **'Now one *should* do, Agathon, as you did ...':** this second reference to Agathon's recommended principle or organization (195a; cf. 199c) reminds us of just how little *else* S. finds to praise in his speech.

e6-7 **'was neither beautiful – by my own account – nor good':** 'by my own account', both because he found himself having to accept the conclusions of Diotima's arguments, and also insofar as they were based on his own presuppositions (cf. 199c5-204c8n.).

e10 **'Take care what you say!'** is a somewhat lame translation of *ouk euphêmêseis*, lit. 'won't you speak words of good omen?' – which usually means keeping one's silence.

202a5-9 **'Don't you recognize ... between wisdom and ignorance?':** 'ignorance', by implication, will include false beliefs about things as well as just not having any inkling of them (the better-known triple division of states of mind in *Republic* 476e ff. is different, and serves a different purpose). It is sometimes suggested that at least some of the views presented by the earlier speakers will fall into the category of correct beliefs. However the primary occupants of this category are the beliefs of *philosophers* – like Love himself, who will be said specifically to be a philosopher, in between wisdom and ignorance (203d6, e5, 204b2-5); and the present passage, while serving to introduce the general idea of intermediates between contraries, also serves as a trailer for this particular, and peculiar, point about Love. The difference Diotima suggests between correct belief and knowledge – that knowledge presupposes the ability to 'give an account': i.e. adequate reasons for holding one's beliefs? – resembles the one proposed by S. in the *Meno* (98a); and while problems are found with this sort of account of knowledge in the *Theaetetus* (201c ff.: true belief plus an account), it looks like a perfectly reasonable working hypothesis. The question will then be whether there is meant to be room in the category of correct belief, alongside whatever beliefs the philosopher (Love, or, more helpfully, S.) holds, for any of the beliefs of an Agathon, an Aristophanes, or an Eryximachus. Given the way that S. appeared to discard Agathon as a philosophical partner, and given that Diotima will reject Aristophanes' main idea outright (205d10-e3, with 192e10-193a1), the omens for at least these two are not good. (The *kaí* in a5 – '*even* without ...' – is not in the papyrus, and some editors bracket it, but though difficult, it can perhaps be taken as emphasizing the difference between *this* type of correct belief and the more obvious type represented by knowledge.)

a6-7 **'how could something irrational be knowledge?'** There is perhaps a pun on *alogos* (alpha negative + *logos*) here: both 'without an account', and 'lacking in reason(s)'.

a9 **'wisdom':** now *phronêsis*, apparently employed as a synonym of *sophia*.

b4-5 **'suppose him to be something *between* these two things':** i.e. given that this alternative exists, and we want to avoid the conclusion that Love is ugly and bad (cf. 201e10-11).

b8 **'by everyone who is ignorant':** cf. 194b-d, 199a2-3.

c5 **'And I said "How can you say that?"'** The Greek has 'I said' twice; there are a number of such cases in *Symp.*, which it does not seem worth trying to reproduce in the translation (the effect is something like 'And I said "How", I said "..."').

c6-7 **'don't you assert that all gods are happy and beautiful?'** What *Agathon* said was that 'while all gods are happy, Love ... is happiest of them, being most beautiful and best' (195a5-7); it does not strictly follow from this, of course, that all the gods are also beautiful, but evidently when S. said the same sort of thing, that is what *he* meant to imply.

c10-11 **'But isn't it those individuals who possess good and beautiful things that you call happy?'** I add 'individuals' to indicate that the question is a general one, not restricted to gods. Again, it might possibly have been inferred from what Agathon said (see preceding n.) – one would have had to check with him – that he thought that happiness in general derived from the possession of beauty and goodness; it is a still further step to saying that it derives from the possession of good and beautiful things in general, but S. is happy to accept that further step, as presumably Agathon would have been (that happiness, *eudaimonia*, consists in possessing good things is almost tautologous, and he explicitly accepted that good things are also beautiful: 201c2-3).

d3 **'Yes, I have agreed to that':** 201a-b (in the Agathon/Socrates version).

d14-e1 **'A great spirit, S.; for everything of the nature of spirits is between god and mortal':** the word *daimôn* is virtually impossible to translate ('demon', its descendant, now suggests something evil); 'spirit' is probably the least bad option, though 'spiritual' for the adjective *daimonios* is not helpful (hence 'of the nature of spirits'). The word can in Greek be used as a synonym for *theos*, 'god', but can also indicate something between gods and men, as here (see e.g. Hesiod, *Works and Days* 122); as Gager says, the cosmos in ancient Mediterranean culture 'literally teemed, at every level and every location, with supernatural beings', and 'although ancient theoreticians sometimes tried to sort these beings into clear and distinct categories, most people were less certain about where to draw the lines between gods, *daimones*, planets, stars ...' (Gager 1992:12). Diotima (P.) here introduces a neat, threefold division of beings (gods, *daimones*, humans) to suit her own purposes; but as rapidly becomes apparent, it is not intended as a literal description of the contents of the cosmos. (On *daimones* in various philosophical contexts, see Kidd 1995.)

e2 **'What function does it have?'** Lit. 'having what power (sc. is it between god and mortal)?'

202e7-203a1 **'It is through this that the whole expertise of the seer works its effects ... the whole realm of the seer and of magic:'** I take it that the three main headings here are not meant to be distinct, but that 2. (priests) overlaps with 1. (seers), while 3. ('those concerned ...') is a more general list which includes both 1. and 2. Diotima is herself perhaps primarily a seer (cf. 201d1-204c8n.), but 201d3-5 also links her with sacrifices, and perhaps also with magic (cf. 203d7n.); later she will reveal certain 'rites' to S. – For the sequence A καί B C τε, see Denniston, *GP* 500.

203a4 **'spirit-like':** *daimonios* again (see 202d14-e1n.); a *daimonios* human being will of course not *be* a *daimôn*, just as a *theios*, 'divine', one will not actually have the attributes of a god.

a6 **'vulgar':** here *banausos*, typically used simply of manual occupations by those considered (and considering themselves) of a higher social status, here apparently extended to any *technê* or expertise other than the ones listed above.

b1 **'It's rather a long story to tell':** not so long, perhaps (only down to about e5), but a lot longer than the usual response to such a question would be. The single most important outcome will be the idea of Love as a perpetual seeker, especially after wisdom: that is, as someone who is by nature perpetually *lacking* (because of his mother, Poverty), and perpetually scheming to get what he lacks (because his father was Resource). This wisdom-seeking, i.e. philosophical, Love also soon begins to bear a remarkable similarity to S. (cf. 219b7-c1, where Alcibiades calls S. a 'truly *daimonios* man' – though without having heard S.'s report of his conversations with Diotima).

b2   '**When Aphrodite was born, the gods held a feast**': evidently, then, it was a normal birth, so not the one resulting from the castration of Uranus (cf. 180d-e); like Pausanias, Diotima selects what she needs from the available material – and if it is missing, invents it (as she does, in fact, with the details of Love's parentage and birth as a whole).

b3   '**Resource, son of Craftiness**': i.e. son of Metis (*mêtis* = 'cunning intelligence'). According to Hesiod,*Theogony* 886 ff., she was Zeus' first wife, knew more than any god or man, and was swallowed by her husband.

b6   '**wine, you see, did not yet exist**': is the suggestion that wine is superior even to nectar, the gods' own drink?

c4   '**by nature a lover in relation to what is beautiful**': *peri* ('in relation to') could in principle mean 'of' (cf. Dover, and *LSJ* s.v. C.5), but given that Diotima will ultimately claim that *erôs* is not of the beautiful (206e2-3), it is probably significant that she avoids committing herself, either here or anywhere else, to the (unambiguous) genitive; at 204d3, the proposition 'Love is of beautiful things' is qualified by an 'as *you* (S.) say'. The 'in relation to' also avoids the difficulty that if Love were love of beauty, then evidently he would be Aphrodite's lover rather than her 'follower and attendant'; and in fact, as we learn, his main attention is directed elsewhere than to Aphrodite.

c7-8 '**far from delicate and beautiful, as most people think he is**': cf. Agathon at 195c ff.

c8   '**barefoot**': this aspect of Love is of course perfectly consistent with his poverty, but it is also a mark of S. and the Socratic (cf. Aristodemus at 173b3; S. at 220b5); the attributes next to be mentioned suggest the ordinary lover (cf. e.g. 183a), but also S. (174d ff., 220a ff.). But in any case poverty is itself a mark of the Platonic S.: he cares nothing about money, and has little of it – of his own (*Apology* 37c, 38b).

d3-4 '**a schemer after the beautiful and good**': the usual ambiguity here (is 'the beautiful', *tôn kalôn*, masculine or neuter?) itself reflects the superficial ambiguity of the behaviour of the Platonic S. – is he after young men, or after something else, which he can achieve in their company? The continuing implicit reference to S. constitutes another reason why S./Agathon had to give way to Diotima/S. (cf. 199c5-204c8n.): to have had S. comparing himself (even implicitly) with a supernatural being would scarcely have been tolerable – though if the fiction of Diotima is as transparent as I have suggested, that is actually what he *is* doing, apparently without noticing it.

d5-7 '**both passionate for wisdom and resourceful in looking for it, philosophizing through all his life**': we might expect *porimos* to mean 'resourceful in *finding* it', but if he 'philosophizes through all his life', then evidently he never finds wisdom (see 204a1-2). 'Passionate for' is literally 'desirer (*epithumêtês*) of'. If Love is passionate for/desires wisdom, he must be a philosopher (because *philo-sophia* is love of wisdom); but why exactly is he passionate for wisdom? Well, we're about to be told, in 204b; but meanwhile it was actually one of Agathon's claims that Love was *sophos*, wise. Here, then, as elsewhere, S./Diotima starts from Agathon: Love is not wise, only a lover of wisdom – a claim so paradoxical, perhaps, that it could scarcely have been introduced by any other route. (According to Denniston, *GP* 290, the first καί, which I translate as 'both', is copulative καί, inserted, unusually, 'in the middle of the series'; and admittedly my 'both ... and' would be easier if ἐπιθυμητής came before φρονήσεως rather than after it. But the main sense will not be affected.)

d7 **'magician, sorcerer, and sophist':** '[t]he sentence, "X is/was a magician!" tells us nothing about the beliefs and practices of X; the only solid information that can be derived from it concerns the *speaker's* attitude toward X ...' (Gager 1992:25). All three Greek terms may have negative connotations, but may also be used positively, depending on the circumstances, and/or (as probably here) with ironic reference to their negative aspect ('Love can do marvellous things, which might make some call him ...'?). On sophists, see 177b2-3n.; and on the danger of confusion between philosophers and sophists, e.g. *Sophist* 230d-231a.

e2 **'when he finds resources':** the opposite of *euporein* ('finding resources') is *aporein*, 'be without resources' (so in e4), but also 'be at a loss', 'be confused' (cf. 199c5-204c8n.); the whole of d7-e5 ('his nature is neither that of an immortal, nor that of a mortal ... so that Love is neither resourceless at any moment, nor rich') will in fact make sense as a metaphorical description of the ups and downs of philosophical discussion – and it is to Love as philosopher, having correct belief rather than knowledge (or ignorance) that Diotima returns at the end of the sentence (e5: 'again [Love] is in the middle ...').

204a1 **'philosophizes, or desires to become wise':** again (see 203d5-7n.) the Greek term *philosophia means* 'loving/desiring wisdom'.

a4-5 **'an admirable person, or a wise one':** 'wise' here is *phronimos* (cf. e.g. 203d6), rather than *sophos*; 'admirable' is *kalos kagathos*, lit. 'beautiful/fine and good' – 'a general laudatory term ...; it differs from "good" in taking account not merely of moral disposition ... but also of attributes (e.g. wealth, good physique and skills) which enhance one's value to the community' (Dover). However here *kalokagathia* is implied to be incompatible with ignorance, which wealth, physique, etc. are self-evidently not. I suggest that it is here in fact standing in for *aretê*, 'goodness' or 'excellence', which on Agathon's own account included wisdom (*sophia*), and incidentally on S.'s actually requires it; the avoidance of the terms Agathon himself used is meant, perhaps, to blunt the edge of a remark which applies, and has been seen to apply (201c), particularly to him. But of course, in the present context, it is supposed rather to apply to *S.* – who obliges with an immediate demonstration of his childlike lack of wit (a7-8, b1).

b3 **'love in relation to what is beautiful':** cf. 203c4n.

c1-2 **'To judge from the things you say, you thought Love to be what is loved, not what does the loving':** *Agathon's* speech, at any rate (but again, S. is supposed to have said similar things), in fact understood Love in terms of 'what loves', insofar as it made Love love of the beautiful; see esp. 197e3-5n. However it is certainly true from the perspective we have now reached, if it was not then (what about all that talk about youth, delicateness, suppleness ...?), that making Love supremely beautiful and good must indeed be to treat him as what is loved rather than as what loves; it is what is loved (or 'lovable', c4) that is really like that (or 'really beautiful, graceful, perfect, and ... blessed', c4-5).

c5 **'counted as blessed':** i.e. called happy.

c7-8 **'Well then, dear visitor – given that you're right: if Love is like this, what use does he have for human beings?'** 'What use is he, if he is like that (sc. not beautiful, graceful, or perfect ...; and a *philosopher*)?' looks like the sort of question Agathon might well ask – and of course S. is still standing in for him. The question launches the next, constructive, stage in Diotima's account. 'Dear visitor': the Greek just has *xenê* ('visitor', 'guest', or 'stranger': cf. 201d1-204c8n.).

204d1-209e4: it will be useful to give a crude summary of the argument in this difficult and crucial passage. Diotima in effect takes S.'s question to mean 'what is *love* for?' 'Why *do* we love the beautiful?' (204d). To make the question easier, she substitutes 'good' for 'beautiful' (204e) – and after all, S. has, like Agathon (201c) accepted that good things are beautiful, so that at least some of the time, when we love beautiful things, we also love good things (but soon she will declare her hand, and say that we love nothing *except* the good). Why do we love good things? Because we want to possess them. What accrues to the person who possesses good things? Happiness. But a permanent desire for happiness is common to everyone; why then do we not say that everyone is a lover (205a-b)? Well, there is a reason for this (205b-c). But in any case everyone *is* a lover, insofar as he loves good things – and in fact, Diotima declares, with S.'s agreement, no one loves anything unless it is good (205e-206a). So: everyone loves, is in love with, the good. Or is it as simple as that? What we are in love with, what we desire, is to *possess* the good (that was agreed before); it is also to possess it *for ever* (206a). So what kind of activity is associated with this loving? It is *giving birth in beauty*, which excites us as promising the permanent possession of the good we desire (206b). You see, says Diotima (and from now on she switches increasingly from question and answer mode to monologue), we are all pregnant, whether female or male, and desperate to give birth, but we can only do so in a beautiful environment (206c-e). In fact (206e), love is after all not, as you, S., think, of the beautiful (that is, insofar as that only provides the environment for the procreation in question?); it is of this birthing in beauty, as the means to the 'immortality together with the good' that we desire (206e-207a). Diotima then sets out to provide evidence for these startling and paradoxical claims: look at how animals behave (207a-b); look at how mortal nature continually aims at a kind of immortality, by replacing what is lost, whether it is bodily tissue or the contents of the mind (207c-208b); and look, finally, at the motive of *love of honour*: doesn't everybody do everything fine and good just because they desire the immortality of fame (208c-209e)? – The whole of 204d1-209e4 is designed primarily to give Diotima what she needs for her description of the final 'mysteries' of love, which will follow in 209e5-212a7. The essential features of this preliminary passage are: 1. the way in which *erôs* is explicitly broadened out – though Agathon's speech itself clearly prepared the way for this step – to include love of, i.e. desire for, the good in general; 2. the way in which, notwithstanding this broadening, *erôs* continues to be understood in terms of sexual passion, so that all of human life is seen – for the moment – in terms of a metaphorical (or sometimes, where real sex is involved, actual) process of reproduction; and 3. an inventiveness and flexibility in the development of Diotima's themes which is likely to leave us breathless as well as sharing the amazement that S. feels and expresses, most directly at 208b8-9 ('are these things *really* so?'). She is dealing in metaphor and paradox, and also, towards the end, when she talks about human behaviour as it is, in irony. But at the same time there is no mistaking the hard and serious core that underlies the play of ideas here; once again, it is important that at no point should S. be allowed to commit himself knowingly to the literal acceptance of anything false.

d1-2 **'This ... is just what I shall try to teach you next':** Nehamas and Woodruff's 'after I finish this' for 'next' ('after this') is misleading; the next sentence in effect sums up, and then gives the starting-point c8 ('[Love] is of beautiful things, according to what you say') for Diotima's answer to S.'s question in c8. We have reached the divide between the treatment of Love's character and that of his 'actions' (see 201d7-e1n.).

d3 **'he is of beautiful things, according to what you say':** not, apparently, as Diotima will say (but see 206e2-3n.).

d5 **'or to put it more clearly':** at this point Diotima and S. more or less stop talking about Love, and talk (directly) about love (i.e. *erôs*).

d6 **'To possess them for himself':** all this talk about 'possession' of the object of love may jar with the reader; but insofar as Diotima is talking about personal relationships at all (which she is, but only as one aspect of 'loving' and desiring), the good whose possession is desired in such a case is not the person but something else, whatever the relationship itself may contribute to that good (i.e. one's overall good/happiness). This, I think, is part of the point of her denial that love is of the beautiful (cf. d3n.).

d7   **'requires'**: lit. 'longs for', 'misses' (*pothei*).

e1-2   **'answer as if someone changed things round, and questioned you using the good instead of the beautiful'**: since S. is committed to the idea that love is of the good as well as of the beautiful, this move is perfectly justified. (The 'as if', I take it, simply refers to the imagined situation: 'suppose someone changed things round; what would you answer then?' In particular, there is no implication that it is still the *same* question after the change of terms.) What either S. or Diotima thinks about the precise relationship between the good and the beautiful is never made clear, and after 205e-206a (which sets up the good as the exclusive object of love and desire) and 206b ff. (which gives beauty a special and subsidiary role in procreation, of whatever sort), it does not much matter to the argument. S. thinks that the good is also beautiful, but also accepts from Diotima that only what is good is an object of love; given the close connection between *erôs* (at least in its original sense of sexual passion) and beauty, this strongly suggests that for him – and for Diotima, to the extent that they move forward together – where beauty begins and ends, so does goodness. But it will then be an open question whether we should think of the good and the beautiful in terms of something like 'coincident classes' (see Dover on 201c2), or in terms of straightforward identity.

e6   **'I'm better placed'**: *euporôteron echô* (cf. e.g. *euporos* at 204b6: '[Love] has a father who is wise and *resourceful*'). For the connection between happiness and the possession of good things, see 202c.

205a2-3 'one no longer needs to go on to ask ...': 'why do you want to be happy?' is as odd a question in English as 'why do you want to be *eudaimôn*?' would be in Greek. (The English would amount to 'why do you want to be content?', the Greek to something more like 'why do you want to have those things that make life worth living?', where the things in question would usually include contentment.)

a6-7   **'and that everyone wishes always to possess good things'**: the 'always', from the order of words in the Greek, seems initially to belong with the possessing, but what Diotima *next* says suggests that it rather belongs with the wishing. But in any case it looks as if she means to claim both (a) that we all wish for permanent possession of good things, and (b) that we all permanently wish to possess them; and if (a) is in fact true, it will be at least harmless (*pace* Dover:144 and Stokes 1986:157-9) to go on to assert (b), since if sometimes even some of us stopped wishing to possess good things, it would no longer be true that everyone wished for permanent possession of them (since some would not wish to possess them at all). Of course one might want to question whether everyone *does* always wish for good things. But it is Diotima's firmly stated view (205e-206a), and the usual view of P.'s S. (see *Republic* 505d-e for a particularly firm statement of it) that 'people love (desire) nothing except the good'; if so, both of them – Diotima, and S. when he has finally stopped playing Agathon (cf. 206a3n.) – will deny that anyone truly desires what will in fact damage himself or herself, and that in itself looks far from being an indefensible position.

b1   **'if in fact everyone loves the same things, and always loves them'**: i.e. if in fact everybody loves good things, and always loves good things. Now in principle there are two possibilities: either the kind of life that is good and happiness-producing may be different for different individuals (while remaining 'the same' insofar as each is good for the individuals concerned), or it is the same for all (while being realized in different lives); the 'final mysteries' will clearly show Diotima plumping for the second alternative, as P.'s S. usually does (there is, for him, just one thing or set of things that constitutes human happiness, pivoting on knowledge and virtue), but for the moment both possibilities are open.

b4   **'as we can now see':** ἄρα (Dover). What Diotima claims about the 'name' *erôs* is only true to the extent that she has made it so (unlike what she says about *poiêsis*, 'creation'/'poetry', in b8-c9); but there is a solid philosophicxal point behind the claim. Cf. e.g. a6-7n.

b7   **'Is there a similar case?'** The Greek actually has something close to 'Like what?', which probably suggests the wrong tone.

b8   **'You're aware that *poiêsis* includes a large range of things':** *poiêsis* is 'making', 'creation', as at 196e-197a, where Agathon himself moved from *poiêsis* 'in the sphere of music' to *poiêsis* of living creatures (a fact presumably not unconnected with Diotima's choice of analogy); it seems marginally more helpful to the reader to leave the Greek word untranslated here.

c7-8   **'This alone is called *poiêsis*, and those to whom this part of *poiêsis* belongs are called poets':** Diotima seems to go on at unnecessary length about a relatively simple idea; but the point which it is supposed to justify (i.e. about what *erôs* really is) is fundamental to the strategy of her account.

d1-3   **'the whole of desire for good things and for happiness is "the supreme and treacherous love", to be found in everyone':** 'treacherous', perhaps, because the 'desire for good things' may lead to wrong choices as well as right ones. If everyone desires the good, do they always look for it in the right place?

d4-5   **'in business, or in their love of physical exercise, or in philosophy':** in business, like Apollodorus' listeners (173c6), and for *philogumnastia* and *philosophia*, see Pausanias at 182b8 (where *philosophia* was 'love of intellectual excellence'; now 'philosophy' is surely meant, introducing the same opposition as in 173c).

d6   **'giving themselves to':** more literally, 'being in earnest about' (*espoudakotes*).

d9   **'Very likely that's true':** this looks like something short of full assent on S.'s part; and after all, whereas all creation just *is* 'making' (*poiêsis*), no convincing reason has – yet, at least – been given for treating *erôs* as anything other than the name for a particular species of desire. Diotima's teaching as it stands depends on the appropriation of the language of *erôs*, but it *could* operate without it. The argument is: what lovers are really in love with/desire is the good (cf. 204d-205a); but that's what we all desire; therefore (let's say) we're all lovers. But she doesn't need to go this way – she could simply say that everyone desires the good, but people pursue it in different ways: through love-affairs, money-making, and so on. Still, after all, this is S.'s contribution to a series of encomia of *Love*. On his account (which he of course got from Diotima), Love is – as Agathon also represented him – a creative force whose influence extends far beyond the sphere of the sexual ... On the face of it, this strategy might seem to take S. perilously close to the very kind of hyperbolic treatment of the subject he complained of the others for giving. However he could plead in his defence that he began by depriving Love not only of beauty and goodness, but divinity as well; what could be less hyperbolic than that? In any case, he is not claiming that Love is really responsible for all our desire, i.e. that all desire is really *erôs*, in the ordinary sense of sexual desire or passion: despite the claims of many modern commentators, Diotima is not advancing anything like a theory of *sublimation* (see Introduction, §3.6). Moreover, if S. is in fact distancing himself, ever so slightly, from her here in d9, as he does perhaps more clearly in 207a-d (see 207c8-9n.) and in 208b-c, he will be able to eat his cake and have it, using partly playful, metaphorical means to express himself -- through Diotima – while also (partly) disowning them. If we strip away the play and metaphor, what is left is a set of ideas which looks familiarly Socratic (see 206a1-2n.), and which, unless he means to contradict his programmatic speech at 198b-199b, he (i.e. the S. of *Symp.*) must believe in. Last but not least, he can claim to be telling the truth about (the real) Love, insofar as his general account of desire and its objects will also apply to ordinary, sexual *erôs* as well.

d10-e1 'there's a story that's told ...': obviously a reference to Aristophanes, whom of course Diotima is not supposed to have heard; but when Aristophanes refers back to what Diotima says here, he says simply 'S. mentioned me' (212c5-6: so evidently *he* isn't fooled by the fiction of Diotima). 'Story' in the Greek is simply *logos*, which could in principle mean no more than 'thing said', and may well mean no more here ('there's something that's said, to the effect that ...'?).

e2-3 'unless, my friend, it turns out actually to be *good*': 'my friend', in the Greek, interrupts the sentence just before 'good', so helping to throw emphasis on it.

e5-6 'that either group is embracing': i.e. either those who allow doctors to amputate their feet and hands, or lovers. For *aspazesthai*, 'embrace', see Aristophanes at 192a6, b5.

206a1-2 'there is nothing else that people are in love with except the good': on the face of it, this might look as if it rules out the tripartite division of the soul we find in the *Republic* (and elsewhere), since that explicitly involves desires that are not for the good (see esp. 439a). However, again (see 205a6-7n.), the claim that desire is always and only for the good appears in the *Republic* itself; if so, it ought on the face of it to be somehow compatible with the partition of the soul (no version of which is mentioned in *Symp.*, perhaps for the same sorts of reasons that the soul's immortality is not mentioned: see 206e8-207a2n.; but in an encomium of Love, there might also be special reasons for excluding the seamier aspects of soul and desire). For a beautifully clear and instructive treatment of the issues, see Kahn 1987, though his own solution still seems to leave us with some desires not directed towards the good. It may well be better, as Terry Penner has proposed to me in conversation, to go in the direction suggested by Prichard: '[t]here is no escaping the conclusion that when P. sets himself to consider not what *should*, but what *actually does* as a matter of fact, lead a man to act, when he is acting deliberately, and not merely in consequence of an impulse, he answers "The desire for some good to himself and that only"' (H.A.Prichard, 'Duty and interest', reprinted in *Moral Obligation*, 2nd edn, Oxford 1968, 218).

a3 'Zeus! I certainly don't': whatever role he may currently be playing, S. is not going to give Diotima trouble over *this* claim (see preceding n.). What she has now done is to give greater precision to what was agreed earlier: in desiring happiness, people love/desire *what is in fact good for them*, what will in fact constitute their happiness; what they want is actually to be happy, not to have things they think will give them happiness but in fact will not. However what precisely it is that *is* in fact good for them has yet to be established. So far as the argument has gone, it might e.g. be money-making or physical exercise as much as philosophy (205d4-5).

a7-8 'But ... oughtn't we to add that what they love includes their possessing the good?' See 204e.

a10 'And then ... not only ...': Diotima picks up the next part of what was agreed earlier (205a).

a12-13 'we can sum up by saying that love is of permanent possession of what is good': not, of course, the 'one kind' of love (*erôs*) with which we normally associate the name, but 'the whole' (205b).

b1-3 'Given, then, that love is always this, ... how will those pursuing it do so, and through what activity ...? What really is this thing that it does?' 'Thing that it does' is *ergon*, 'work', as at 201e1 (Diotima is presently in the thick of discussing 'what Love does'). This is a crucial passage, which produces sharp differences between those commentators who think that it marks a return to the subject of sexual *erôs*, and those (including myself) who insist that it does not, and cannot. Waterfield belongs to the first group: 'so now Diotima reverts to discussing the specific kind of love which we commonly call "love", rather than the generic kind she has outlined. Even the specific kind must be love of goodness, of course, but this will manifest [itself?] in a specific fashion' (Waterfield:86). If this is right, Diotima is from this point on no longer developing a universal theory of human motivation. But can it be right? I believe not. (a) It isn't clear, if there is a transition back to 'specific' *erôs*, why S. should be stumped, as he is (b5-6), for an answer to the question about what sort of activity goes with *erôs* (obviously, *sex*). (b) What Diotima goes on to talk about *isn't* actually what 'we commonly call "love"', i.e. *erôs*, even if it starts from that (see e.g. 207b: animals' 'erotic' impulse is '*first*' towards intercourse, but *then also* towards feeding and preserving their offspring – which in itself anticipates the structure of the 'ascent of love' for human beings: see 210a1 ff.). (Argument (b) will hardly persuade those who believe Diotima to be advancing a theory about the sublimation of sexual desire: cf. 205d9n. But that whole reading itself appears to depend on finding a return to the subject of specific love here in b1-3 – which argument (a) alone seems sufficient to block.) Sier's argument, ad loc., that there is no clear sign of any transition (in b1-3) back from generic to specific love, won't quite work, since those who detect such a transition presumably find it in *tôn tina tropon diôkontôn auto ... hê spoudê kai hê suntasis erôs an kaloito* ('how will those pursuing it do so, ... if their intense eagerness in pursuing it is to be called love?'); 'those pursuing it' (*tôn ... diôkontôn auto*) itself looks as if it should pick out a particular class of lovers, and 'intense eagerness' ('zeal and exertion', Dover) seems precisely to refer to the 'intense eagerness' of lovers in the ordinary sense – as Sier himself acknowledges. But he is surely right in insisting on a tight connection with 205d: Diotima has told S. who ought to be called lovers, and it is natural to suppose that she is now building on that. Those on Waterfield's side of the argument would have a stronger point if she had said '*is* called *erôs*' (... *erôs kaleitai*) rather than '*would/could/should be* called *erôs*' (*erôs an kaloito*). What she is doing is to pick out *an aspect* of *erôs* as commonly understood (its 'intense eagerness'), and ask what generic activity exhibits it, maybe on the not (wholly) unreasonable assumption – if it is granted that ordinary *erôs* is a genuine species, and that such *erôs* is essentially passionate and intense – that it will be a genuine mark of *erôs* as a whole, i.e. of 'generic' *erôs*. Or alternatively, and more straightforwardly, sexual desire simply becomes a metaphor for all desire: after all, 'we are all lovers': see 204d1-209e4n. ('Those pursuing it' then merely marks a change of subject, from *erôs* itself to those who experience it.) Diotima's whole question here is certainly a 'feed' (cf. Dover on 205b7): what she wants is a particular description of (what she claims is) the sort of 'activity' in which all *erôs* issues, and the convoluted sentence is primarily a means of getting to that, *via* the puzzled response from S. that it elicits. It marks the introduction of the (again, intentionally paradoxical) idea which treats all human striving in terms of sexual *erôs*; that is, which treats all human desire *as if* it had the structure, and followed the pattern, of sexual desire. For a more continuous account of the reading of Diotima's strategy proposed here, see Rowe, 'Socrates and Diotima ...'. – In b1 some editors emend *touto* ('love is this') to *toutou* ('love is of this'), on the grounds that 'it' (in 'those pursuing it') must refer to the object of love; in fact 'it' is better taken as referring to love, or perhaps rather 'this thing that love is' (so that 'those pursuing it' more or less = 'lovers' – obviously in the 'generic' sense), as it will naturally do if we keep the reading of the mss.

b7-8 **'It's giving birth in the beautiful':** *en kalôi* (lit. 'in (something) beautiful'?), but this is evidently identical in meaning to *en tôi kalôi*, i.e. with the definite article (c4-5, e5).

b9   **'It would take a seer ...':** which Diotima of Mantinea probably is (cf. 201d1-204c8n. above).

c5-6   **'The intercourse of man and woman is in fact a kind of giving birth':** 'a kind of' is supplied in the translation, to avoid the un-English 'a giving birth' (*tokos*); in any case human heterosexual intercourse will in fact turn out to be far from the only case of 'giving birth'. Diotima appears to mean that intercourse literally *is* giving birth – as if the male were pregnant and his semen the offspring (Dover:147 also refers to evidence in Aristotle for the belief, among some Greeks, that the female too 'emitted semen, necessary for conception, at the moment of orgasm'). This idea of male pregnancy may perhaps have been less odd for a Greek than it is for us (cf. e.g. Pender 1992), and would certainly not have looked odd at all to some 'preformationists' in eighteenth-century Europe; but its chief purpose in the present context in *Symp.* – to which any points of contact with actual theories of reproduction are largely incidental – is to prepare the way for the introduction of the other kind of procreation, effected by those 'pregnant in soul' (208e ff.), and without a long period of gestation. In any case ejaculation rather than the ultimate birth of offspring is what at least the male of the species (and perhaps the female too, if Diotima agrees with Aristotle) is under normal circumstances most immediately 'intensely eager' (b2-3) about.

c6   **'This matter of giving birth is something divine':** explained by what immediately follows (it offers a kind of immortality).

d1-2   **'beauty is both Fate and Eileithyia for coming-into-being':** for the presence at births of Fates, as well as Eileithyia (goddess of childbirth), see e.g. Pindar, *Olympians* 6.41-2, *Nemeans* 7.1.

d3   **'gracious':** *hileôs* (cf. Agathon at 197d5, of Love).

d4-6   **'melts ... contracts ... curls up':** Dover suggests that the latter two verbs, plus *spargônti* ('swelling', e1; 'full to bursting' in the present translation), 'describe equally the reactions of the male and of the female genitals to sexual stimulus or revulsion', while 'melts' is 'more appropriate to the female'. In my own view 'melts (with joy)' looks equally applicable to, and *spargônti* more obviously appropriate to, the male; the whole passage seems designed to allow the male gradually to appropriate virtually the whole female function in reproduction. Cf. following n., and Pender 1992:74-6 (unlike Pender, however, I believe that Diotima then goes on to operate entirely with the idea of male 'pregnancy' and 'giving birth', whether physical or 'spiritual'). But the whole context is more impressionistic, and more concerned to destabilize, than it is precise, so that no firm conclusion here is likely to be possible; the descriptions in question are of course themselves at least as much metaphorical as literal ('becomes gracious ... frowning with pain ...').

d7-e1   **'This is why what is pregnant ... in proximity to the beautiful':** ordinary female pregnancy here seems actually to be excluded (even if the birth of a child is something beautiful, at least to its parents, Greek women would be no more likely to have given birth 'in beauty', i.e. in a beautiful environment, than their modern equivalents). But paradox is part of, not an obstacle to, Diotima's presentation of her thesis. 'In proximity to' translates the same *peri* + acc. which was earlier translated as 'in relation to': see 203c4n., etc. (with e2-3n. below).

e1-2   **'because of the fact that the beautiful person frees it from great pain':** lit. 'because of the fact that the one who has [it, sc. the beauty: *ton echonta*] frees [it, sc. what is pregnant: *to kuoun*] from great pain'; the Greek could also mean 'because of the fact that it frees from great pain the one who has it (the great pain)', but 'the one who has it' seems in this case lame, even redundant – and Diotima has so far preferred to keep the pregnant subject in the (generalizing) neuter (so at least in d3, and it is then natural to take *tôi* *kuounti te kai ... spargônti*, 'what is pregnant and already full to bursting', also as neuter). This is because she is already moving away from physical 'giving birth'. The word for 'pain' here is also, but not exclusively, used for 'birth-pangs' (cf. *Theaetetus* 151a).

e2-3 'love is not, as you think, of the beautiful': cf. 204d3 (Diotima herself has carefully avoided committing herself to the idea: see 203c4n., 204b3). Given the immediately preceding reference to 'the one who has it (beauty)' (see last n.), 'the beautiful' might in principle have the same ambiguity it has had before (see 197b4-5n., b7-c1n., 201e5, 203d3-4n.), between beauty (the property) and the beautiful *individual*; but in fact it is surely Diotima's point here precisely that the lover's *erôs* is not of his partner. If this strikes us as bizarre, it is still wholly consistent with her teaching so far; after all, it is the *good* we love, and if what excites us is the prospect of procreation (not so much for itself as for the 'offspring' produced: see following n.), the beautiful person in whom we procreate will apparently be no more than a means to that, even if she/he will have the compensation of knowing that we couldn't have done it without them – or someone else beautiful. (But at the same time, if it still holds that – as Agathon admitted at 201c, and as S. himself no doubt also accepts – the good is also beautiful, then in a way *erôs* is still of *beauty*.)

e5 'Of procreation and giving birth in the beautiful': 'procreation' (*gennêsis*) adds nothing that is not already in 'giving birth' (*tokos*); love is of procreation, as it is of giving birth, because of the offspring, or rather because of what the offspring bestow on us (i.e. some kind of permanent possession of the good).

e6 'All right': this is Waterfield's translation of *eien* – 'recognising the establishment of a situation and suggesting that the next step should be considered', Dover on 176a5. S. now signals that he is beginning to understand what he failed to understand in b7-10.

e7 'Why, then, is it of procreation?' Cf. 204d 'why does the person who loves love beautiful things?' In effect Diotima now repeats her question, having modified S.'s account of the object of *erôs*; and the same answer comes back – or rather an interesting variant on it.

206e8-207a2 'it is immortality, together with the good, that must necessarily be desired, according to what has been agreed before – if indeed love is of permanent possession of the good': the last clause repeats 206a12-13, with minor variations; interestingly, the placing of the 'always' (*aei*, which underlies 'permanent' in the translation) allows the clause simultaneously to recall the two other things that have been said to be always the case, i.e. (1) that we are always in love with possession of the good (205a-b), and (2) that love is always love of permanent possession of/always possessing the good (206b1). While it is reasonable enough to say that someone who desires (literally) permanent possession of something must also desire immortality, it might seem less reasonable to suggest that it is immortality that we desire; S. next, in 207a5-209e4, reports how Diotima once tried to convince him that we do. Of course, as she has admitted in 206e7-8, actual immortality lies beyond the reach of the mortal, and all her evidence relates to substitutes for that: the production of offspring that are like ourselves (207a5-208b6: see following n.), or achievements which will be remembered by others (208c2-209e4). One might feel inclined to ask her just what *these* sorts of 'immortality' have to do with the immortality that would be the condition of our literally possessing the good for ever; she would reply, I think, that she is only trying to show that our behaviour, and that of mortal nature in general, shows a tendency to try to overcome the limitations set on us by our mortality (thus even the highest kind of life, described in her account of the 'higher mysteries', must ultimately fall short of true immortality, i.e. the kind that belongs to the divine: see 212a6-7n.). But it remains the case that the inference, from permanent possession of the good to immortality, is not a happy one. All the more interesting, then, that S. does not actually record himself as agreeing to it: see 207c8-9n.

– One of the standing puzzles about *Symp.*, and one that figures prominently in the secondary literature, is that for all Diotima's talk about immortality, and her apparently close familiarity with Socratic-Platonic philosophy, she has not the slightest word to say about the *immortality of the soul*, a theme which bulks large in a number of dialogues which, on the usual dating, belong to roughly the same period in P.'s writing career: *Phaedo*, *Republic*, and *Phaedrus* (see e.g. Hackforth 1950). Here is one case where the relative dating of *Symp.* does seem to matter (see Introduction, §5): does *Symp.* perhaps date to a time before these other dialogues, and before P. made the commitment they apparently signal to the idea of an immortal soul? Or is it just that, within the strategy of Diotima's argument as he has designed it, it is superfluous to requirements? On the grounds of economy alone, the second alternative seems the more attractive; there is in fact nothing in her account which actually rules out the possibility that the soul is immortal, since even if it is, human beings as such will still be mortal (S., along with all the others, will still die *qua* composite of soul and body), and the only question raised is how, given the fact of our mortality, we can – through the kind of life we live – transcend it. Even if it happened to be true that part of us will survive death anyway, that either does not affect the question or, if it does, it would mean opening up an entirely new front, and introducing a degree of complexity out of place, perhaps, in the context of the dinner-party. It is one of the features of P.'s use of the dialogue form that what his characters say tends to be constrained by the dramatic situation.

207a4-5 'All these things she taught me ... whenever she talked about matters to do with love, and on one occasion she asked me ...': S. supports his fictions with circumstantial details, just as P. does his. What follows is really of a piece with what went before this break, and, as it seems from c5 ('as I said just now'), which refers back directly to 206b5-6, actually followed either it, or a conversation very similar to it, on the very occasion S. now goes on to describe ('and on one occasion she asked me ...'). But – whatever else it may do: see c8-9n. – the brief interlude serves to remind us where we are (with S. telling us a story). 'Matters to do with love' are of course 'erotics', *ta erôtika*, as at 177e1, etc. (and c3).

207a5-208b6: the main function of this passage (see 206e8-207a2n.) is to offer support for the view of love as directed towards 'procreation in beauty', now understood (also) as a means to immortality (207a2-3). It falls into two parts. Diotima first points out how passionate animals are, not just about the procreation of offspring, but about feeding and generally rearing them (207a6-b6); she then explains the reason for this passion, in terms of the general drive of mortal nature towards (a kind of) immortality through replacement (207c8-208b6: see esp. 208b4-6). At the same time the passage provides a smaller-scale rival to Eryximachus' account of the working of Love on the cosmic scale: by implication, even at the level of physiological processes, everything is driven by something analogous to our (human) desire for the good. Such teleological ideas are themselves endemic in P.'s dialogues (most notably, of course, in the *Timaeus*, which contains his single most concentrated account of the physical world in all its aspects).

a6 'the cause of this love, and this desire': or 'responsible for ...' (*aition*), as e.g. at 193d1; but for *aitia* in b8, and c7, which has a similar reference to that of *aitia* here, see 205b9, where 'cause' is the most natural translation. For the pairing 'this love, and this desire', see 197a8, 200a6, e5-6.

a7 'all animals': *thêria*, contrasted with human beings, *anthrôpoi*, b7.

b1-3 'all of them stricken with the effects of love, first for intercourse with one another, and then also ...': thus even animals 'love' (desire) something beyond intercourse itself (i.e., ultimately, immortality). ('For' here is 'in relation to', *peri* + acc.: here too Diotima will strictly want to avoid saying quite that animals' desire is *of* intercourse, etc., itself. – cf. a6n., 206d7-e1n.)

b8-c1 **'so powerfully affected by love'**: i.e. that they do what they do to rear their offspring.

c5 **'as I said just now'**: see a4-5n.

c8-9 **'if you are confident that what love is of ... is what we have agreed many times that it is'**: i.e. that love is of the good, and therefore (?) of immortality (206e7-207a3; cf. c9-d2); the 'often' must refer to the many times they have talked about the subject (a4-5). But in fact S. has noticeably *omitted* (or Aristodemus, or Apollodorus, has omitted) any reference to his actually having agreed to the inference from love of the good to love of immortality. Is this a sign that he might want to leave her on her own this time (as he would have good reason to do: see 206e8-207a2n.)? On the purpose of such distancing, see 205d9n. More than one commentator has suggested (and several people have urged on me in conversation) that any separation between Socrates and Diotima should be interpreted as marking a boundary between the Socratic and the Platonic. However it seems to me that whatever reservations S. has about Diotima's 'teaching' ought also to have been shared by P., just because of S.'s overall commitment to the truth. That the new elements of that teaching were vouchsafed to him on only a single occasion (while the rest she taught him many times over: see a4-5n.) is perhaps itself an indication of their more provisional – and occasional – nature: cf. Introduction §2.4.

d3 **'coming-into-being'**: *genesis*, as at 206d2. – **'because it always leaves behind something else that is new'**: or 'insofar as on each occasion/in each case it leaves behind ...'.

d4-5 **'is said to be alive and to be the same individual'**: 'is said to be' (similarly in d5, d7), because from another – and, Diotima suggests, equally valid – point of view (given that parts are constantly being renewed, d6 ff.), it might be said to have perished and been replaced by a different individual. Underlying this passage is a standing problem about identity (see Sier 238, and esp. Plutarch, *Theseus* 23.1), which probably begins its life with Heraclitus (see d7n.). ('Individual' is supplied, as is 'person' in the next line; the Greek has 'the same'.)

d6 **'he's never made up from the same things'**: does this mean (1) take any point in a person's life later than another by more than a moment or two, and at least some part of him will have changed; or (2) from one moment to the next, literally no part of him will stay the same? The next sentence, which uses more or less the same formula (e4-5) perhaps suggests that (1) is more likely (at any rate a person's 'traits' and 'habits' could hardly be said to change *all* the time).

d7 **'always being renewed'**: the Greek can also – and no doubt *does* also – mean 'always becoming *young*'; for the paradoxical coincidence of old and young, see Heraclitus fr. 88 Diels-Kranz.

e3 **'its traits, habits'**: the sentence is meant to report something 'strange' (see the beginning of the next one), and this strangeness is perhaps most obviously in the idea that even what we think of as lasting – traits and habits – themselves change over time; we are likely to have different patterns of life as old people, or adults, from those we have as children (cf. d5-6). As a general observation, this seems fair enough, even if there may be unfortunate exceptions to the rule.

e6 **'It's much stranger even than this with the pieces of knowledge we have'**: *knowledge* is something we would expect to be especially stable; after all, isn't it a matter of grasping something which itself won't change (the truth)? P.'s S. has his own take on this, in the *Meno* (98a): it's opinions that shift around, even true ones, because we can be persuaded out of them, or they can just 'run away' (like a mindless slave); but when true opinion is 'tied down' ('by reckoning of the cause/reason why'), then they 'become, first, knowledge, and then stable (*monimoi*)', i.e. they won't 'run away from you'. But of course, as Diotima points out, we may at any time forget anything we currently know, so that while knowledge *qua* what is known will not change, and is a paradigm of stability, our possession of it is, sadly, not so reliable. 'Pieces of knowledge' translates *epistêmai*, the plural of *epistêmê*, 'knowledge': the plural indicates *cases* of knowledge/knowing (so regularly with abstract nouns), as the *Meno* passage illustrates – the Greek there for 'true opinions become knowledge' is 'true opinions become *epistêmai*'. Sier is surely wrong to suggest that Diotima is referring to a popular conception of knowledge (Sier:244-5); in principle, she suggests, *anyone* can forget something, because that is what human knowing is like. Someone with complete, perfect, knowledge (which allowed him or her to make sense of everything, and connect any item with any other) might well not forget any part of it – but then he or she would have joined the company of the gods.

208a2 **'the things we know'**: i.e., again, 'our knowledges' (see preceding n.).

a3 **'what we call "going over" things'**: or 'practising', 'rehearsing' ('unrehearsed' in the first line of the dialogue comes from the same root).

a6 **'in such a way as to make it seem the same'**: i.e. when it is actually not, according to the perspective of 207d-e (see 207d4-5n.).

b2 **'of the same sort that it was'**: this point, of course, is what allows us to talk of things as retaining their identity, despite the fact that they are changing; it is also what connects this topic with the question we started with in 207b8-c1, about why animals feel so passionately about their offspring. Answer (b4-6): because their offspring, being like themselves, give them a kind of immortality.

b5-6 **'this eagerness, this love, that attends on every creature is for the sake of immortality'**: i.e. 'this eagerness which *is* love' (cf. Dover); Diotima echoes the phrasing in the original question at 206b1-3, which the one at 207b8-c1 (see preceding n.) repeated at a more specific level – why do animals feel so passionately about procreating (the act, but also, and for the sake of, its products: 207b2-3)?

b7 **'I was indeed surprised'**: S. might well be surprised, especially if he is still partly playing Agathon's role (see 209e5-210a1n.), at the idea that all the passion associated with *erôs* (still here standing for all desire, but – because of the excursion into the animal world – with the emphasis on its sexual variety) is 'for the sake of' immortality.

b8-9 **'Well now, most wise Diotima: is what you say really true?'** The closest parallel for this *eien* ('well now') is likely to be at *Republic* 350e: 'I'll say "Well now" to you, as one does to old women telling tales, and I'll nod my head in agreement – and take it back at the same time' (contrast *eien* at 206e6, and even more the example at 176a5: 'well then', simply introducing a new subject). 'Most wise' has much the same effect, referring to S.'s position as Diotima's pupil, but (from his perspective as *narrator*: cf. Sier) with a tinge of irony; he maintains his distance from at least *this* aspect of her account (cf. 207c8-9n.).

c1 **'Like an accomplished sophist'**: for the expression 'perfect sophist' (*teleos sophistês*, written as if 'sophist' were just like any other sort of occupation) see *Cratylus* 403e, where it is used of of Hades, as a good speaker, a benefactor, able to make people better people ... But this *Cratylus* passage is itself a complex one, in a complex context. 'Sophist' remains a thoroughly slippery term, ranging in connotation from 'expert' to 'sophistical', 'tricksy' (cf. 177b2-3n.); here S. plays on both ends of the spectrum – Diotima speaks like a complete expert, but (given the tricksy nature of some of what will follow) in a way also like a complete sophist, in the negative sense. So when she replies 'You can be sure of that, S.' (c1-2), he cannot, quite, be sure of it (see preceding n.), and he is indicating as much, while also setting the tone for the next part of what she (supposedly) said (208c2-209e4). It is not that she will tell lies, because after all she *is* Socrates' teacher, but on the other hand she will frequently not mean quite what she appears to say, and her tone will be less than completely serious. (Thus, for example, we find her almost immediately trumping Phaedrus' flabby conceits, and parodying his methods – or at least appearing to do so: d2 ff.)

208c2-209e4: the final 'evidence' for Diotima's thesis about the object of our desire (see 206e8-207a2n.). She now returns directly to human beings: her thesis is demonstrated by the very way they behave – always, and in everything (so she says), motivated to procreate (whether in soul or in body: we are, of course, all pregnant in both, 206c) by the love of honour; for being honoured by others on the right scale itself represents a kind of immortality. By implication, she will treat all human creative achievement as the outcome of the working of *erôs*: that is, again, 'generic' *erôs*, but presented as if it followed the pattern of specific *erôs* (and so involving a beautiful partner, who provides the necessary environment for 'giving birth'). The general theme is one of Agathon's – Diotima specifically includes poets in her account, as well as legislators (the latter perhaps suggesting Aristophanes' manly politicians at 192a: see 209c4-7n.). But there is one important difference: she will implicitly question how real the achievements are. (Dover:151 suggests that *philosophical* achievements are included at 209c4-7, which if true would radically alter the case; but see my n. on the passage.)

c3-4 **'you'd be surprised ... in relation to what I've talked about':** i.e. the treatment of offspring (c4 'how terribly ...'; cf. 207a7 'how terribly all animals are affected ...'); Diotima's vagueness is because she is about to reintroduce a different, non-physical, kind of 'children' (209a-e). Clearly, we need some sort of explanation of people's 'irrational' love of honour, given that human beings are supposed to be rational (207b7-8); it is another question whether Diotima's proposed explanation, in terms of a universal desire for immortality, is – or is meant to be taken as – the right one.

c5-6 **'"of laying up immortal glory for all time to come"':** a hexameter of unknown provenance (but might S., in his role as Agathon, be breaking into verse on his own account?).

d1-2 **'they'll spend money, undergo any suffering you like, give up their lives':** as lovers do ...

d3-6 **'Alcestis ... Achilles ... Codrus ...':** Diotima simultaneously corrects and goes one better than Phaedrus. 'Do you think they would have done what they did if they hadn't thought they would acquire immortal fame for it?' suggests that at the least Phaedrus gave an incomplete account of their motivation; Codrus' 'dying before' (*proapothanein*) improves (?) on Phaedrus' 'not just a case of dying for (*huperapothanein*), but of dying on top of (*epapothanein*)' (180a1). – Dover comments on this whole section that in it 'love of an individual for the individual's sake is decisively rejected' (Dover:152). But it might well be said that it was rejected as soon as *erôs* was said to be of *the good*, i.e. of what is good for the agent (and especially not of the beautiful person, 206e2-3?); and the present context could actually be taken rather as *mitigating* that position, since Diotima's descriptions of Alcestis' and Codrus' actions (and perhaps by implication of Achilles') still include a reference to doing things *for others* ('do you think she would have died for Admetus if she hadn't ...?'). While the agents in these cases may not be seen as doing things exclusively for the sake of others, there is nothing here to make us suppose that the (real) good desired will exclude reference to the good of others, and positive evidence that such a reference may in fact (at least sometimes) be included. However Alcestis and company will ultimately turn out to be poor models: since they presumably have not encountered Beauty Itself, they cannot procreate 'true virtue' (212a5-6, with the preceding context). Nothing much of a substantive sort can therefore be derived from their cases, and it still remains to be seen just to what extent, and how, individuals may still be the objects of love in the new context of 'the final revelation' (see esp. 210c2n., c8-d3n.). The one thing that seems to be ruled out is that they should emerge as the sole objects of (even) the best kind of love/desire, insofar as love is always of the good. But that is, anyway, surely a hard condition to lay down for any kind of love.

d4 **'your Codrus':** i.e. 'your Athenian Codrus' (once again Diotima's status as a foreigner is marked, or at least acknowledged: see 201d1-204c8n.), a mythical king of Athens who deliberately allowed himself to be killed by the Dorian enemy, knowing that an oracle had foretold that they would take the city if they did not kill him (so the scholiast). The detail that he died early in order to preserve the kingship for his children is presumably invented on the spot, not just for the sake of adding to the sequence dying for/on top of (see preceding n.), but perhaps also because of the interesting collision with the idea that people are *even more* prepared to die for glory than for their children (c7-d1). Here is someone who does both, but then apparently glory will have been his first consideration (and after all, it is immortality/the good that we desire ...).

d5-6 **'their own courage':** *aretê* is probably 'courage' here, but must be 'virtue' in d7; it would be implausible even to begin proposing that 'everyone does everything for the sake of immortal courage'.

d7-e2 **'I imagine it's for the sake of immortal virtue and this sort of glorious reputation that everyone does everything, the more so the better people they are':** 'for the sake of immortal virtue' = 'for the sake of a virtue which will go on existing because always remembered'; the virtue itself is then evidently desired because of the glory it will bring. The claim that (literally) everyone does (literally) everything for the sake of fame and reputation sounds not just un-Socratic, and un-Platonic, but plainly false – and indeed the cases that have been listed are likely in themselves to throw doubt on it, just as Phaedrus' own list of examples did on his thesis (that only lovers die for others). So is this just a parody of Phaedrus? (Diotima was not there to hear him; but by now she is surely a fiction that has worn paper thin.) Perhaps it is a parody, or is meant to suggest one. However the last words of the lemma still have to be accounted for: 'the more so the better people they are'. This introduces a qualification to 'everyone ... everything', along the lines of 'well, some more than others, i.e. better people more than inferior ones'. The argument might then go as follows. 'Everyone desires immortality, which is why they aim at the reputation that comes from virtue – if they are sufficiently good; and the better they are, the more they aim at that. But there are some people who aim lower ... So my (Diotima's) thesis is supported by the phenomenon of "love of honour" (*philotimia*), which operates in the case of better people ...' What she proposes here is something which both (a) is likely to appeal to the vanity of those present and (b), if (a) is taken into account, will cease to be a worryingly false description of actual behaviour, provided that 'the good' is reinstated in place of 'immortality' (which, according to the fiction, was in any case introduced – perhaps – without S.'s actually agreeing to it: see 207c8-9n.). We all do everything for the sake of the good. So if anyone does things for the sake of fame, that is because they think fame a good thing (cf. e5 'as they think') – and if people who think that are the better sort, then the better we are, the more likely we shall be to do things for the sake of fame; but whether they really *are* the better sort still remains to be seen.

e2 **'because they are in love with immortality':** or 'with what is immortal'.

e2-3 **'Those, then ... who are pregnant in their bodies':** according to 206c1-3, 'all human beings ... are pregnant both in body and in soul'; 208e6-209a2 suggests that those who are 'pregnant in soul' will all be pregnant in body too, but it is now not so clear that (some degree of) pregnancy in soul always accompanies pregnancy in body.

e3-4 **'more towards women'**: i.e than towards boys ('in' whom only the other, non-physical, kind of offspring can be produced).

e4-6 **'securing immortality, a memory of themselves, and happiness, as they think, ... through having children'**: though apparently 'everyone' would prefer children of a different sort, when they consider the great men of the past (209c7 ff.). But the 'final mysteries' will propose that 'everyone', too, is looking in the wrong direction (see 212a3-5n.).

209a3-4 **'Wisdom and the rest of virtue; of which all the poets are, of course, procreators'**: presumably an ironic compliment to Agathon, and Aristophanes, both of whom might like to think of themselves as having some sort of wisdom (here *phronêsis*, as at 202a9, 203d6), of the sort generally attributed to Homer and Hesiod (cf. d3-4n.), but neither of whom has actually managed to show much evidence of wisdom. Whatever we suppose to be P.'s general view of poets, the handling of the two actually present in *Symp.* renders it actually impossible that 'of which all the poets are procreators' could be taken as seriously and literally meant – unless, of course, Diotima is a real and independent individual, whose actual views S. (P.) is reporting. Since the evidence against this is overwhelmingly strong, the ironic reading – for which *Apology* 22a-c would provide good background reading – seems inevitable.

a4-5 **'along with all those craftsmen who are said to be inventive'**: for the term *heuretikos* ('inventive'), see *Politicus* 286e, 287a, where it means 'capable of discovery'. I provisionally suggest that just as Diotima/S. has just made indirect reference to Agathon and Aristophanes, and compared them to the greatest poets of all, so now s/he refers, equally indirectly, to Eryximachus (cf. *dêmiourgos*, 'craftsman', used by him of the doctor at 186d5), comparing him to the great inventors of the past – like Asclepius, mentioned by him as founder of medicine at 186e (contrast Agathon's attribution of the invention of medicine to Apollo, and other inventions to other gods, at 197a-b: according to Homer – and Eryximachus is relying on 'the poets' – Asclepius was a mortal). The starting-point will perhaps be Eryximachus' own claims to expertise, which certainly seem to have some rather ill-defined connection with the 'fathering' of virtue (186b ff.).

a5-b1 **'But by far the greatest and most beautiful kind of wisdom ... which is called "moderation" and "justice"'**: cf. *Protagoras* 322e ff., where P. has Protagoras similarly pair justice and moderation as the basis of good government; Diotima seems here to be drawing on (idealized) ordinary views of the 'political art'.

b1 **'When someone is pregnant with these things'**: 'these things', I take it, are the sorts of things that poets, craftsmen and politicians (supposedly) 'bring to birth', i.e. 'wisdom and the rest of virtue'.

b2 **'by divine gift'**: lit. 'being divine/godlike' (*theios*). For the idea, Bury compares *Meno* 99c-d, where the same word *theios* is applied to all sorts of people, including poets and politicians, who (seem to) manage to get things right without knowing what they are doing; and after all, it is a puzzle how things come so easily to this particular pregnant lover ('he is immediately full of resource when it comes to things to say about virtue', b8) when it involves so much time and effort for the philosophical lover Diotima will go on to describe. (The answer, surely, is that his 'achievement' is not quite what he, and we, might think it to be.) – Editors have sometimes preferred to emend θεῖος to ἤθεος, in the sense of 'unmarried', 'bachelor': '... from youth on, when the right age comes and he is without a partner ...'. If this emendation is accepted, it is probably easiest then, with Dover, to keep the mss. reading ἐπιθυμεῖ in b3, making it a main verb, with a full stop after it; but to my eye the emendation looks more ingenious than convincing, not least because θεῖος seems to render up the right sense without too much difficulty.

b3 **'then I imagine he too'**: i.e. presumably like those attracted to women.

b5-6 'he warms to beautiful bodies': it does not make much sense here to ask whether this means having sex with them, because Diotima is talking, not specifically about actual lovers (though them too: cf. c3-4n.), but about people like poets, craftsmen and politicians, who create what they do out of a desire for immortality – creation, again, being seen for the moment as procreation. ('Warm to' translates *aspazesthai*, often 'embrace', but often in the sense of welcoming or greeting; i.e. not necessarily implying sexual contact. Cf. 205e5-6n.) In any case Diotima moves on immediately to the idea of the lover as moral educator of the beloved; the lover's teaching, or attempt to teach (c2), becomes the central metaphor for creative activity.

b7-8 'to this person he is immediately full of resource when it comes to things to say about virtue': but how so? (Cf. b2n., and c2 '*tries* to educate him'.)

c1 'what sort of thing the good man must be concerned with, and the activities such a man should involve himself in': this pair of subjects mirrors those that preoccupy S./Diotima – what is our goal, and by what activities is it achieved? (For 'activities', i.e. *epitêdeuein/epitêdeumata*, see esp. 210c4-5n.).

c3-4 'both when he is present with him and when he is away from him but remembering him': this serves to underline the point, perhaps teasingly obscured by the language of 'warming to'/'embracing', and of 'contact with', that actual contact is unnecessary for the process of mental 'bringing to birth'. But there is a point behind the teasing: even if we are being given a metaphorical description of desiring and creating in general, still real lovers (devotees of Pausanias' Heavenly Love, presumably: cf. c5-7, which refers to one of Pausanias' favourite themes, about the fidelity of such lovers) are included, and there is no reason to suppose that *they* are abstaining from physical contact.

c4-7 'and he joins with the other person ... children of a more beautiful and more immortal kind': so this is Diotima's 'explanation' of the genesis of great works of poetry, great achievements in the crafts, in politics ... – men pregnant with ideas look for a beautiful partner in/with whom to give birth, for the sake of immortality. ('So here too the evidence is consistent with my theory of desire.') And who wouldn't prefer offspring of *this* kind over those of the other, when they look at the examples of Homer and Hesiod, Lycurgus and Solon (c7 ff.)? But now these great figures are themselves, by implication, drawn into the same account: their works, too, are their 'offspring' (*ekgona*, d3) and 'children' (*paides*, d6), and so presumably were 'procreated' in the same way. Diotima does not push her luck by actually claiming as much, but we have only been given one account of how procreation takes place: they too must have found beautiful partners 'in whom' to give birth. Strange stuff, indeed, but no stranger than much of what the other speakers proposed (on whom it also draws, in a variety of ways), and the invention is more controlled. Diotima pursues her idea relentlessly to its limits and beyond them, and yet – I suggest – a careful reading shows us exactly where we are, and (most importantly) where the truth is supposed to lie.

c7-d2 'Everyone would prefer the birth to them of children of this sort to that of human children': that is, because the first sort are 'more beautiful and more immortal'. Surely not everyone, we might reply – but Diotima is ahead of us; would our answer be the same, if our soul-children were like Homer's, or ... (d2 ff.)?

d3-4 'the sort of offspring they leave behind them': the present, natural enough in a general statement (about all good poets), also teasingly offers Agathon and Aristophanes the possibility of comparing themselves with Homer and Hesiod (cf. a3-4n.).

d5-8 'the sort of children Lycurgus left behind for himself in Sparta ... Solon too, here in Athens ...': that Lycurgus' achievement as lawgiver should be privileged in this context over Solon's makes sense; after all, his laws lasted in a way that Solon's did not – while it would still be possible, indeed normal, to say in the late fifth century that Sparta's laws dated back to the 'half-legendary' Lycurgus (Dover), and so at least to the seventh century, the early sixth-century Solonian constitution at Athens, however important and long-lasting its effects, was in many respects itself a distant memory. But what of the implication that Sparta was 'saviour of Greece'? Athens would herself have a good claim to the title (what of Marathon?), and considerable grounds for rejecting Sparta's (her defeat by Sparta in the Peloponnesian War, e.g., hardly saved *her*). Moreover, as a Mantinean, Diotima ought perhaps to have special reason to hate Sparta: see 193a2-3n. Is she simply suggesting, provocatively, that from outside Athens Sparta's achievement – in the Persian Wars – looks the more impressive? Since the subject in hand is immortality and memory, this would be to the point, and perhaps especially insofar as it raises questions of perspective: Diotima has yet to give her real, final, verdict on Sparta, Athens, the great lawgivers and the great poets. This will come at the very end of her speech, where by implication she treats all the 'offspring' described here as mere 'shadowy images of virtue' (see 212a4-5n.). But for the moment they have their use, as part of the evidence ('evidence') for her thesis about immortality.

e2-3 **'for having achieved many conspicuously beautiful things, and procreated virtue of all sorts':** 'of all sorts' refers to the variety of different fields in which men have achieved things; 'excellence' might well be better here for *aretê* than 'virtue', but that would obscure the undoubted connections and contrasts with 212a, where 'virtue' is unavoidable.

e3-4 **'and in fact in many cases cults have been set up to them ...':** thus (1) 'immortality', of a superior variety, really is available, and (2) everyone would surely desire it more than that other sort (cf. c7 ff.); so (3) we can see again that the desire for immortality is what really drives us. The term *hiera* ('cults') 'denotes temples and sanctuaries as well as rites and sacrifices' (Dover). For the case of Lycurgus, see e.g. Herodotus 1.66.1; on Asclepius, see a4-5n.

209e5-212a7: the so-called 'ascent' passage, which introduces a new metaphor, that of the mysteries (mainly those of Eleusis), and combines it with the one already in play ('generic' desire for the good as *erôs*). However there is no real sense of strain in the combination, partly because the latter theme is not entirely a metaphor: just insofar as the passage is – like what precedes it – about desire as a whole, it must also be, and is, about sexual desire, though just as an account of that subject it might well seem distinctly thin. This passage is probably, on balance, the most difficult part of the whole dialogue. However if it is read closely with, and as representing the climax and end-point of what precedes it, its general sense and shape seem to emerge clearly enough. The first and most obvious point (because Diotima announces it) is that this new passage is about the *correct* way to go about the business of erotics – that is, what our goal should be, or rather, what our goal *really is*, and how we should set about achieving it, both in life as a whole and in our erotic relationships. The central figure is that of the lover, the *paiderastês* (see 211b6), who is 'led' by someone else (210a6, c8, e3) through various stages of understanding of beauty, each stage issuing in his 'procreating' *logoi* ('words', 'things to say': so e.g. at 210a7), apparently to a beloved. This already gives us enough to recognize that Diotima is still working (as we should expect) with the same idea as before, i.e. of human beings as desiring immortality, which they can achieve vicariously through their 'offspring'. Now one of the outcomes of 208c2-209e4 was that these offspring may vary in quality, and in the degree of 'immortality' that they offer (see esp. 209c7 ff.); another outcome was that this quality differs with the degree of beauty 'in which' they are procreated (see 209b3-c2). The chief function of the leader is to ensure the lover's exposure to ever-increasing degrees, and quantities, of beauty, and the result is (we may suppose) a steady increase in the quality of his offspring. Since his development is a philosophical one, it seems reasonable to suppose that he is a philosopher, and that 'the one leading' is also a philosopher, only more experienced than him (see 210a6-7n.). But if his progress charts the 'correct' way of doing erotics, he is also a model for all of us – that is, if 'erotics' is really about ourselves as desiring beings, who desire the good but need to learn the direction in which it lies. Next, he will require a partner (or, as it may emerge, partners), for how else can one procreate if not with a partner? Well, one might answer, the beauty the philosopher will encounter will actually mostly not be in his partner(s); so why should he not go off and somehow procreate 'in' that? Still, if what the lover is procreating is in the form of words, as at least most of the time it is, he will need someone to address those words to. In any case, he is a *lover*, and what is a lover without a beloved? Thus at the same time the lover's progress is a model of how we should organise our erotic selves (in the ordinary, common or garden sense). The philosopher in love (and again, we all need to be philosophers) will get over his attachment to particular bodies early on, and even before he has done so he will confine himself to procreating beautiful words (210a5-7). The message here is both negative and positive: 'do not waste time on physical affairs; do use your time with the beautiful young to do philosophy'. This is hardly a complete lesson in *erôs*, from any point of view. But neither is it meant to be one. It is a response, in part, to a type of view which sets (from a Socratic perspective) too much value on simple forms of satisfaction – those relevant to, and normally perhaps offered by, the institution of the symposium – and too little on reflection; in this respect the lesson about (ordinary) love is a stand-in for a larger lesson about life as a whole. – There is, no doubt, much in this interpretation, and in the detailed notes that follow, with which different readers will wish to take issue; and indeed there are already many readers who have interpreted the passage along quite different lines (the literature on this part of the dialogue is, understandably, even more plentiful than it is on other parts). However I have described what I believe, at least for the moment, to be the most satisfactory interpretation, measured by its explanatory power both in relation to the actual language of the passage and, equally importantly, in relation to the passage's context as the last part of long and apparently structured piece of writing. No reading is likely to be successful which fails to explain the development of the argument from at least as far back as Agathon's speech (since Diotima incontrovertibly starts from there), and the way in which the ascent passage develops out of that. Whatever else we may say of the other speakers, the signs are that the composite figure of S./Diotima knows precisely where he is going, and it is our business to try to map his journey with equal precision. (For an alternative, and sympathetic, treatment of the passage, which also engages with other important parts of the secondary literature, see ch.2 of Price 1989.)

209e5-210a1 'Into these aspects of erotics, perhaps, S., you too could be initiated': evidently (see e.g. *Gorgias* 497c, with scholiast; and Burkert 1983:266) initiation into the Lesser (or 'Small') Mysteries, at Agrae ('in the city'), was a necessary qualification for initiation into the Great(er), at Eleusis; and on any account it must be true that S. will have needed to learn what has gone before in order even to begin to grasp what follows. But Diotima's main point is just about the relative importance, and difficulty, of the two sets of ideas; it hardly matters that the real Greater Mysteries were evidently not particularly difficult ('[t]he Athenians were, as a rule, mustai', i.e. were initiates, Burkert 1983:254). *Pace* Riedweg 1987:2-29, it is unnecessary to go back and re-read Diotima's preliminaries in the light of the new image, which is suggested above all by the idea of the final vision of Beauty (210e-212a). – 'Perhaps, S., you too': or 'perhaps even you', but the less extreme version seems more in place. It will not be surprising if S.'s listeners find the final stretch hard to understand; his way of introducing it (in the role of

Diotima's slow pupil: so no ordinary 'Socratic mock-modesty', as Dover calls it) among other things signals just how hard it will be.

210a1-2 'those aspects relating to the final revelation ... if one approaches these correctly': 'those aspects ...' reads literally 'the final and *epoptika* (things)', *ta telea kai epoptika*, i.e. those corresponding to the vision of the sacred object(s), the *epopteia*, which represented the high point of the Eleusinian Mysteries. But they are also 'final' in that they are the things 'for the sake of which I have taught you the rest' (lit. 'for the sake of which *these* are': emphatic καί). 'These' (the rest that I've taught you) are 'for the sake of' what is to follow in the sense that what Diotima has told S. so far will help him understand the next part, if he treats the lesson so far in the right spirit ('if one approaches these correctly'), i.e., I take it, if he understands it as a basic lesson about the nature of human motivation; and in particular, if he retains the notion of *erôs* as directed towards 'giving birth in beauty', for the sake of immortality. He must also apparently be prepared to consider abandoning his existing views about how immortality is best to be achieved – and in fact this might after all be the main point of the conditional clause in a2: see next n. (The Greek actually leaves the object of 'approaches' in a2 unexpressed; I have taken it to be 'these things', i.e. 'what I have taught you up to now', 'the rest', but it could, just, also be 'the final and *epoptika* things', in which case it will refer simply to the proper conduct of the final rites of love.)

a4-5 'The person who turns to this matter correctly': this looks as if it is meant to echo a2 'if one approaches these correctly' (see previous n.); if so, and if 'this matter' is loving/*erôs* (cf. 211b8), we should perhaps take a2 too to refer primarily to attitudes, priorities, etc. (Everything from here in a4 down to d7 makes up a single and frequently awkward sentence in the Greek, depending on the initial word *dei*: 'It is necessary/ required that ...'. Is Diotima perhaps meant to be recalling some list of ritual instructions, like the one referred to in the n. on a6-7?)

a5 'must begin': 'the next stage', following this one, starts in b6.

a6-7 'if the one leading him leads him correctly, he must fall in love with a single body ...': if we follow out the metaphor of the Mysteries, 'the one leading him' will be a *mustagôgos*, someone who guides the new initiates. In the real Mysteries, this will apparently have been a person already initiated and responsible for keeping the new initiates both in order and informed (see the first-century B.C. inscription from Eleusis published by J.H.Oliver in *Hesperia* 10 (1941), with Plutarch, *Moralia* 795e); in the present context the 'mystagogue' will be someone already initiated in, i.e. experienced in, 'loving correctly', but also, insofar as the initiate's progress will be a philosophical one (see e.g. d4-6n.), in philosophy. His 'correct leading' will in the present case perhaps consist not so much in pointing the initiate towards beautiful bodies, and instructing him to fall in love with one of them – in which he might be supposed to need little encouragement – as in causing him only to 'procreate beautiful words', rather than to indulge in physical sex, and helping him 'realise for himself that the beauty that there is in any body whatever is the twin [lit. 'brother'] of that in any other', and so on (a8 ff.). If so, we perhaps need not inquire too closely what the 'beautiful words' might consist in; but in any case the apprentice lover will presumably, like his counterpart at 209a-c, be 'still more pregnant in soul than in body', and so teeming with things to say. But even in this first stage he will apparently leave that counterpart behind; there is no sign that the non-initiate of 209a-c will learn the lesson(s) the initiate learns (he has no guide or leader, and is not even at the Mysteries). – Editors have raised problems about αὐτόν in both a7 (where one of the principal mss. has αὐτῶν) and a8. With some hesitation I take αὐτόν in a7 as signalling the return to the original (logical) subject of the sentence after the conditional cause; αὐτόν in a8, by contrast, seems to me to mark the difference between the 'leader' and an ordinary teacher – the lover/pupil comes to see what is the case '*for himself*' (something which is in any case a requirement of his progress as a philosopher). Cf. e.g. *Cratylus* 438b, *Alcibiades I* 110d; and des Places 1981 (1961):40-42.

b7-c2 **'so that if someone who is decent in his soul has even a slight physical bloom, even then it's enough for him':** is the thought that 'decency of soul' is not quite enough to constitute beauty, so that the lover is prompted by the thought that beauty in the soul is more valuable than beauty in the body to set about producing some (as the presence of 'even a slight physical bloom' will permit, according to the theory of 'giving birth in beauty')? (Alternatively, if decency of soul does constitute beauty, the 'small physical bloom' will simply indicate the absence of actual ugliness, which would inhibit any sort of procreation ...)

c2 **'he loves and cares for the other person':** 'for the other person' is supplied; the Greek intends it, but can do without it. Again (see 208d3-6n.), love of other people evidently *does* have a part in P.'s scheme, though what that part is still needs further clarification. (At least one can say that the relationship of lover to beloved in the present case is quite complex – if the first interpretation suggested in the last n. is right: (a) the lover is attracted, if only a little, by the beloved's body; (b) he is attracted by the potential represented by the beloved's soul; and (c) he 'cares for' the beloved, in the sense of seeking his good, while also (d) not being preoccupied exclusively with him, because 'he gives birth to, and seeks for', words which will make young men in general better men (c2-3); on the other hand (e), there is no indication that the lover will ever desert the beloved, even if his love turns out to include others as well. The beloved will not be the same as the recipient of the 'beautiful words' at the last stage (b7-c1 seems to indicate a new encounter), but then from the lover's current perspective that was a stage he has grown out of (it was 'when he was young', a5); there is no reason for him to abandon his new love – and indeed he will need at least one in which to procreate his soul-offspring.)

c2-3 **'and gives birth to the sorts of words – and seeks for them – that will make young men into better men':** the words 'and seeks' (delayed also in the Greek) are frequently bracketed by editors, but on inadequate grounds. Thus Dover says 'the ... seeker has already found his partner ..., he does not "seek" arguments [*logoi* in the Greek: it seems better to keep the more neutral 'words'], and *toioutous* ['the sorts of'] obviously looks forward to *hoitines* ... ['that will ...']'; but as Sier sees, it is exactly the lover's *seeking* for things of the right kind to say that will '*compel*' him 'to contemplate beauty as it exists in kinds of activity ...' (c4: he will *have* to look at the different kinds of things people do, etc., if he is going to 'care for' his beloved), and it is also what makes sense of 'that *will* make young men into better men'. (The general point was seen by Stallbaum and Rettig in the last century; Bury unfortunately rejects their defence of 'and seeks' as 'futile'.) Since the lover is being guided and taught, it surely fits that he shouldn't have the right sorts of *logoi* off pat – he's bursting with ideas, but will also need to do some *seeking*, *inquiring* (presumably with his guide, but no doubt also with his beloved). If Love, and the lover, is a philosopher (see d4-6n.), this should hardly come as a surprise; contrast the lover of 209b8-c1, or indeed our lover at the beginning (210a7), both of whom do have things off pat, in a way distinctly unlike Diotima's picture of the perpetually indigent Love. In short, removing 'and seeks' is not only unjustified, but does some damage to the argument.

c4-5 **'in order that he may be compelled in turn to contemplate beauty as it exists in kinds of activity and in laws':** 'kinds of activity' renders the fairly indefinite term *epitêdeumata*, for which the key parallel in the present context is probably *Republic* 444e 'isn't it true (too? *kai*) that fine *epitêdeumata* lead to the acquisition of virtue, shameful/dishonourable ones to the acquisition of vice?'; see also c8–d3n. The 'compulsion' to contemplate beauty in these new locations evidently comes from the lover's interest – acquired under the supervision of his 'guide' – in methods of moral improvement: it is the laws, and the right kinds of activities (at least primarily virtuous actions, as prescribed by the laws), that would normally, and reasonably, be thought of as the chief means to moral education. But it is the 'correct' lover's philosophical ascent that – if it could be completed – would lead to *true* virtue.

c5-7 **'and to observe that all of this is mutually related, in order that he should think beauty of body a slight thing':** while presumably retaining his higher evaluation of beauty of soul ('beauty of body' is 'beauty in relation to' [*peri*] body: see 203c4n.). So by the end of the present stage – the description of the next begins immediately with c7 'After activities ...' – the lover has understood that where beauty exists in 'kinds of activities and laws', it is all one; that then enables him to recognise that bodily beauty in general is something slight, presumably by comparison with the newly-comprehended beauty – from which will derive the means to increasing beauty of soul, itself already discovered to be 'more valuable' than beauty of body (b6-7).

c7-8 **'After activities, he must lead him to the different kinds of knowledge':** the translation here accurately represents the Greek in not identifying either the subject or the object of the 'leading', but the Greek even omits the 'he' and the 'him'. In a way no explicit identification is needed; we *know* who is doing the leading (the leader) and who is being led (the lover). However the sudden use of the transitive verb, with no subject, and with the likely candidate for the role last mentioned seventeen lines ago (in a6), is striking (that the object is unspecified is less so, since the obvious candidate for *that* role has been present all the time). Nor, if there are *two* relationships involved (guide/lover, lover/beloved), is the question 'who must lead who?' obviously otiose. In that case, it is not unreasonable to suspect a deliberate ambiguity: perhaps both guide must lead lover, and lover the beloved (that is, on separate occasions)? It is already fairly clear, after all, that both lover and beloved will progress; and if they do, they presumably do in the same way. See further c8–d3n., 211b8–c1n. – 'The different kinds of knowledge': the plural of *epistême* again, as in 207e6 ff., but with a different sense, i.e. branches of knowledge (cf. d7). What branches of knowledge will Diotima, or S., consider as containing beauty? At 211c5-6, Diotima will talk instead about beautiful *mathêmata* ('sciences' in the translation); in later literature *mathêmata* becomes specialized in the sense of 'mathematics', but evidently it has not done so yet (see Burkert 1972:207 n.80, 422). In any case Diotima immediately goes on to talk about a *mathêma* of Beauty (211c6–d1), and while a mathematical science of the beautiful cannot be ruled out, that is surely not what is at issue here. What she means by *mathêmata* is what would at this time generally have been meant by it, i.e. 'branches of learning' (hence 'sciences'). However if we ask what 'sciences' P.'s S. prefers elsewhere, mathematical ones would certainly be on the list (*Republic* 521c ff.), along with the *mathêma* of the good (*Republic* 504d ff.: 'the greatest and most fitting *mathêma*'). What she has said earlier suggests that Diotima would include the expertise of the seer, along with e.g. some sort of 'magic' (see 202e–203a); whether S. (or P.) would have gone along with her is at least an open question.

c8-d3 **'and, gazing now towards a beauty which is vast, and no longer slavishly attached to the beauty belonging to a single thing – a young boy, some individual human being, or one kind of activity – may cease to be worthless and petty, as his servitude made him':** 'one kind of activity' perhaps refers primarily to sexual intercourse; the whole contrast is between a growing understanding of beauty as a whole, on the one hand, and on the other the obsessive behaviour of the ordinary, common or garden lover, revolving around sex. (But at the same time, insofar as the whole is a metaphor for our striving for the good, 'one kind of activity' should also refer to anything to which we mistakenly devote ourselves in preference to what in fact will conduce to our good.) That the primary reference is to sex is suggested, at any rate, by the emphasis on the idea of *slavery* (one thinks again of Pausanias at 183a). But the person who already understands that beauty of soul is more to be valued than beauty of body (b6-7) is already freed from such slavery – insofar as his horizon now includes the question 'what will make young men better?' (c2-3), i.e. not just a particular young man (as in Pausanias' account). What he is leaving behind is not so much a particular individual as *slavery to* a particular individual; in other words there is no suggestion here that the beloved has been unceremoniously dumped, though the latter might well find that he is now having to share his lover (and tutor) with others. The inclusion of 'some individual human being' in the list of (single) items to which 'he' is no longer enslaved is significant. Diotima is not just thinking of the lover's relationship to his younger beloved ('a young boy'), but generalizing beyond that: at this point, the lover will recognize freedom from slavery to *any* individual human being (or other item). But so too, perhaps, will the beloved (see c7-8n.); Alcibiades – who has himself evidently not even begun the climb into the foothills of love, on Diotima's reckoning – will later describe his slavery to his (putative) lover S. (219e4-5, with 215e6, 216b3-5, 217a1-2, 217e ff.). The choice in d1 of the verb *agapô* ('attached to' in the translation), a verb which unlike *erô* can cover any form of affection for another individual, is likely itself to be significant in the context, i.e. as potentially including the beloved's feeling for his lover (cf. 180a7-b4n., on *agapan* at 180b3). The general upshot is that the conversion away from the individual – whether lover or beloved? – is an epistemological process, involving the acquisition of that ability to grasp the general/generic which is blocked by too great an attachment to the particular; that is, so the context seems to tell us, to particular, physical, instantiations of beauty. – According to Reeve 1971:326 the whole of d1-2 ὥσπερ ... ἑνός is to be bracketed as 'an expansion of τῷ [Schleiermacher, for the mss. τὸ] παρ' ἑνί ... δουλεύων' (giving the sense 'gazing ..., and no longer enslaved to the individual, may cease to be ...'). If Reeve is right, everything said above on the lines in question will be otiose. However I see no reason for regarding the passage as 'incoherent', or for seeing τὸ παρ' ἑνί ... ἀγαπῶν παιδαρίου κάλλος as impossible Greek (while it may stretch the normal rules, it is not too difficult to suppose a slight dislocation – of the sort indicated by my dashes in the translation – which is of a piece with the somewhat telegraphic style of the whole passage).

d3-4 **'turned towards the great sea of beauty'**: i.e. beauty as it has spread/washed over all the beauties contemplated before?

d4-6 **'may bring to birth many beautiful, even magnificent, words and thoughts in a love of wisdom that grudges nothing'**: 'love of wisdom' is, of course, *philosophia*; and c3 ('and seeks for', with the text as transmitted) has reminded us of the connection Diotima made earlier – in her description of Love the philosopher – between philosophy and *searching*. Given that this searching will take place in the presence of someone else, and will issue in 'words', it is only a short step to the Socratic notion of philosophy as conversation (*dialegesthai*); and also to the near-total metamorphosis of the relationship between lover and beloved into one between philosopher and pupil (or between an experienced and a less experienced philosopher). But that is just what S.'s own 'eroticism' will turn out to amount to – the drive towards wisdom, and more 'procreation in beauty'. – 'That grudges nothing': Dover comments '"ungrudging", hence "unlimited"', but in a context that has aspects of a donor-recipient relationship, it seems reasonable to allow room for the literal sense of the word.

d7 'which has for its object a beauty of a sort I shall describe to you': lit. 'of such a kind that it is the the the science of a beauty ...' (Dover).

e1 '"Try", she said, "to pay as much attention to me as you can"': as often, the 'she said' marks that a particularly important point is about to be, or is being, introduced (similarly with the apostrophe in e5 and elsewhere, i.e. where Diotima suddenly addresses S. by name).

e2-3 'whoever is led by his teacher ': the person normally led by a *paidagôgos*, or taught, is (as the word suggests) a boy (*pais*); thus although *paidagôgein* can be used generally of teaching, it positively encourages us to think of the relationship between lover and beloved rather than, or at least as well as, that between the lover and his 'leader' (cf. c7-8n.). Cf. 183c4-6, where fathers instruct their sons' *paidagôgoi* to prevent them from talking to their lovers.

e3 'contemplates the various beautiful things in order and in the correct way': the emphasis again is on correct procedure.

e3-4 'will come now towards the final goal of matters of love': cf. a1 'those aspects [of love matters/erotics] relating to the final revelation', where 'final' (*teleos*) like 'end' (*telos*) here includes the senses both of ending/completion and of end/goal.

e5-6 'that very beauty, in fact, ... that all his previous toils were for': i.e. those Diotima has been describing since a4. The description may have been short, but the ascent itself is long and arduous; indeed some of the things Diotima has said earlier (see esp. 203e-204a) suggest that mere human beings may not be capable of completing it at all (cf. 212a6-7n., 211b7-8n.). The beauty in question is, of course, 'the (Platonic) form of beauty': see Introduction, §§3.6, 7.

210e6-211a2 'first, a beauty that always is, and neither comes into being nor perishes, neither increases nor diminishes': 'is', i.e. 'is (just what is)'; an example of what Kahn – appropriately enough – calls the 'stative-durative value' of the Greek verb 'to be', *einai* (Kahn 1988:249).

211a2-5 'secondly, one that is not beautiful in this respect but ugly in that ... because some people find it beautiful while others find it ugly': the first point (210e6-211a2) contrasted the stability of the beauty in question with the perishability and changeability of other beauties/beautiful things; this second one contrasts the absoluteness of its beauty with the relative nature of that of other beauties. That the form of beauty should itself be beautiful is both essential to Diotima's argument, and in itself unproblematical – if there *were* such a thing as Beauty Itself, which somehow encapsulated all beauty, from and for all time, it would no doubt be an astounding thing to grasp. If other forms too turned out to instantiate themselves – as is suggested by certain ways P.'s S. has of talking about them – then the consequences would frequently be catastrophic (e.g. Largeness Itself would turn out to be perfectly large, Equality perfectly equal, and so on); however it is probably now generally agreed, not least because the consequences in question are so blatantly obvious, that statements of the type 'Largeness Itself is large' are not to be taken as indicating such simple 'self-predication' of forms, but in some more technical way – thus e.g. Alexander Nehamas is cited by Kahn 1988:257 n.42 as taking '"the F is F" as meaning "The F is *what it is to be* F"' ('"what (being) [F, e.g.] beautiful truly is"'). In short, if one wants to know what it is to be beautiful, one should find a way of 'moving upwards', 'ascending' – as *Symp.* describes it (b6, c2) – to a 'vision' of Beauty Itself. Cf. 'what beauty is, itself' (*auto ... ho esti kalon*) in d1. – 'Because some people find it beautiful ...': people's *thinking* something beautiful presumably won't be enough to make it actually beautiful (if there are objective standards of aesthetic judgement, in principle founded on the objective reality of the forms, it will be possible to make aesthetic judgements that are actually *false*); the point is just that the beauty in question isn't *that* sort of beauty (the sort that depends on mere taste).

a5-6 '**nor again will beauty appear to him the sort of thing a face is':** or '... appear to him such as a face (is, or appears)', i.e. some face or other. I take the point to be that the lover now ceases to *identify* beauty with the things that merely share in beauty, or are qualified by it.

a7 '**or a speech, or a piece of knowledge':** i.e., again, some particular (*tis*) speech (*logos*), some particular piece of knowledge (*epistêmê*). The term *logos* here could also mean all sorts of other things, especially perhaps 'piece of reasoning' (Waterfield), but a further (covert) reference to the context, in which the relationship – or lack of relationship – between speech-making and knowledge bulks fairly large, seems to fit well. (But the choice must to some extent be arbitrary; and given that there are hardly any clues, no doubt we should conclude that this is another case of deliberate ambiguity – with the difference here that nothing much hangs on it.)

a7-b2 '**nor as having a location in some other thing, such as a living creature ...':** i.e. not as being immanent in anything, so that one could discover it in that thing ('having a location': lit. 'being somewhere'). But that it is also said not to be 'in the earth, or the heavens' also suggests that it is not located anywhere at all. In the myth of the *Phaedrus*, the forms exist outside the heavens (247c-e), but it is unlikely that this is to be taken literally, not least because it is doubtful whether there is, for P., any place outside the heavens (how, after all, *could* there be anything beyond the universe, 'the all'?). If so, we should also avoid any temptation to take the idea of 'moving upwards' in b6 and c2 in anything other than a strictly metaphorical sense. (Nor is it helpful to think of the forms as existing in some other 'world', whether parallel or transcendent; they are simply without location.)

b2 '**itself by itself, in its own company':** this is probably the idea that is expressed by one of the standard expressions for a form, *auto to* F, '(the) F itself', as in *auto to kalon* in d3 (so: the form of beauty is *just* beauty, not beauty combined with anything else). ('In its own company': lit. 'with itself'.)

b2-5 '**uniform, with all the other beautiful things sharing in it ... nor is it affected in the slightest':** Diotima's description here in effect returns to its starting-point (the unchangeable nature of the form), while also introducing the crucial idea of the 'participation' (*metechein*) in Beauty of particular (changeable) beautiful things. Quite what relationship is indicated by this notion of 'participation' is unclear (as S. himself is elsewhere represented as admitting: see *Phaedo* 100d); but that there must be *some* sort of relationship is clear enough – not least because, if there were not, no amount of contemplation of beautiful particulars, over however wide a range, would be capable of leading towards an insight into Beauty Itself, in the way Diotima envisages in the present context.

b6 '**away from these things, through the correct kind of boy-loving':** 'these things' are 'the other beautiful things', but – because of the reference to 'boy-loving' (*paiderastein*) – especially, or as represented by, the particular beautiful *body*. Diotima's account continues its shift away from the relationship between 'leader' and lover, towards that between lover and beloved (cf. 210e2-3n.); but both will surface again together in b8-c1.

b7-8 '**he would practically have the final goal within his reach':** the optative + *an* ('would') reflects the tone of circumspection introduced by Diotima's 'practically' (*schedon ... ti*), and also by her 'begins to' ('*begins* to catch sight of that beauty', b7). It is, evidently, an elusive object (cf. 210e5-6n.).

b8-c1 '**For this is what it is to approach love matters, or be led by someone else in them, in the correct way':** i.e. this is how a lover should behave in relation to his beloved, or (rather) be guided to behave; I take it that Diotima here marks the reintroduction of the idea of the 'leader', who has been left out of the picture for a little while (cf. b6n.; and O'Brien 1984:198 n.36).

c3-6 'from one to two and from two to all beautiful bodies ... to beautiful activities ... to beautiful sciences': significantly there is no mention of 'souls' in this list; a further indication, perhaps, that the lover never moves beyond his attachment to souls, that is, to 'caring for' and improving them (210c2-3).

c6-d1 'and finally ... what beauty is, itself': there is surely something wrong with the transmitted text here (see apparatus: the sudden break into subjunctives looks hardly possible); none of the editorial solutions to the problems looks particularly attractive, but none makes much difference to the sense. The solution I have adopted, following Dover and others, gives that sense straightforwardly: the final clause at the end ('in order that one may finally know what beauty is, itself') simply brings us back to the crucial point of the *purpose* of the whole ascent ('for the sake of that beauty', c1-2). 'What beauty is, itself': or 'what is (truly) beautiful, (by) itself', or 'that very thing that is beauty', or ... (for what is in Greek a closely similar formula, see 199e4 'just insofar as he is a brother'); in any case the sense of the formula is given by the preceding description, in 210e6-211b5.

d2-3 'if anywhere': lit. 'if indeed/really anywhere else'; but see Dover (in any case, to insist that Diotima means 'if, and at least as much as, anywhere else' would hardly be consistent with her passionate tone). The same sort of formula appears at 212a6-7 (lit. 'if indeed to any *other* human being').

d3-4 'if ever you see it': that S. has not yet 'seen' beauty itself is not just part of the present fiction based around Diotima (see following n.); the whole dialogue pictures him as the needy, philosophical lover (and one may ask: if S. hasn't completed the ascent, who has?).

d4-5 'gold, and clothes, and the beautiful boys and young men that now drive you out of your mind ...': 'gold and clothes' hardly interest the real S. (whose spruce appearance for the dinner-party was unusual enough to occasion comment), and Alcibiades' speech will also confirm that he is no ordinary lover, starving himself for a glimpse of his beloved. But the message, of course, is really for the others present (evidently S. is still at least partly playing the role of Agathon).

d6-8 'so that both you and many others ... and be with them': 'Diotima' here plainly picks up ideas from Aristophanes' speech – esp. in 'if somehow it were possible' – in order to contrast her vision of human eroticism with his. 'Be with them': on *suneinai* and its possible sexual connotations, see 176e8-9n.

e1 'if someone succeeded': more literally, 'if it happened to someone (to ...)'.

e1-3 'pure, clean, unmixed, and not contaminated ... much other mortal nonsense': 'not contaminated ...', sc. as the beauty of beautiful boys and young men is: here once more the emphasis falls decidedly on the rejection of *bodily* beauty (cf. 210c8-d3n.). What is mortal is here 'nonsense' ('tomfoolery', i.e. not to be taken with the slightest seriousness) only by comparison with the divine; for most of us, unfortunately, if not all of us (including S.: note the remote conditional, '*if someone succeeded ...*', sc. no one probably will?), it is all we have. 'Pure' (in the sense of 'unalloyed', 'unmixed'): for the corresponding adverb, see Pausanias at 181c8 ('genuinely').

212a2 'with the faculty he should use': lit. 'with what he must (contemplate)', i.e. the soul/mind, not the body; if he uses the body, he will 'contemplate' only physical beauty.

a3 'as he sees beauty with what has the power to see it': lit. 'with (that to) which it is visible'.

a4-5 'bringing to birth, not phantoms of virtue ... because he is grasping the truth': i.e. because he is 'grasping' true beauty (beauty itself) instead of what is merely a 'phantom' beauty (mere physical, or individual, particular, beauty), he will 'bring to birth' true virtue instead of a phantom virtue ('phantom' is *eidôlon*, perhaps 'shadowy imitation'; the best-known *eidôla* are the shades of the dead, insubstantial likenesses of their living originals). 'Because he is grasping the truth': that is, because he 'has intercourse with' true beauty (cf. a2 'and is able to be with it': *suneinai* again). It might look as if something has gone wrong with the image here: shouldn't the *beloved* be what the lover 'is with', and supply the beauty in which the lover 'gives birth'? In fact, however, it was only in the very first stage that the beauty required for procreation was in the beloved (when the lover 'came to' beautiful bodies). Since then, the source of beauty has all along been the things 'contemplated' rather than the beloved (kinds of activity, laws, ...), and it is these things to which the lover's attention has been directed, for the sake of the 'offspring' that they enable him to produce (also to the benefit of the beloved). Their beauty is what corresponds to the physical beauty, or in the best cases the combination of beauty of body and soul, which enabled the 'pregnant in soul' in 208e6-209e4 to give birth to their 'offspring'; contemplation of these new 'beauties' allows the gradual realization, dawning finally and conclusively with the vision of beauty itself, that the other kind of beauty, rooted in the individual and particular, was a mere 'phantom', and that any 'offspring' procreated in it were 'phantoms of virtue'. (The difference between phantom and reality here in fact seems to be essentially a matter of degree: cf. 211e1-3n. But then it is an *extraordinary* difference of degree, as Diotima has emphasized – the difference, I take it, that philosophy makes, allowing us to perceive and to pursue the real good, the real object of our 'love' and desire. The whole ascent passage describes the process which might lead to that, away from our current – and mistaken – preoccupations.) If this interpretation is right, all those 'great achievements' referred to in the earlier passage – those of Homer and Hesiod, Lycurgus and Solon – are written off as insubstantial; but so they must be, by implication, in any case, since Homer and the rest lack the vision of true beauty that enables the philosophical lover to procreate true virtue. And that is the usual, uncompromising verdict of P.'s S. on all poets, politicians, and others who operate without devoting themselves to the philosophical search for truth (for the case of the poets, see esp. Janaway 1995).

a5-6 **'and that when he has given birth to and nurtured true virtue':** for 'nurturing', cf. 209c4, but especially 207a ff., on the care that animals take to rear their offspring; like them, the lover nurtures *his* offspring, and sees to it that they flourish – because after all, what he desires is the 'immortality' they are going to provide for him (a6-7). The virtue he gives birth to, if we may judge by the parallel case in 208e-209e (as we surely may, if that passage describes a 'shadowy imitation' of the procreation of virtue), will be both his beloved's (209c4-7 with 208e6-209a3; cf. 210c) and his own.

a6-7 **'it belongs to him to be loved by the gods, and to him, if to any human being, to be immortal':** his 'immortality', according to Diotima's theory, will stem from his offspring, whose true value will be recognized by the gods (and not by mere mortals, like those of the politicians and poets); there is no immortality in the strict sense for human beings – how could there be, when they are mortal? On the absence from *Symp.* of the notion of the immortality of the soul, see 206e8-207a2n.; what the Eleusinian Mysteries themselves offered was not immortality, but some altogether vaguer promise of better things for the initiate after death (see Burkert 1997:323-4). ('If to any human being': see 211d2-3n.)

b1-3 **'that's what Diotima said, and I am persuaded by her; since I am persuaded, I try to persuade everyone else too':** so S. is committed to the truth of what Diotima told him (or rather, presumably, what hides beneath its metaphorical garb); he has evidently lived up to *his* notion of what an encomium should be (198b ff.). The sequence Diotima-S.-

everyone else echoes that of guide-lover-beloved – or guide-lover-beloveds (see 210c2n., 210c8-d3n.). 'Everyone else' (lit. 'the others', 'the rest') may be taken literally, since in principle everyone needs to learn Diotima's lessons (everyone needs to know how to direct their desire for the good), but there is perhaps also a special reference to the present company, who have just been addressed as 'Phaedrus and everyone else'.

b3-4 **'for acquiring this possession one couldn't easily get a better co-worker with human nature than Love is':** thus we return to the notion of love or desire as the operation of Love. 'This possession' must be immortality, which is after all, according to Diotima, what we all desire, always; if it is Love who works within us to direct our actions, then it will be an understatement to say 'one couldn't easily get a better co-worker than Love ...' At 218d1-3 Alcibiades will attribute a similar role to S. himself: 'for me there's nothing more important than my becoming as good a person as possible, and in this I don't think there's any more effective collaborator for me than you'. But Love stands for 'what loves' (Diotima at 204b-c), and Alcibiades' encomium as a whole implicitly identifies S. with the lover who has already turned his back on beautiful bodies – as he does more or less literally on Alcibiades' – and directed himself to the improvement of the young.

b4-5 **'That's why I declare that everyone must honour Love':** 'everyone' is lit. 'every man' (*pant' andra*), but this phrase can in principle be used to include both genders – and insofar as Diotima's theory was about *human* desire, it ought also to apply to women, though S. shows rather little interest in the fact.

b5-6 **'I myself honour what belongs to him and practise it':** 'what belongs to him', i.e. *ta erôtika* ('erotics'). Love, of course, like S., is a philosopher; and all lovers need to be philosophers, if they're to realize Love's/love's goal. (All philosophers will also be lovers – but only insofar as *everyone* is a 'lover'; once we return to ordinary categories, then still all lovers will need to be philosophers, but not all philosophers will need to be lovers. One *can*, fortunately, do philosophy without being in love with one's colleagues.)

b7-8 **'and both now and always I eulogize the power and courage of Love to the best of my ability':** the idea of Love's *courage* here is surely meant to take us back to the arduousness (*ponoi*, 210e6) of the ascent; but it is also significant that courage is the *only* virtue which S. attributes to Love – the other virtues, wisdom, justice and moderation, with which the pregnant in soul in 209a-b were supposedly teeming, are left out. If Love stands for the process of striving for the goal, is 'in the middle', is the philosopher, and so on, that is exactly what we should expect: (true) virtue is an *outcome* of the process. (So, once again, the high achievers of 208e-209e cannot actually have achieved what people at large believe them to have achieved, awarding them honours and even cults ...). – 'Eulogize' is *enkômiazô* ('offer an encomium to').

b8-c3 **'So, Phaedrus, if you like, ... name it like that':** S. plays with a formula often used in prayers and hymns – 'I address you, X, or Y, or whatever name it pleases you to go under' (Sier usefully compares *Cratylus* 400e, which refers to the practice, and *Protagoras* 358a-b, which plays with it in a different way from the present passage). However there is also a serious point. If an encomium of a subject means praising it, S.'s actual, direct encomium is more or less restricted to the statement 'both now and always I eulogize the power and courage of Love to the best of my ability', plus the few lines before that. (Almost: 'you want me to praise love – well, I do'?) The rest is mainly an extended essay in how best to use his gift to us, and some of it is distinctly unflattering to the god; but that, one must suppose, is the cost of telling the truth. Perhaps the case simply is that giving encomia and telling the truth are incompatible activities – and if so, there is no doubt about which S. will choose.

c4 **'When S. finished, the others praised his speech':** contrast the raucous reception given to Agathon's speech.

c4-6 **'but Aristophanes was trying to say something, because S. while speaking had mentioned him and *his* speech'**: or just 'mentioned his speech'; but the translation attempts to take account of the early position of *autou* ('him'/'his') – which has the effect of making it look, until we get to *peri tou logou*, as if what's being said is just that S. mentioned *him*. That is, after all, the main point. (The mid./pass. of *mimnêskô* in the use in question can be followed either by the genitive of what is mentioned, or by *peri*.)

c6-7 **'Suddenly there was a loud banging from the door to the court'**: 'round which the house was built', Dover; the outside door is clearly meant.

c7-d1 **'and an *aulos*-girl's voice could be heard'**: just as the suspension of normal sympotic behaviour was marked by the sending away of one *aulos*-girl (176e), so its resumption – with the arrival of revellers – is accompanied by the arrival of another. 'Suddenly' (*exaiphnês*): compare/contrast the 'suddenness' (*exaiphnês*) with which the lover caught sight of Beauty at 210e4; Alcibiades will accuse S. of suddenly (*exaiphnês*) appearing when least expected (213c1).

d7 **'to be taken ... taken in'**: the verb in both cases is *agein*, the verb used in Diotima's mystery-story at 210c8 ('he must lead him to the different kinds of knowledge ...'), 211c1.

d8-9 **'by some other attendants of his'**: 'people who were with him' (Waterfield), 'companions' (Nehamas/Woodruff); but 'attendants' (slaves) seems the natural way of taking *akolouthos* (cf. 203c3 *akolouthos kai therapôn*, 'follower and attendant', and *akolouthos* = 'slave-attendant' at 217a7, b1), and that the glorious Alcibiades is having to be helped in by slaves – and the *aulos*-girl – gives additional point to the detail.

e1 **'wreathed with a thick wreath of ivy and violets'**: I take the αὐτὸν after ἐστεφανώμενον simply as marking the change of subject (and delayed to avoid the pattern ἄγειν ... αὐτὸν ..., καὶ ἐπιστῆναι αὐτόν ...). Cf. αὐτόν at 210a7.

e3 **'Greetings, gentlemen'**: or just 'men'; also at 213e7 and 214a4.

e7-8 **'the wisest and most beautiful man – that's my proclamation'**: 'that's my proclamation' (ἀνειπὼν οὑτωσί) is an editor's emendation for the transmitted, and impossible, ἐὰν εἴπω οὑτωσί, 'if I speak thus'.

213a1 **'all the same I *know* I'm telling the truth'**: i.e. in saying Agathon is the wisest and most beautiful man – but he will quickly acknowledge that he *isn't* telling the truth; S. is both wiser and, in his own way, more beautiful. Is Alcibiades' insistence here, and the suggestion that the others might laugh at him for saying what he's said, just the slightest of hints that everyone really knows that Agathon overvalues himself (cf. 194e4-197e8n.)? Or is it just that he's drunk?

a1-2 **'Tell me at once ... Will you drink with me or not?'** Alcibiades is not only drunk but aggressive.

b1-2 **'S. had moved over when *he* caught sight of *him*'**: has he moved over so that Alcibiades can sit next to Agathon, or so that Alcibiades can sit next to him (i.e. is his move motivated by politeness, or by *erôs* ?)? Alcibiades and Agathon, at least, would take it in the second way; we – perhaps – know better. The text of the mss. has καθίζειν ('so as to give him a seat'?), but κατιδεῖν looks more likely, not least because it allows us to give an explanation of sorts for ἐκεῖνον (we might have expected αὐτόν, especially after ἐκείνου in the line before, referring to Agathon): Alcibiades didn't see S. (a6-7), but S. certainly saw *him*. Cf. Dover. For ὡς + inf. just like this, see 174e4-5 ὡς ἰδεῖν τὸν Ἀγάθωνα ('when Agathon saw him', i.e. Aristodemus).

b7 **'person joining in our drinking'**: lit' 'fellow-drinker' ('symposiast').

b8 **'Heracles!'** Heracles is frequently called on to avert evil of any sort. Burkert 1985:75 compares the modern 'Jesus!' ('Greeks regularly call on 'fitting divine names').

b9-c2 'You were lying there to ambush me again, showing up suddenly as you always used to, where I least expected you to be': Alcibiades and S., as we shall discover, used to be closer than they are now. But S. counts himself as still being in love with Alcibiades (see c8 ff.); the enduring nature of *his* love, as well as the form it takes – caring and talking, as at 210c2-3? – may well be part of the point we are meant to discover in Alcibiades' encomium.

c3-4 'I see you didn't choose to be next to Aristophanes, or someone else we laugh at, and who wants to be laughed at': '(someone else) we laugh at' is lit. 'who is laughable' (*geloios*: 'funny', 'amusing', as at 189b6, and in the right context, 'ridiculous', 'absurd'). On the expression 'is ... and wants/is willing to' (*esti te kai bouletai*), Dover comments 'considered as an object or as a functioning unit of society, a man may be good or bad through no doing of his; to add "... and he is willing to be so" is to double the praise or blame (e.g. Eur. *Helen* 998 "I am by nature pious and I am willing to be so", Andocides I.95 "who is the worst of men and willing to be so").' That Aristophanes is a comic poet would not, presumably, in itself make him personally an object of laughter – but perhaps that's the joke?

c8-d2 'From the time I fell in love with him ... *he* **gets jealous and resentful':** if so (but it is of course mere banter), Alcibiades misunderstands S.'s love for him, and the nature of his 'talk' (*dialegesthai* again).

d5-6 'his mad attachment to being loved': lit. 'his madness and attachment to lovers'; *philerastia* is a rare word for a (perhaps) not so rare condition (cf. *philerastês* at 192b5, 'someone who shows affection to lovers'; and Aristotle, *Rhetoric* 1371b24), but one that may have a special importance in the light of the 'final mysteries' – if, that is, they leave room for the beloved's, as well as the lover's, need to be taught a proper attitude towards individual beauty (see 210c7-8n., c8-d3n., etc.). Alcibiades' problem will turn out to be that he cannot separate love from sex; someone (like S.) who doesn't want to have sex with him is insulting his beauty.

214a2 'eight *kotulai'***:** nearly half a gallon. According to Davidson 1997:48 Alcibiades' taking the wine-cooler means that he is drinking *unmixed* wine into the bargain; but the next sentence ('when he'd had this filled') might suggest that it was empty when he saw it, and was then filled from the mixing-bowl. (The chief emphasis, in any case, is surely on the quantity of wine he downs.)

a7   'S. drank from it': whereas in a3 Alcibiades '*drained* it'.

b3-4 'Best of sons to the best and most sensible father – greetings to you!' 'Sensible' translates *sôphrôn*, previously translated as 'moderate' (cf. e.g. 209a7); evidently Alcibiades treats Eryximachus as interfering with serious drinking.

b7   '"For a medical man is worth as much as many other men together"': *Iliad* 11.514.

b10-c1 'each of us in turn ... the most beautiful he could manage': more or less exactly the words he used at 177d2-3.

c3   'you've finished your drink': Alcibiades is hardly likely to think so.

d2-3 'if ever I praise anyone in his presence, whether a god or a human being, other than him': Alcibiades, of course, was not there for Diotima's demonstration that Love is not a god.

d5   'Take care what you say': for the expression, cf. 201e10n. This *could* be S. joining in the banter, and Alcibiades seems to take it that way, but it is also an objection to the idea that he puts himself on the level of the gods. On the other hand, as Alcibiades' speech will amply demonstrate, S. is no ordinary human being either (see esp. 221c-d).

d6   'By Poseidon': 'frequent in comedy but otherwise unexampled in P.; it may have had 'bullying overtones' (Dover); or is Alcibiades punning on *posis*, 'drinking' (Bury)?

d6-8 'don't you even try stopping me, because there just isn't anyone else I'd praise in your presence': but in any case the S. he describes in his speech will bear a remarkable resemblance to Love as Diotima described him. 'Don't you even try stopping me (sc. from praising you)': for λέγειν πρός in this kind of sense, see *Protagoras* 345c.

e4-5 'Will you praise me to amuse everybody?' After all, what is there to praise about *him*? (Lit. 'will your praise be on the amusing side?' 'Amusing' is *geloios*, 'laughable': cf. 213c3-4n.)

e6 'I'll tell the truth. Do I have your permission?' Alcibiades is warning S. that he means to reveal some intimate details; at the same time, without knowing it, he is asking permission to do what S. himself not only always recommends but specifically recommended, before Alcibiades arrived, in the case of eulogies (198c-199b).

214e10-215a1 'if ever I say anything that isn't true, break in on me then and there, if you like, and say it's untrue': a point on which he goes on insisting (216a1-2, 217b2-3, 219c2, 220e3-4) – appropriately enough, perhaps, given that he is addressing someone who denies as a matter of course that he's any better than anyone else; but what he has to relate is so strange that anyone might think he was making it up anyway.

215a2 'if as I'm speaking my memory gets jumbled up': lit. 'if I speak recalling this from here, that from there (sc. in the wrong order).

a3-4 'recount the details of your strangeness': 'recount the details of' is lit. 'enumerate'; for S. as behaving 'strangely', see 175a10.

a6 '*he* will probably think it's meant to amuse everybody': picking up what S. said at 214e4-5.

215a5-222b7: Alcibiades' speech. The structure of the speech is straightforward enough: S. is like an 'opening silenus' with a god inside (see 215a8-b1n.), and like Marsyas (215b3-c6). His 'piping', though, as Alcibiades himself can testify, has an even greater effect on people than Marsyas' (215c6-216c3). As for the other comparison, what is inside S., and its contrast with his exterior, is extraordinary: especially his moderation (216c5-219e5), illustrated by the long story of Alcibiades' failed attempt, as younger party, to seduce him (216e8-219d2), and his endurance and courage, illustrated by descriptions of his behaviour on campaign (Potidaea: 219e6-220e7; Delium, 220e7-221c1). But the most extraordinary thing about S. is that there is just no one to compare him with, past or present, god or man – except silenuses and satyrs (221c2-d7). Not just the man himself but his words are like those opening silenuses: listen to them, and they sound amusing, but once one gets inside them ... (221d8-222a6). Alcibiades himself finishes by emphasizing his own 'maltreatment' at S.'s hands, and the way he – and others – have been forced to change their roles from recipient of advances to maker of them (222a7-b4); he warns Agathon to be careful that he doesn't get treated in the same way. However the chief effect of the speech as a whole (unbeknownst to Alcibiades) is to confirm the picture of S. as Love, and as the lover who has completed some part of the ascent described by Diotima. He is the lover who is able to improve his beloved (or rather his beloveds, because he plainly does not confine his attentions to one only). But of course he can only work his effect if the beloved is prepared to stay and listen, as Alcibiades is not – with the result that he fails to understand at all the real nature of S.'s relationship with him. So, by implication, what Alcibiades became (according to many, a 'traitor guilty of inflicting great and deliberate harm on Athens', Dover) had nothing to do with S.: Alcibiades could have stayed, listened, and become a better man, but chose not to (note the carefully placed past tense already at 213c1: 'You were lying there to ambush me again, showing up suddenly *as you always used to*'). This is no doubt in itself one purpose of the speech – to clear S., in this central case, of part of what he was charged with at his trial, 'corrupting the young'. See further below. But within the context and argument of *Symp.* itself, the case of Alcibiades fits readily into the broader picture of S.'s concerns. Here it is the necessarily unspoken connection between the great man and the *daimôn* Love which matters (n.b. the description of S. as *daimonios*, 'superhuman', at 219c1): S. as representing a life informed by philosophy, and therefore turned towards the real object of *erôs*, love and desire; barefoot, hardy, always seeking, poised between ugliness and beauty, ignorance and knowledge; co-worker with others towards the goal of permanent posession of the good (218d2-3, with 212b3-4); and so on. If Alcibiades claims that S. is not only moderate and courageous (219d5), but even wise (219d6), that perhaps should be taken with about the same degree of seriousness as the charge against him of *hubris* (215b7, 219c5, 222a8; which of course prevents him from adding justice to the list); someone who mentions everyone present along with S. as having 'shared in the madness and Bacchic frenzy of philosophy' (218b1-4) is unlikely to be meant to be much of a judge of wisdom. Meanwhile, of course, P. can have it both ways: if the dialogue has told us what to make of Alcibiades' judgement, nevertheless the dialogue more or less ends with it. At the same time we have an indication of sorts about S.'s own attitude towards that judgement, in the shape of his insistence that the prize for bravery should go to Alcibiades rather than to him (220d6-e7): in the case of courage, at least, evidently he would not press his own claims. – Further on S. and Alcibiades: one of the notorious events that took place not long after the dramatic date of *Symp.* was the profanation of the Mysteries, one source on which – Plutarch, *Alcibiades* 22 (recording a formal charge against Alcibiades himself) – has it occurring in Alcibiades' own house. It is a nice coincidence, at the least, that S.'s partial enactment of Diotima's 'mysteries' (cf. Alcibiades' reference to the 'uninitiated' – of course quite differently motivated – at 218b7) should take place in the same house, and perhaps even the same room, in which Alcibiades and his friends were said to have profaned the Mysteries by private performance. On the nature and significance of the historical event, see Murray, 'The affair ...', in Murray 1990. This crime, along with the mutilation of the herms (see Osborne 1985), took place shortly before the departure of Athenian forces on the expedition to Sicily; the conversation between Apollodorus and his friends is taking place after Athens' final defeat in the Peloponnesian War, towards which the ill-fated Sicilian episode heavily contributed. Alcibiades is probably the leading character in the whole sequence of events: might we speculate that P. wishes to suggest, not only that S. was not responsible for Alcibiades' behaviour, but that if only Alcibiades and others like him had been more prepared to follow S. and his example, the city might never have been defeated?

215a8-b1 'those silenuses that sit in the statuary-shops': '[p]erhaps this was a temporary fashion in late fifth-century Athens; no examples have survived, nor are there any references to such a type of statue except in late passages dependent on this one' (Dover). But it is difficult to see how on earth such a fashion – why *gods* inside a silenus-figure? – should ever have arisen, even if there was a sober side to the Silenus-figure as well as the goatish, lewd side: for the second, see Lissarague 1990, and for the first, Zanker 1995:34 ff. (Silenuses as a type appear to be indistinguishable from satyrs like Marsyas; there is, however, 'Old Silenus' himself, who can be represented as a teacher – which might or might not help with the connection with S., but hardly with the question at issue here, i.e. about gods *in* silenuses.) This makes Peters's suggestion distinctly attractive (Peters 1976): that the reference is to *moulds* for the making of statues, in which there would need to be holes (*surinx*, 'pipe', in b2 can also mean 'anything like a pipe': *LSJ*) for the draining of wax and/or the extrusion of air; that such moulds should have looked like malformed silenuses is not so unlikely – maybe (I add) 'silenus' was even a name for them?

b4   '**Marsyas**': so good a musician that he challenged Apollo to a competition (and ended up being flayed alive).

b4-5 '**you're like them in your physical appearance**': see the discussion in Zanker 1995 (a8-b1n. above). Alcibiades stops short of saying that S. is ugly, which would make him unlike Love (however little Alcibiades may know or care about *that* identification). But then, S. argues (unsuccessfully, to those present) in Xenophon's *Symp.* (5.1 ff.), it all depends on what one's criteria are for judging physical beauty.

b7   '**Your behaviour is criminal – or do you deny it?**' The (root) term here is again *hubris* (see e.g. 175e8, where Agathon says exactly the same thing, but in an altogether lighter tone: cf. 215a5-222b7n.); used of silenuses/satyrs, it has connotations, perhaps, of 'mischief-making' (cf. 221e3) – however unsavoury their behaviour, associated e.g. with permanent erection, it is after all mythical, and so (maybe) harmless.

c2-3 '**since what Olympus used to play, I call Marsyas', because Marsyas taught Olympus**': presumably a little joke, since even if certain tunes were attributed to him (Dover), Olympus appears to have no more of a historical context than Marsyas.

c5-6 '**indicate those who stand in need of the gods and their initiation-rites**': the underlying sense seems to be that if people react to them, then they were in need of divine intervention (cf. Dover's note on the 'Corybantes' at e1: 'the special feature of their cult was the drum- and pipe-music which induced a curative frenzy in those who were "possessed" in the sense "deranged"'). But the idea also surely connects closely with the effects of S.'s 'music', as 'indicating those who stand in need of' a different sort of initiation-rites (i.e. Diotima's); Alcibiades claims that he had to stop his ears to prevent his being kept there, with *this* musician, for ever (216a6-8).

d3-4 '**or your words being spoken by someone else, even if the speaker is extremely poor**': is P. here slyly referring to himself? (But of course in *Symp.* it is rather Aristodemus, and then Apollodorus, who are reproducing S.'s words ...)

d6-7 '**if it weren't for the fact that I'd appear totally drunk, I'd have told you on oath**': is the point that what he has to say is so strange that a sworn statement might be needed – but only someone completely drunk could be thought capable of swearing to such (strange) things? (One alternative is perhaps that Alcibiades *is* just drunk and losing track here; but otherwise he seems to be surprisingly clear, even eloquent, despite just having consumed his half-gallon on top of what he'd had before.)

e1   '**the Corybantes**': cf. c5-6n.

e6   '**my condition was that of a slave**': cf. 210c8-d3n.

215e7-216a1 '**I was frequently reduced to thinking that**': more literally 'I was very often put into the sort of state to make it appear to me that'.

216a3 '**prepared to listen to him**': lit. 'prepared to offer him my ears'.

a4-5 '**For he forces me to admit that although there's much that I lack myself**': cf. Diotima's lessons about Love's lack; what Alcibiades needs to do, and what he won't do (because he shuts his ears to S.) is some philosophy ...

a6   '**I ... do the Athenians' business**': sc. as a politician (and general).

b3-4 '**I'm not capable of arguing against ...**': cf. Agathon at 201c6-7, where the point as well as the language is almost identical.

b6   '**because of what's been agreed between us**': cf. a4-6.

c1   '**gone from this world**': lit. 'not being among human beings'

d2   '**is in love with beautiful young men**': lit. 'is erotically disposed towards' them ('young' is supplied). The plural is itself suggestive: cf. e.g. 210c2n.

d3   '**overwhelmed**': cf. 215d5.

d4   '**Isn't this silenus-like?**' The point is not that a drunken satyr/silenus wouldn't be expected to know anything; what is described is Socratic ignorance, which is like the

sculptor's silenus (d5-6) when combined with the other features of him we're told about –
his (apparent) lewdness, and the implied difference ('so far as his appearance goes')
between what he looks like on the outside and what he is inside.

d6-7 **'how completely full he is, fellow-drinkers, of moderation'**: lit. 'with how much
(*posês*) moderation he is full'; 'fellow-drinkers', *sumpotai*, no doubt plays on *posês*
(suggesting *posis*, 'drink'). 'Moderation': or 'self-control' (*sôphrosunê*); the juxtaposition
of the word with 'fellow-drinkers' plays with the same complaint Alcibiades made
against Eryximachus (see 214b3-4n.).

e1-2 **'which he looks down on to a greater degree than anyone could possibly suppose'**:
Alcibiades anticipates the story of his attempted seduction of the man.

e2-3 **'nor if he possesses anything else ...'**: lit. 'nor if he possesses any other honour from
among those called blessed by the majority'.

e5-6 **'spends his whole life continually pretending and playing with people'**: Vlastos 1987
objects to the translation of *eirôneuomenos* (lit. 'ironizing'?) as 'pretending', broadly on
the grounds that it suggests *deliberate deceit*. It is certainly unlikely that Alcibiades
would be suggesting that S. was a lifelong deceiver; however 'pretending', especially
followed by 'playing', hardly suggests anything so negative, especially since both verbs
together are contrasted with *spoudazein* (in the aorist, 'come to be in earnest') in the
following sentence. Alcibiades almost immediately gives an example of the kind of
behaviour he means, in the shape of what he reports S. as saying, *eirônikôs* (i.e.,
eirôneuoumenos: 218d7), in 218d8-219a5. But this passage is itself for the most part
only an elaborate variation of S.'s famous claim that he knows nothing (216d3-4) –
which Alcibiades certainly treats as a pretence, since it forms part of what he calls S.'s
outer covering. But there is nothing malicious or hostile about the verb *eirôneuesthai*
here, as there certainly is when Thrasymachus uses the corresponding noun of S. – in a
quite different tone of voice – in *Republic* 337a. P.'s S. is so often ironic, and so often
teasingly paradoxical (or both together), that even those who feel an attachment to him
can think he is just playing with them, while those hostile to him, like Thrasymachus,
can treat it all as deliberate dissimulation (even deceit). So in 218d8-219a5 Alcibiades
thinks he is merely pretending to have nothing to offer, when in fact there is something
that he *genuinely* wants to deny he possesses, even if that something is not quite what
Alcibiades thinks it is (see 218d7n., 219a6n.).

e7 **'I don't know if any one of you'**: 'of you' is supplied.

217a3 **'the way I looked at my age'**: a laborious attempt to get the effect of the Greek *hôra*,
which combines the ideas of '(right) season', and (so) 'youth', 'flourishing', and 'beauty'
(see Dover).

a4-5 **'because I was in a position ... if I granted him my favours'**: so Alcibiades had in
mind the usual kind of reciprocal exchange, with S. the usual kind of lover and teacher
(see Pausanias at 184b ff.).

b3 **'S., *you* challenge me ...'**: the verb is *exelenchein*; cf. *elenchein*, translated as 'examine',
at 201e5.

b4-5 **'I'd be contentedly thinking'**: lit. 'I'd be thinking ..., and I'd be happy (about it)'.

c5 **'try a direct assault'**: lit. 'attack according to strength' (cf. Dover).

d1-2 **'He wasn't quick to accept this invitation from me either'**: presumably, by now,
realizing what was on Alcibiades' mind, and (as the sequel shows), genuinely not
wanting to go along with it. This is no coyness; what interests S. is evidently, as Diotima
put it, 'giving birth in beauty' by *talking*.

e3-4 **'if first of all – as the saying goes – the truth weren't in the wine, whether without
slaves present or with them'**: more literally 'if ... wine both without *paides* and with
paides weren't true'. Waterfield offers a workable explanation involving an original

proverb (cited by a very late source) along the lines of 'truth comes from wine and children (*paides*)', and a play by Alcibiades on *paides* – (1) 'truth comes from wine, whatever one says about *paides* ('children')', and (2) 'truth will come out because of the wine, whether or not there are *paides* ('slaves') present'. But Rösler 1990:107 suggests interesting connections with Alcaeus fr. 366 Voigt *oinos, ô phile pai, kai alathea* ('wine, my dear boy ['adolescent'] and truth/true things'), where the reference is to 'the compulsion on the *sumpotês* to expose his thoughts frankly and completely' in what is – on Rösler's reading – a pedagogic situation before it is an erotic one. Cf. Introduction, §3.1. (So 'wine leaves out nothing, whatever one says about Alcaeus' boy'?) On the whole Waterfield seems to catch Alcibiades' tone better, but one could perhaps have Alcaeus' boy in place of Waterfield's (Photius) children/slaves.

e4-5   'to leave a proud achievement of his in obscurity': the word translated 'proud' here, *huperêphanos*, can easily tip over into 'arrogant', as the corresponding noun clearly has – with help from the (mainly playful) context – by 219c6.

e6   'what people feel when they've been bitten by the snake': 'the snake' means 'the proverbial snake' (cf. Rückert, cited by Bury – we might immediately think of what a snake did to Sophocles' Philoctetes), or as Dover puts it, 'the snake assumed by the popular notion expounded in the next sentence'. There is perhaps also some etymological play (*echis ... echei*, or if not here, certainly in 218a6 (... *echontai echidnês* ...).

218a1-2 'will understand and be forgiving': *gnôsomenois te kai sungnôsomenois* – another piece of word-play likely to be invisible in any English translation.

a4-5   'because it's in my heart, or my soul, or whatever one's supposed to call it': 'Alcibiades' uncertainty reflects the readiness with which "heart" and "soul" are interchangeable in many Greek expressions', Dover. Maybe, but Alcibiades was happy about using them interchangeably before (215e2, 6), so why should uncertainty grip him *here*? One possibility is that he starts with 'heart' as the natural way of continuing the metaphor of 'biting', but then switches to 'soul' in deference to S., because he is about to mention *philosophy* (a5-6); for S., after all, philosophy is nothing if it is not the medicine of the soul. (The 'or whatever one's supposed to call it' – lit. 'or what one must name it' – might then itself be an indication of the slightness of Alcibiades' engagement with philosophy, to which he openly admits.)

a5-6   'the words that philosophy brings with her': *tôn en philosophiai logôn*; cf. *Diotima's logous ... en philosophiai aphthonôi* (in the translation, 'words ... in a love of wisdom that grudges nothing') at 210d5-6.

a7-b1   'make you do or say anything whatever': i.e. things like what he's about to recount; the sentence is as disturbed as no doubt he is meant to to be (by embarrassment?).

b2   'Aristodemus and Aristophanes': the *te ... kai* here, linking the last two members of an otherwise 'asyndetic' series (i.e. 'Phaedrus, Agathon, Eryximachus, Pausanias, Aristodemus *te ... kai* Aristophanes'), is paralleled by a similar use in the anodyne list 'earth, fire, water *te ... kai* air' at *Timaeus* 82a (see Denniston, *GP* 501), and therefore does not indicate any special relationship between these two items in the list. Nevertheless, the listing of Aristophanes (and indeed Phaedrus and the others) together with Aristodemus, a genuine 'lover' of S. (173b), and then immediately with S. himself, as among those who 'have shared in the madness ... of philosophy' (b4) is surely in itself enough to suggest how little Alcibiades understands of that 'madness'. (Whatever got to him, it was not that.)

b5-6   'you'll forgive both what I did then and what I'm saying now': i.e. my actions then, and the fact that I'm telling you about them now (because they're so shaming).

b6-7 **'and anyone else here who's uninitiated'**: i.e., perhaps, both uninitiated in the 'Bacchic frenzy' of philosophy (standing in for Diotima's 'mysteries'?), and lacking in the kind of sensitivity needed to understand the reasons for his behaving as he is about to describe ...

c4 **'I'm certainly not'**: i.e. 'I'm too aroused to sleep', which will have different meanings for Alcibiades and for S., if we interpret the latter's behaviour in terms of Diotima's lessons (he will be bursting with *logoi* only, in the presence of beauty).

c7-8 **'the only worthy lover I've had'**: i.e. worth having (and worthy of me).

c9-10 **'gratify you ... in this matter '**: i.e. give you what a normal lover would want, though that as usual remains delicately unspecified.

d1-2 **'For me there's nothing more important than my becoming as good a person as possible'**: Alcibiades' description of himself here is as like Pausanias' portrait of the ideal beloved as S.'s actual behaviour is like that of Diotima's 'correct kind of boy-loving' (211b6).

d2-3 **'and in this I don't think there's any more effective collaborator for me than you'**: cf. 212b3-4.

d7 **'with great pretence of seriousness'**: *mala eirônikôs*. See 216e5-6n. From Alcibiades' point of view the disclaimer that follows is mere pretence (as his response to it in 219a6-7 shows), while from S.'s it is a gently teasing statement of something he takes to be true (that he has nothing he can directly exchange for Alcibiades' beauty). No doubt he is also being ironic in our sense, insofar as he knows that Alcibiades is starting from a different viewpoint, and does nothing to stop him from missing the point; but *Alcibiades* is surely not calling him 'ironic', since that would mean that he actually understood what S. was saying.

d8-e1 **'you must really be a person of no mean quality'**: 'almost "no fool"' (Dover).

e2-3 **'and there is in me some power which could make you a better man'**: in a sense there is – the power of philosophy. But that by itself will not make Alcibiades a better person; he has also to want to be improved.

218e6-219a1 **'truly beautiful things in return for only apparently beautiful ones'**: lit. 'truth of beautiful things in return for appearance'.

219a1-2 **'a true exchange of "gold for bronze"'**: what S. would have to offer would be more 'golden' – an epithet already applied by Alcibiades to the statues inside the silenus S. (216e8) – than Glaucus' armour (S. quotes from the last line of the episode between Glaucus and Diomedes in *Iliad* 6.119-236).

a2 **'my fine friend'**: *ô makarie*, a form of address 'capable of conveying correction, rebuke ...' (Halliwell 1995:107).

a3 **'and I'm really nothing'**: cf. 216e4.

a3-5 **'The sight of the mind, I assure you, first sees sharply when the sight of the eyes starts [?] to fade from its prime'**: what P. means Alcibiades to say here is clear enough, but what he actually wrote is less clear (ἐπιχειρεῖν means 'undertake', 'try', not 'start').

a6 **'On my side, things are as I've said'**: so evidently Alcibiades still thinks they can do a deal (see 218d7n.); whereas in fact S. is (among other things) genuinely denying that he has what *Alcibiades* thinks he has (cf. 218e2-3n.).

b1-2 **'both in relation to the present situation and in relation to everything else'**: lit. 'both about these (things) and the others'. If Alcibiades takes this as evidence that he has 'wounded' S. (b4), he must think it refers to the offers he made in 218c9-d1. What S. actually means – I imagine – is that they should consider what to do now in the context of a general consideration of their overall good ('what will contribute to our happiness?').

b3 **'when I'd heard this response to what I'd said'**: lit. 'having heard and said these things'.

b5 'my himation': an outside garment, which could evidently double as a blanket; heavier than S.'s *tribôn* ('short cloak', b6).

b7-c1 'he – this person here – this truly superhuman ... man': 'him' on its last two occurrences has also been lit. 'this (man)', which gives four uses of 'this' in three lines – 'the repeated demonstratives ... are like a jabbing finger; Alcibiades speaks half in exasperated admiration, half in denunciation', Dover'. Denunciation, albeit playful, is the main element in the use of the same demonstrative at 222b5. 'Superhuman': *daimonios*, so *'daimôn*-like', 'spirit-like'; the same word that Diotima used at 203a4 – 'the person who is wise about such things [sc. involving intercourse between gods and men] is a spirit-like man'. In Alcibiades' mouth it will have its ordinary sense (something like 'marvellous'?) rather than the special sense Diotima gave it, but given all the other connections between Alcibiades' speech and Diotima's account of Love (and love), it seems reasonable enough to suppose that we are meant to understand that S. is also 'like a *daimôn*', i.e. like Love (an identification which was, of course, already implied in Diotima's own speech: Alcibiades unwittingly confirms something he was not there to hear).

c4-5 'laughed at my beauty, treated it criminally': 'beauty' is *hôra* again (see 217a3n.); 'treated it criminally' translates *hubrisen*.

c5-6 'gentlemen of the jury': or 'gentlemen judges' (*dikastês*: see 175e9-10n.).

c6 'S.'s arrogance': *huperêphania* (see 217e4-5n.).

e1-2 'I knew perfectly well that he was much more invulnerable to money, from any quarter, than Ajax was to iron weapons': is Alcibiades seriously suggesting that he'd thought of trying to *bribe* S. into having sex with him? Well, maybe; but perhaps he is just using the opportunity to bring in another aspect of 'this amazing man'. (He noticeably omits the possibility of using argument, which one might have expected to be a more obvious choice for dealing with S.; it wouldn't have worked, of course, but why could he not at least have thought of it?)

e5-6 'For after all of these things had happened to me, we served together on the expedition to Potidaea': lit. 'for (both) all these things had happened for me previously, and after them ...'. The 'for' indicates that what follows is a further explanation of Alcibiades' sense of 'enslavement' to S. The expedition in question lasted from the summer of 432 to the end of 430 (see Dover).

220a2 'the rest of them were nowhere': lit. '... were nothing'; cf. 216e4, 219a3, c5. The idea of 'being something' obviously means a lot to Alcibiades (which only goes to illustrate what Diotima said in 208c ff.).

a4 'at drinking when he didn't want to, whenever he was forced to, he beat everyone': the repetition of 'whenever ... forced' (see 219e8-220a1) jokingly makes drinking to excess (when forced) another military hardship along with going without food (when forced). Hence 'again, as for feats of endurance in the cold of winter' in a7: Alcibiades has just described two contexts which demonstrate S.'s endurance, and now he'll mention another. – On the construction of the Greek, I have adopted Bury's suggestion – 'regard πίνειν as a kind of accus. of respect ("at drinking") with ἐκράτει; if this meat is too strong, one can retreat to taking the infinitive as belonging after ἐθέλων. (But the point will be the same.)

a5-6 'no person on earth has ever yet seen S. drunk': this is perhaps not just a matter of his 'having a head for' drink, but of judgement (cf. 214a7n.). As in the case of Alcibiades' advances, the picture is one of complete (and unnerving) rational control.

a6-7 'put to the test': a rather different kind of 'testing' (*elenchus*) from the sort that concerns S.

c2 '"what a thing *this* was that our enduring hero dared to do"': adapted from *Odyssey* 242, 271. The type of behaviour Alcibiades now goes on to describe recalls the episode with S. in the neighbours' doorway (174d ff.).

c4-5 'when he couldn't make progress with it': lit. 'when it didn't go forward for him'.

c5 'looking for a way forward': the Greek limits itself to 'looking (for)' (*zêtein*, as e.g. at 191d5, 210c3).

d1 'some of the Ionians': i.e. from an allied contingent. Is the implication perhaps that Athenians would have been familiar with this sort of behaviour of S.'s?

d5 'with a prayer to the sun': so P.'s S. (or P.'s Alcibiades' S.) believes the sun is a god (see *Apology* 26d for a charge that he – S. – did not).

d5-6 'Or again, in the battles': lit. 'and if you wish (sc. to hear what I have to say about his behaviour) in the battles'.

e1 'when I'd been wounded': the verb is the same as the one used at 219b4 ('I thought he'd been *hit*').

e4 'you won't ... blame me': despite what he said about S. in 216e ('he thinks ... possessions worthless'), Alcibiades seems still half to believe that he must care about such things as prizes and recognition (see further 221a8-b1n.).

221a1-2 'when the army was withdrawing in retreat from Delium': the Athenians were defeated there (in Boeotia) in 424.

a8-b1 'how much more composed he was than Laches': lit. 'how superior he was to L. in/by being composed'. Laches himself (elected general before and after Delium), in the dialogue P. names after him, describes his own observation of S.'s exemplary behaviour in the battle (*Laches* 181a-b). When S. is said to have been 'composed' ('with his wits about him', *emphrôn*), he is also presumably being said to have been courageous; we might perhaps think of detecting a covert reference here to the *argument* of the *Laches*, which ends up with a suggested account of courage (formally rejected) in purely intellectual terms – but then of course Alcibiades would not have known anything about that. In any case, what stands out is once again mainly the degree of S.'s rational control. (Alcibiades is not implying that Laches was a coward; rather he means that S. was even braver than L. – whatever S. may have thought: see 215a5-222b7n.)

b2-3 '"swaggering and casting his eyes this way and that"': adapted from Aristophanes' *Clouds*, 362.

c3 'the other aspects of his behaviour': 'aspects of behaviour' translates *epitêdeumata*, the word translated as 'activities' in Diotima's account of the 'final mysteries' (210c4, etc.).

c7 'Brasidas': the choice of this Spartan figure – killed leading an army in 422 – might be another sign of Diotima's non-Athenian origins; on the other hand, the evidence suggests that he was an outstanding military commander, who could have been on anybody's list. (So according to Alcibiades' account, S. stands in the same sort of relationship to the sorts of people normally accepted as great men as Diotima's 'correct lover' would to the lovers, and 'lovers', of 208e6-209e4?)

d1 '(and there are others as well)': 'others', i.e. other public speakers. It is not clear who else Alcibiades could be thinking of but himself.

d3 'so strange is he, both in himself and in the things he says': 'so strange is he' is, lit. 'in respect to his strangeness'; 'the things he says' are his *logoi* ('words', in 215c7, etc.). Similarly in (221)d7, d9, e1, 222a1.

d5 'if one were to compare him to the figures I'm talking about': so Alcibiades neatly returns to the point from which he started.

e1 'For if one were willing to listen to what S. says': which Alcibiades himself is not, now (216a-c). (But an alternative reading in the mss. would give 'if one *is* willing ...'.)

e2-3 'such are the terms and expressions in which it is clothed': cf. 199b4-5.

e3 'mischief-making': *hubristês.*

222a3 'of the things one hears': i.e. 'of what is said', 'things said' – *logoi* again.

a6 'a person of quality': *kalos kagathos* (cf. 204a4-5n.). (In terms of what Diotima says at 204a Alcibiades must himself count as ignorant; and it will be just that ignorance, and in particular his lack of self-knowledge, that has prevented him from sticking to philosophy.)

a8 'the crimes he committed': *ha hubrisen.*

b1-2 'Charmides, son of Glaucon, Euthydemus, son of Diocles': on Glaucon, or Glaucons, see 172a3n. P. named a dialogue after this Charmides; but this Euthydemus is not the one after whom he named the *Euthydemus.*

b5 'not to be deceived ... by this man': see 219b7-c1n.

b6-7 'not – as the proverb runs – to learn like a fool, by suffering': Alcibiades ends on a mock-epic/mock-tragic note (for the 'proverb', see e.g. *Iliad* 17.32, 20.198; Aeschylus, *Agamemnon* 177). Alcibiades himself, of course, has learned nothing from his 'suffering'.

c1 'Aristodemus said' is supplied; the Greek merely continues in *oratio obliqua.*

c2-3 'he seemed still to be affected by love for S.': *erôtikôs echein* is chosen instead of *eran* ('love'/'be in love with') perhaps because the latter will be used (by S.) to describe S.'s relationship to Alcibiades (d1); however strangely confused the roles of lover and beloved may have been in their case, still S. is the older man and the one who loves, the lover (or, from Alcibiades' point of view, at the time of the incident, his 'lover'). Similar periphrasis for *eran* occurs, for different reasons, at 207b2, b8-c1, 208c4, e4.

c7-d1 'as if you didn't say everything for this reason, just to cause trouble between me and Agathon': this and what follows is banter – and how else is S. to respond to Alcibiades' praise, unless by boorishly criticizing the detail? **d3-4** 'this satyr-play of yours, or silenus-play': so it was a mere play ('[t]he satyr-play, humorous in tone and normally using a chorus dressed as satyrs, rounded off each set of three tragedies at the City Dionysia', Dover); and like S.-silenus, amusing on the outside (all those stories about him) but with serious content (jealousy)?

d7-8 'Why, S., I believe you're right': the translation is taken from Denniston, *GP* 355 (commenting on *kai mên*: indicating 'a generally favourable reaction to the words of the previous speaker', 353). Is Agathon really taking S. seriously, or is he just joining in the joke? Or is he doing a bit of both?

e2 'I'll come and recline beside you': at present the order is Agathon, Alcibiades, S.; S. invites Agathon to take the place 'below' him (e3-4), which would mean Alcibiades having S. next to him with Agathon on S.'s far side. Alcibiades proposes instead that Agathon should be between them (e7), but S. immediately rejects that idea (e8-11); Agathon gets up to move to S.'s other side, but apparently never gets there (223b1 ff.).

e6 'He thinks he's got to get the better of me in every way': Alcibiades attributes his own motivation to S. (whose attitude towards such *philotimia*, or 'love of honour', is presumably the same as Diotima's: i.e., as I understand it, that it is *erôs* misdirected).

e7 'my wonderful friend': Alcibiades' use of *thaumasios* here clearly has a certain edge to it, while also referring back to his speech; S. was *thaumastos* at 219c1, did *thaumasia* things at 221c3 (both 'amazing' in the translation). See also following n.

e11 'Come on, man': *ô daimonie* is apparently a perfectly ordinary form of address (see Halliwell 1995:109-10); in P. it is perhaps tends to be used in contexts of mild remonstration. 'Man' fits in this sense, but in another it is a totally inadequate translation, for it blots out the echo of Alcibiades' description of S. as 'truly *daimonios*' at 219c1. In S.'s mouth here the word acquires – maybe – a gentle irony, matching Alcibiades' 'wonderful' (*thaumasios/thaumastos*, also in 219c1).

223a1 **'the boy':** even if Agathon left his 'boyhood' some time ago, to my ear the description
sounds entirely in place – just here, and in S.'s mouth. But see 194e4-197e8n.

a1-2 **'I'm absolutely longing to give him an encomium':** presumably on the terms outlined
in 198b ff. In the event the encomium is not given; but see d2-5n. 'I'm longing' is
epithumô, the standard word for 'desire', as in Diotima's account of love. (So here is S., in
the proximity of beauty, bursting to talk ...)

a7 **'to get their share of beauties':** *tôn kalôn*, the gender of which (as so often) might in
principle be either masculine or neuter (or feminine); Alcibiades, at any rate, means the
masculine.

a8-9 **'how resourceful he was ... lie beside *him*':** should one make anything of the apparent
echo of the idea Poverty's lying down with Resource (203c1-2), and if so, what?

b7 **'Eryximachus and Phaedrus':** Eryximachus is the one who is against too much
drinking on professional grounds (176c-d; cf. Alcibiades' greeting to him at 214b3-4),
Phaedrus his friend (177a ff.).

c1 **'since the nights were long':** as they would be in January (cf. 173a5-6n.; the City
Dionysia were held around March).

c6 **'Well, S. was having a conversation with them':** a particularly apt way of putting it, as
it soon turns out (S. is very much in charge).

d2 **'S. was also forcing them to agree':** *prosanankazein* can evidently mean either just
'force' (so at 181e5), or 'force *in addition*', and it is surely the second that is meant here –
they are already being forced to drink heavily (b6), and actually 'drinking from a large
cup' (c5, where 'from left to right' confirms that they are all drinking, and steadily); S. is
now forcing them to do something else, namely a bit of philosophy. Aristodemus is in
effect reporting S.'s passing the test Alcibiades predicted at 220a6-7, of his unrivalled
capacity for putting up with the rigours of hard drinking. These evidently interrupt S.'s
'searching' no more than did the more obvious rigours of winter at Potidaea. (The
passage from c2 to the end of the dialogue is almost Aristodemus' own encomium of S. –
suitably small and inconspicuous.)

d2-5 **'it belongs to the same man ... an expert tragic poet is also a comic poet':** here we get
some idea of what might have been in S.'s 'encomium' of Agathon. Since Agathon was
exclusively a tragic poet, and playwrights evidently did not as a rule switch between the
two genres, then by implication, when he agrees to S.'s proposition (d5), he will be in
danger of agreeing that he is not an expert tragic poet (lit. 'a tragic poet by
expertise/skill'). Of course the same point will also apply, *mutatis mutandis*, to
Aristophanes – and to all existing dramatic poets, to the extent that they did not display
talent in both tragedy and comedy. In the *Republic*, at 395a, S. uses their inability to do
so to illustrate a general point about the *dangers* of a man's combining different roles.
But there he is referring to poets as they actually are; here in *Symp.* he is making a point
(developing an argument: this is clearly the sense in which he is using 'force') rather
about what dramatic poets *should* be, as it were in principle. We are left to guess what
his argument might have been, but it is not too difficult to reconstruct it, if we start from
Diotima's claims about the good, and from the role of poets as educators of society (cf.
187d2n.): tragic poets and comic ones will both need – will they not? – to compose, in
their different ways, on the basis of a knowledge of the true ends of human life. (A more
detailed argument can be constructed using especially *Laws* 816c ff. and *Philebus* 48b
ff., but the general upshot is the same.) If we ask who *does* combine equal ability in the
areas both of the tragic, or serious (an equation made in the *Laws* passage and
elsewhere), and the comic, then one answer is S. himself: it was precisely his
combination of the comic and the serious, and his ability to move between them (see esp.
216e6 'as soon as he comes to be in earnest'), that gave Alcibiades the theme for his

speech. Another answer is *P.*, who after all is the one who puts S. on the stage (but P., of course, is not there). On the issues here, see Clay 1975, Patterson 1982.

d5-6 **'Even as they were being forced to agree to this, and not following too well, they were nodding off':** so, if anything, they were nodding off because they were not following, not failing to follow because they were nodding off? If so, this might help explain why it was Aristophanes who fell asleep first (d6-7): Agathon has shown at least some ability to follow an argument, and certainly more than Aristophanes (see 212c4-6n.). (But perhaps this is to press the text too hard?)

d7-8 **'So S., having put them to sleep, got up and left':** after all, he no longer has anyone to 'converse with' (*dialegesthai*).

d9 **'the Lyceum':** a sanctuary of Apollo in one of his guises (*Lukeios*), with a gymnasium attached. *Symp.* might help to explain why that would have made it so attractive a place to S. – that is, because it would also be a natural gathering-place for young males (the beginning of the *Euthyphro* suggests that the Lyceum was a place where one might regularly expect to find him; cf. also *Lysis* 203a). Or at any rate, *Symp.* might help to explain why the Lyceum was so attractive to *P.*'s S.; once again, how much of the real S. is in this one we can never quite be sure.

Select Bibliography

1. Texts and editions

Burnet, J., *Platonis opera* (Oxford Classical Texts), vol. II, Oxford 1901
Bury, R.G., *The Symposium of Plato* (2nd edn), Cambridge 1932 (= 'Bury')
Dover, K.J., *Plato: Symposium*, Cambridge 1980 (= 'Dover')
Hommel, A., *Platonis Convivium*, Leipzig 1834
Hug, A., *Platons Symposion*, Leipzig 1884
Reitig, G.F., *Platonis Symposion*, Halle 1876
Robin, L., *Platon. Oeuvres complètes*, t. IV.2: *Le banquet* , Paris 1966
Rückert, L.I., *Platonis Convivium*, Leipzig 1829

2. Translations into English

Allen, R.E., *The Dialogues of Plato*, vol. II: *The Symposium* (translated with comment), New Haven 1991 (= 'Allen')
Hamilton, W., *Plato, The Symposium* (Penguin), Harmondsworth 1951 (= 'Hamilton': completely revised version, by C.Gill, forthcoming 1999)
Nehamas, A., and Woodruff, P., *Plato: Symposium* (translated, with introduction and notes), Indianapolis 1989 (= 'Nehamas and Woodruff')
Waterfield, R., *Plato: Symposium* (World's Classics), Oxford 1994 (= 'Waterfield')

3. Works of reference

Ast, F., Lexicon Platonicum sive Vocum Platonicarum Index, Leipzig 1835 (reprinted Bonn 1956)
Brockmann, C., *Die handschriftliche Überlieferung von Platons Symposion* (Serta Graeca: Beiträge zur Erforschung griechische Texte, Band 2), Wiesbaden 1992
Denniston, J.D., *The Greek Particles* (2nd edn), Oxford 1954 (= 'Denniston, *GP*')
Diels, H. and Kranz, W., *Die Fragmente der Vorsokratiker* (6th edn), Berlin 1951 (= 'Diels-Kranz')
Dover, K.J., *Greek Popular Morality in the Time of Plato and Aristotle*, Oxford 1974
Goodwin, W.W., *Syntax of the Moods and Tenses of the Greek Verb* (2nd edn), London 1889 (= 'Goodwin, *MT*')
Greene, W.C., *Scholia Platonica* (American Philological Association Monograph Series, 8), Haverford, PA, 1938

Kock, T., *Comicorum Graecorum Fragmenta*, Leipzig 1880-8

Nauck, A., *Tragicorum Graecorum Fragmenta* (2nd edn), Leipzig 1889

Liddell, H.G, Scott. R., and Jones, H.S., *A Greek-English Lexicon* (9th edn, Oxford 1940 (= *LSJ*)

Page, D.L., *Poetae Melici Graeci*, Oxford 1962

Voigt, E.M., *Sappho et Alcaeus*, Amsterdam 1971

4. Other works

Bacon, H., 'Socrates crowned', *Virginia Quarterly Review* 35 (1959), 415-30

Belfiore, E., '*Elenchus, epode* and magic: Socrates as Silenus', *Phoenix* 34 (1980), 128-37

Belfiore, E., 'Dialectic with the reader in Plato's *Symposium*', *Maia* 36 (1984), 137-49

Boardman, J., '*Symposion* furniture', in Murray 1990, 122-31

Bowie, A.M., 'Thinking with drinking: wine and the symposium in Aristophanes', *Journal of Hellenic Studies* 107 (1997), 1-21

Bremmer, J.M., 'Adolescents, *symposion*, and pederasty', in Murray 1990, 135-48

Brink, C.O., 'Plato on the natural character of goodness', *Harvard Studies in Classical Philology* 63 (1958), 193-8

Brock, R., 'Plato and comedy', in E.M.Craik (ed.), *Owls to Athens: essays on classical subjects presented to Sir Kenneth Dover*, Oxford 1990, 39-51

Burkert, W., *Lore and Science in Ancient Pythagoreanism* (tr. E.L.Minar, Jr), Cambridge, MA, 1972

Burkert, W., *Homo Necans: the anthropology of ancient Greek sacrificial ritual and myth* (tr. P.Bing), Berkeley 1983; 2nd (German) edition, 1997

Burkert, W., *Greek Religion: archaic and classical* (tr. J.Raffan), Oxford 1985

Burkert, W., *Ancient Mystery Cults*, Cambridge, MA 1987

Burnett, A.P., *Three Archaic Poets: Archilochus, Alcaeus, Sappho*, London 1983

Burnyeat, M.F., 'Socratic midwifery, Platonic inspiration', *Bulletin of the Institute of Classical Studies* 24 (1977), 7-17; reprinted in H.H.Benson (ed.), *Essays on the Philosophy of Socrates*, Oxford 1992, 53-65

Burnyeat, M.F., 'First words: a valedictory lecture', *Proceedings of the Cambridge Philological Society* 43 (1997), 1-20

Calame, C. , *L'Éros dans la Grèce antique*, Paris 1996

Calogero, G., *Il 'Simposio' di Platone* (versione e saggio introduttivo), Bari 1928

Clarke, W.M., 'Achilles and Patroclus in love', *Hermes* 106 (1978), 381-96

Clay, D., 'The tragic and comic poet of the *Symposium*', *Arion* n.s. 2 (1975), 238-61

Clinton, K., *The Sacred Officials of the Eleusinian Mysteries* (*Transactions of the American Philosophical Society* 64.2), Philadelphia 1972

Cohen, D., *Law, Sexuality and Society: the enforcement of morals in classical Athens*, Cambridge 1991

Cornford, F.M., 'The doctrine of eros in Plato's *Symposium*', reprinted in G.Vlastos (ed.), *Plato: A collection of critical essays*, vol. 2, New York 1971, 119-31

Cotter, J., 'The *Symposium*: Plato's title and intent', in E.N.Borza and R.W.Carrubba (eds), *Classics and the Classical Tradition. Essays presented to Robert E.Dengler*, University Park, PA, 1973, 33-50

Daux, G., 'Sur quelques passages du *Banquet* de Platon', *Revue des études grecques* 55 (1942), 236-71

Davidson, J., *Courtesans and Fishcakes: the consuming passions of classical Athens*, London 1997

des Places, E., 'La langue philosophique de Platon: Le vocabulaire de l'accès au savoir et de la science' (1961), in des Places 1981, 36-55

des Places, E., *Études platoniciennes 1929-1979*, Leiden 1981

de Vries, G.J., 'Mystery terminology in Aristophanes and Plato', *Mnemosyne* 26 (1973), 1-8

de Vries, G.J., 'Marginal notes on Plato's *Symposium*, *Mnemosyne* 33 (1980), 349-51

Dorter, K., 'The significance of the speeches in Plato's *Symposium*', *Philosophy and Rhetoric* 2 (1969), 215-34

Dover, K.J., 'Eros and nomos (Plato, *Symposium* 182a-185c)', *Bulletin of the Institute of Classical Studies* 11 (1964), 31-42

Dover, K.J., 'The date of Plato's *Symposium*', *Phronesis* 10 (1965), 2-20

Dover, K.J., 'Aristophanes' speech in Plato's *Symposium*', *Journal of Hellenic Studies* 66 (1966), 41-50

Dover, K.J., *Greek Homosexuality*, London 1978

Dover, K.J., 'Greek homosexuality and initiation', in *The Greeks and their Legacy = Collected Papers*, vol. 2, Oxford 1988, 115-34

Edelstein, L., 'The role of Eryximachus in Plato's *Symposium*', *Transactions of the American Philological Association* 76 (1945), 83-103

Fasce, S., *Eros. La figura e il culto*, Genoa 1977

Erbse, H., 'Sokrates und die Frauen', *Gymnasium* 73 (1966), 201-20

Feeney, D.C., 'Towards an account of the ancient world's concept of fictive belief', in C.Gill and T.P.Wiseman, *Lies and Fiction in the Ancient World*, Exeter 1993, 230-44

Ferrari, G.R.F., 'Platonic love', in Kraut 1992, 248-76

Fierro, M.A., 'Socratic *elenchos* in Plato's *Symposium*' (unpublished paper)

Foucault, M., *Histoire de la sexualité 2. L'usage des plaisirs*, Paris 1984

Frede, D., 'Out of the cave: what Socrates learned from Diotima', in Rosen, R.M., and Farrell, J. (eds.), *Nomodeiktes: Greek studies in honor of Martin Ostwald*, Ann Arbor 1993, 397-422

Friedländer, P., *Plato* (trans. H.Meyerhoff), vols 1 & 2, Princeton 1958/68

Gagarin, M., 'Socrates' *hubris* and Alcibiades' failure', *Phoenix* 31 (1977), 22-37

Gager, J.G., *Curse Tablets and Binding Spells from the Ancient World*, New York 1992

220 BIBLIOGRAPHY

Gilbert, W., 'Der zweite Teil des Logos der Diotima in Platons Gastmahl (cap. 24-29, pag. 204C-212A)', *Philologus* n.f. 22 (1909), 52-70

Gill, C., 'Platonic love and individuality', in Loizou, A., and Lesser, H. (eds), *Polis and Politics: essays in Greek moral and political philosophy*, Aldershot 1990, 69-88

Golden, M., 'Slavery and homosexuality at Athens', *Phoenix* 38 (1984), 308-24

Golden, M., '*Pais*, "child" and "slave"', *L'antiquité classique* 54 (1985), 91-104

Gould, T., *Platonic Love*, London 1963

Graf, F., *Eleusis und die orphische Dichtung Athens in vorhellenistischer Zeit*, Berlin 1974

Greifenhagen, A., *Griechische Eroten*, Berlin 1951

Guthrie, W.K.C., *A History of Greek Philosophy*, vol.4: *Plato, the Man and his Dialogues*, Cambridge 1975

Hackforth, R., 'Immortality in Plato's *Symposium*', *Classical Review* 64 (1950), 43-5

Halliwell, S., 'Forms of address: Socratic vocatives in Plato', in F.de Martino and A.H.Sommerstein (eds), *Lo spettacolo delle voci*, Bari 1995, parte seconda, 87-121

Halperin, D.M., 'Platonic *erôs* and what men call love', *Ancient Philosophy* 5 (1985), 161-204

Halperin, D.M., 'Plato and erotic reciprocity', *Classical Antiquity* 5 (1986), 60-80

Halperin, D.M., Winkler, J.J., and Zeitlin, F.I. (eds), *Before Sexuality: the construction of erotic experience in the ancient Greek world*, Princeton 1989

Halperin, D.M., 'Why is Diotima a woman?', in Halperin (ed.), *One Hundred Years of Homosexuality and Other Essays on Greek Love*, New York 1990, 113-51, 190-211

Halperin, D.M., 'Plato and the erotics of narrativity', in J.C.Klagge and N.D.Smith (eds), *Methods of Interpreting Plato and his Dialogues* (Oxford Studies in Ancient Philosophy supplementary volume), Oxford 1992, 93-129

Hard, R., *Eros and Athanasia: a critical analysis of Socrates' themes in Plato's Symposium*, diss. University of Reading, 1992

Irwin, T., *Plato's Ethics*, Oxford 1995

Isenberg, M.W., *The Order of the Discourses in Plato's Symposium*, diss. University of Chicago 1940

Janaway, C., *Images of Excellence*, Oxford 1995

Kahn, C.H., 'Plato's theory of desire', *Review of Metaphysics* 41 (1987), 77-103

Kahn, C.H., 'Being in Parmenides and Plato', *La parola del passato* 43 (1988), 237-61

Kahn, C.H., 'Aeschines on Socratic eros', in Vander Waerdt 1994, 87-106

Kahn, C.H., *Plato and the Socratic Dialogue: the philosophical use of a literary form*, Cambridge 1996

Kidd, I., 'Some philosophical demons', *Bulletin of the Institute of Classical Studies* 40 (1995), 217-24

Konstan, D., and Young-Bruehl, E., 'Eryximachus' speech in the *Symposium*', *Apeiron* 16 (1982), 40-6

Kosman, A., 'Platonic love', in Werkmeister, W.H. (ed.), *Facets of Plato's Philosophy*, Assen 1976, 53-69

Kranz, W., 'Diotima von Mantineia', *Hermes* 61 (1926), 437-47

Kraut, R. (ed.), *The Cambridge Companion to Plato*, Cambridge 1992

Krüger, G., *Einsicht und Leidenschaft. Das Wesen des platonischen Denkens* (4th edn), Frankfurt 1973

Kurke, L., 'Inventing the hetaira: sex, politics and discursive conflict in archaic Greece', *Classical Antiquity* 16 (1997), 106-50

Lang, B., *The Anatomy of Philosophical Style*, Oxford 1990

Lasserre, F.,'Ερωτικοὶ λόγοι', *Museum Helveticum* 1 (1944), 169-78

Levi, A., 'Sulla demonologica platonica', *Athenaeum* 24 (1946), 119-28

Levy, D., 'The definition of love in Plato's *Symposium*', *Journal of the History of Ideas* 40 (1979), 285-91

Levin, S., 'Diotima's visit and service to Athens', *Grazer Beiträge* 3 (1975), 223-40

Lissarague, F., 'De la sexualité des satyres', *Métis* 2 (1987), 63-79 [cf. Lissarague, F., 'The sexual life of satyrs', in Halperin, Winkler and Zeitlin 1989]

Lissarague, F., 'Un rituel du vin: la libation', in Murray and Tecusan 1995, 126-44

Loraux, N., *The Invention of Athens. The funeral oration in the classical city* (tr. A Sheridan), Cambridge, MA 1986

Loraux, N., *Les expériences de Tirésias. Le féminin et l'homme grec*, Paris 1989

Lowenstam, S., 'Paradoxes in Plato's *Symposium*', *Ramus* 14 (1985), 85-104

MacDowell, D.M., *Gorgias: Encomium of Helen*, Bristol 1982

Mackenzie, M.M., 'Impasse and explanation: from the *Lysis* to the *Phaedo*', *Archiv für Geschichte der Philosophie* 70 (1988), 15-45

Markus, R.A., 'The dialectic of eros in Plato's *Symposium*', *Downside Review* 73 (1955), 219-30; reprinted in Vlastos, G. (ed.), *Plato: a collectiion of critical essays*, vol. II, New York 1971, 132-43

Mason, H.A., *Fine Talk at Agathon's: a version of Plato's Symposium*, Cambridge 1992

Mattingly, H.B., 'The date of Plato's *Symposium*', *Phronesis* 3 (1958), 31-9

McGrath, E., '"The Drunken Alcibiades": Rubens's picture of Plato's *Symposium*', *Journal of the Warburg and Courtauld Institutes* 46 (1983), 228-35

Moravcsik, J.M.E., 'Reason and eros in the "ascent"=passage of the *Symposium*', in Anton, J. and Kustas, G. (eds), *Essays in Ancient Greek Philosophy*, Albany, NY, 1971, 285-302

Morrison, J.S., 'Four notes on Plato's *Symposium*', *Classical Quarterly* 14 (1964), 42-55

Murray, O. (ed.), *Sympotica: a symposium on the symposion*, Oxford 1990

Murray, O., 'Sympotic history', in Murray 1990, 2-13

Murray, O., 'The affair of the mysteries: democracy and the drinking group', in Murray 1990, 149-61

Murray, O., 'Histories of pleasure', in Murray and Tecusan 1995, 3-17

Murray, O., and Tecusan, M. (eds), *In Vino Veritas*, London 1995

Mylonas, G.E., *Eleusis and the Eleusinian Mysteries*, Princeton 1961

Neumann, H., 'Diotima's concept of love', *American Journal of Philology* 86 (1965), 33-59

Nightingale, A.W., *Genres in Dialogue: Plato and the construct of philosophy*, Cambridge 1995

Nussbaum, M.C., *The Fragility of Goodness*, Cambridge 1986 (earlier version of ch.6 = 'The speech of Alcibiades: a reading of Plato's *Symposium*', *Philosophy and Literature* 3 (1979), 131-72)

O'Brien, D., 'L'Empédocle de Platon', *Revue des études grecques* 110 (1997), 381-98

O'Brien, M.J., '"Becoming immortal" in Plato's *Symposium*', in D.E.Gerber (ed.), *Greek Poetry and Philosophy: studies in honour of Leonard Woodbury*, Chico, CA, 1984, 185-205

Osborne, C., *Eros Unveiled: Plato and the god of love*, Oxford 1994

Osborne, R., 'The erection and mutilation of the Hermai', *Proceedings of the Cambridge Philological Society* n.s.31 (1985), 47-73

Oscar Velásquez, J., 'En torno a "subitamente" en el *Banquete* de Platon', *Revista Chilena de Literatura* 27/28 (1986), 67-76

Parker, R., *Athenian Religion: a history*, Oxford 1996

Parsons, P., 'Eels tomorrow, but sprats today' (review of Davidson 1997), *London Review of Books* 18 September 1997, 6-7

Patterson, R., 'The Platonic art of comedy and tragedy', *Philosophy and Literature* 6 (1982), 76-92

Patterson, R., 'The ascent in Plato's *Symposium*', *Proceedings of the Boston Area Colloquium in Ancient Philosophy* 7 (1991), 193-214

Pender, E.E., 'Spiritual pregnancy in Plato's *Symposium*', *Classical Quarterly* 42 (1992), 72-86

Penner, T., *The Ascent from Nominalism: some existence arguments in Plato's middle dialogues* (Philosophical Studies Series, 37), Dordrecht 1987

Penwill, J.L., 'Men in Love: aspects of Plato's *Symposium*', *Ramus* 7 (1978), 143-75

Peters, W.J.Th., 'The sileni of Alcibiades. An archaeological commentary on Plato, *Symposium* 215 A-B', in J.S.Boersma et al., *Festoen. Opgedragen aan A.N.Zadoks-Josephus Jitta bij haar zevenstige verjaardag* (Scripta Archaeologica Groningana 6), Groningen 1976, 475-85

Pickard-Cambridge, A.W., *The Dramatic Festivals of Athens*, rev. J.Gould and D.M.Lewis, Oxford 1968, (with supplement) 1988

Price, A.W., *Love and Friendship in Plato and Aristotle*, Oxford 1989 (second edition, with 'Afterword', 1997)

Plass, P., 'Anxiety, repression and morality: Plato and Freud', *Psychoanalytic Review* 65 (1978), 533-56

Plass, P., 'Plato's "pregnant" lover', *Symbolae Osloenses* 53 (1978), 47-55

Reale, G., *Platone: Simposio* (Italian translation, with a bibliography on the dialogue by E.Peroli, covering the last fifty years), Milan 1993

Reeve, M.D., 'Five notes', *Classical Review* n.s. 21 (1971), 324-9

Renehan, R., 'Three places in Plato's *Symposium*', *Classical Philology* 85 (1990), 120-6

Riedweg, C., *Mysterienterminologie bei Platon, Philon und Klemens von Alexandrien*, Berlin 1987

Rist, J.M., *Eros and Psyche. Studies in Plato, Plotinus and Origen* (*Phoenix* Supplement 6),Toronto 1964

Robin, L., *La théorie platonicienne de l'amour*, Paris 1908

Roochnik, D.L., 'The erotics of philosophical discourse', *History of Philosophy Quarterly* 4 (1987), 117-30

Rosen, S., *Plato's Symposium*, New Haven 1968 (2nd edn 1987)

Rosenmeyer, T., 'Eros-erotes', *Phoenix* 5 (1951), 11-22

Rösler, W., 'Wine and truth in the Greek *symposion*', in Murray and Tecusan 1995, 106-12

Rowe, C.J., *Plato: Phaedrus*, Warminster 1986

Rowe, C.J., 'The speech of Eryximachus in Plato's *Symposium*', forthcoming (1999) in J.J.Cleary (ed.), *The Neoplatonic Sage*

Rowe, C.J., 'Socrates and Diotima: eros, creativity and immortality', forthcoming in *Proceedings of the Boston Area Colloquium in Ancient Philosophy* 14 (1998)

Santas, G.X., *Plato and Freud: two theories of love*, Oxford 1988

Saxonhouse, A.W., 'Eros and the female in Greek political thought: an interpretation of Plato's *Symposium*', *Political Theory* 12 (1984), 5-27

Schofield, M., *The Stoic Idea of the City*, Cambridge 1991

Sheffield, F.C.C., 'Philosophical creativity in Plato's *Symposium*' (unpublished paper)

Sider, D., 'Plato's *Symposium* as Dionysian festival', *Quaderni urbinati di cultura classica* 33 (1980), 41-56

Sier, K., *Die Rede der Diotima. Untersuchungen zum platonischen Symposion*, Stuttgart 1997 (= 'Sier')

Skinner, Q., 'Meaning and understanding in the history of ideas', *History and Theory* 8 (1969), 3-53

Sokolowski, F., *Lois sacrées des cités grecques*, Paris 1969 (supplement, 1962)

Solmsen, F., 'Parmenides and the description of perfect beauty in Plato's *Symposium*', *American Journal of Philology* 92 (1971), 62-70

Stannard, J., 'Socratic eros and Platonic dialectic', *Phronesis* 4 (1959), 120-34

Stehle, E., *Performance and Gender in Ancient Greece*, Princeton 1997

Stokes, M.C., *Plato's Socratic Conversations: drama and dialectic in three dialogues*, London 1986

Szlezák, T.A., *Platon und die Schriftlichkeit der Philosophie*, Berlin 1985

Taylor, A.E., *Plato: the man and his work* (7th edn), London 1960

Tecusan, M., '*Logos sympotikos*: patterns of the irrational in philosophical drinking: Plato outside the *symposion*', in Murray and Tecusan 1995, 238-60

Tomin, J., 'Socratic midwifery', *Classical Quarterly* 37 (1987), 97-102

Vander Waerdt, P.A. (ed.), *The Socratic Movement*, Ithaca, NY1994

Vernant, J.-P., 'One ... two ... three: *erôs*', in Halperin, Winkler and Zeitlin 1989, 465-78

Vlastos, G., 'The individual as an object of love in Plato', in Vlastos, *Platonic Studies* (2nd edn), Princeton 1981, 3-42

Vlastos, G., 'Socratic irony', *Classical Quarterly* 37 (1987), 79-96

von Blanckenhagen, P.H., 'Stage and actors in Plato's *Symposium*', *Greek, Roman and Byzantine Studies* 34 (1993), 1-18

Warner, M., 'Love, self, and Plato's *Symposium*', *Philosophical Quarterly* 29 (1979), 329-39

West, M.L., *The Orphic Poems*, Oxford 1983

West, M.L., *Greek Lyric Poetry*, Oxford 1993

White, F.C., 'Love and beauty in Plato's *Symposium*', *Journal of Hellenic Studies* 109 (1989), 149-57

Winkler, J.J., *The Constraints of Desire: the anthropology of sex and gender in ancient Greece*, New York 1990

Wippern, J., 'Eros und Unsterblichkeit in der Diotima-Rede des Symposions', in Flashar, H. and Gaiser, K. (edd.), *Synousia. Festgabe für W.Schadewaldt*, Pfullingen 1965, 123-59

Yunis, H., *A New Creed: fundamental religious beliefs in the Athenian polis and Euripidean drama* (*Hypomnemata* 91), Meisenheim 1988

Zanker, P., *The Mask of Socrates: the image of the intellectual in antiquity* (tr. A.Shapiro), Berkeley 1995

Index

(to Introduction and Commentary)

ARIS & PHILLIPS
CLASSICAL TEXTS

AESCHYLUS
EUMENIDES ed. A.J. Podlecki *(1989)*
PERSIANS ed. E. Hall *(1996)*

ARISTOPHANES ed. Alan H. Sommerstein
ACHARNIANS *(1980)*
BIRDS *(1987)*
CLOUDS *(1982)*
FROGS *(1997)*
KNIGHTS *(1981)*
LYSISTRATA *(1990)*
PEACE *(1985)*
THESMOPHORIAZUSAE *(1994)*
WASPS *(1983)*

ARISTOTLE
ON THE HEAVENS I & II ed. S. Leggatt *(1995)*
ON SLEEP AND DREAMS ed. D. Gallop *(1996)*

AUGUSTINE
SOLILOQUIES *and* IMMORTALITY OF THE SOUL ed. G. Watson *(1990)*

CAESAR
CIVIL WAR I & II ed. J.M. Carter *(1991)*
CIVIL WAR III ed. J.M. Carter *(1993)*

CASSIUS DIO
ROMAN HISTORY Books 53.1-55.9 ed. J.W. Rich *(1990)*

CATULLUS
61–68 ed. J. Godwin *(1996)*

CICERO
TUSCULAN DISPUTATIONS I, ed. A.E. Douglas *(1985)*
TUSCULAN DISPUTATIONS II & V ed. A.E. Douglas *(1989)*
ON FATE with **BOETHIUS** CONSOLATION V ed. R.W. Sharples *(1992)*
PHILIPPICS II, ed. W.K. Lacey *(1986)*
VERRINES II,1 ed. T.N. Mitchell *(1986)*
ON STOIC GOOD AND EVIL ed. M.R. Wright *(1991)*
LAELIUS ON FRIENDSHIP and THE DREAM OF SCIPIO ed. J.G.F. Powell *(1991)*
LETTERS (43 B.C.) ed. M. Willcock *(1996)*

EURIPIDES
ALCESTIS ed. D. Conacher *(1988)*

ANDROMACHE ed. M. Lloyd *(1995)*
BACCHAE ed. R. Seaford *(1996)*
ELECTRA ed. M.J. Cropp *(1988)*
HECUBA ed. C. Collard *(1991)*
HERAKLES ed. S. Barlow *(1996)*
HIPPOLYTUS ed. M.R. Halleran *(1995)*
ION ed. K.H. Lee *(1997)*
ORESTES ed. M.L. West *(1987)*
PHOENICIAN WOMEN ed. E. Craik *(1988)*
TROJAN WOMEN ed. S. Barlow *(1986)*
FRAGMENTARY PLAYS VOLUME I eds C. Collard, M.J. Cropp & K.H. Lee

GREEK ORATORS
I ANTIPHON, LYSIAS ed. M. Edwards & S. Usher *(1985)*
III ISOCRATES PANEGYRICUS and TO NICOCLES ed. S. Usher *(1990)*
IV ANDOCIDES ed. M. Edwards *(1995)*
V DEMOSTHENES On the Crown ed. S. Usher *(1993)*
VI APOLLODORUS Against Neaira ed. C. Carey *(1992)*

HELLENICA OXYRHYNCHIA ed. P.R. McKechnie & S.J. Kern *(1988)*

HOMER
ODYSSEY I & II ed. P.V. Jones *(1991)*
ILIAD VIII & IX ed. C.H. Wilson *(1996)*

HORACE
SATIRES I, ed. P. Michael Brown *(1993)*
SATIRES II ed. Frances Muecke *(1993)*

JOSEPH OF EXETER
THE TROJAN WAR I-III ed. A.K. Bate *(1986)*

LIVY
Book XXXVI ed. P.G. Walsh *(1991)*
Book XXXVII ed. P.G. Walsh *(1992)*
Book XXXVIII ed. P.G. Walsh *(1994)*
Book XXXIX ed. P.G. Walsh *(1995)*
Book XL ed. P.G. Walsh *(1996)*

LUCAN
CIVIL WAR VIII ed. R. Mayer *(1981)*

LUCIAN
A SELECTION ed. M.D. McLeod *(1991)*

LUCRETIUS
DE RERUM NATURA III ed. P. Michael Brown (1998*)*
DE RERUM NATURA IV ed. J. Godwin *(1987)*
DE RERUM NATURA VI ed. J. Godwin, *(1991)*

MARTIAL
EPIGRAMS V ed. P. Howell *(1996)*

MENANDER
SAMIA ed. D.M. Bain *(1983)*
THE BAD-TEMPERED MAN ed. S. Ireland *(1995)*

OVID
AMORES II ed. J. Booth *(1991)*
METAMORPHOSES I-IV ed. D.E. Hill *(1985)*
METAMORPHOSES V-VIII ed. D.E. Hill *(1992)*

PERSIUS
THE SATIRES ed. J.R. Jenkinson *(1981)*

PINDAR
SELECTED ODES ed. S. Instone *(1996)*

PLATO
APOLOGY ed. M. Stokes *(1998)*
MENO ed. R.W. Sharples *(1985)*
PHAEDRUS ed. C.J. Rowe *(1986)*
REPUBLIC V ed. S. Halliwell *(1993)*
REPUBLIC X, ed. S. Halliwell *(1988)*
THE STATESMAN ed. C.J. Rowe *(1995)*
SYMPOSIUM ed. C.J.Rowe *(1998)*

PLAUTUS
BACCHIDES ed. J.A. Barsby *(1986)*

PLINY
CORRESPONDENCE WITH TRAJAN FROM BITHYNIA ed. W. Williams *(1990)*

PLUTARCH
LIVES OF ARISTEIDES AND CATO, ed. D. Sansone *(1989)*
LIFE OF CICERO ed. J.L. Moles *(1989)*
MALICE OF HERODOTUS ed. A.J. Bowen *(1992)*
LIFE OF THEMISTOCLES ed. J, Marr *(1998)*

THE RUODLIEB ed. C.W. Grocock *(1985)*

SENECA
LETTERS: A SELECTION ed. C.D.N. Costa *(1988)*
FOUR DIALOGUES, ed. C.D.N. Costa *(1994),*

SOPHOCLES
AJAX ed. A. Garvie *(1998)*
ANTIGONE ed. A.L. Brown *(1987)*
PHILOCTETES ed. R.G. Ussher *(1990)*

SUETONIUS
LIVES OF GALBA, OTHO & VITELLIUS ed. D.C.A. Shotter *(1994)*

TACITUS
ANNALS IV ed. D.C.A. Shotter *(1989)*

TERENCE
THE BROTHERS ed. A.S. Gratwick *(1987)*
THE SELF-TORMENTOR ed. A.J. Brothers *(1988)*
THE MOTHER-IN-LAW ed. S. Ireland *(1990)*

THUCYDIDES
HISTORY Book II ed. P.J. Rhodes *(1988)*
HISTORY Book III ed. P.J. Rhodes *(1994)*
PYLOS 425 BC: Book IV, 2-41, ed. J. Wilson *(1979)*

WILLIAM OF NEWBURGH
THE HISTORY OF ENGLISH AFFAIRS I ed. P.G. Walsh & M. Kennedy *(1988)*

XENOPHON
HELLENIKA I-II.3.10 ed. Peter Krentz *(1989)*
HELLENIKA II.3–IV.2.8 ed. Peter Krentz *(1995)*